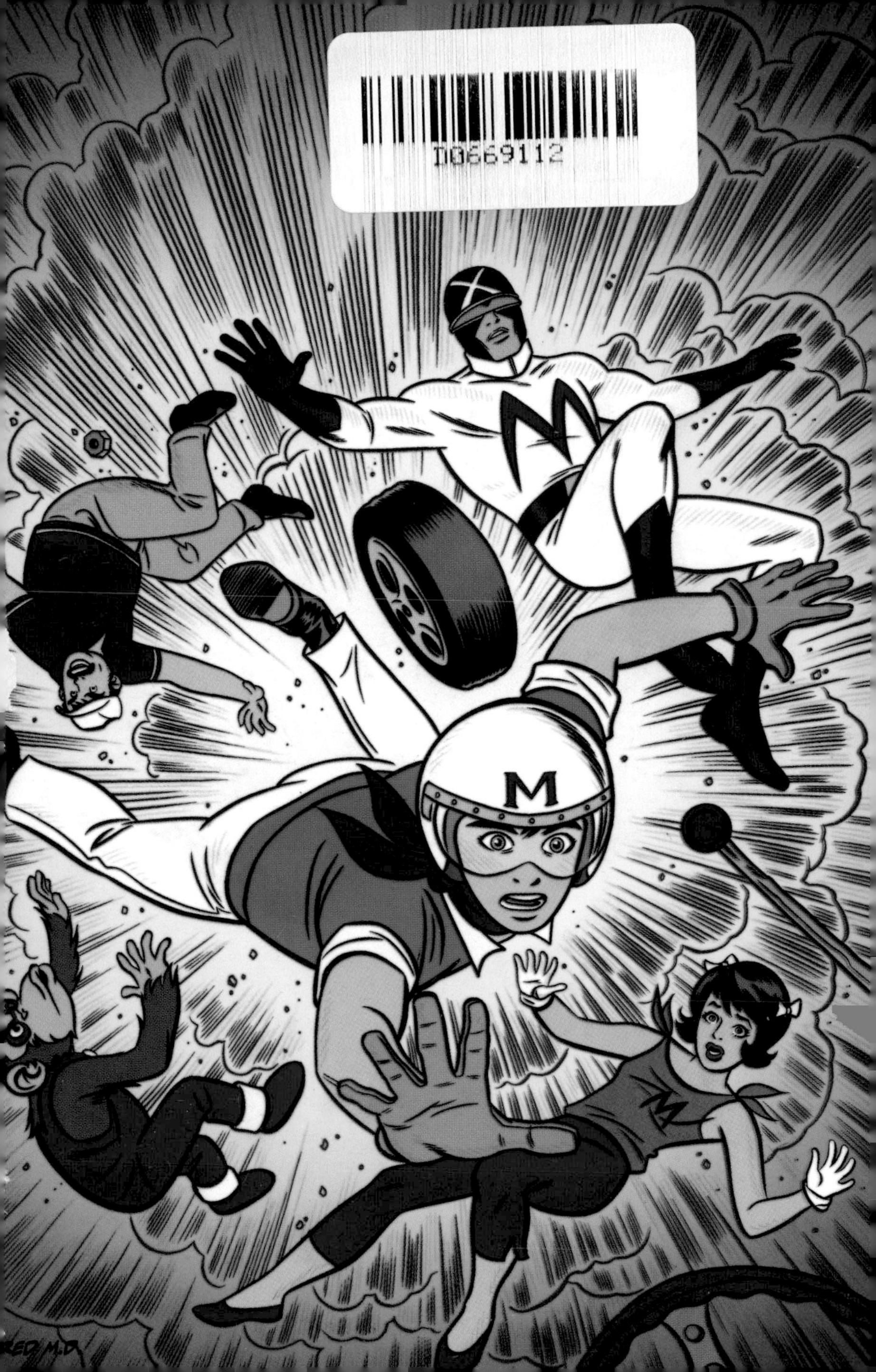

STORY BY

Dwayne Alexander Smith

ART BY

Elmer Damaso

SPEED RACER™

story by
Dwayne Alexander Smith

art by
Elmer Damaso

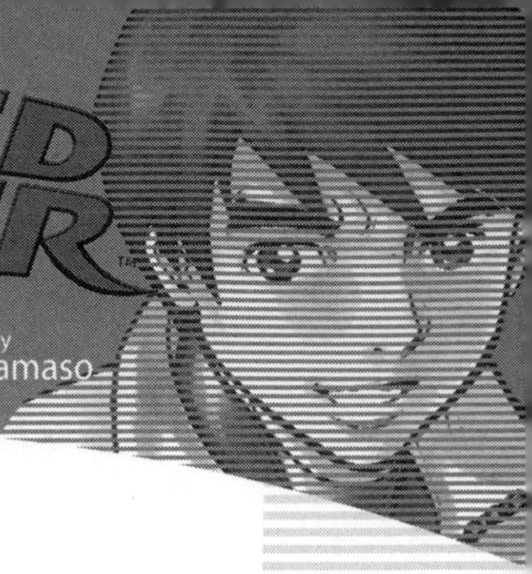

STAFF CREDITS

toning	**Ludwig Sacramento**
lettering	**Jon Zamar**
graphic design	**Jon Zamar**
cover design	**Nicky Lim**
copy editor	**J. W. Coffey**
assistant editor	**Adam Arnold**
editor	**Jason DeAngelis**
publisher	**Seven Seas Entertainment**

Visit us online at www.gomanga.com.

ISBN 978-1-933164-33-5

Printed in Canada

First printing: December, 2007

10 9 8 7 6 5 4 3 2 1

Seven Seas

CONTENTS

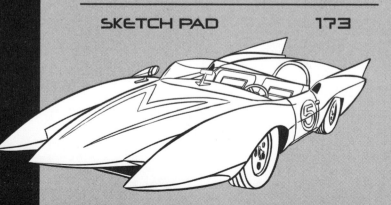

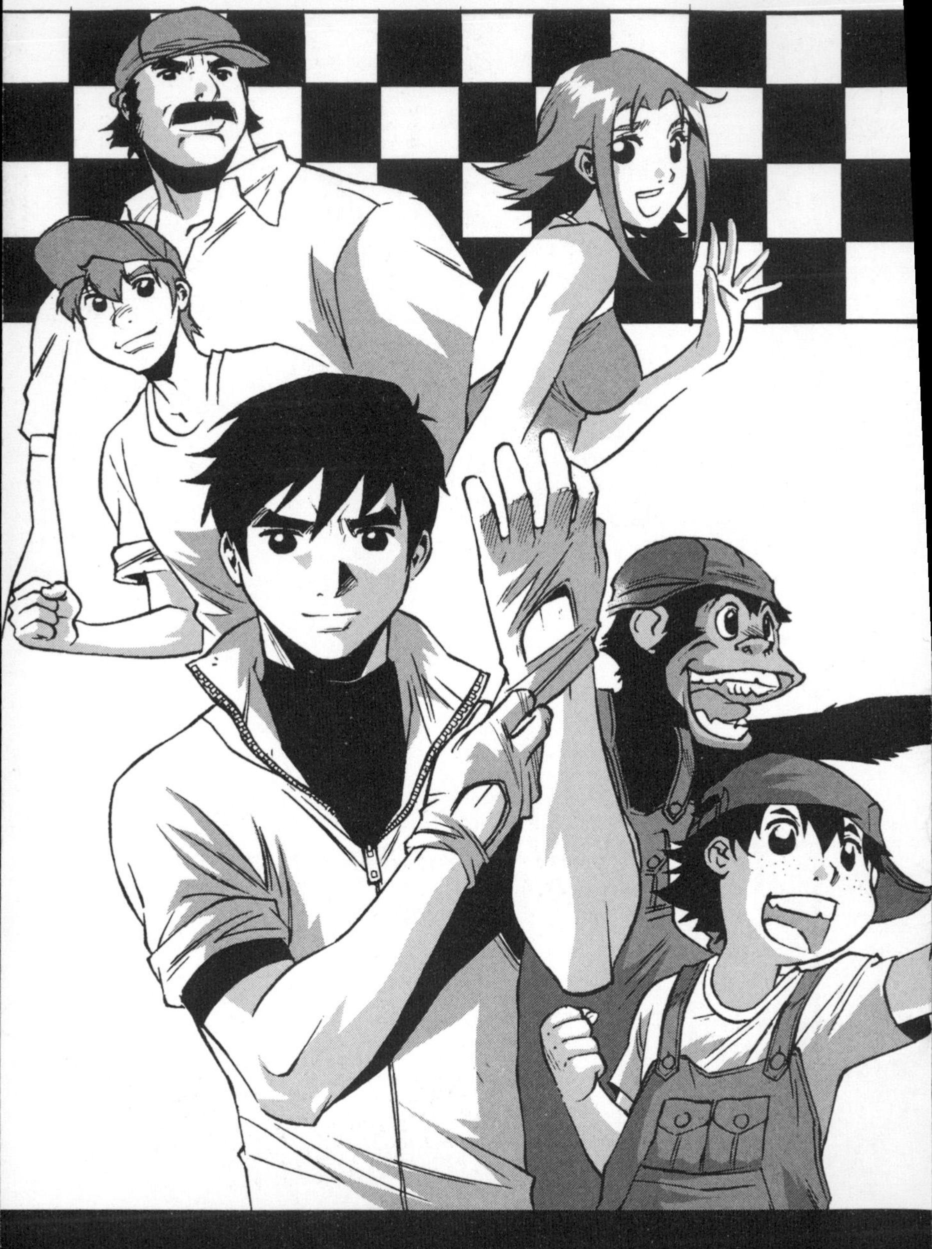

CHAPTER ONE

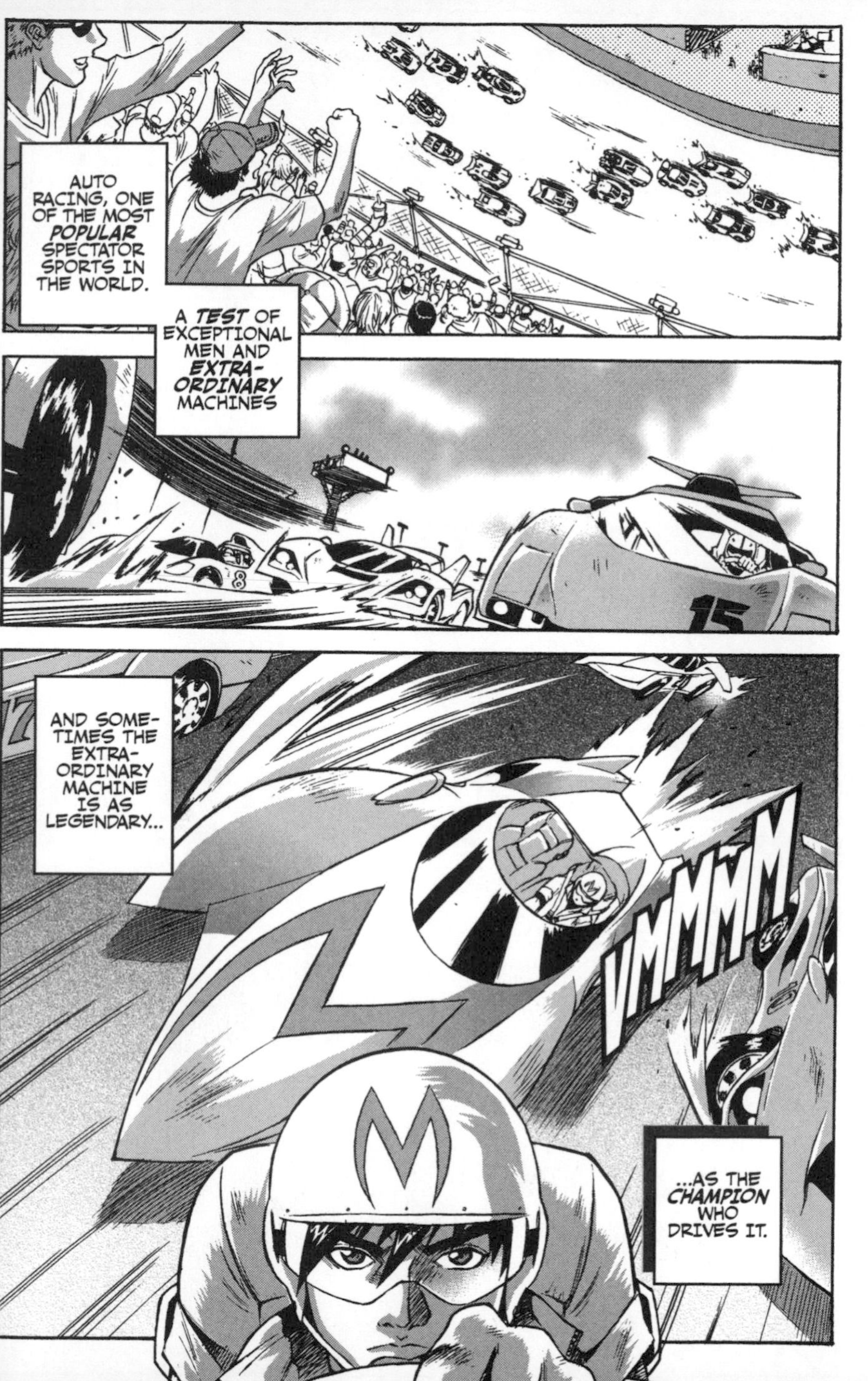
AUTO RACING, ONE OF THE MOST *POPULAR* SPECTATOR SPORTS IN THE WORLD.
A *TEST* OF EXCEPTIONAL MEN AND *EXTRA-ORDINARY* MACHINES
AND SOME-TIMES THE EXTRA-ORDINARY MACHINE IS AS LEGENDARY...
VMMMM
...AS THE *CHAMPION* WHO DRIVES IT.

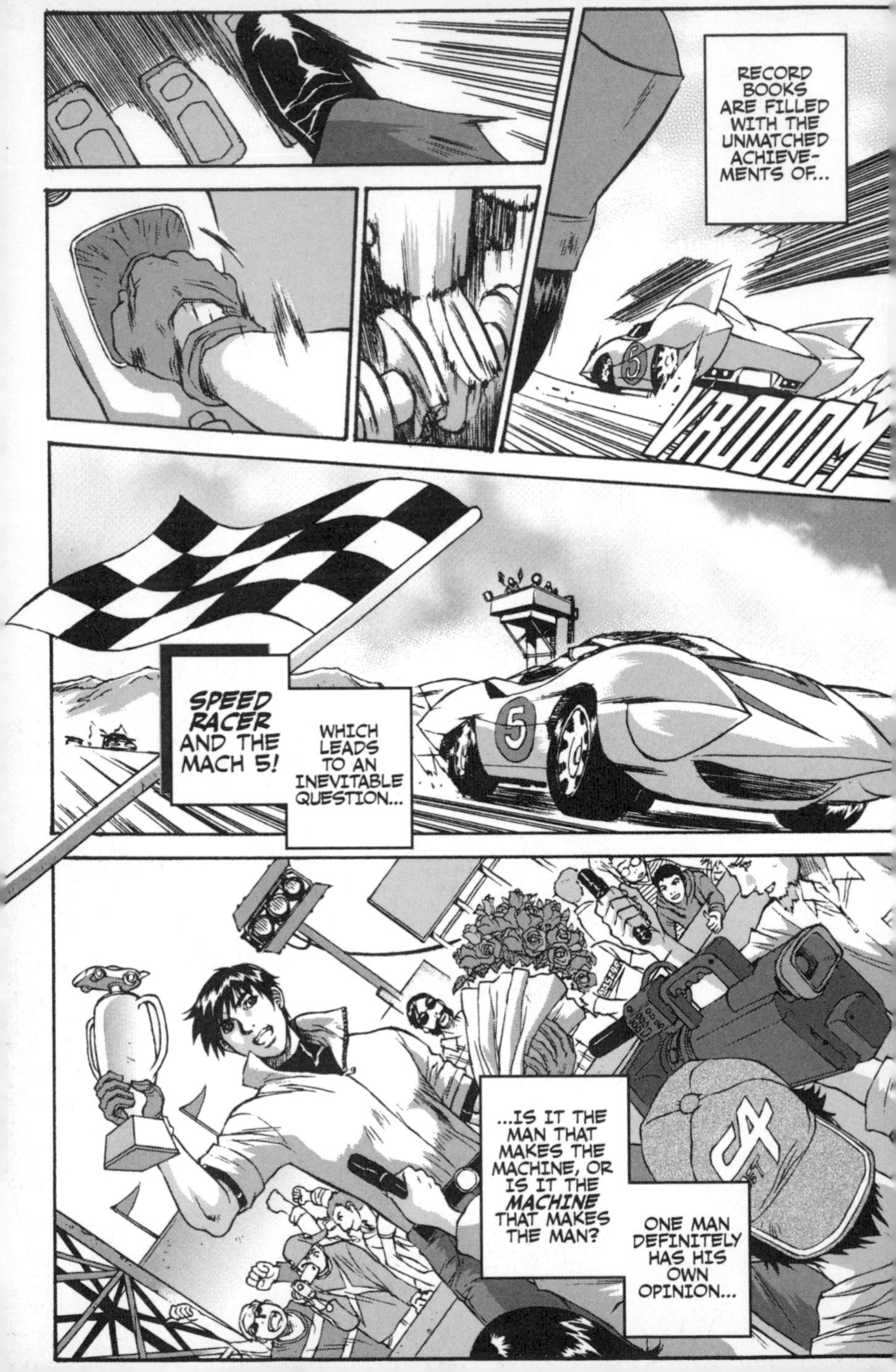

RECORD BOOKS ARE FILLED WITH THE UNMATCHED ACHIEVE-MENTS OF...
VROOM
SPEED RACER AND THE MACH 5!
WHICH LEADS TO AN INEVITABLE QUESTION...
...IS IT THE MAN THAT MAKES THE MACHINE, OR IS IT THE MACHINE THAT MAKES THE MAN?
ONE MAN DEFINITELY HAS HIS OWN OPINION...

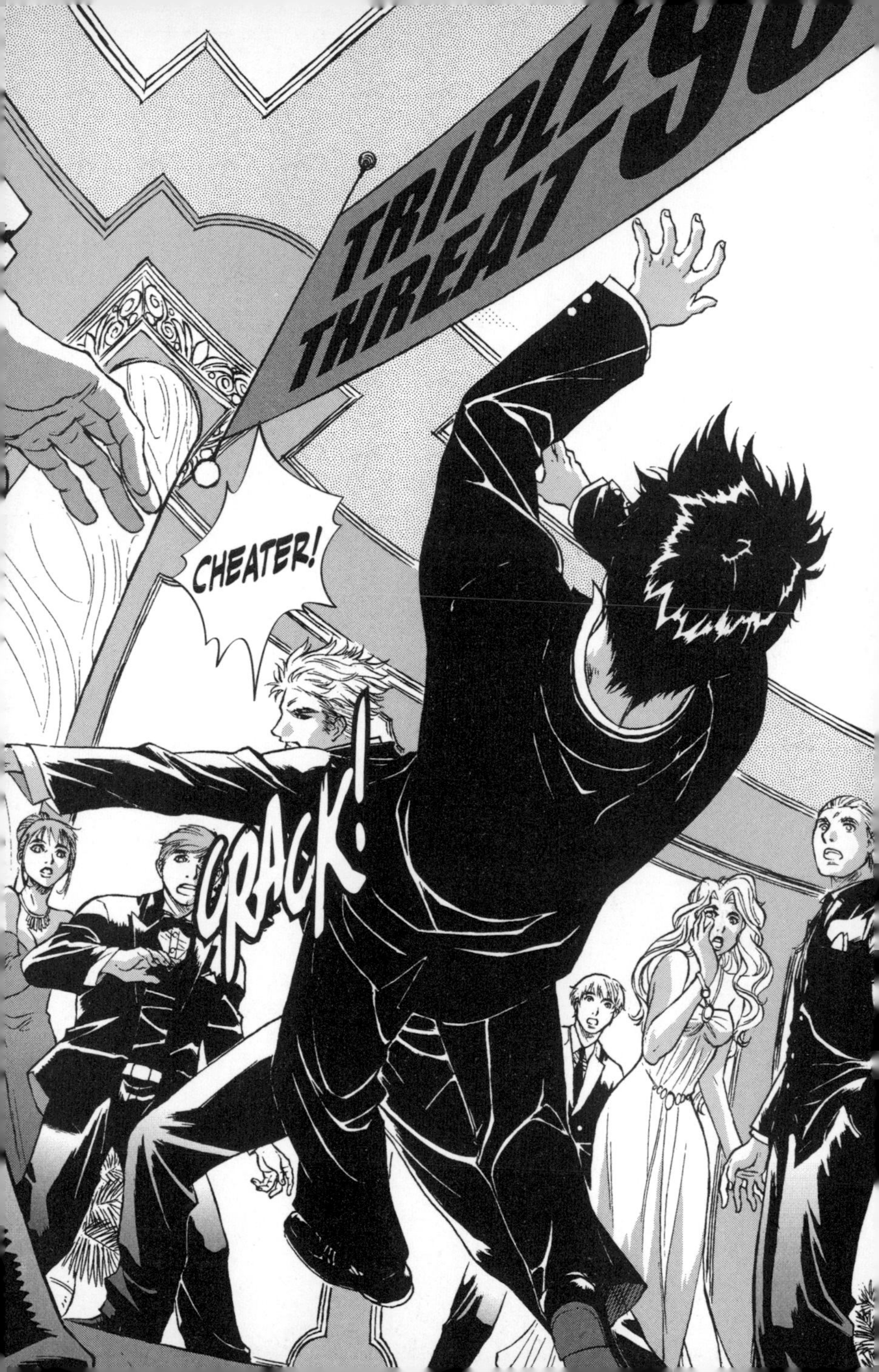
TRIPLE THREAT
CHEATER!
CRACK!

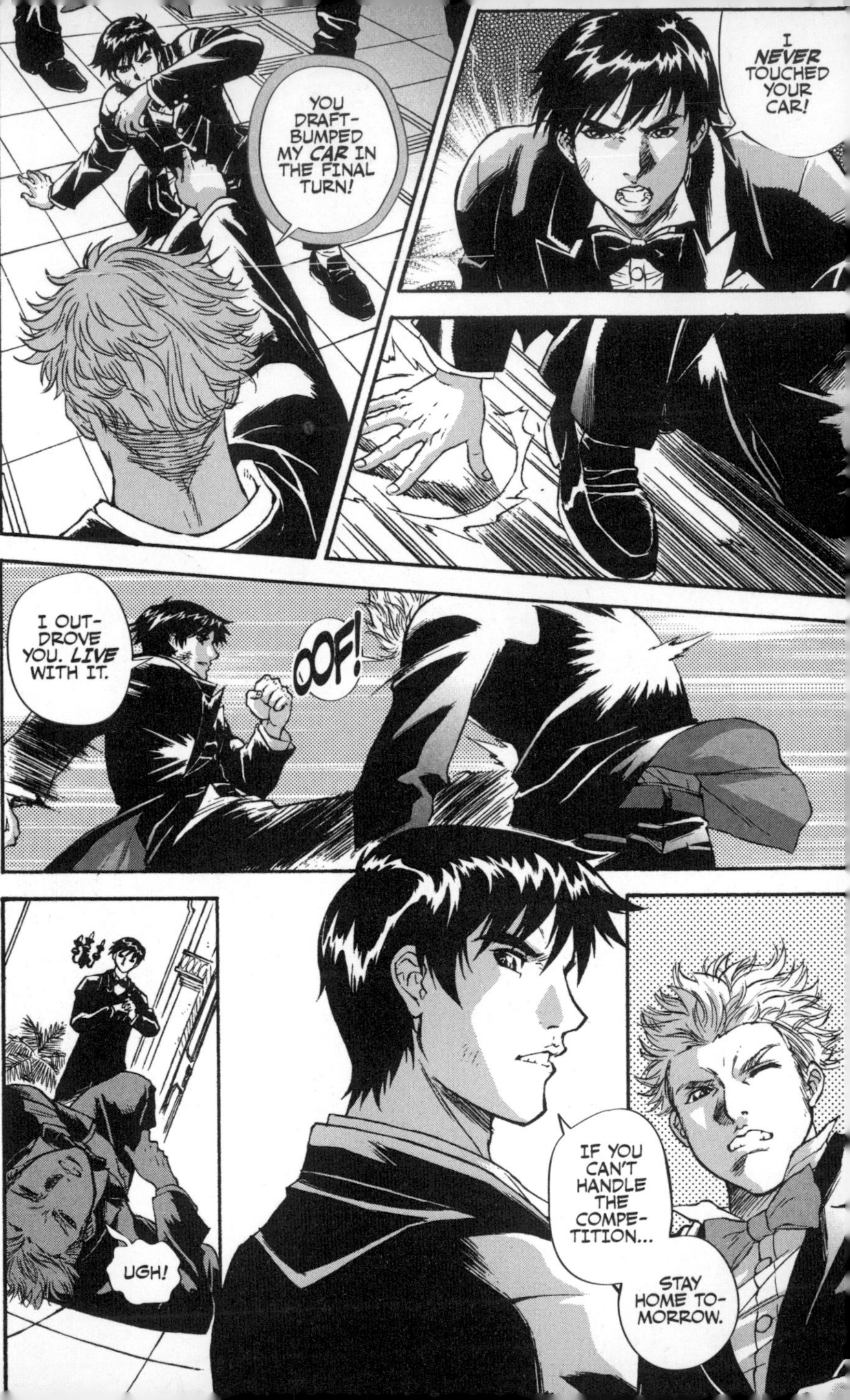
YOU DRAFT-BUMPED MY CAR IN THE FINAL TURN!
I NEVER TOUCHED YOUR CAR!
I OUT-DROVE YOU. LIVE WITH IT.
OOF!
UGH!
IF YOU CAN'T HANDLE THE COMPETITION...
STAY HOME TOMORROW.

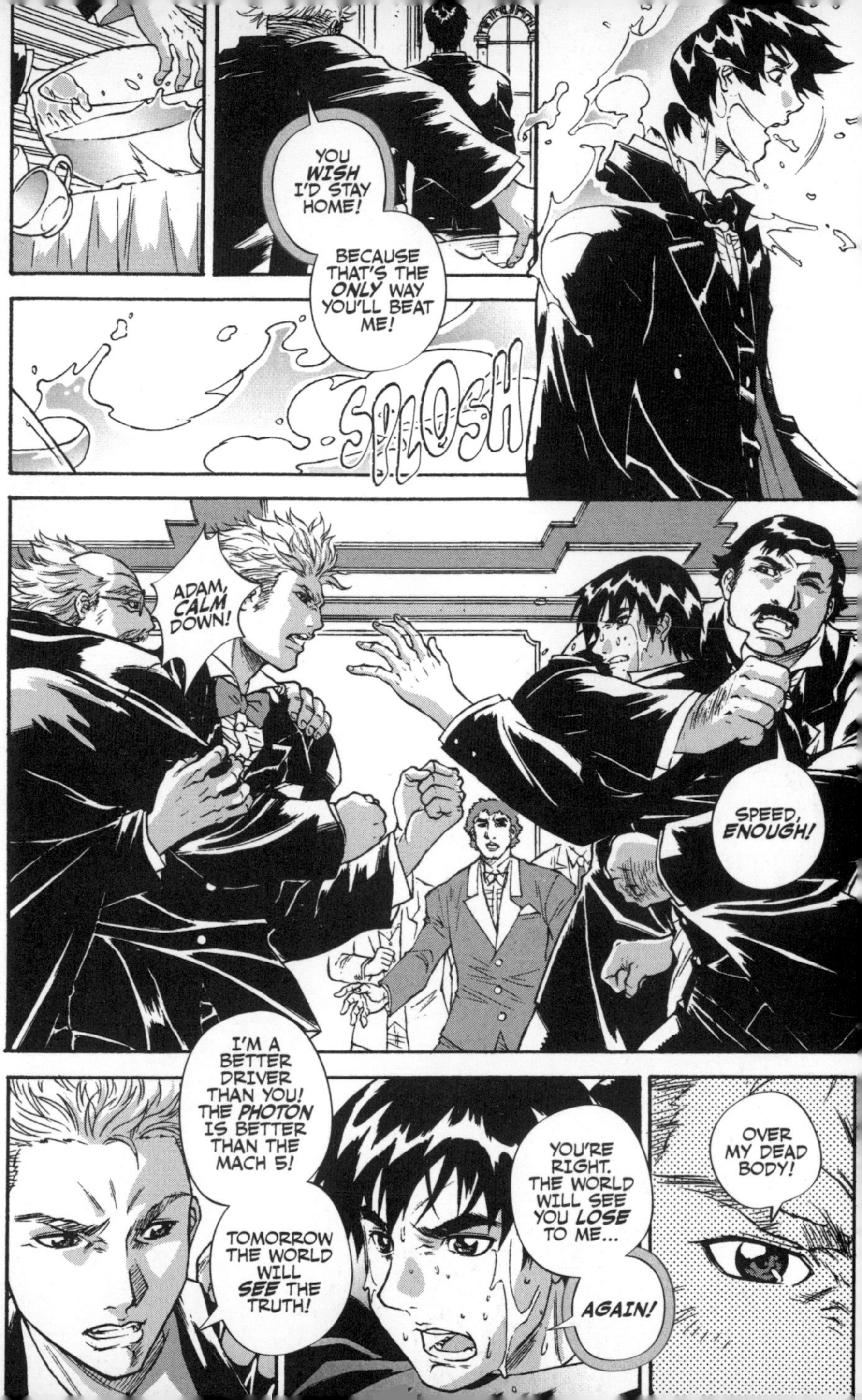
YOU WISH I'D STAY HOME!
BECAUSE THAT'S THE ONLY WAY YOU'LL BEAT ME!
SPLOSH
ADAM, CALM DOWN!
SPEED, ENOUGH!
I'M A BETTER DRIVER THAN YOU! THE PHOTON IS BETTER THAN THE MACH 5!
TOMORROW THE WORLD WILL SEE THE TRUTH!
YOU'RE RIGHT. THE WORLD WILL SEE YOU LOSE TO ME...
AGAIN!
OVER MY DEAD BODY!

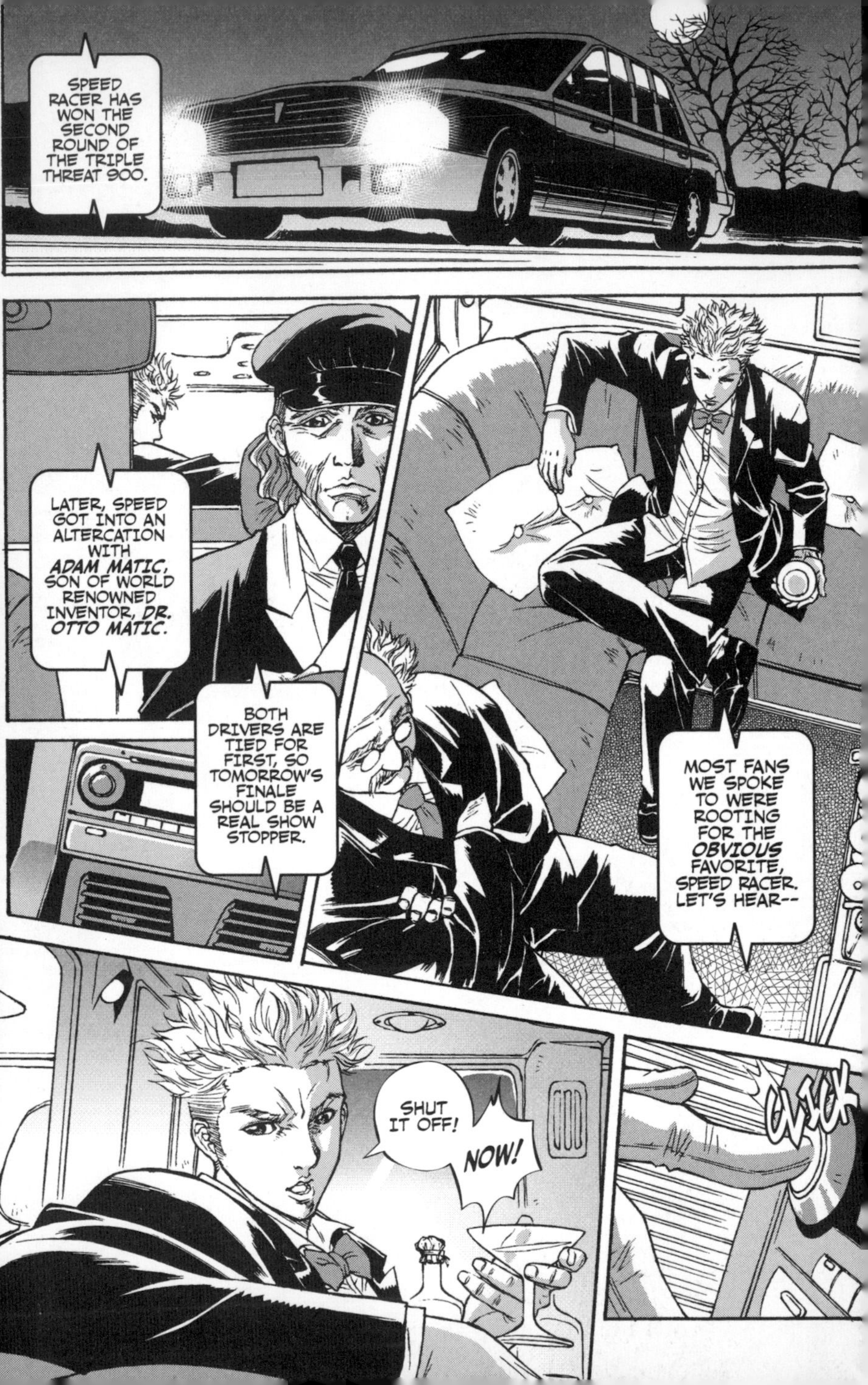
SPEED RACER HAS WON THE SECOND ROUND OF THE TRIPLE THREAT 900.
LATER, SPEED GOT INTO AN ALTERCATION WITH ***ADAM MATIC***, SON OF WORLD RENOWNED INVENTOR, ***DR. OTTO MATIC***.
BOTH DRIVERS ARE TIED FOR FIRST, SO TOMORROW'S FINALE SHOULD BE A REAL SHOW STOPPER.
MOST FANS WE SPOKE TO WERE ROOTING FOR THE ***OBVIOUS*** FAVORITE, SPEED RACER. LET'S HEAR--
SHUT IT OFF!
NOW!
CLICK

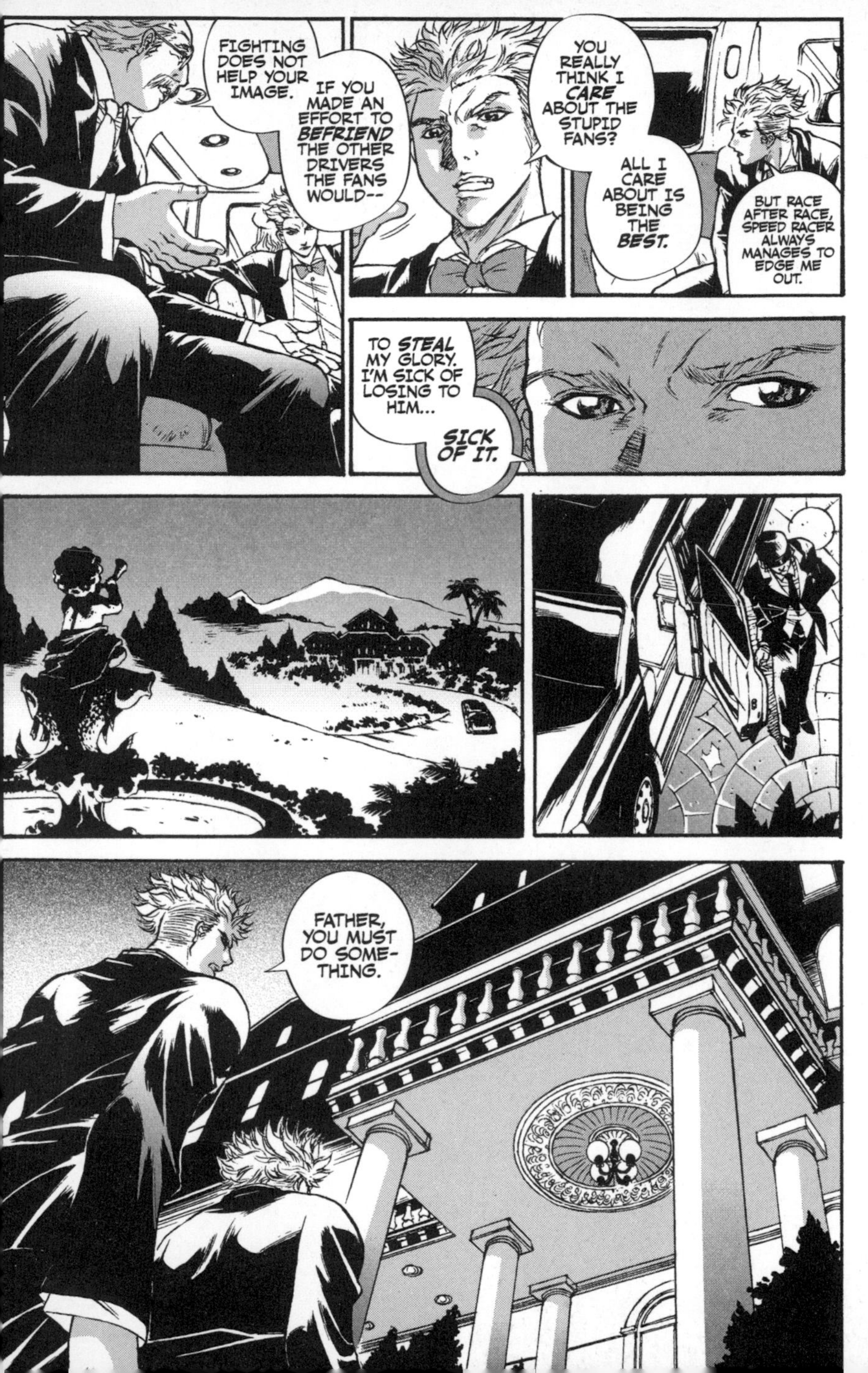
FIGHTING DOES NOT HELP YOUR IMAGE.
IF YOU MADE AN EFFORT TO *BEFRIEND* THE OTHER DRIVERS THE FANS WOULD--
YOU REALLY THINK I *CARE* ABOUT THE STUPID FANS?
ALL I CARE ABOUT IS BEING THE *BEST.*
BUT RACE AFTER RACE, SPEED RACER ALWAYS MANAGES TO EDGE ME OUT.
TO *STEAL* MY GLORY. I'M SICK OF LOSING TO HIM...
SICK OF IT.
FATHER, YOU MUST DO SOME-THING.

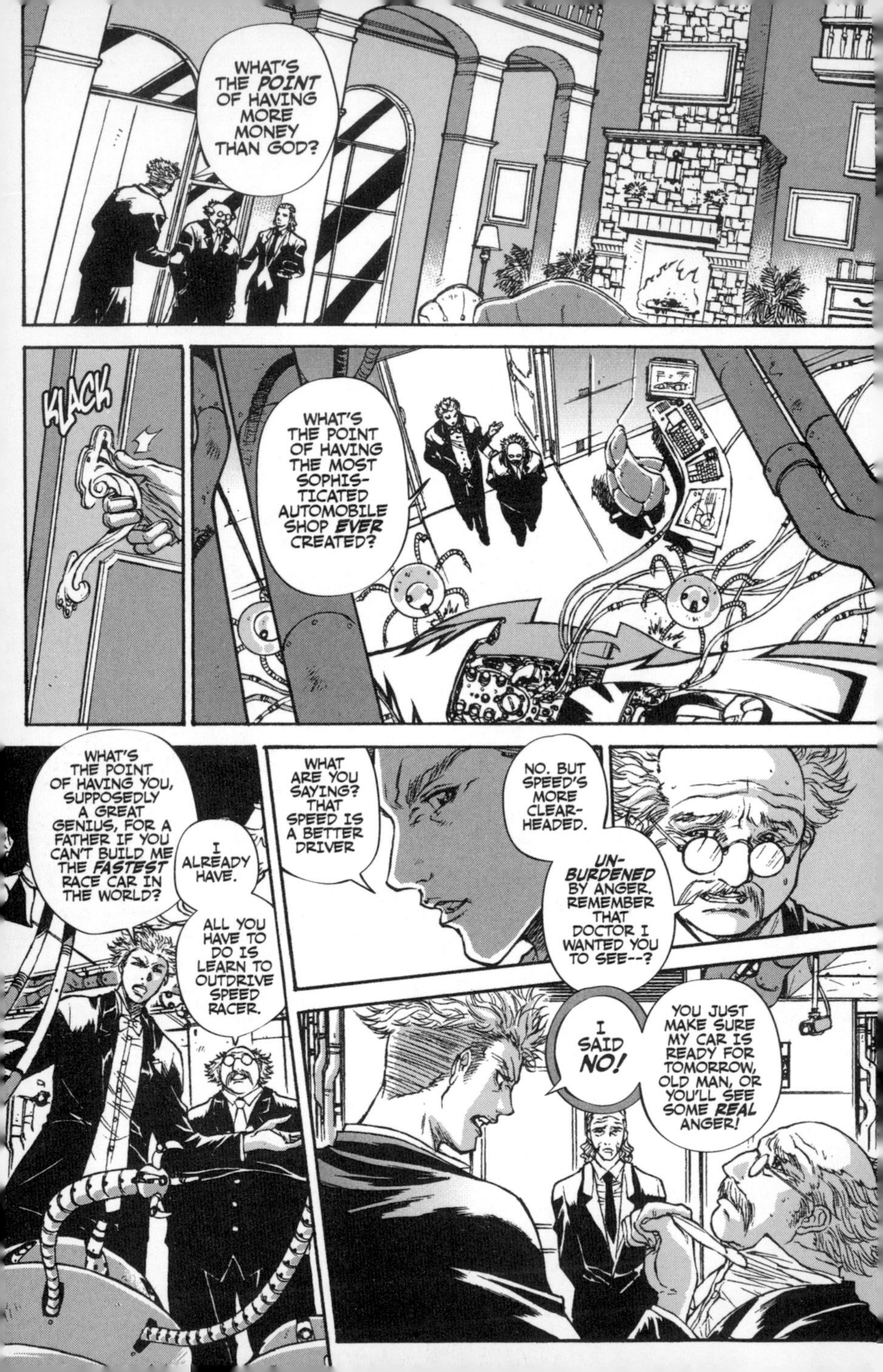
WHAT'S THE *POINT* OF HAVING MORE MONEY THAN GOD?
KLACK
WHAT'S THE POINT OF HAVING THE MOST SOPHISTICATED AUTOMOBILE SHOP *EVER* CREATED?
WHAT'S THE POINT OF HAVING YOU, SUPPOSEDLY A GREAT GENIUS, FOR A FATHER IF YOU CAN'T BUILD ME THE *FASTEST* RACE CAR IN THE WORLD?
I ALREADY HAVE.
ALL YOU HAVE TO DO IS LEARN TO OUTDRIVE SPEED RACER.
WHAT ARE YOU SAYING? THAT SPEED IS A BETTER DRIVER
NO. BUT SPEED'S MORE CLEAR-HEADED.
UN-BURDENED BY ANGER. REMEMBER THAT DOCTOR I WANTED YOU TO SEE--?
I SAID *NO!*
YOU JUST MAKE SURE MY CAR IS READY FOR TOMORROW, OLD MAN, OR YOU'LL SEE SOME *REAL* ANGER!

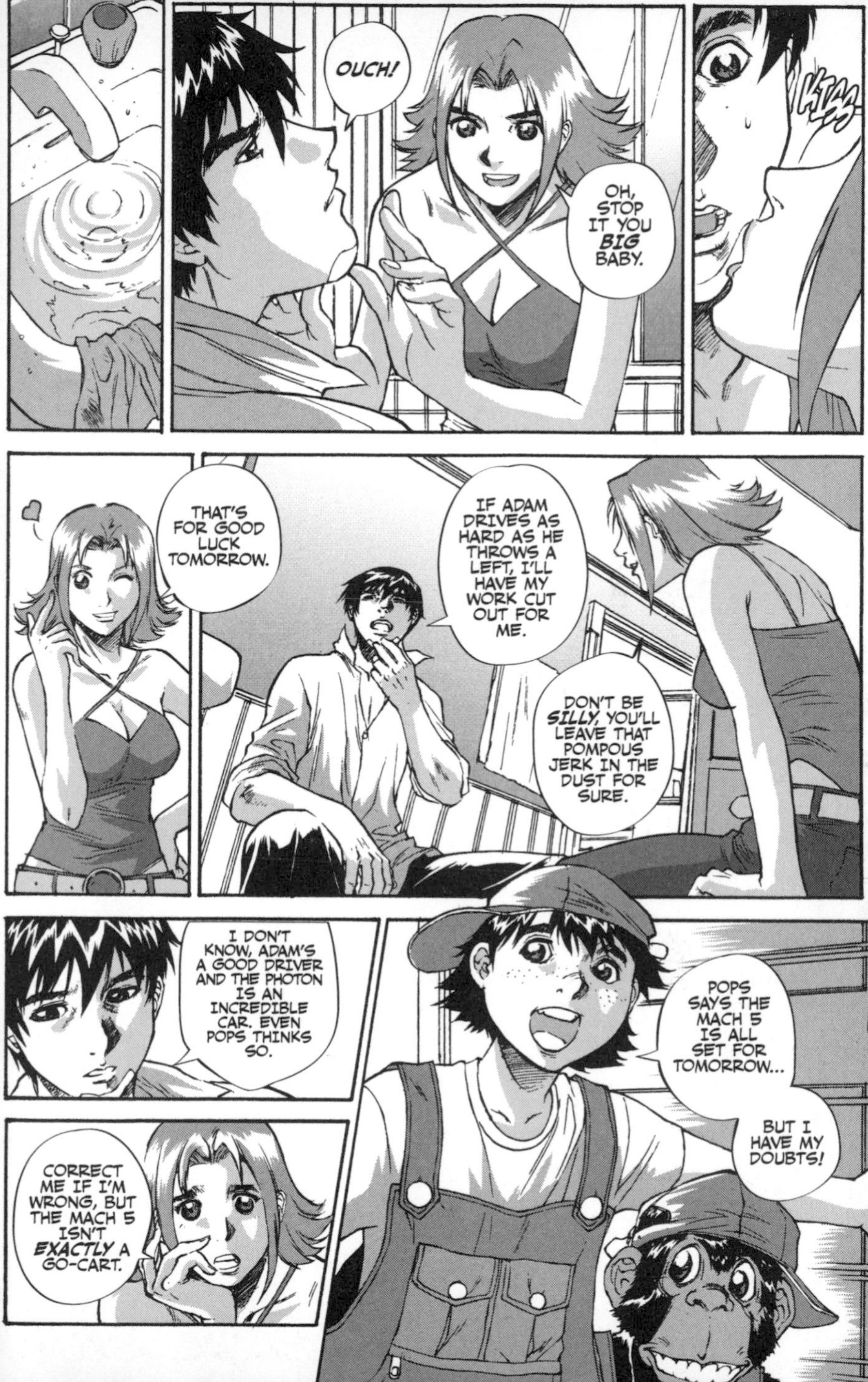
OUCH!
OH, STOP IT YOU *BIG* BABY.
KISS
THAT'S FOR GOOD LUCK TOMORROW.
IF ADAM DRIVES AS HARD AS HE THROWS A LEFT, I'LL HAVE MY WORK CUT OUT FOR ME.
DON'T BE *SILLY*, YOU'LL LEAVE THAT POMPOUS JERK IN THE DUST FOR SURE.
I DON'T KNOW, ADAM'S A GOOD DRIVER AND THE PHOTON IS AN INCREDIBLE CAR. EVEN POPS THINKS SO.
CORRECT ME IF I'M WRONG, BUT THE MACH 5 ISN'T *EXACTLY* A GO-CART.
POPS SAYS THE MACH 5 IS ALL SET FOR TOMORROW...
BUT I HAVE MY DOUBTS!

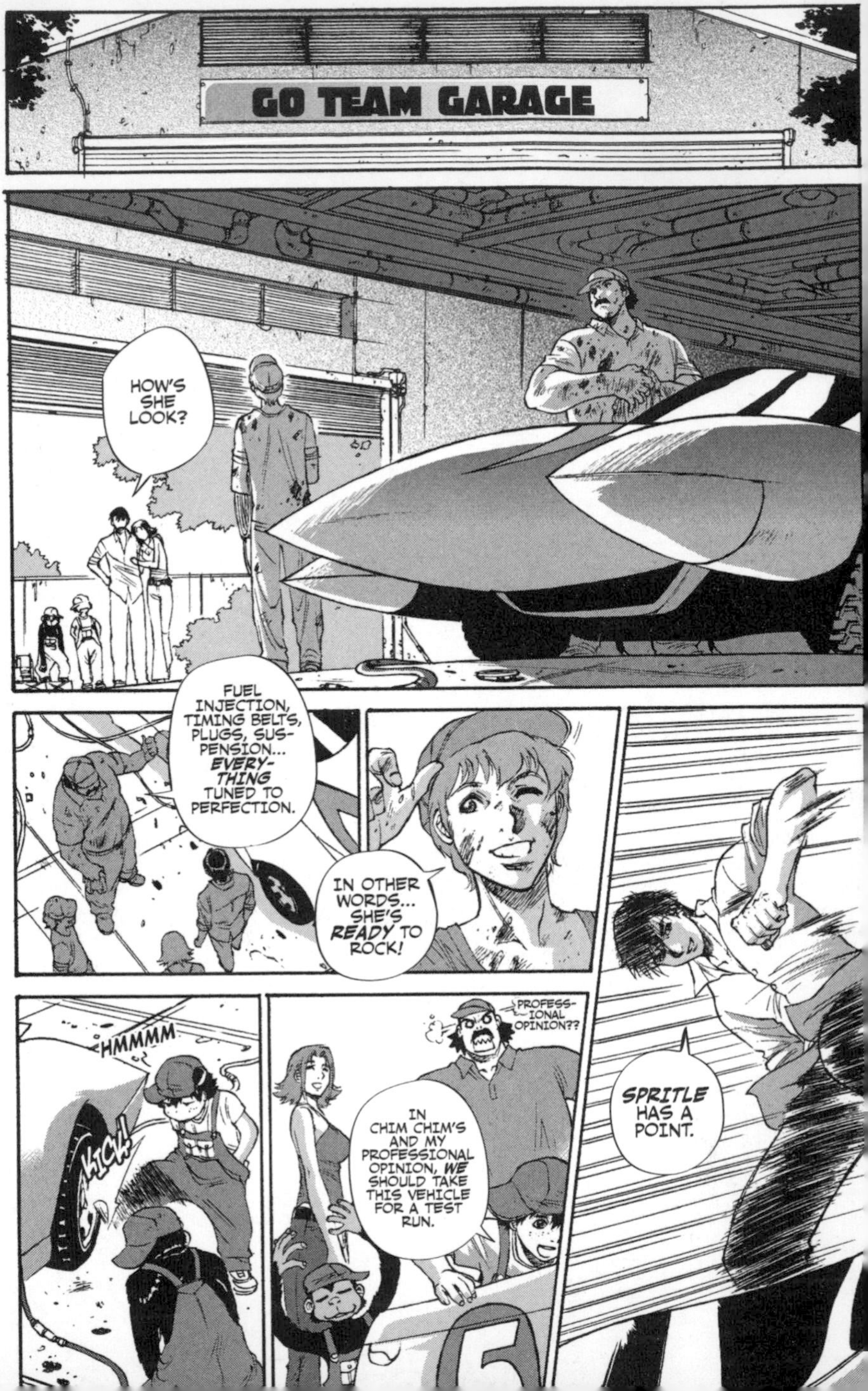
GO TEAM GARAGE
HOW'S SHE LOOK?
FUEL INJECTION, TIMING BELTS, PLUGS, SUSPENSION... *EVERYTHING* TUNED TO PERFECTION.
IN OTHER WORDS... SHE'S *READY* TO ROCK!
HMMMM
KICK!
PROFESSIONAL OPINION??
IN CHIM CHIM'S AND MY PROFESSIONAL OPINION, *WE* SHOULD TAKE THIS VEHICLE FOR A TEST RUN.
SPRITLE HAS A POINT.

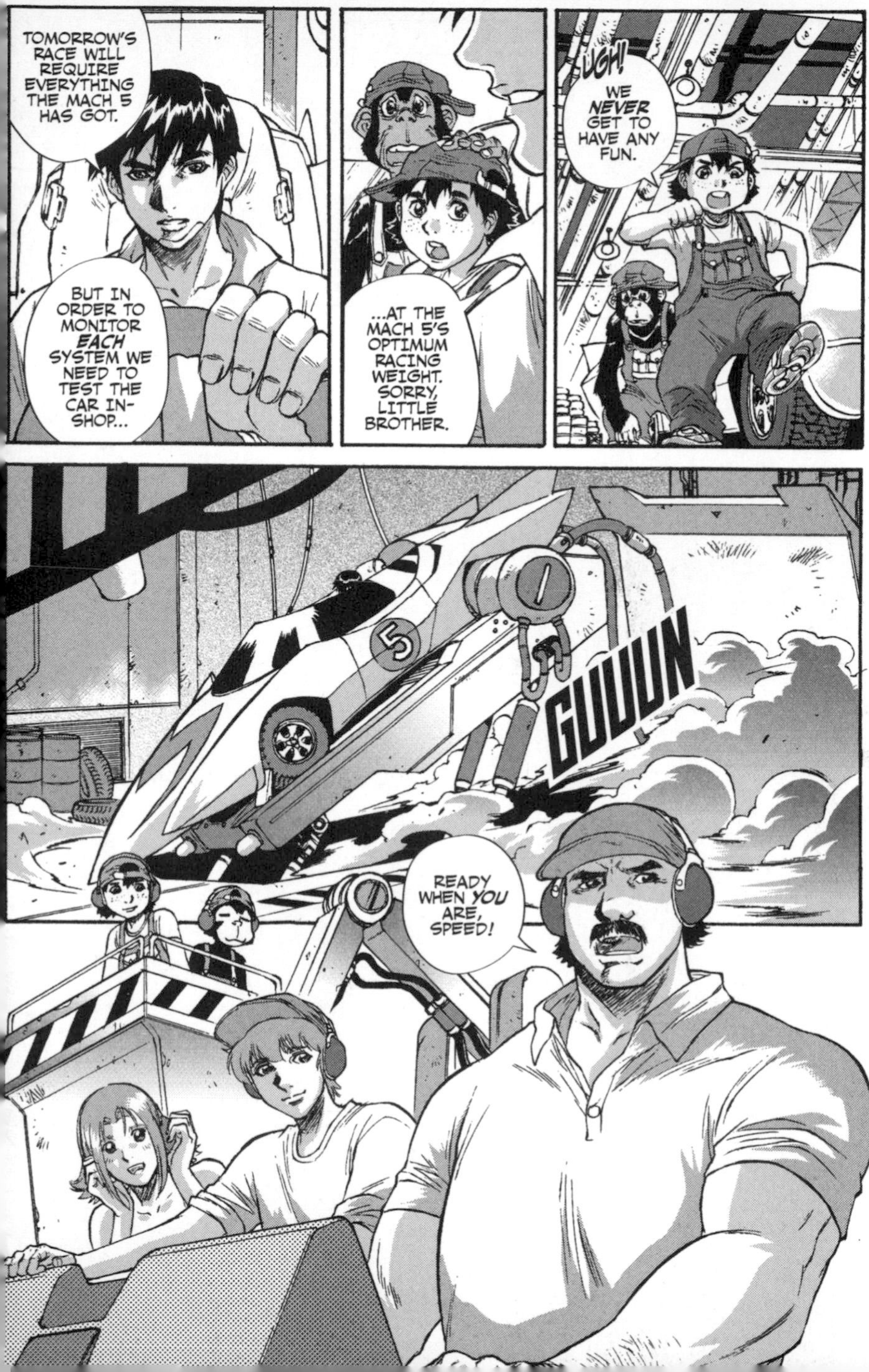
TOMORROW'S RACE WILL REQUIRE EVERYTHING THE MACH 5 HAS GOT.
BUT IN ORDER TO MONITOR EACH SYSTEM WE NEED TO TEST THE CAR IN-SHOP...
...AT THE MACH 5'S OPTIMUM RACING WEIGHT. SORRY, LITTLE BROTHER.
UGH!
WE NEVER GET TO HAVE ANY FUN.
GUUUN
READY WHEN YOU ARE, SPEED!

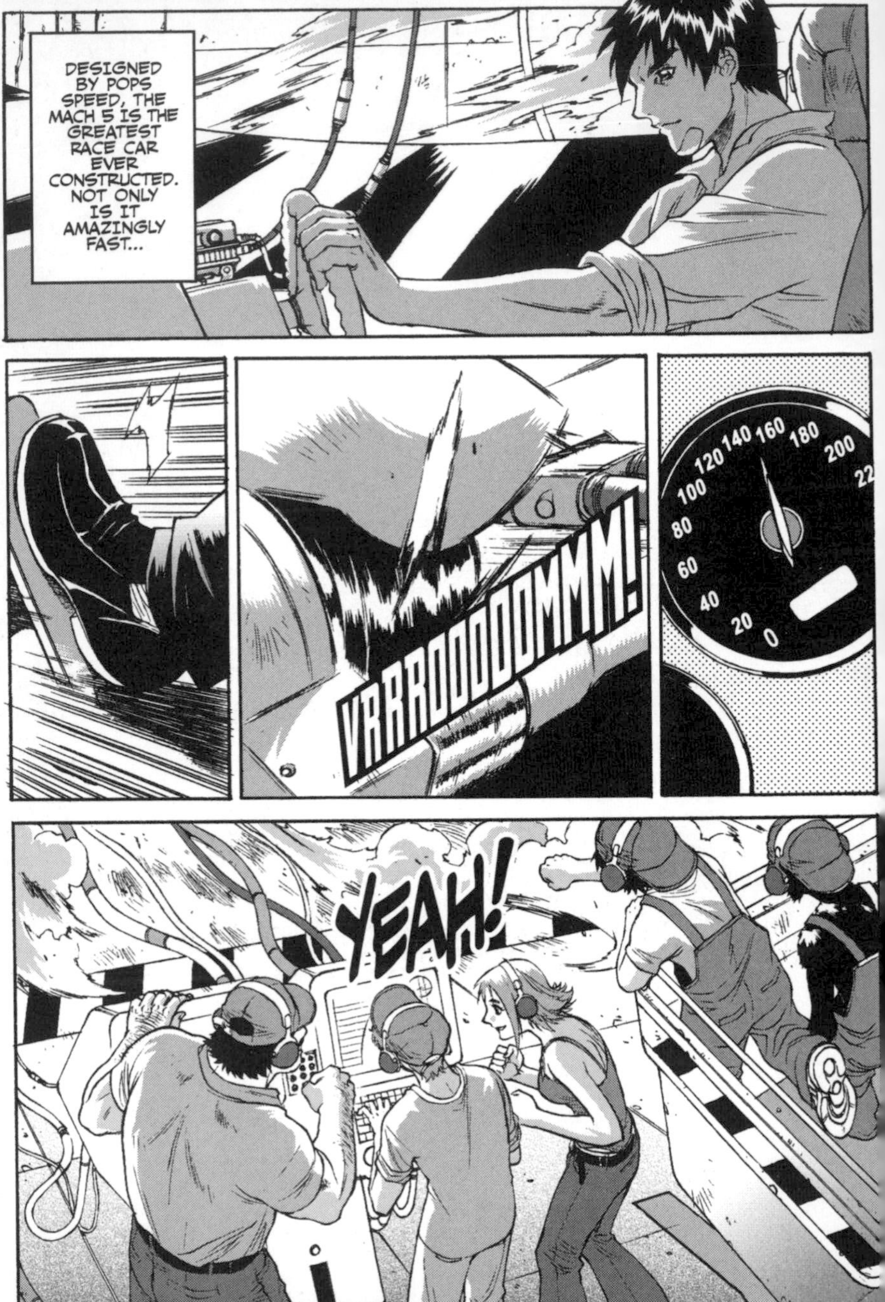
DESIGNED BY POPS SPEED, THE MACH 5 IS THE GREATEST RACE CAR EVER CONSTRUCTED. NOT ONLY IS IT AMAZINGLY FAST...
VRRROOOOOMMM!
0 20 40 60 80 100 120 140 160 180 200
YEAH!

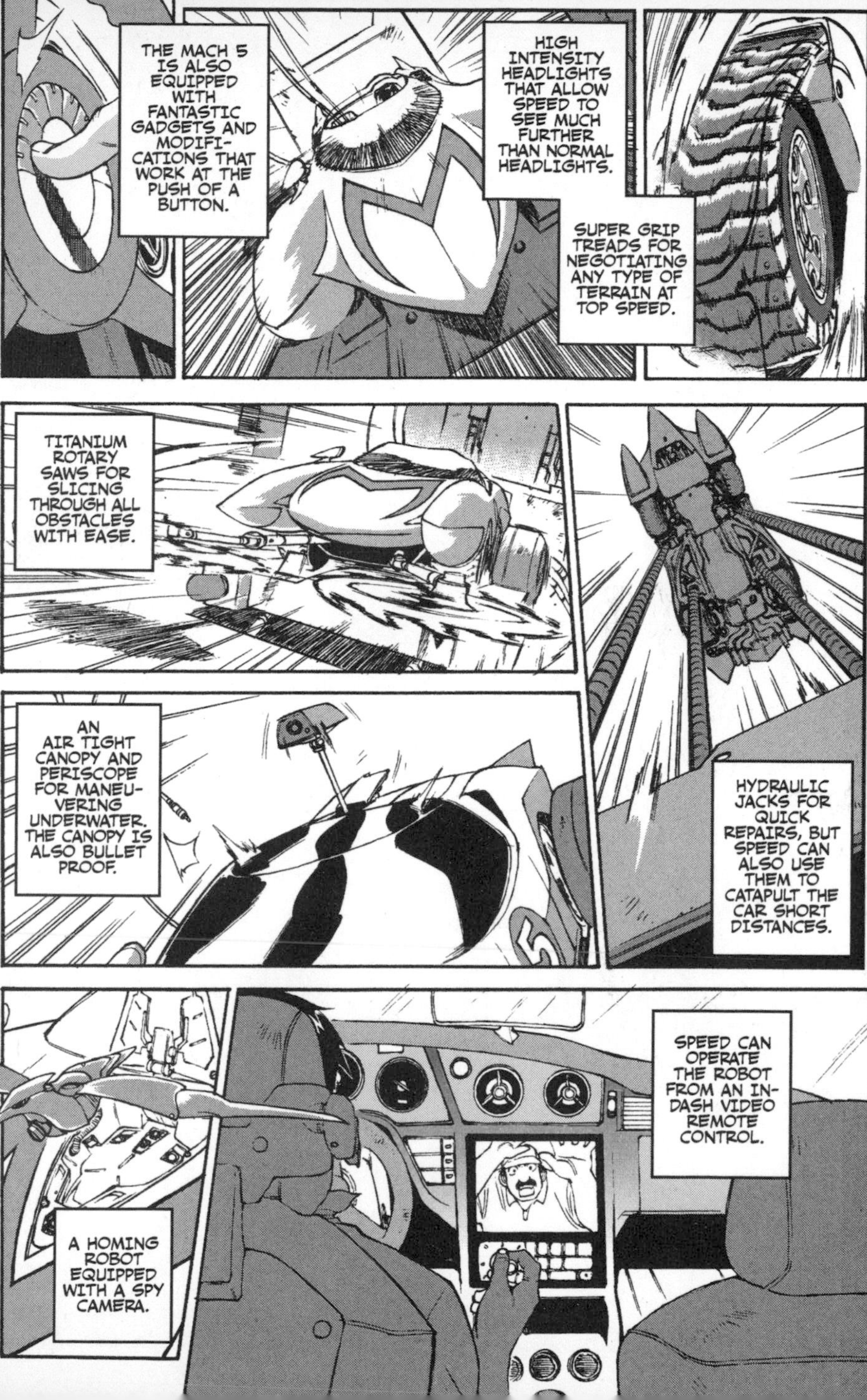
THE MACH 5 IS ALSO EQUIPPED WITH FANTASTIC GADGETS AND MODIFI-CATIONS THAT WORK AT THE PUSH OF A BUTTON.
HIGH INTENSITY HEADLIGHTS THAT ALLOW SPEED TO SEE MUCH FURTHER THAN NORMAL HEADLIGHTS.
SUPER GRIP TREADS FOR NEGOTIATING ANY TYPE OF TERRAIN AT TOP SPEED.
TITANIUM ROTARY SAWS FOR SLICING THROUGH ALL OBSTACLES WITH EASE.
AN AIR TIGHT CANOPY AND PERISCOPE FOR MANEU-VERING UNDERWATER. THE CANOPY IS ALSO BULLET PROOF.
HYDRAULIC JACKS FOR QUICK REPAIRS, BUT SPEED CAN ALSO USE THEM TO CATAPULT THE CAR SHORT DISTANCES.
A HOMING ROBOT EQUIPPED WITH A SPY CAMERA.
SPEED CAN OPERATE THE ROBOT FROM AN IN-DASH VIDEO REMOTE CONTROL.

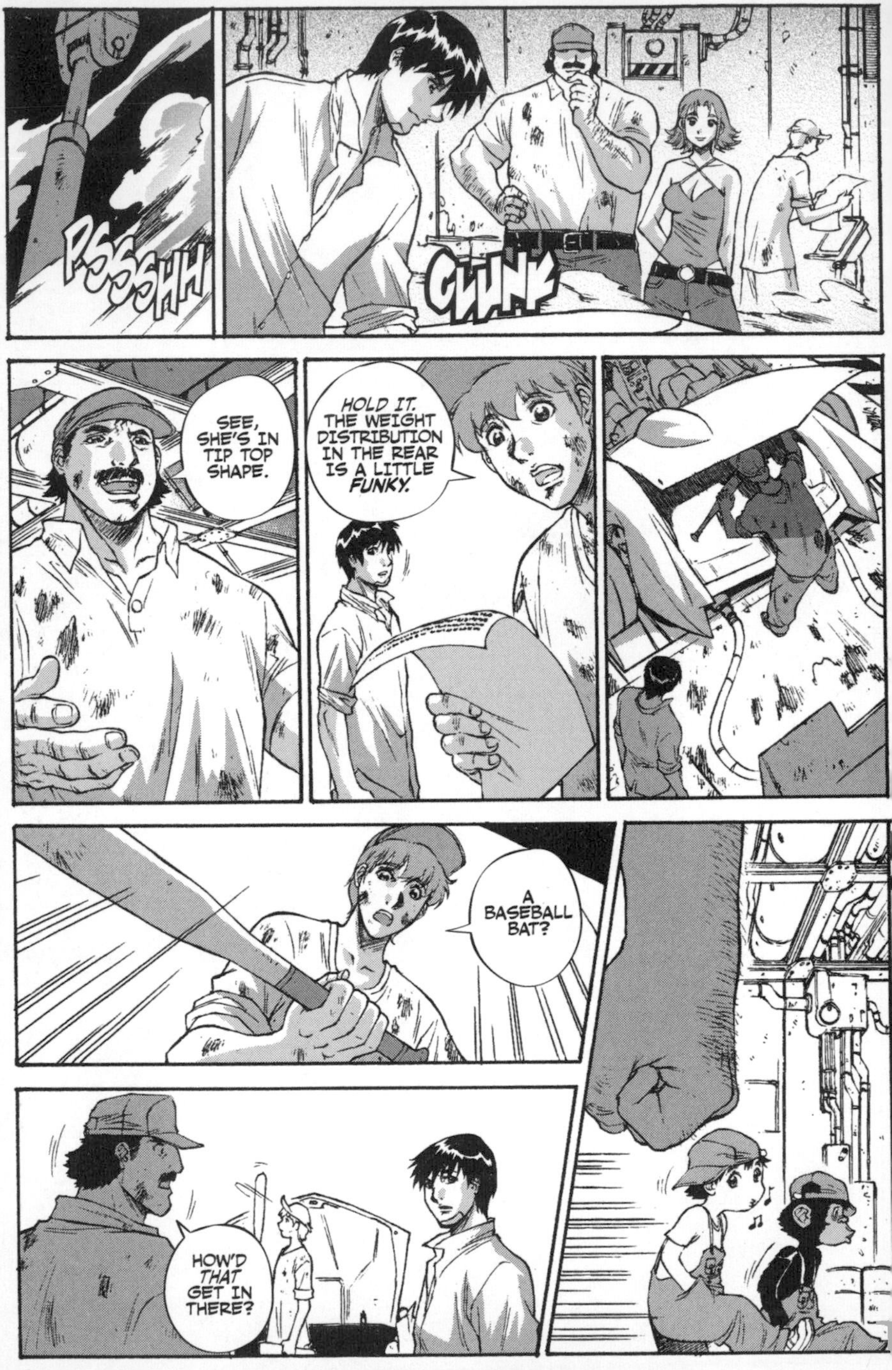
PSSSHH
CLUNK
SEE, SHE'S IN TIP TOP SHAPE.
HOLD IT. THE WEIGHT DISTRIBUTION IN THE REAR IS A LITTLE FUNKY.
A BASEBALL BAT?
HOW'D THAT GET IN THERE?

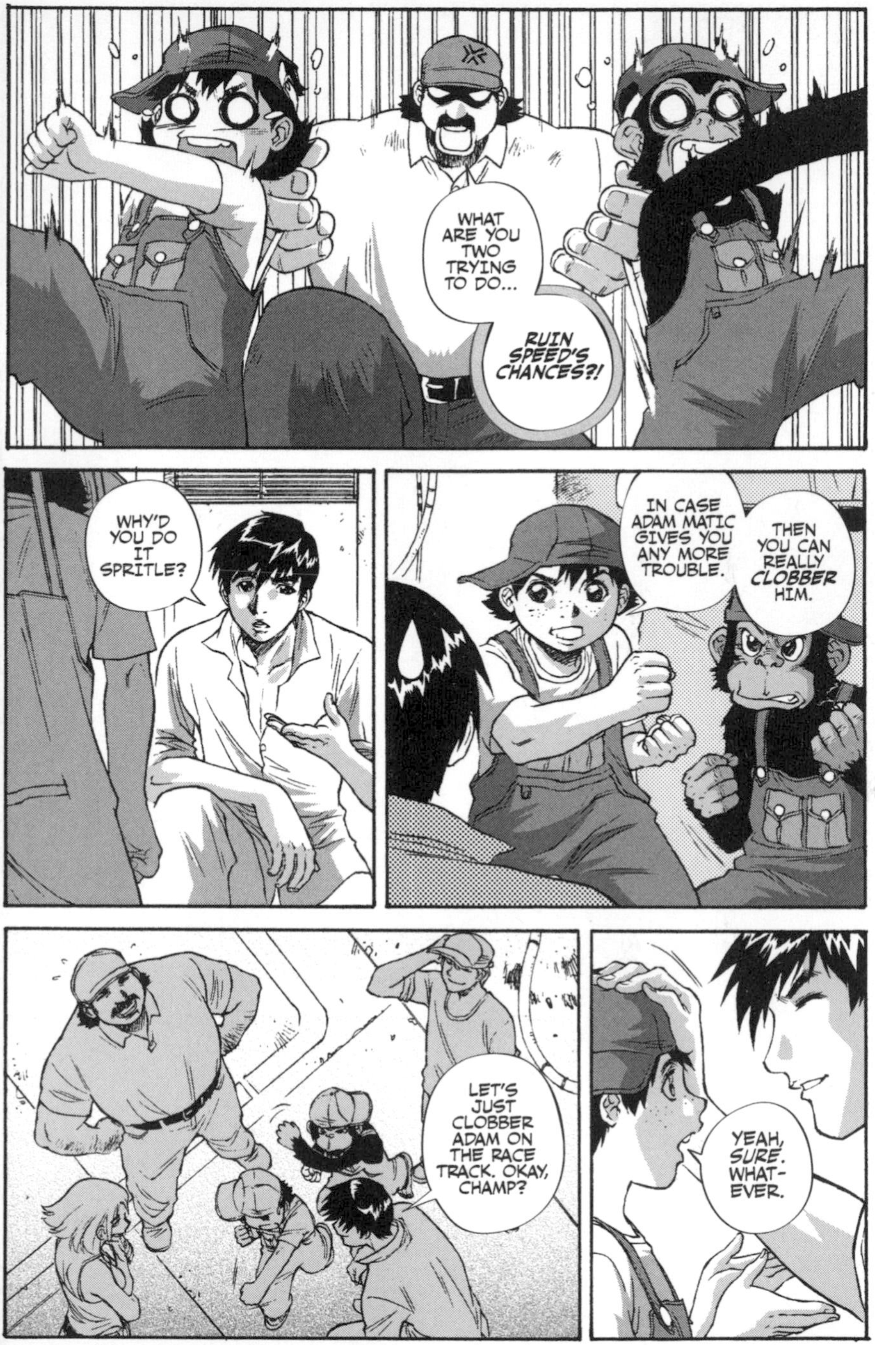
WHAT ARE YOU TWO TRYING TO DO...
RUIN SPEED'S CHANCES?!
WHY'D YOU DO IT SPRITLE?
IN CASE ADAM MATIC GIVES YOU ANY MORE TROUBLE.
THEN YOU CAN REALLY CLOBBER HIM.
LET'S JUST CLOBBER ADAM ON THE RACE TRACK. OKAY, CHAMP?
YEAH, SURE. WHAT-EVER.

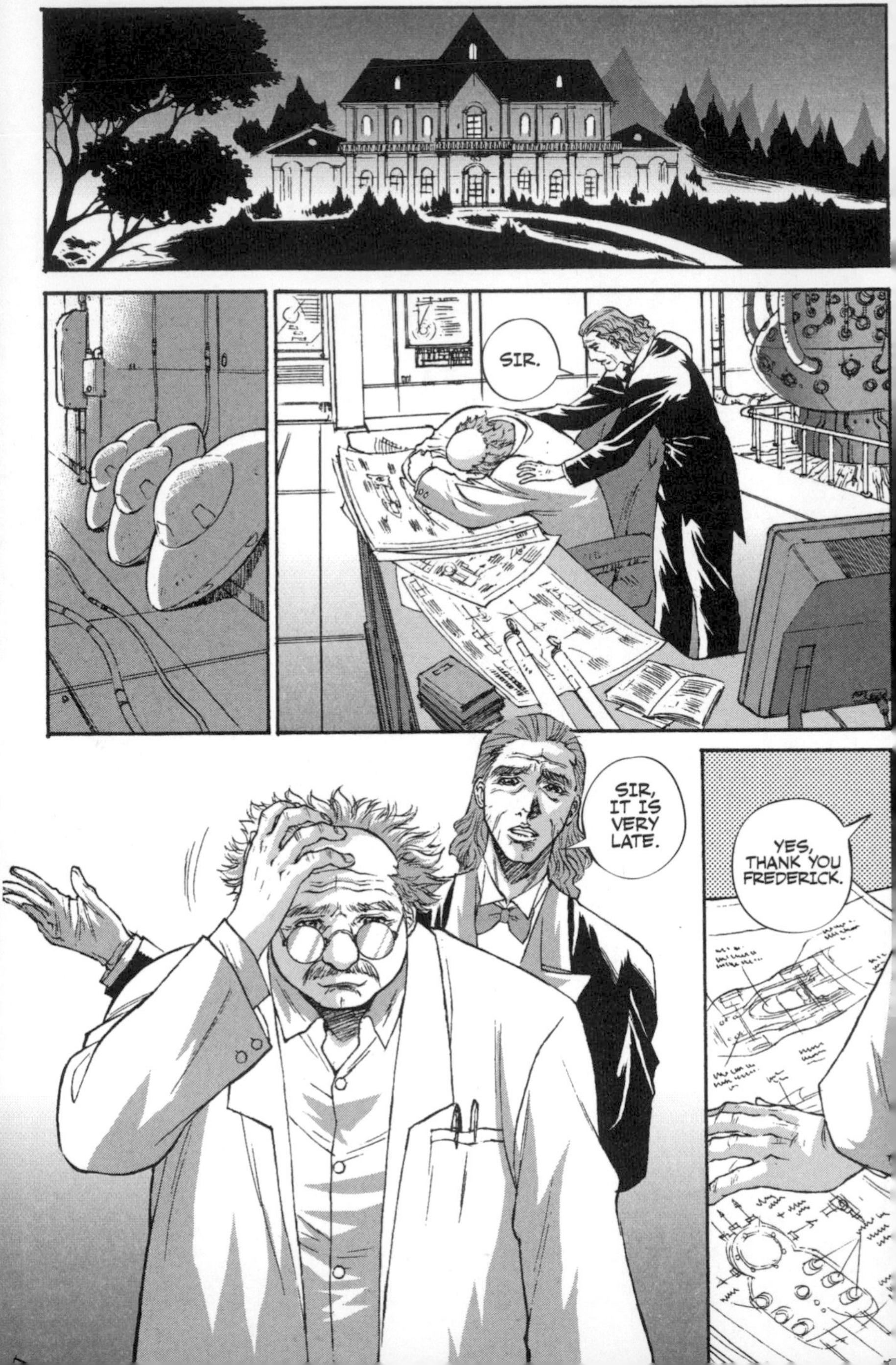

SIR.
SIR, IT IS VERY LATE.
YES, THANK YOU FREDERICK.

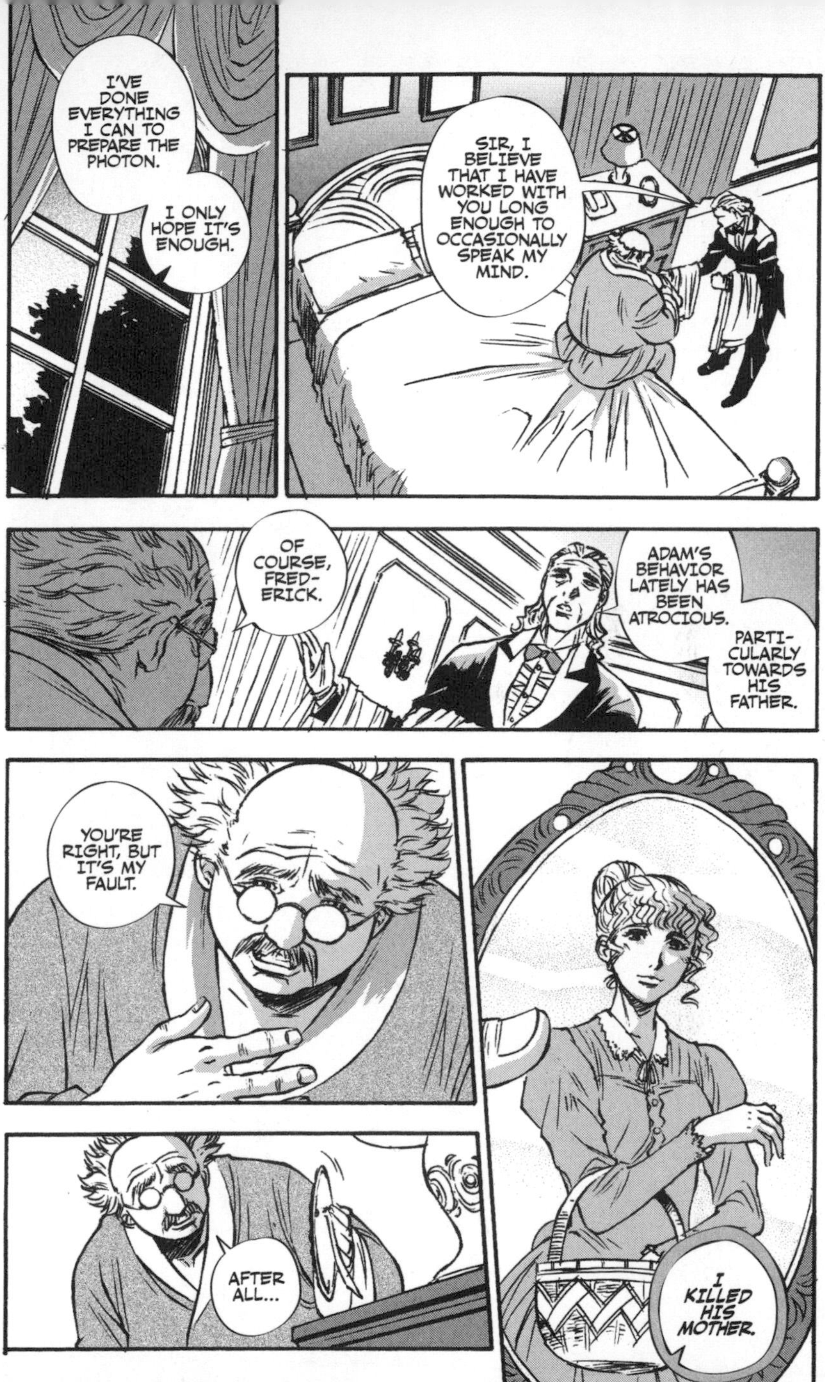
I'VE DONE EVERYTHING I CAN TO PREPARE THE PHOTON.
I ONLY HOPE IT'S ENOUGH.
SIR, I BELIEVE THAT I HAVE WORKED WITH YOU LONG ENOUGH TO OCCASIONALLY SPEAK MY MIND.
OF COURSE, FRED-ERICK.
ADAM'S BEHAVIOR LATELY HAS BEEN ATROCIOUS.
PARTI-CULARLY TOWARDS HIS FATHER.
YOU'RE RIGHT, BUT IT'S MY FAULT.
AFTER ALL...
I KILLED HIS MOTHER.

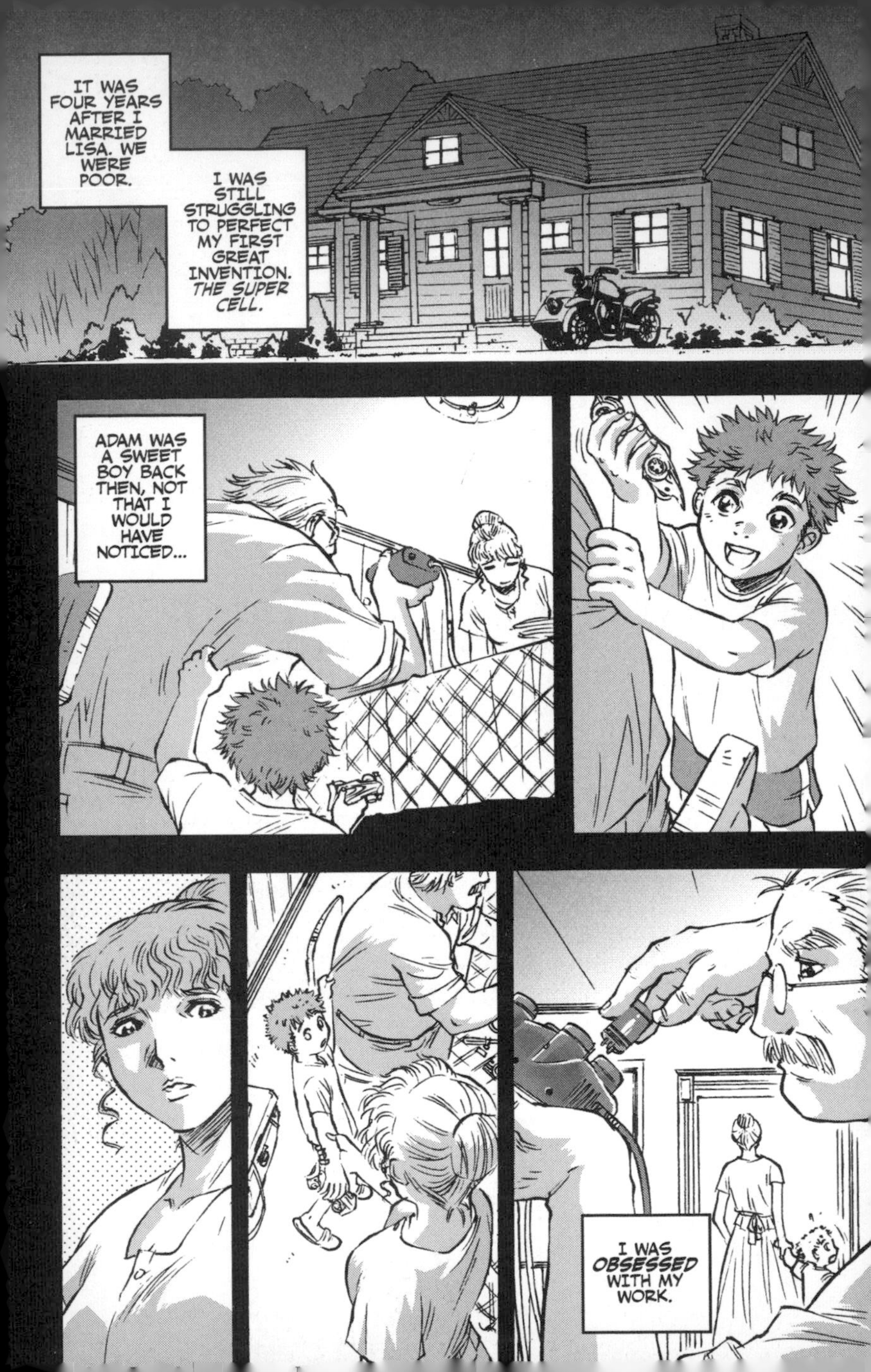
IT WAS FOUR YEARS AFTER I MARRIED LISA. WE WERE POOR.
I WAS STILL STRUGGLING TO PERFECT MY FIRST GREAT INVENTION. THE SUPER CELL.
ADAM WAS A SWEET BOY BACK THEN, NOT THAT I WOULD HAVE NOTICED...
I WAS OBSESSED WITH MY WORK.

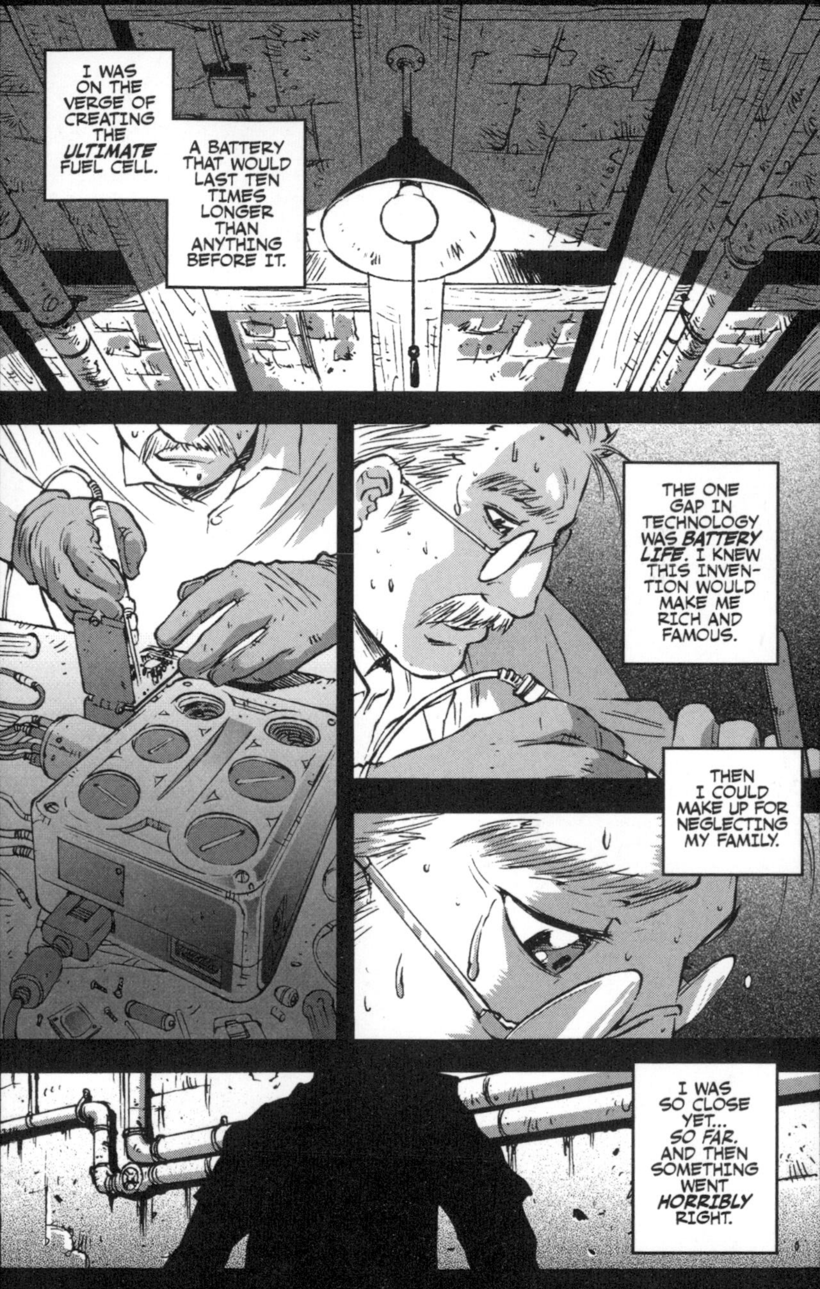
I WAS ON THE VERGE OF CREATING THE *ULTIMATE* FUEL CELL.
A BATTERY THAT WOULD LAST TEN TIMES LONGER THAN ANYTHING BEFORE IT.
THE ONE GAP IN TECHNOLOGY WAS *BATTERY LIFE*. I KNEW THIS INVENTION WOULD MAKE ME RICH AND FAMOUS.
THEN I COULD MAKE UP FOR NEGLECTING MY FAMILY.
I WAS SO CLOSE YET... *SO FAR*. AND THEN SOMETHING WENT *HORRIBLY* RIGHT.

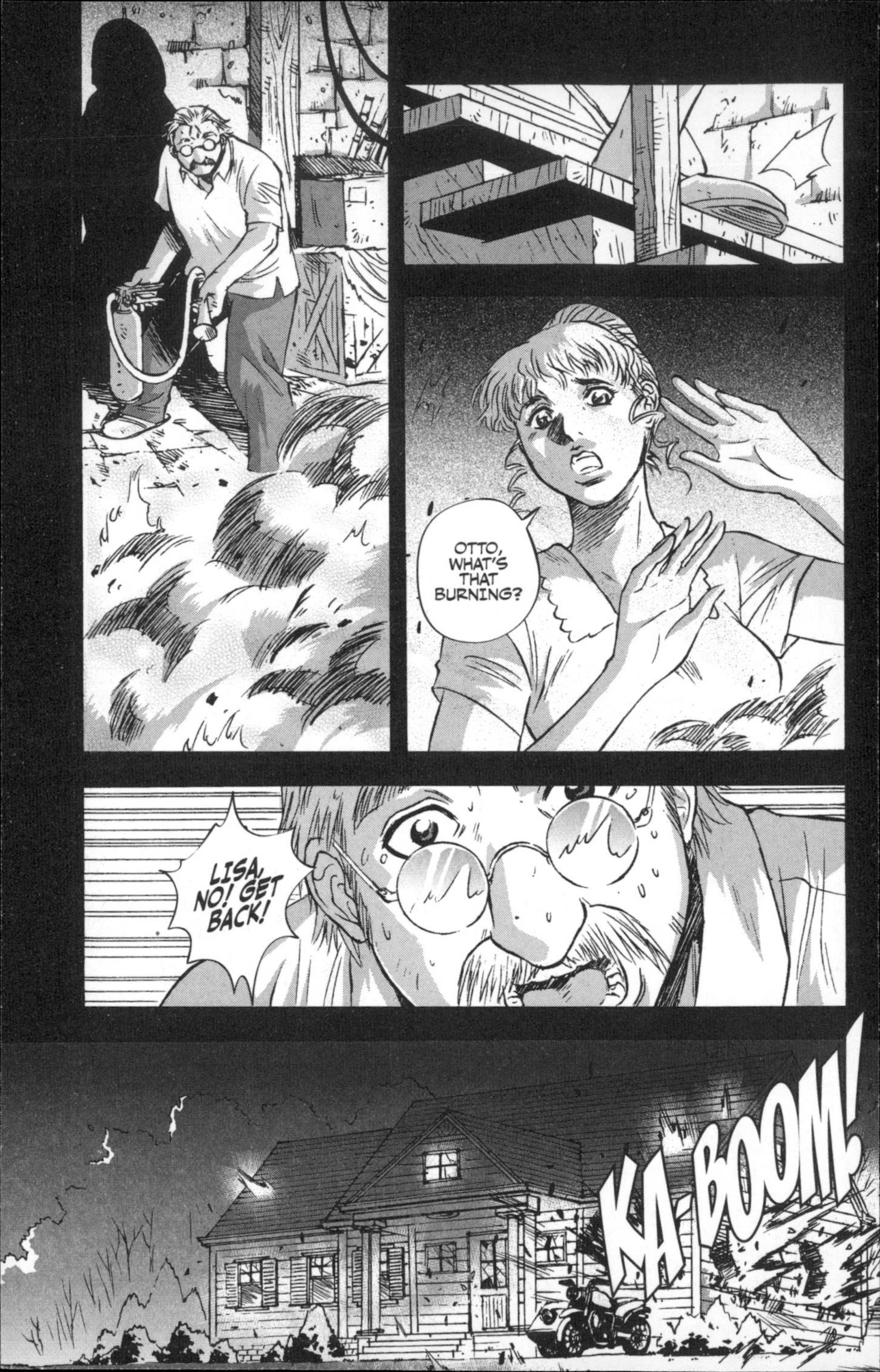
OTTO, WHAT'S THAT BURNING?
LISA, NO! GET BACK!
KA-BOOM!

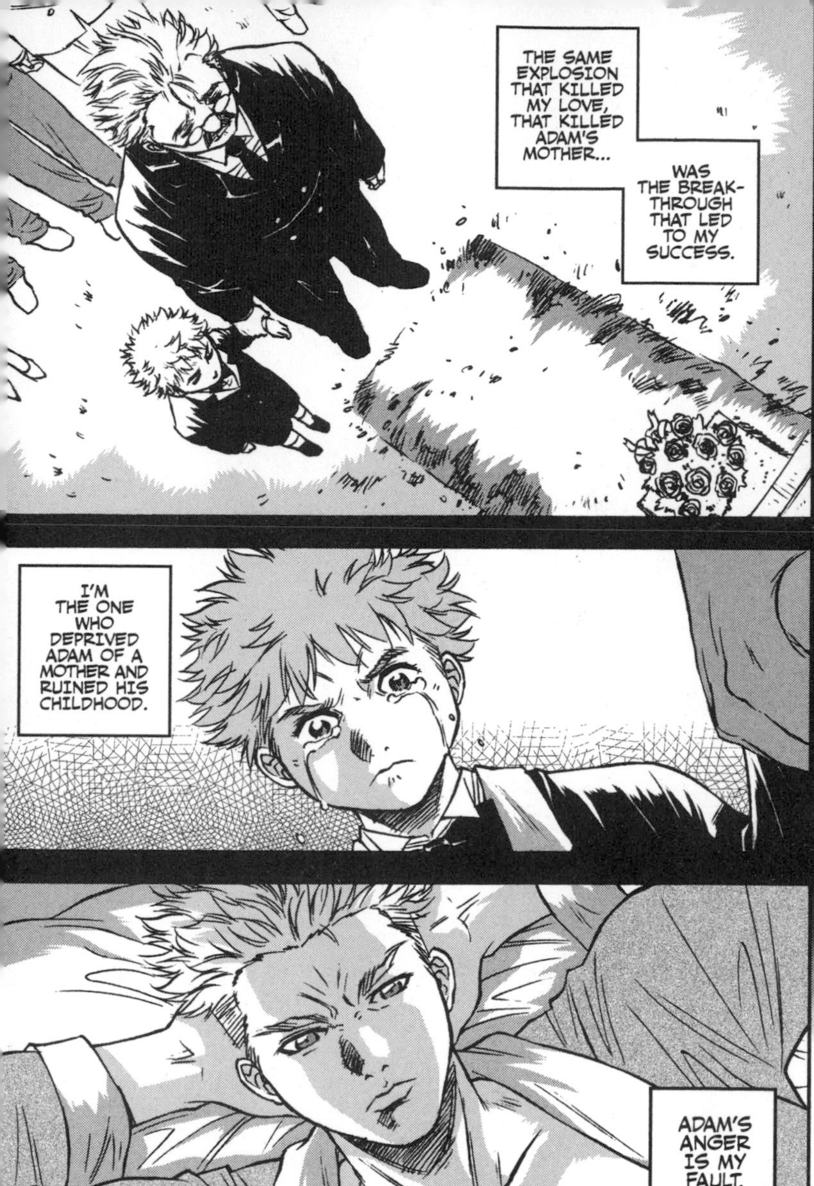
THE SAME EXPLOSION THAT KILLED MY LOVE, THAT KILLED ADAM'S MOTHER...
WAS THE BREAK-THROUGH THAT LED TO MY SUCCESS.
I'M THE ONE WHO DEPRIVED ADAM OF A MOTHER AND RUINED HIS CHILDHOOD.
ADAM'S ANGER IS MY FAULT.

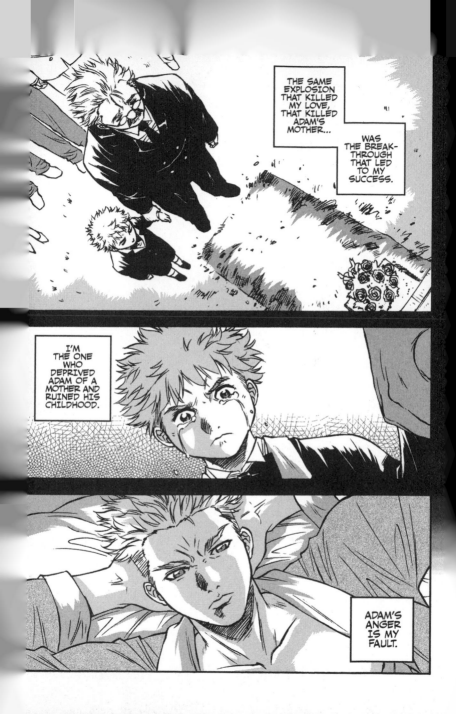

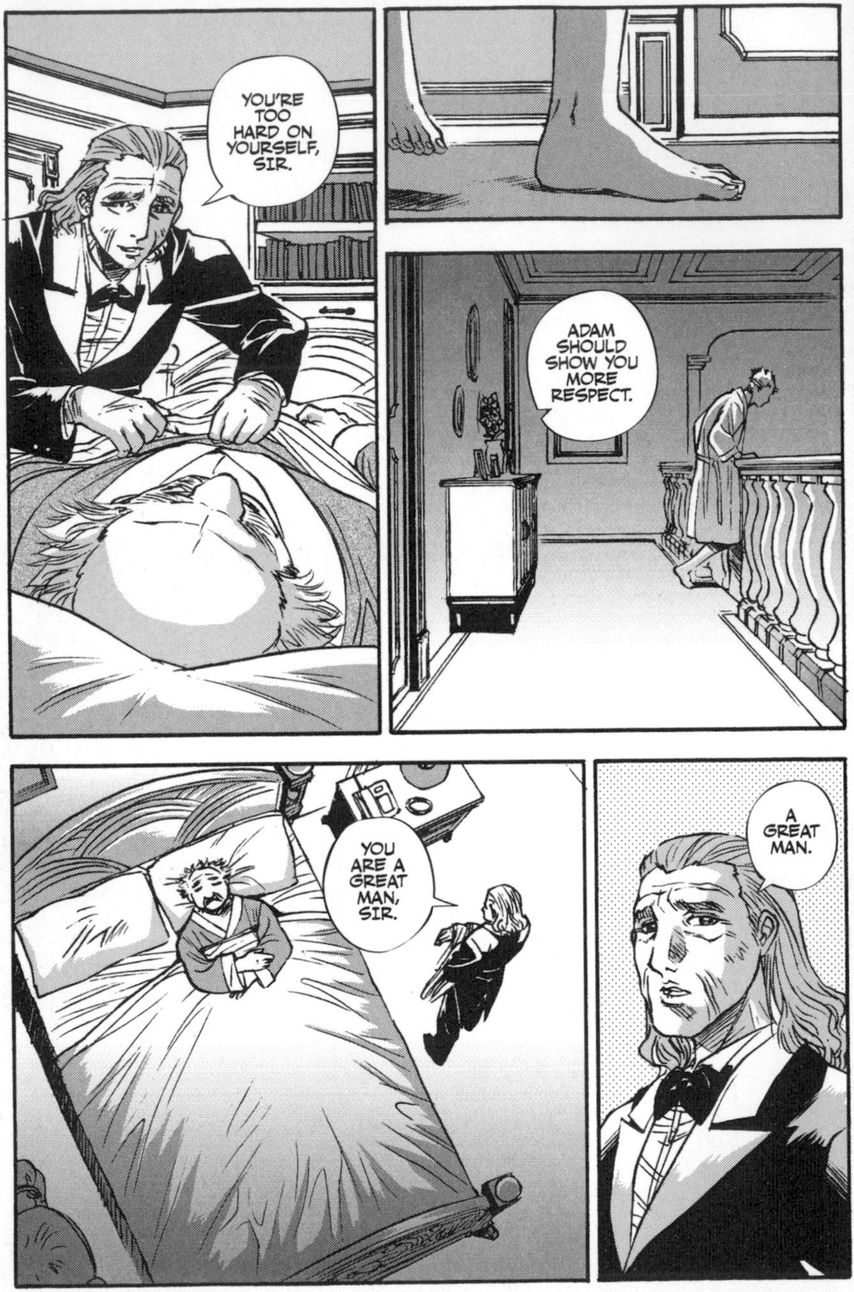
YOU'RE TOO HARD ON YOURSELF, SIR.
ADAM SHOULD SHOW YOU MORE RESPECT.
YOU ARE A GREAT MAN, SIR.
A GREAT MAN.

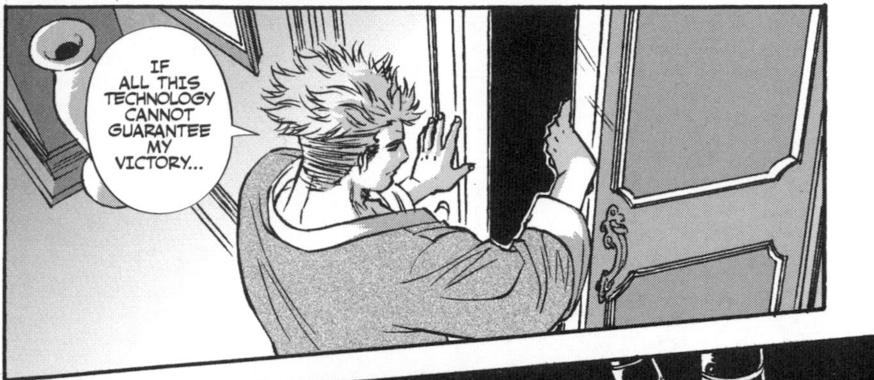
IF ALL THIS TECHNOLOGY CANNOT GUARANTEE MY VICTORY...
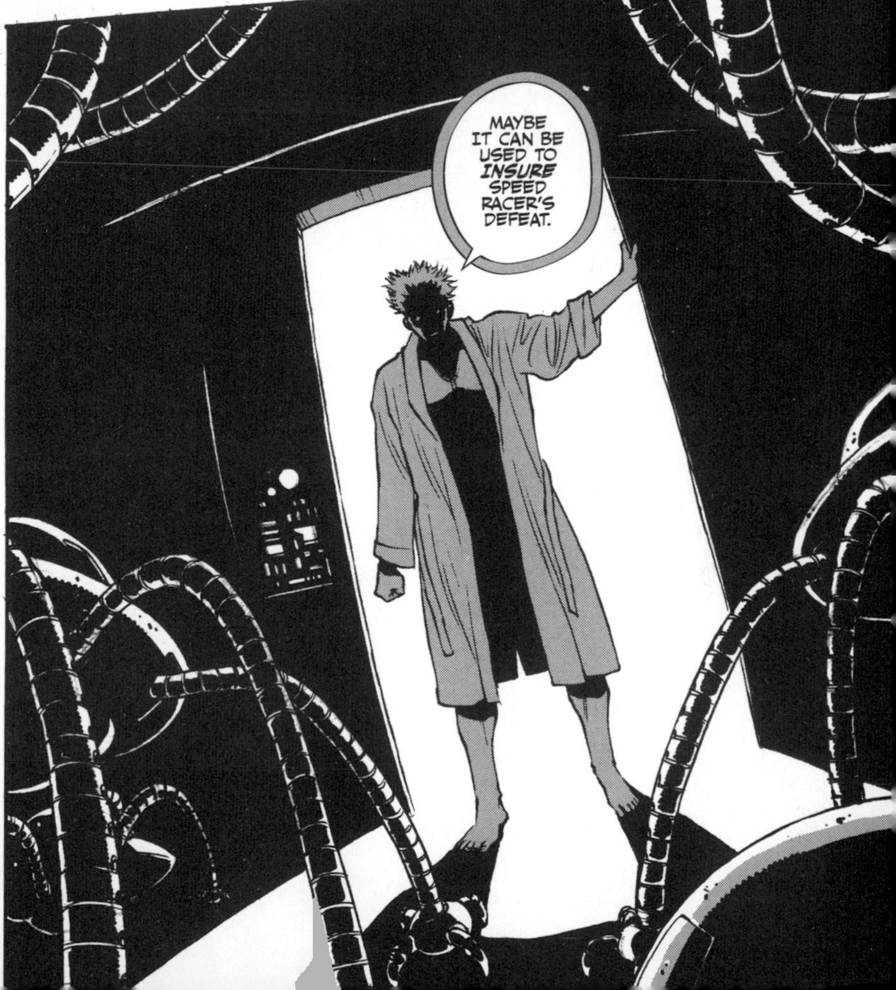
MAYBE IT CAN BE USED TO INSURE SPEED RACER'S DEFEAT.

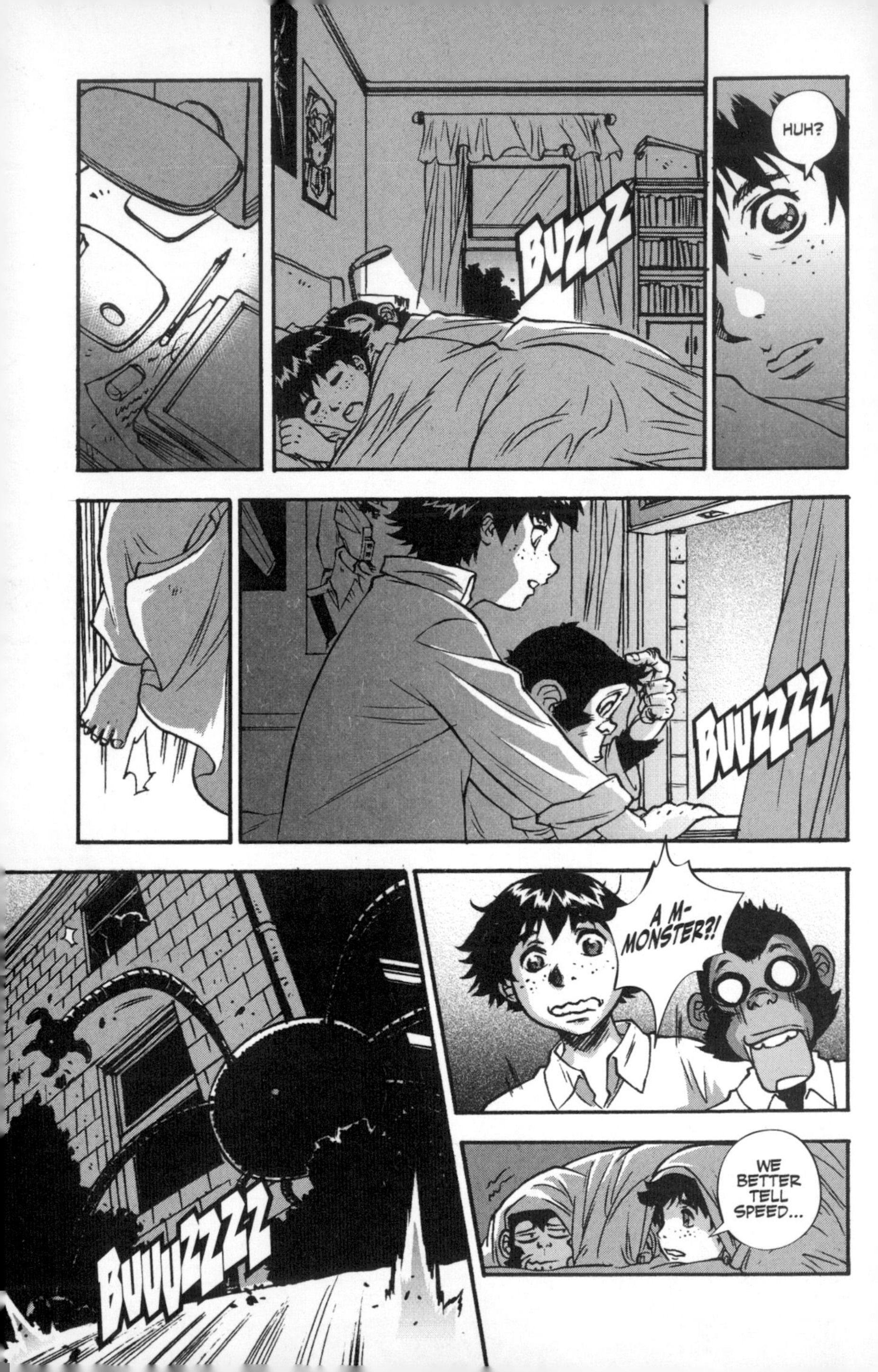
BUZZZ
HUH?
BUUZZZZ
BUUUZZZZ
A M-MONSTER?!
WE BETTER TELL SPEED...

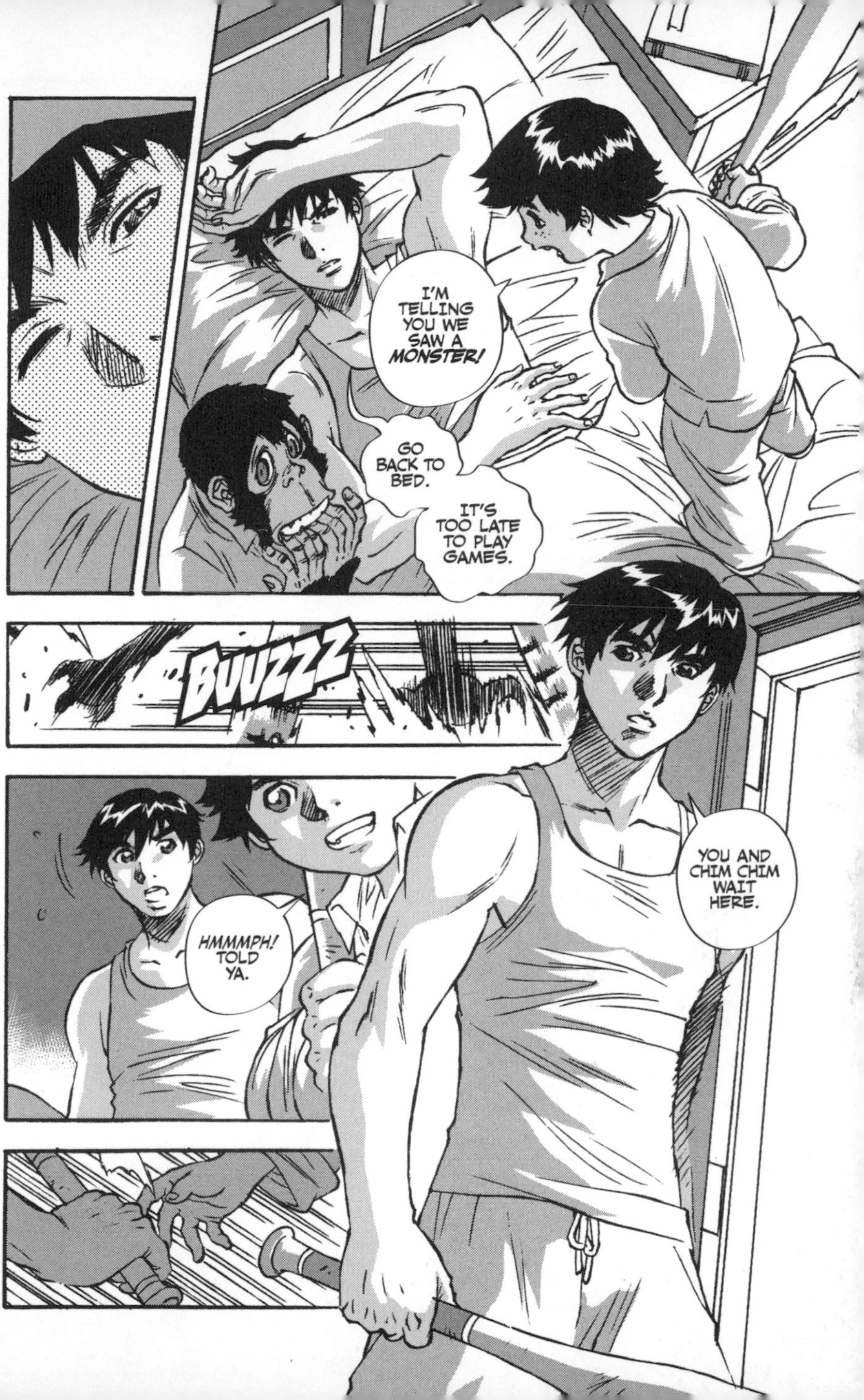
I'M TELLING YOU WE SAW A *MONSTER!*
GO BACK TO BED.
IT'S TOO LATE TO PLAY GAMES.
BUUZZZ
HMMMPH! TOLD YA.
YOU AND CHIM CHIM WAIT HERE.

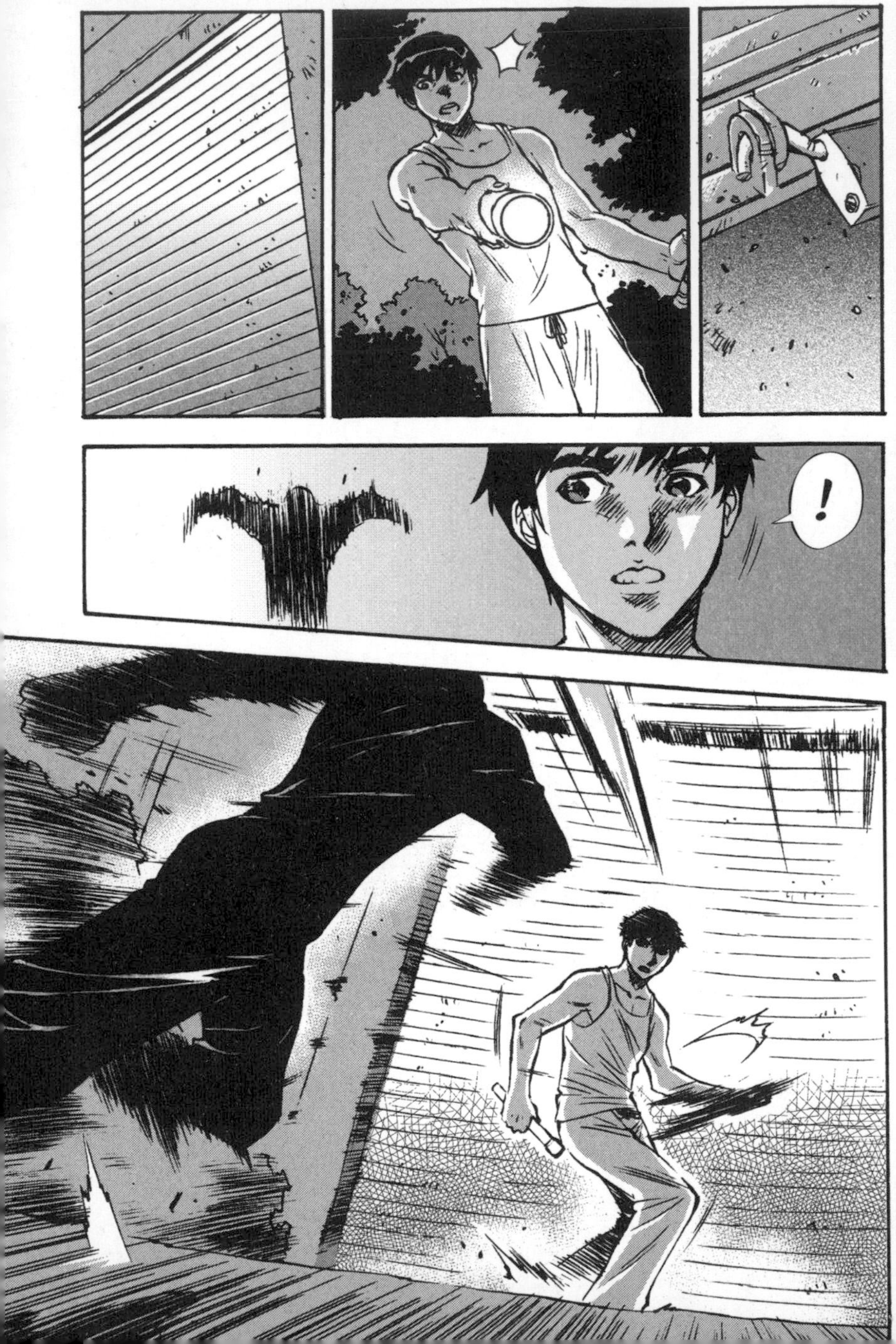
!

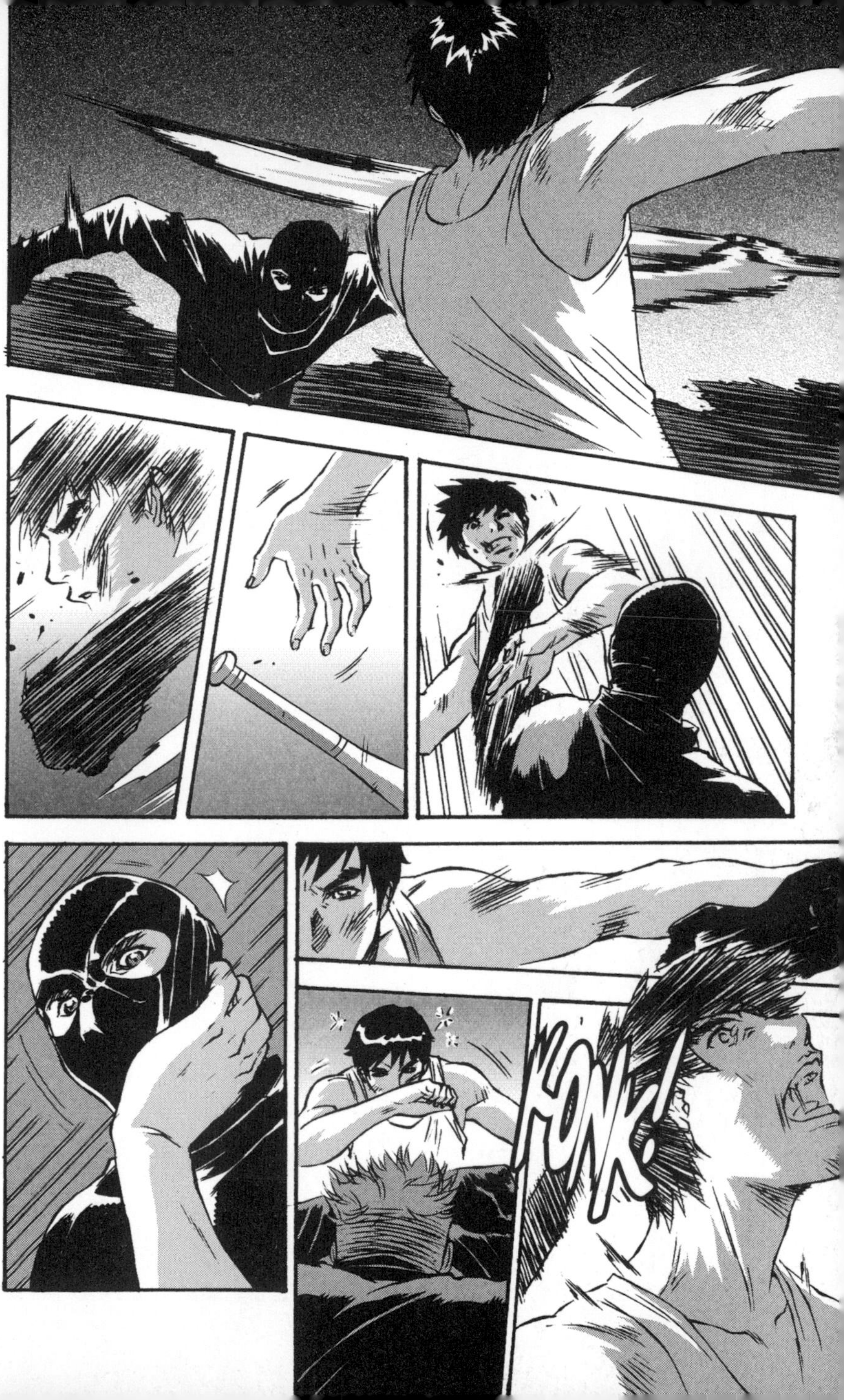
PONK!

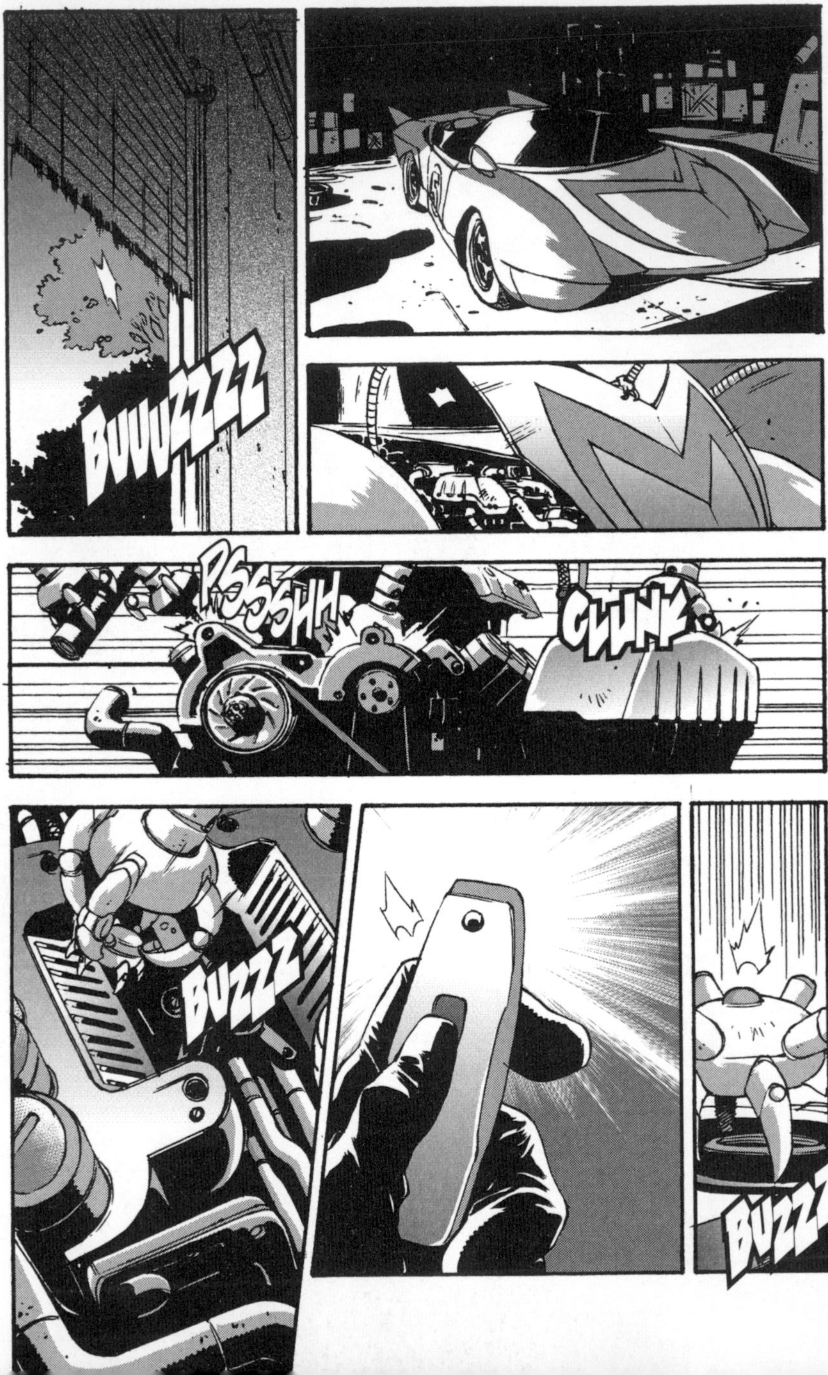
BUUZZZZ
PSSSHH
CLUNK
BUZZZ
BUZZZ

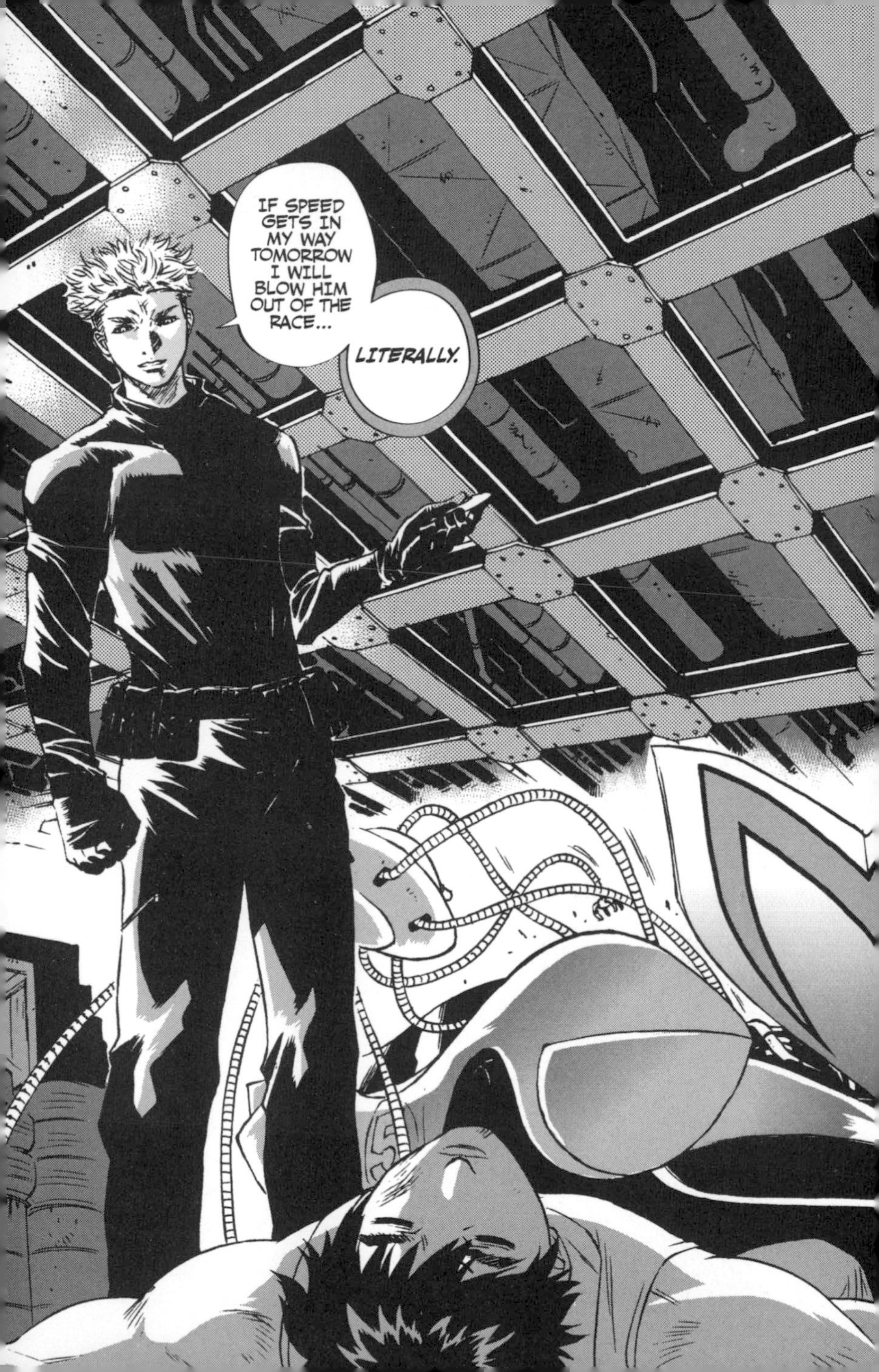
IF SPEED GETS IN MY WAY TOMORROW I WILL BLOW HIM OUT OF THE RACE...
LITERALLY.

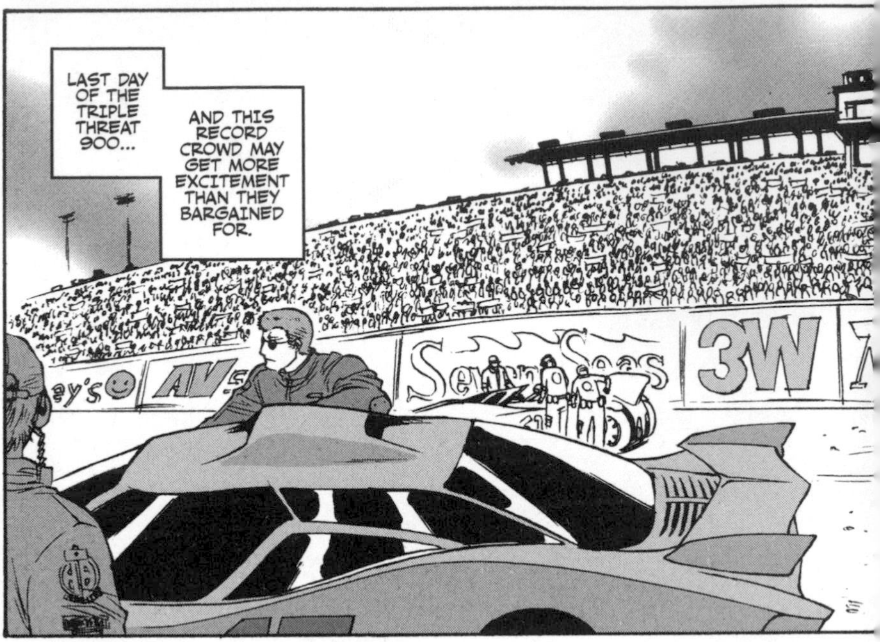
LAST DAY OF THE TRIPLE THREAT 900...
AND THIS RECORD CROWD MAY GET MORE EXCITEMENT THAN THEY BARGAINED FOR.
3W

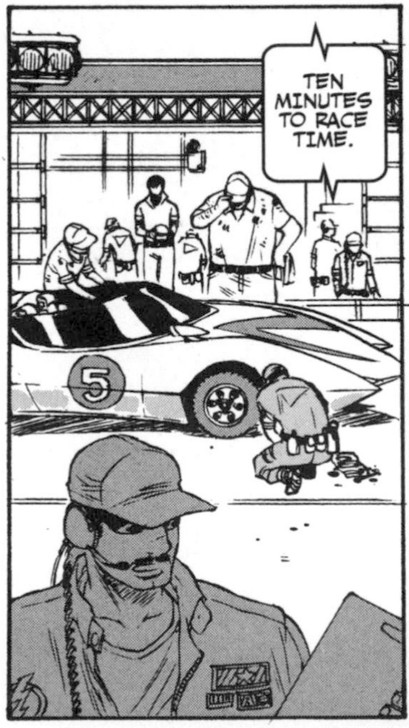
TEN MINUTES TO RACE TIME.
5

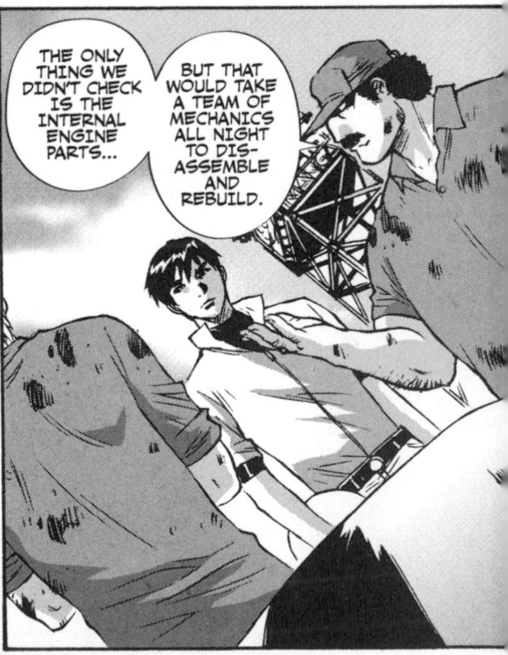
THE ONLY THING WE DIDN'T CHECK IS THE INTERNAL ENGINE PARTS...
BUT THAT WOULD TAKE A TEAM OF MECHANICS ALL NIGHT TO DIS-ASSEMBLE AND REBUILD.

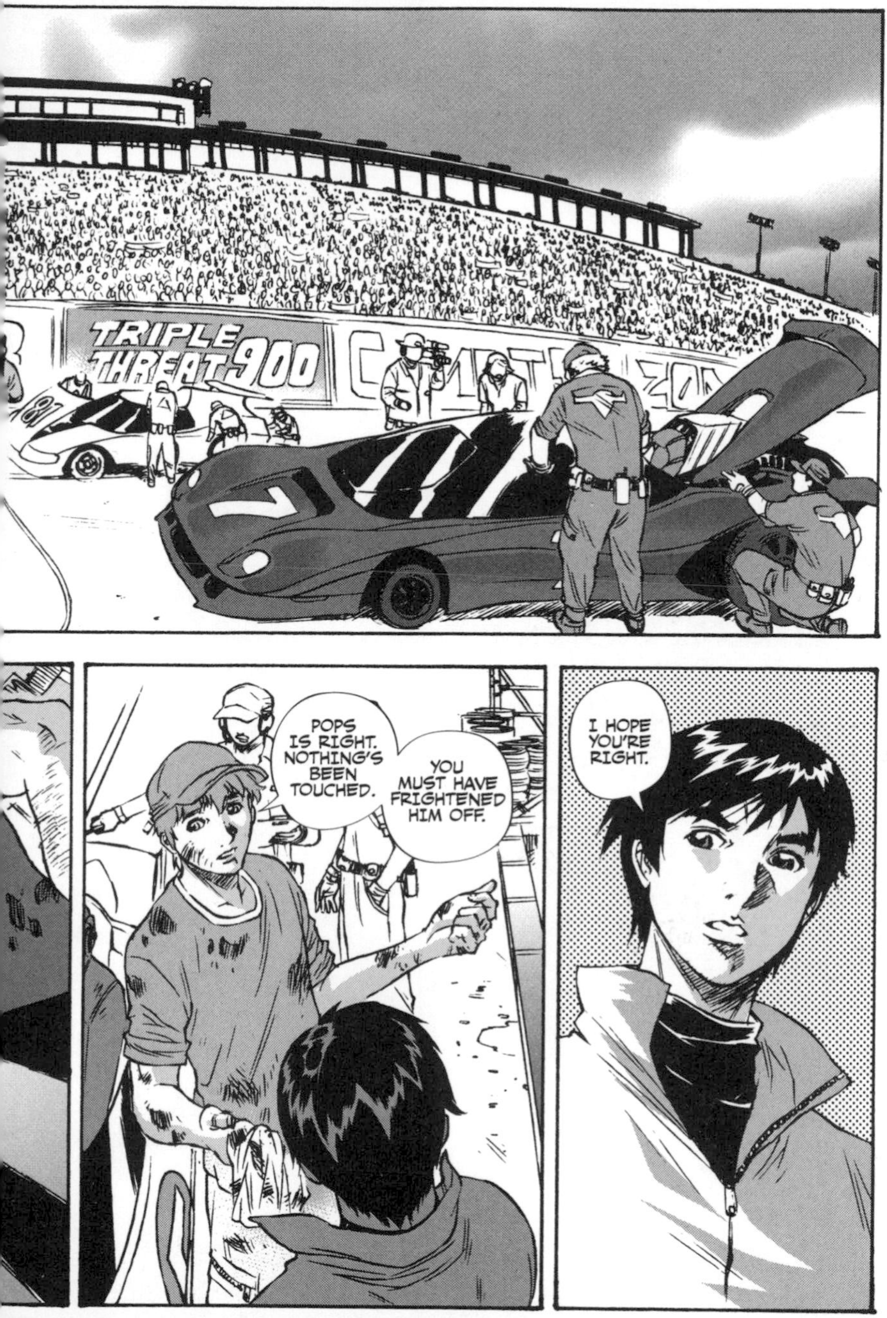
TRIPLE THREAT 900
POPS IS RIGHT. NOTHING'S BEEN TOUCHED.
YOU MUST HAVE FRIGHTENED HIM OFF.
I HOPE YOU'RE RIGHT.

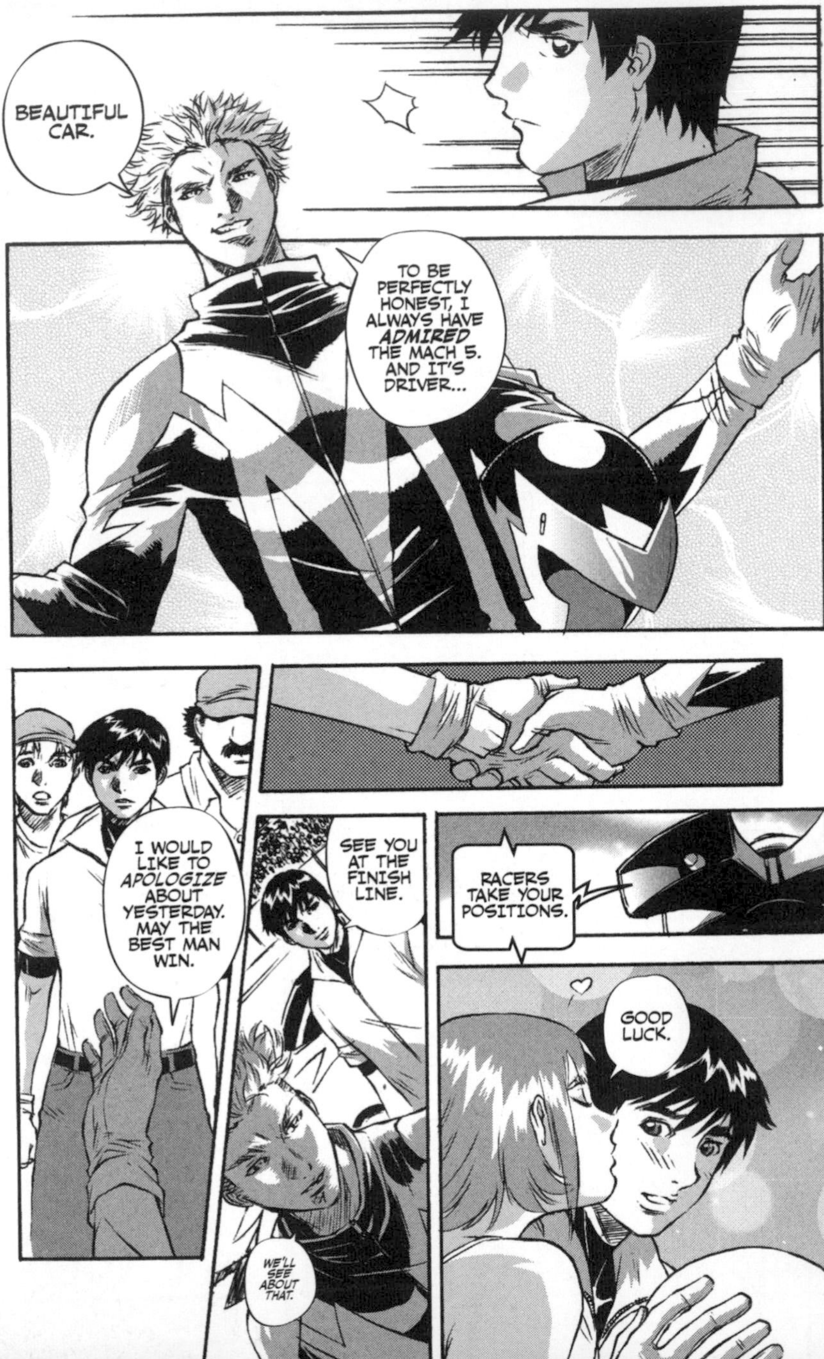
BEAUTIFUL CAR.
TO BE PERFECTLY HONEST, I ALWAYS HAVE ADMIRED THE MACH 5. AND IT'S DRIVER...
I WOULD LIKE TO APOLOGIZE ABOUT YESTERDAY. MAY THE BEST MAN WIN.
SEE YOU AT THE FINISH LINE.
WE'LL SEE ABOUT THAT.
RACERS TAKE YOUR POSITIONS.
GOOD LUCK.

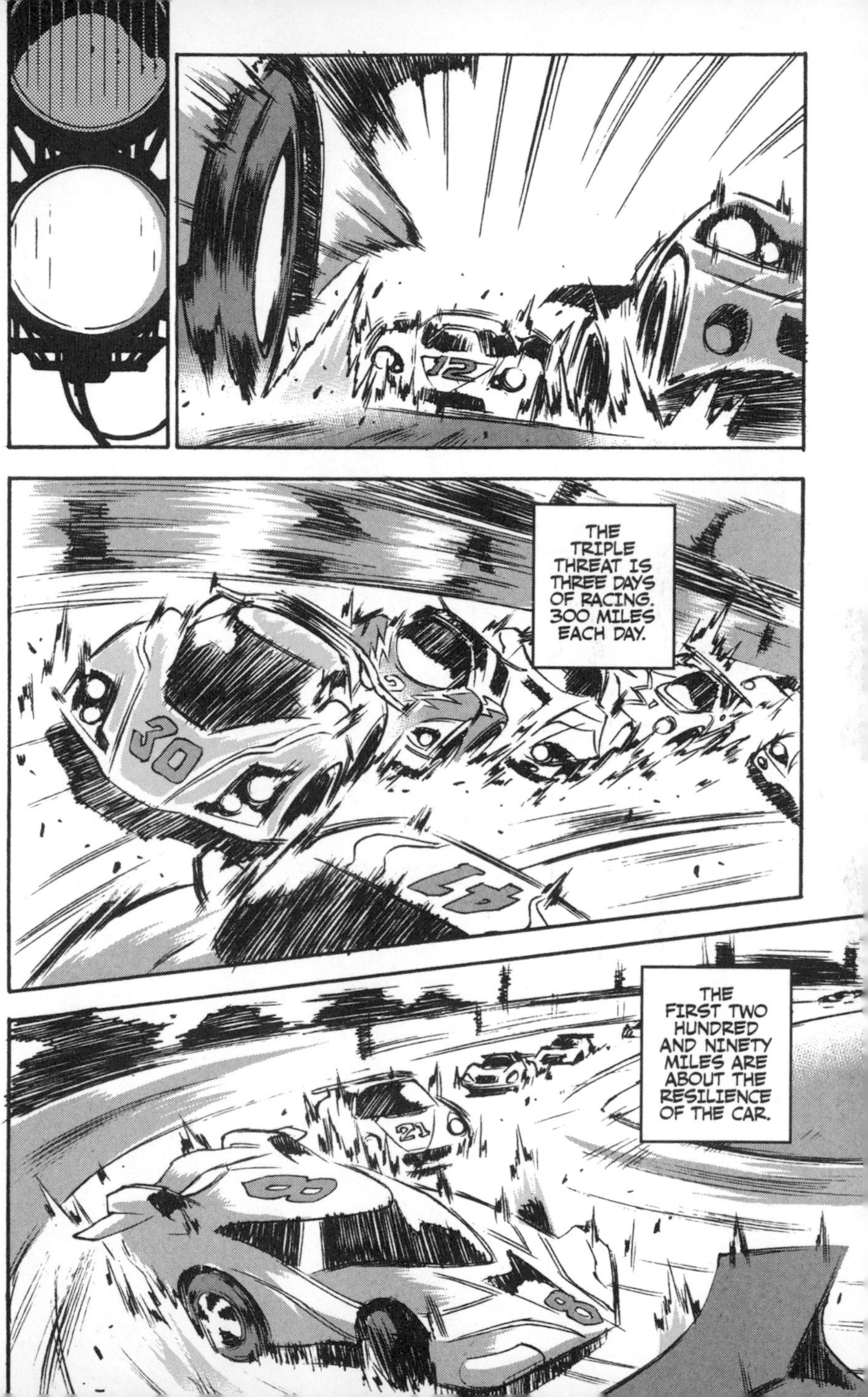
THE TRIPLE THREAT IS THREE DAYS OF RACING. 300 MILES EACH DAY.
THE FIRST TWO HUNDRED AND NINETY MILES ARE ABOUT THE RESILIENCE OF THE CAR.

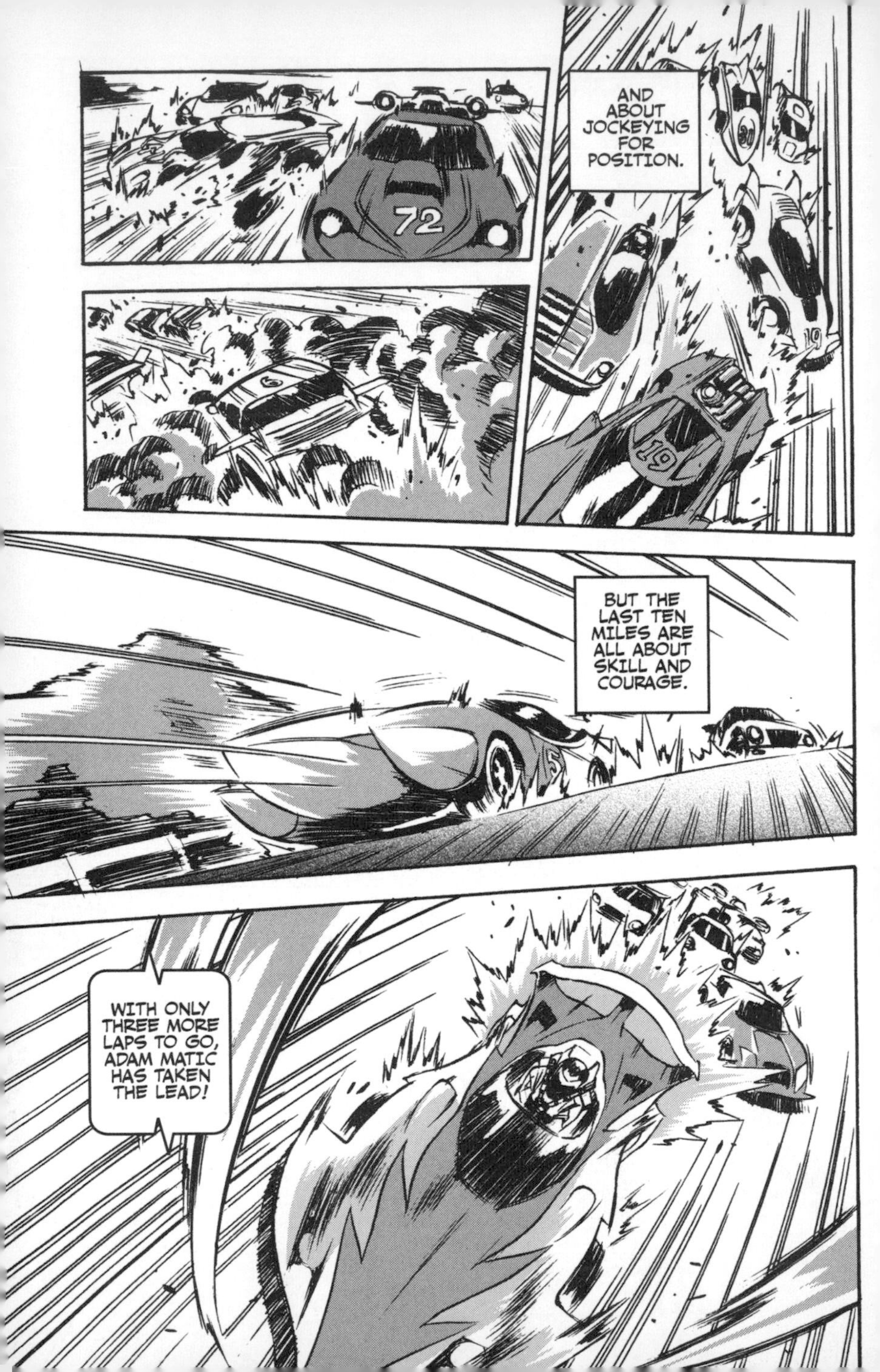
AND ABOUT JOCKEYING FOR POSITION.
BUT THE LAST TEN MILES ARE ALL ABOUT SKILL AND COURAGE.
WITH ONLY THREE MORE LAPS TO GO, ADAM MATIC HAS TAKEN THE LEAD!

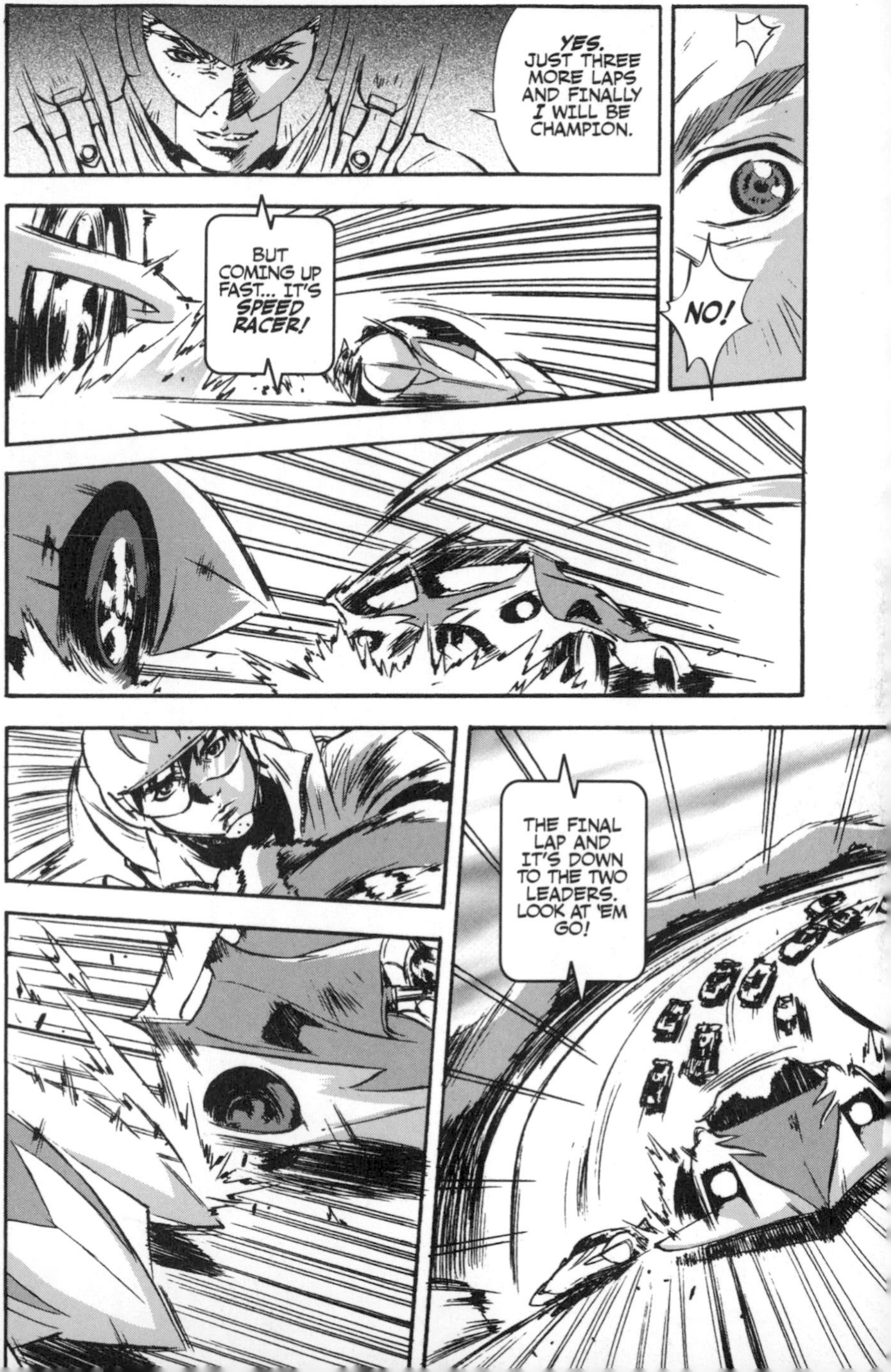
YES. JUST THREE MORE LAPS AND FINALLY I WILL BE CHAMPION.
BUT COMING UP FAST... IT'S SPEED RACER!
NO!
THE FINAL LAP AND IT'S DOWN TO THE TWO LEADERS. LOOK AT 'EM GO!

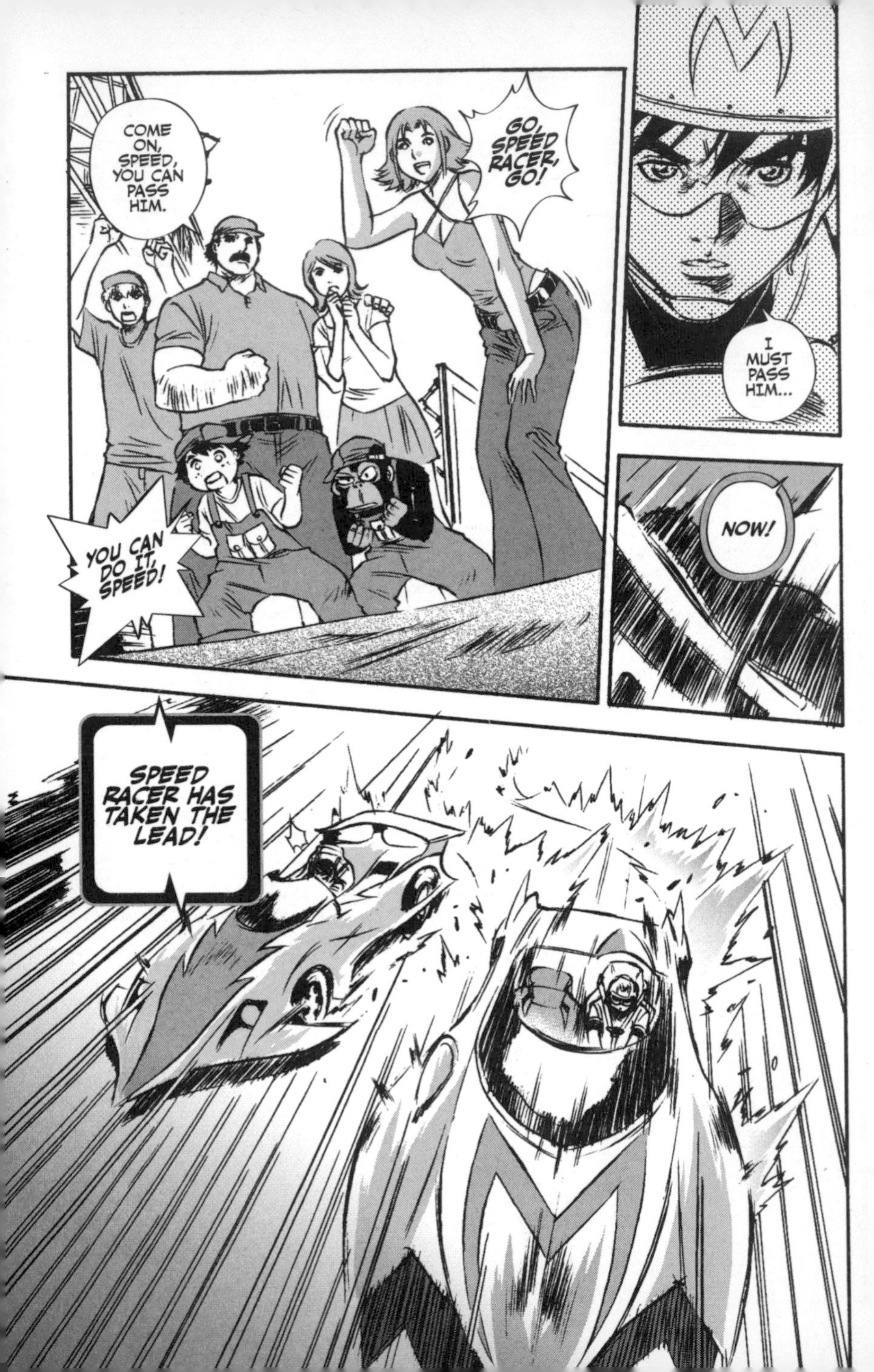
COME ON, SPEED, YOU CAN PASS HIM.
GO, SPEED RACER, GO!
YOU CAN DO IT, SPEED!
I MUST PASS HIM...
NOW!
SPEED RACER HAS TAKEN THE LEAD!

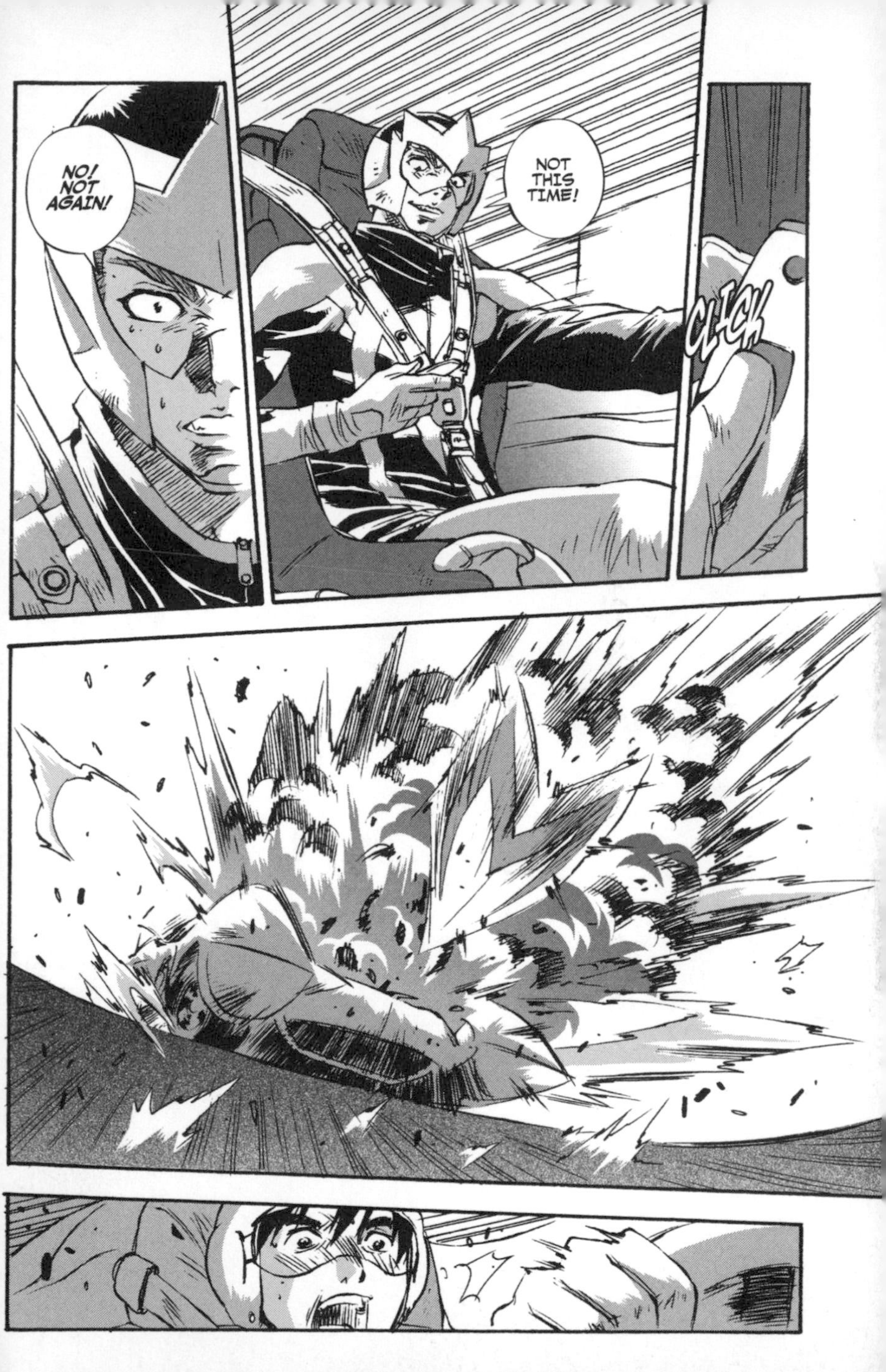
NO! NOT AGAIN!
NOT THIS TIME!
CLICK

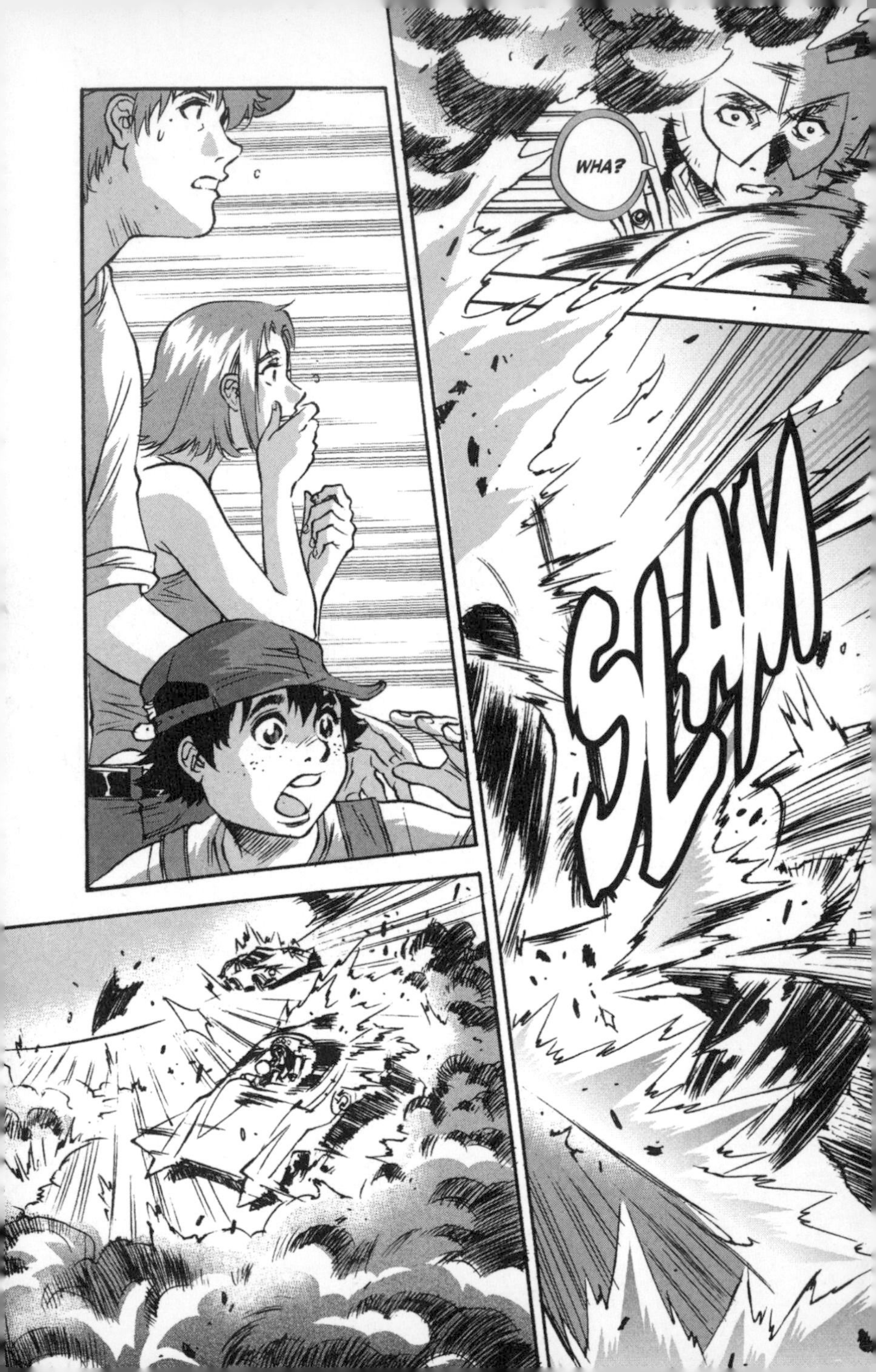
WHA?
SLAM

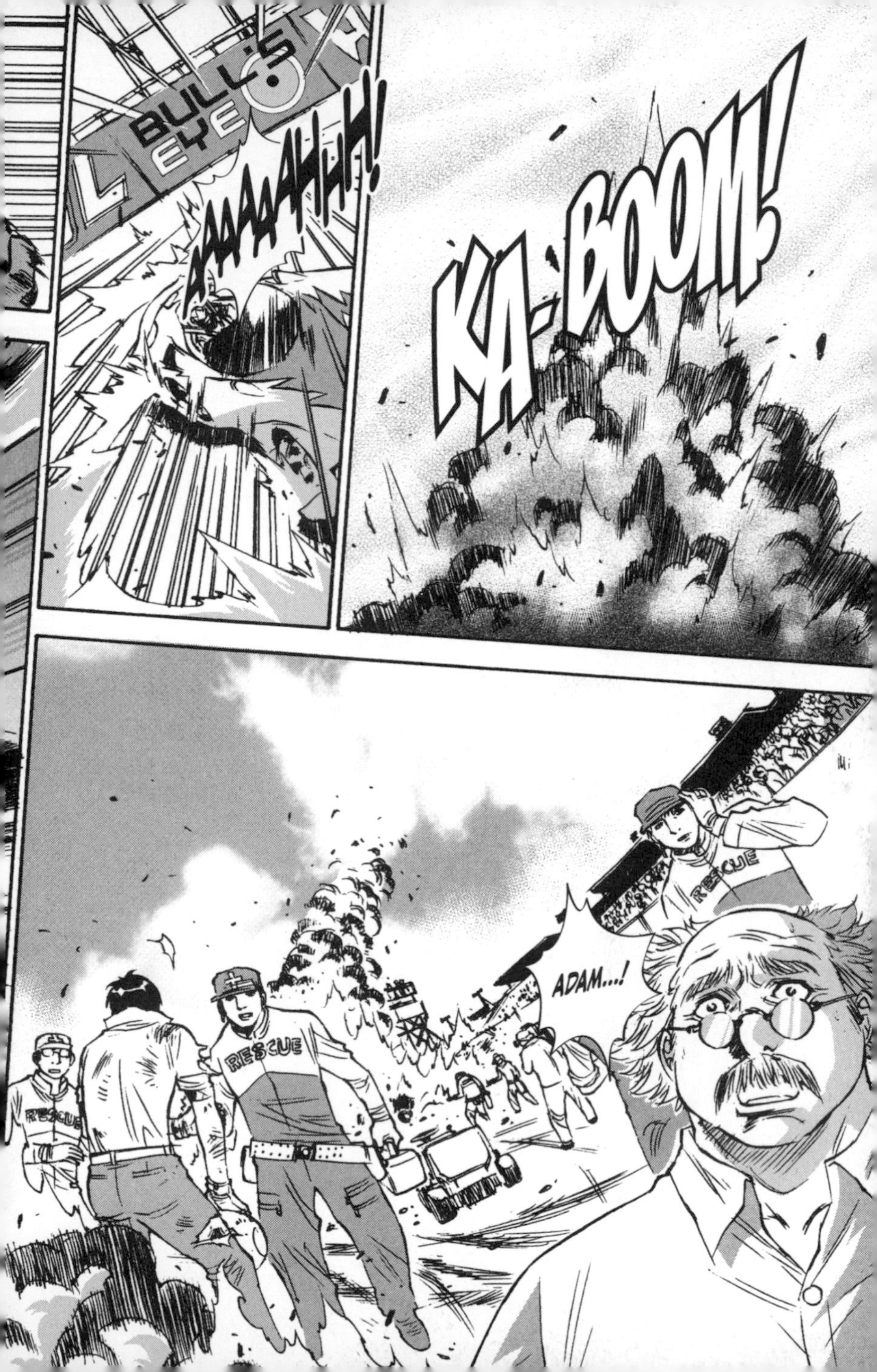

BULL'S EYE
AAAAAHHH!
KA-BOOM!
RESCUE
RESCUE
RESCUE
ADAM...!

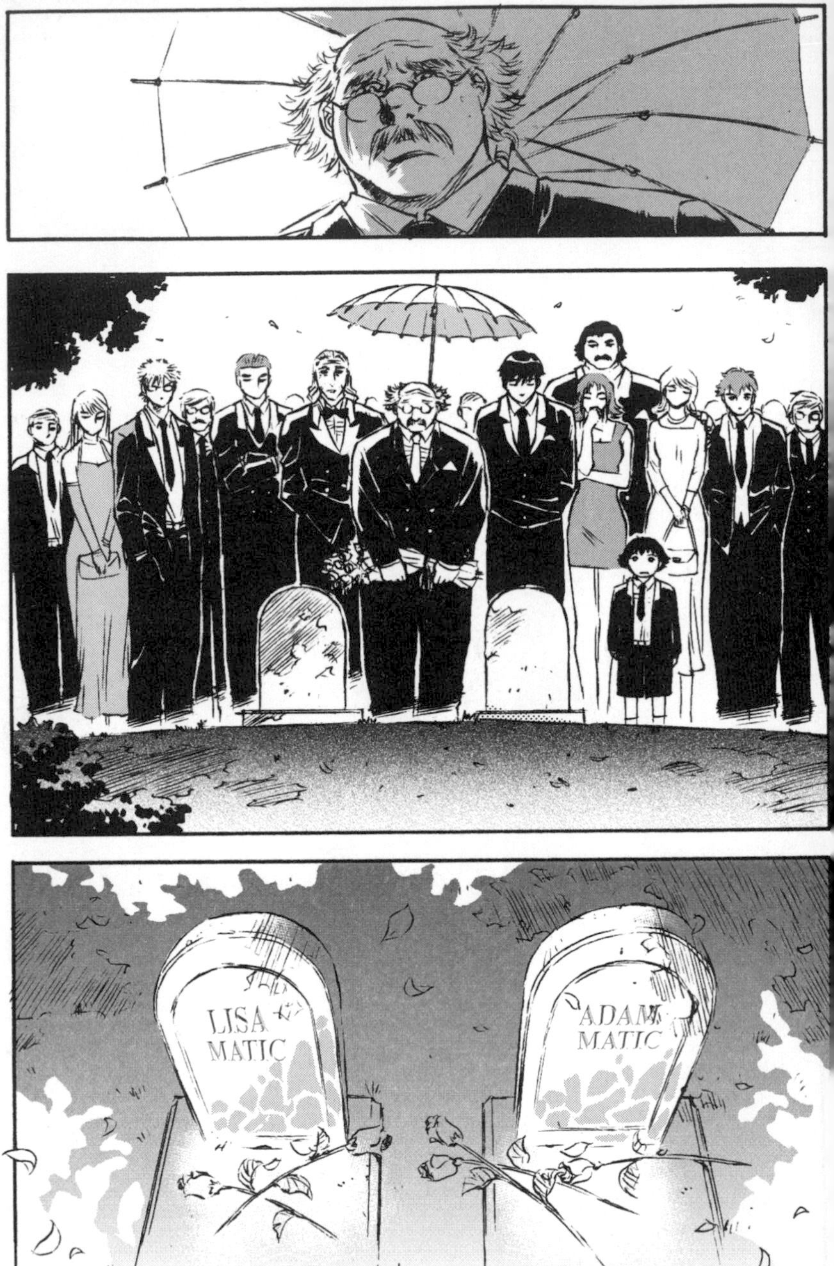
LISA MATIC
ADAM MATIC

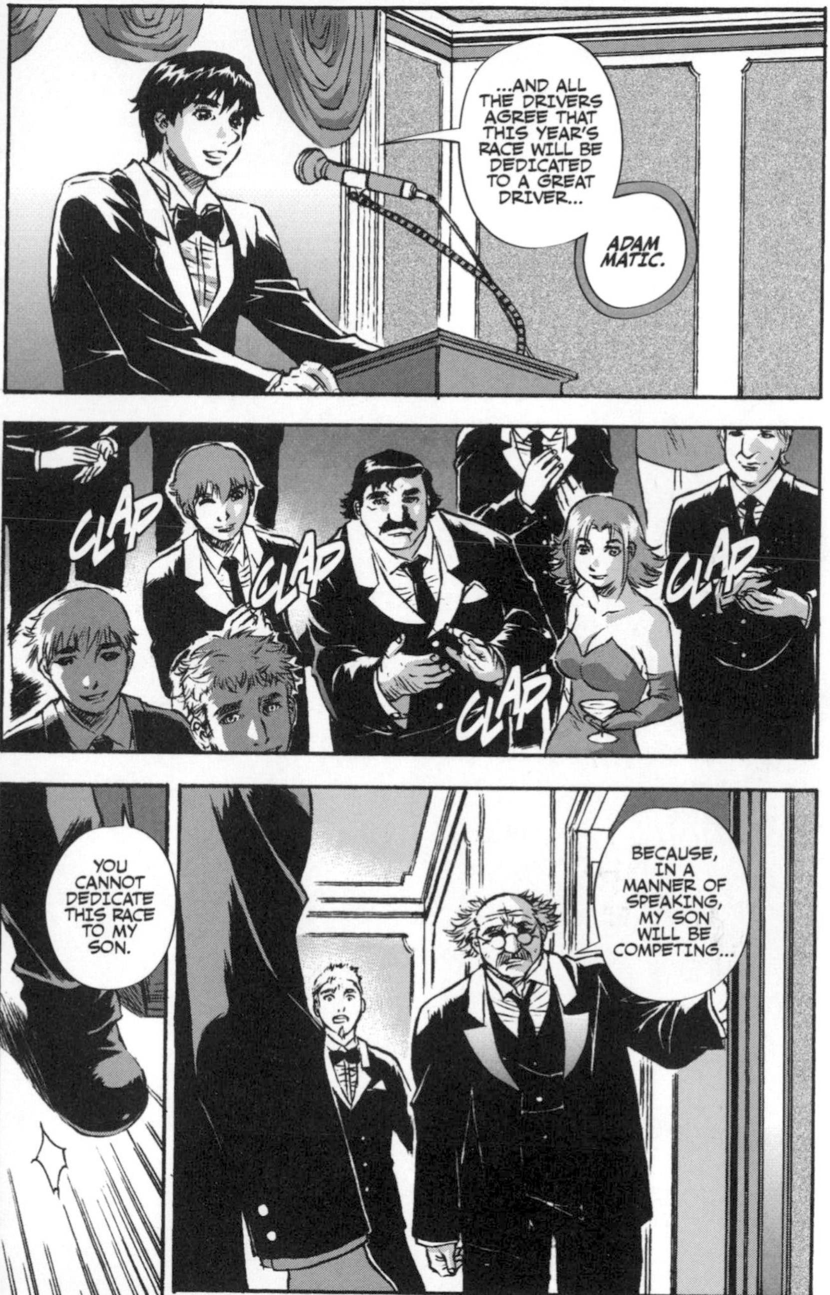
...AND ALL THE DRIVERS AGREE THAT THIS YEAR'S RACE WILL BE DEDICATED TO A GREAT DRIVER...
ADAM MATIC.
CLAP
CLAP
CLAP
CLAP
YOU CANNOT DEDICATE THIS RACE TO MY SON.
BECAUSE, IN A MANNER OF SPEAKING, MY SON WILL BE COMPETING...

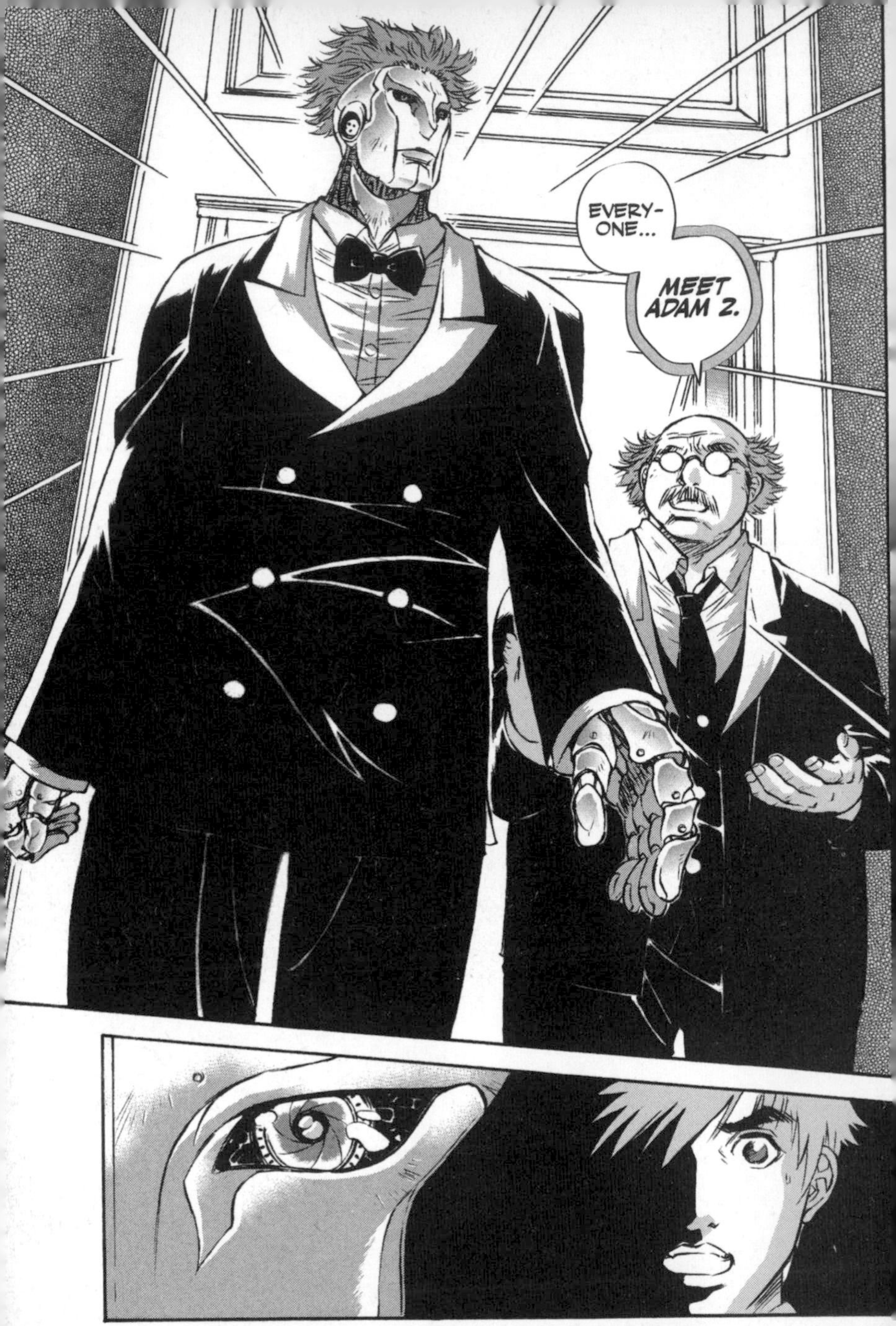
EVERY-ONE...
MEET ADAM 2.

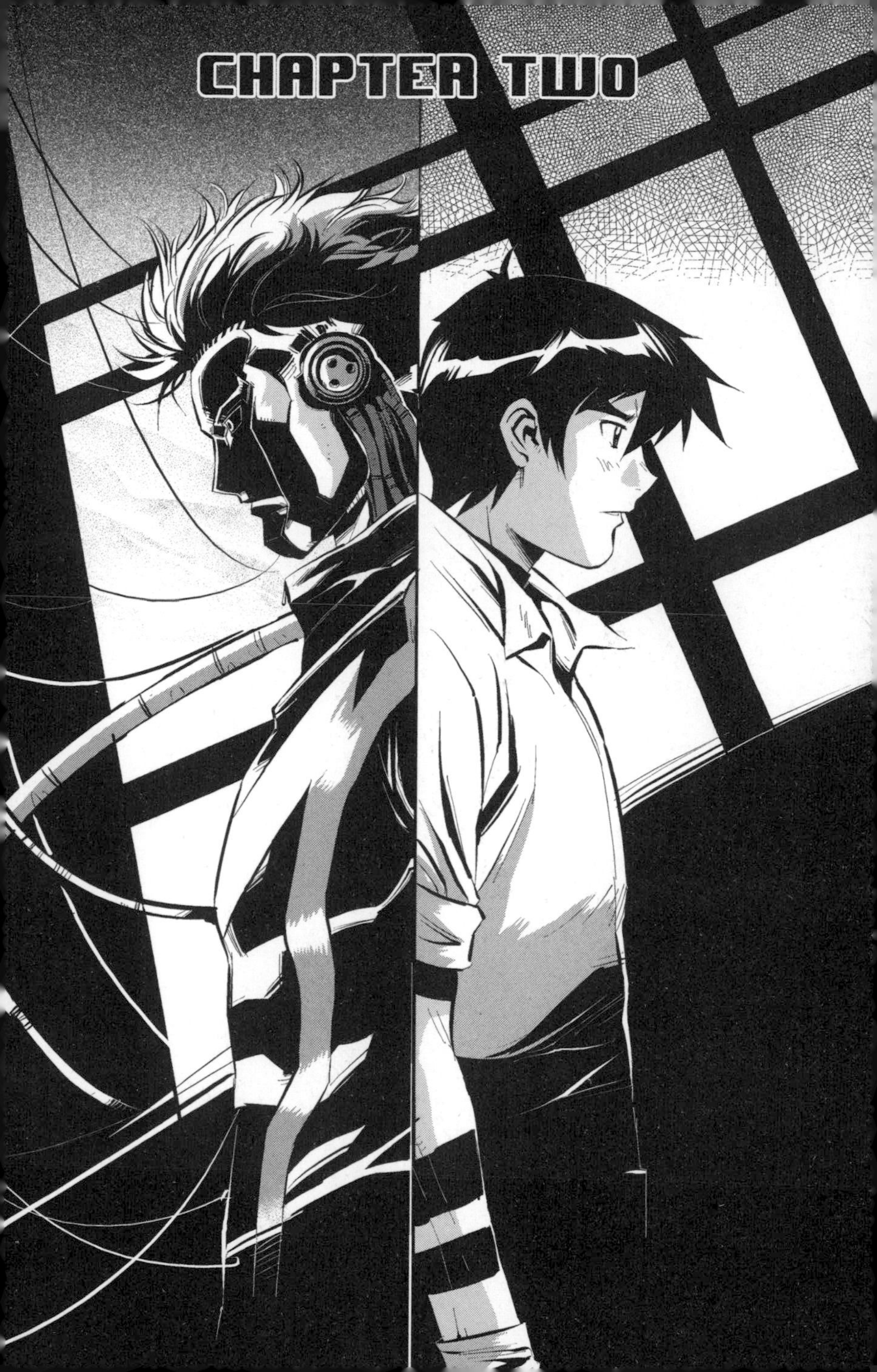
CHAPTER TWO

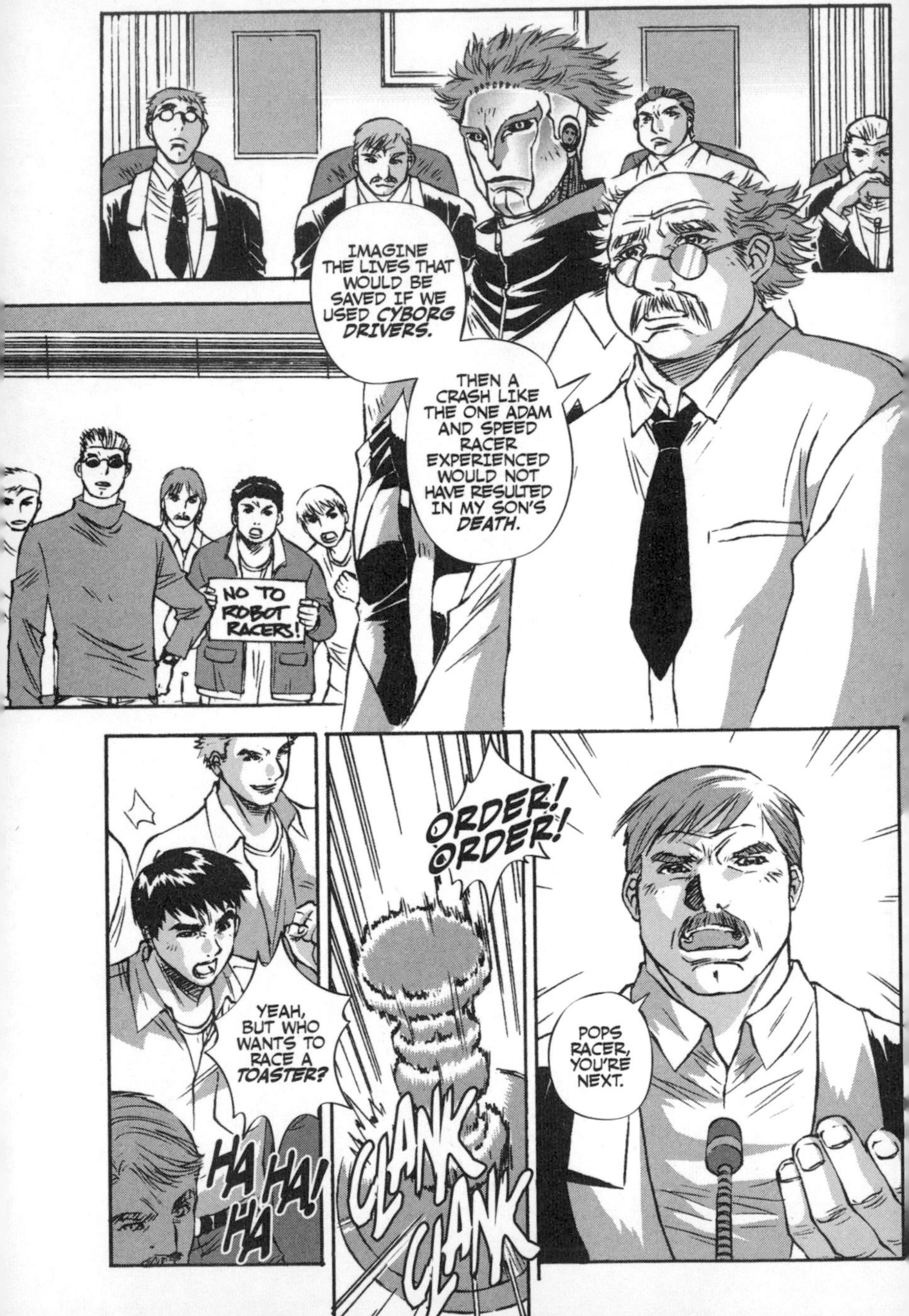
IMAGINE THE LIVES THAT WOULD BE SAVED IF WE USED CYBORG DRIVERS.
THEN A CRASH LIKE THE ONE ADAM AND SPEED RACER EXPERIENCED WOULD NOT HAVE RESULTED IN MY SON'S DEATH.
NO TO ROBOT RACERS!
YEAH, BUT WHO WANTS TO RACE A TOASTER?
HA HA! HA
ORDER! ORDER!
CLANK CLANK
POPS RACER, YOU'RE NEXT.

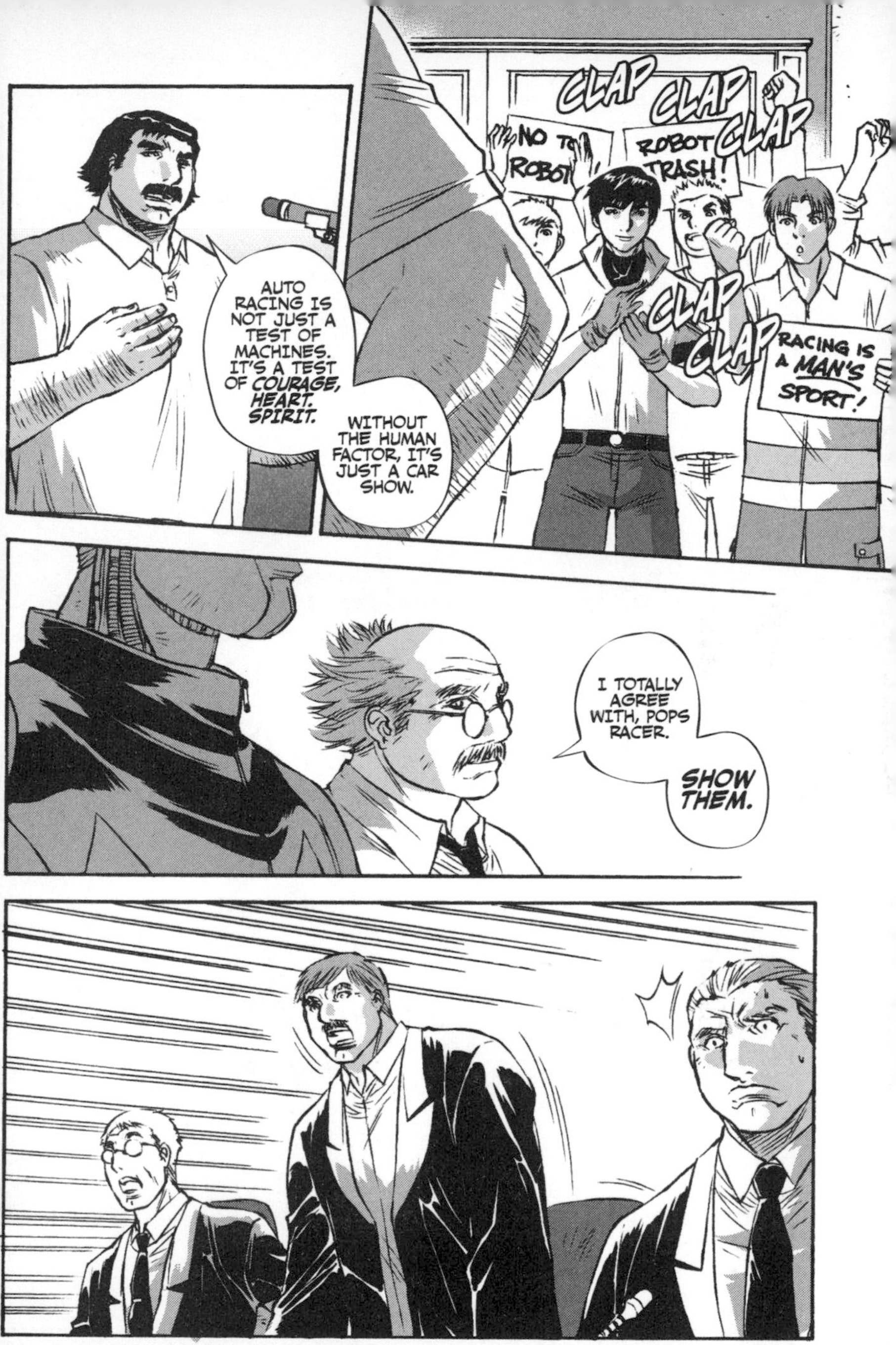
AUTO RACING IS NOT JUST A TEST OF MACHINES. IT'S A TEST OF COURAGE, HEART. SPIRIT.
WITHOUT THE HUMAN FACTOR, IT'S JUST A CAR SHOW.
CLAP CLAP CLAP
NO TO ROBOT
ROBOT TRASH!
CLAP CLAP
RACING IS A MAN'S SPORT!
I TOTALLY AGREE WITH, POPS RACER.
SHOW THEM.

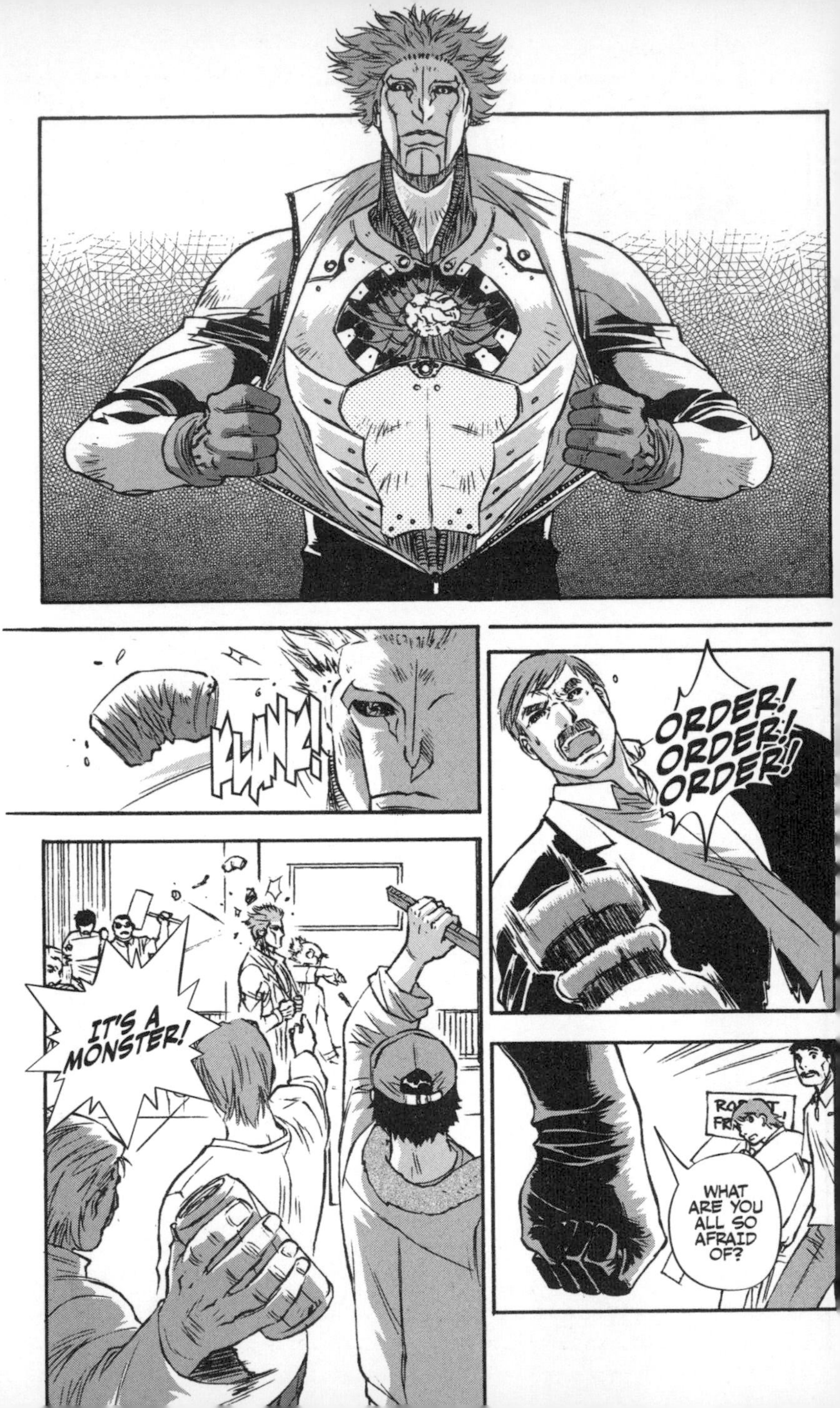
KLANK!
ORDER! ORDER! ORDER!!
IT'S A MONSTER!
WHAT ARE YOU ALL SO AFRAID OF?

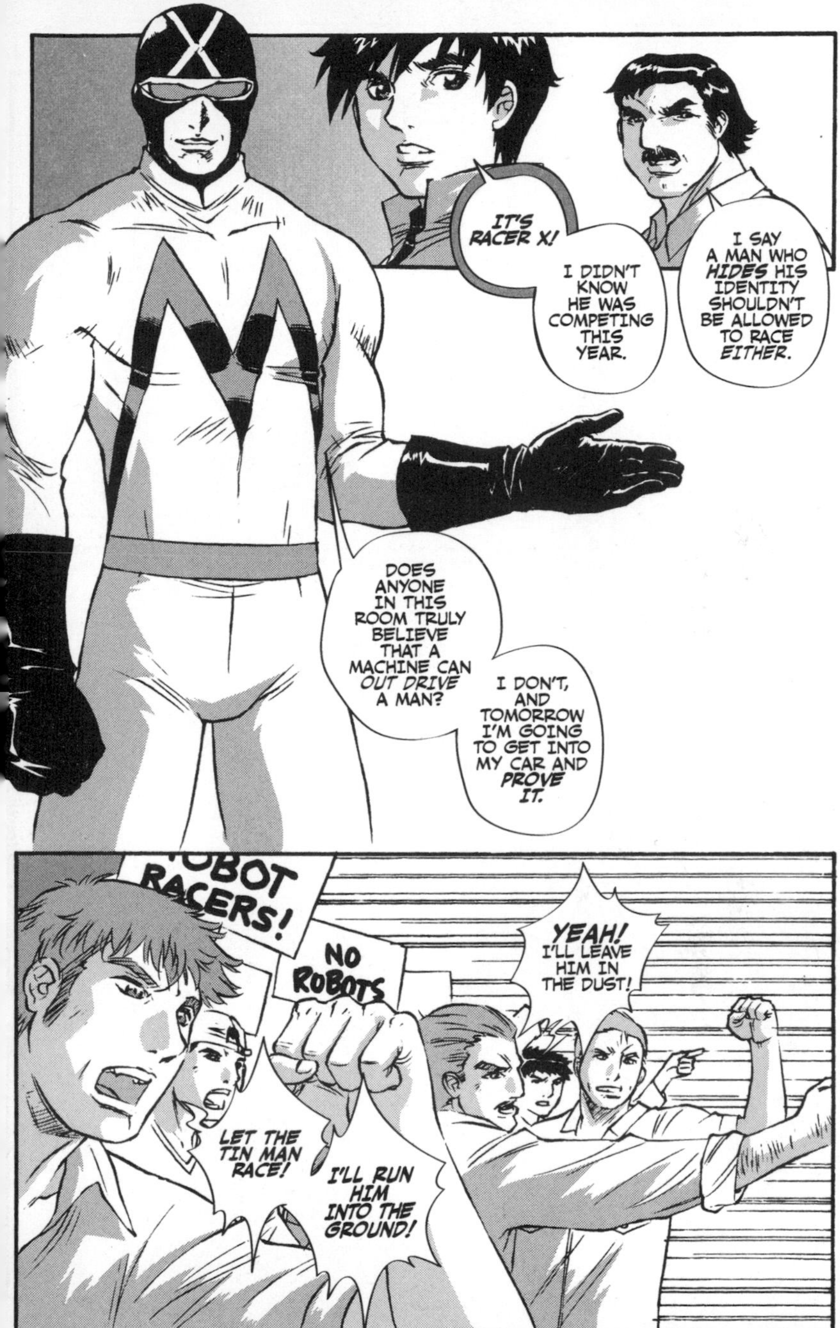
IT'S RACER X!
I DIDN'T KNOW HE WAS COMPETING THIS YEAR.
I SAY A MAN WHO *HIDES* HIS IDENTITY SHOULDN'T BE ALLOWED TO RACE *EITHER.*
DOES ANYONE IN THIS ROOM TRULY BELIEVE THAT A MACHINE CAN *OUT DRIVE* A MAN?
I DON'T, AND TOMORROW I'M GOING TO GET INTO MY CAR AND *PROVE IT.*
OBOT RACERS!
NO ROBOTS
YEAH! I'LL LEAVE HIM IN THE DUST!
LET THE TIN MAN RACE!
I'LL RUN HIM INTO THE GROUND!

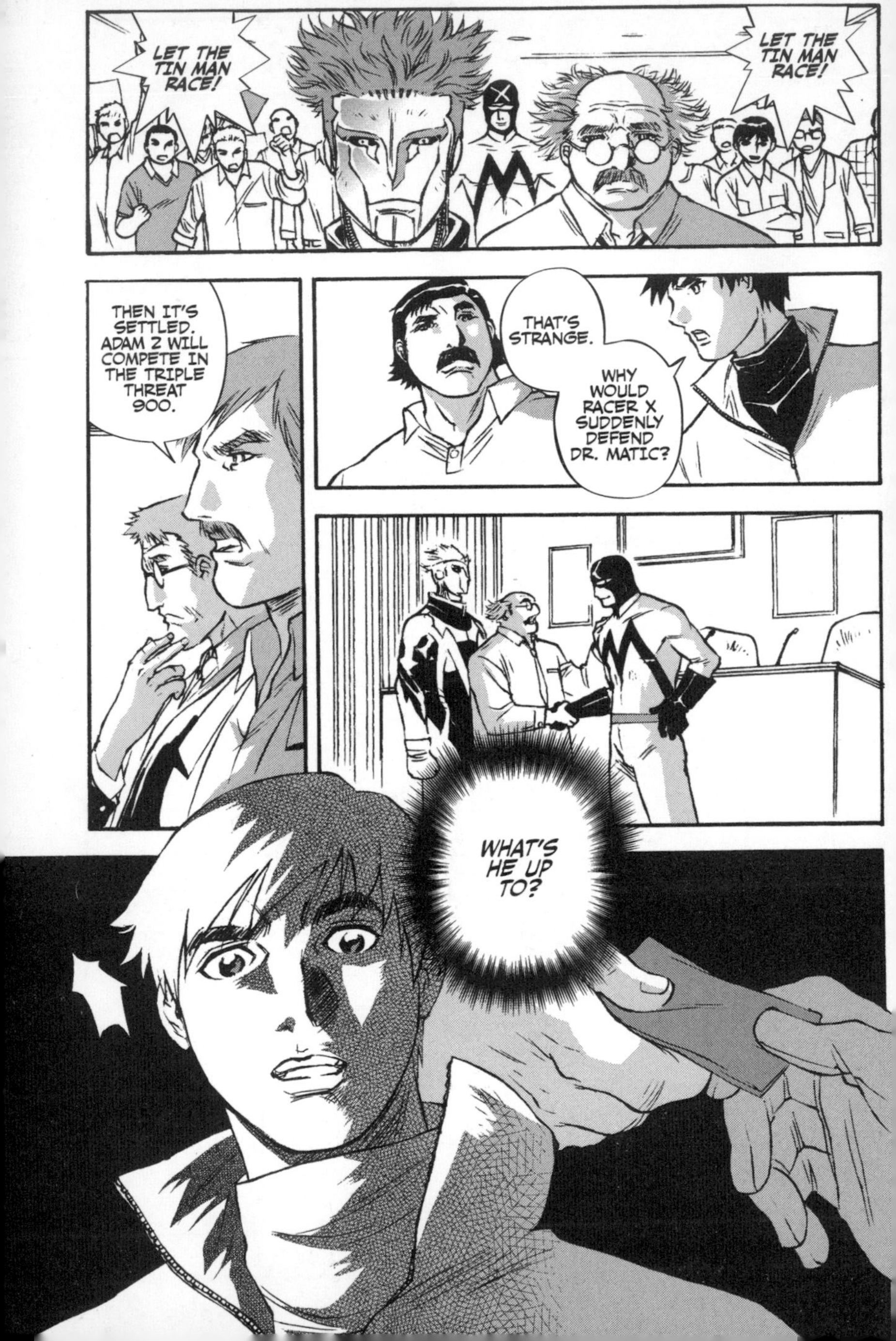
LET THE TIN MAN RACE!
LET THE TIN MAN RACE!
THEN IT'S SETTLED. ADAM 2 WILL COMPETE IN THE TRIPLE THREAT 900.
THAT'S STRANGE.
WHY WOULD RACER X SUDDENLY DEFEND DR. MATIC?
WHAT'S HE UP TO?

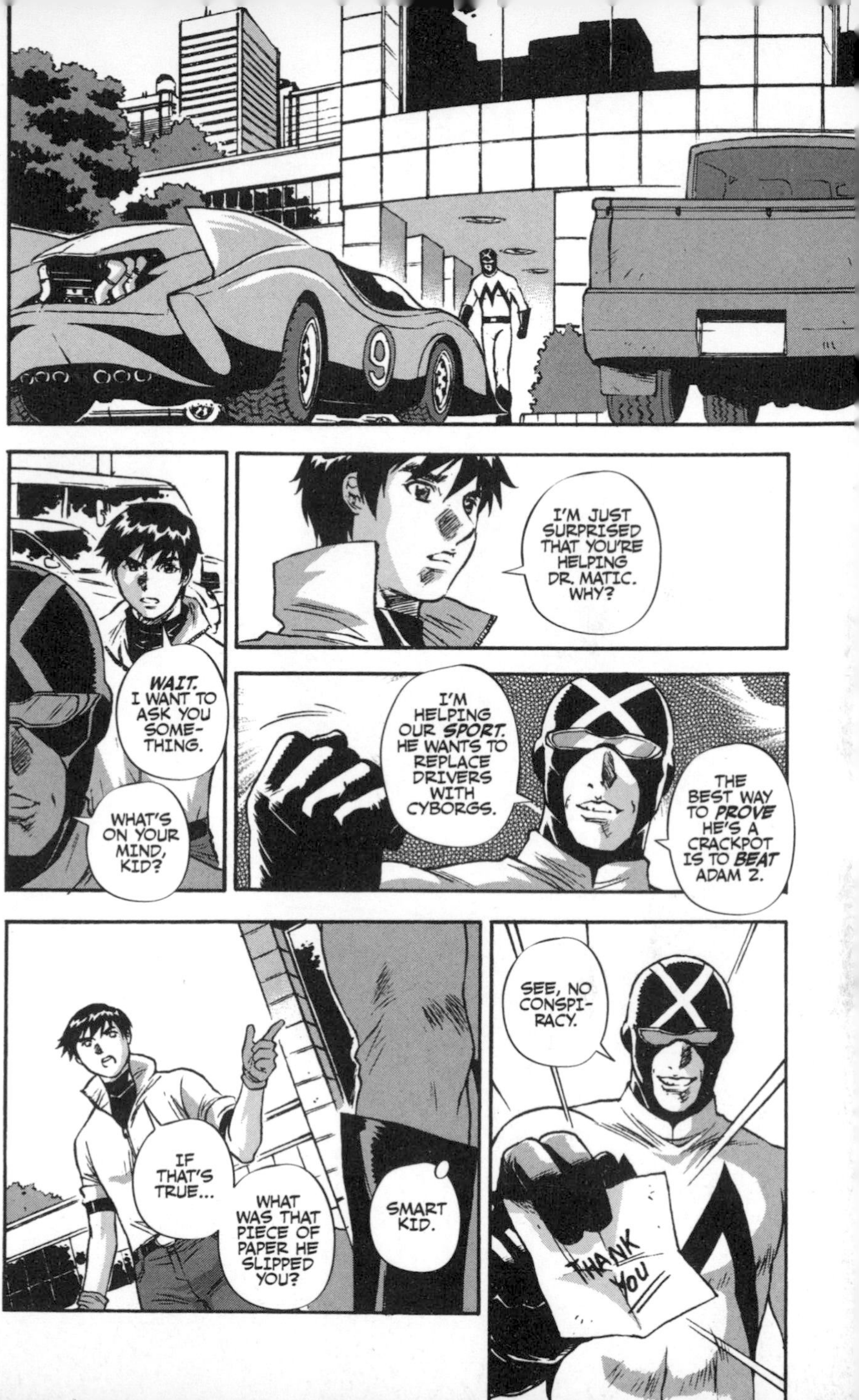
WAIT. I WANT TO ASK YOU SOMETHING.
WHAT'S ON YOUR MIND, KID?
I'M JUST SURPRISED THAT YOU'RE HELPING DR. MATIC. WHY?
I'M HELPING OUR SPORT. HE WANTS TO REPLACE DRIVERS WITH CYBORGS.
THE BEST WAY TO PROVE HE'S A CRACKPOT IS TO BEAT ADAM 2.
IF THAT'S TRUE...
WHAT WAS THAT PIECE OF PAPER HE SLIPPED YOU?
SMART KID.
SEE, NO CONSPIRACY.
THANK YOU

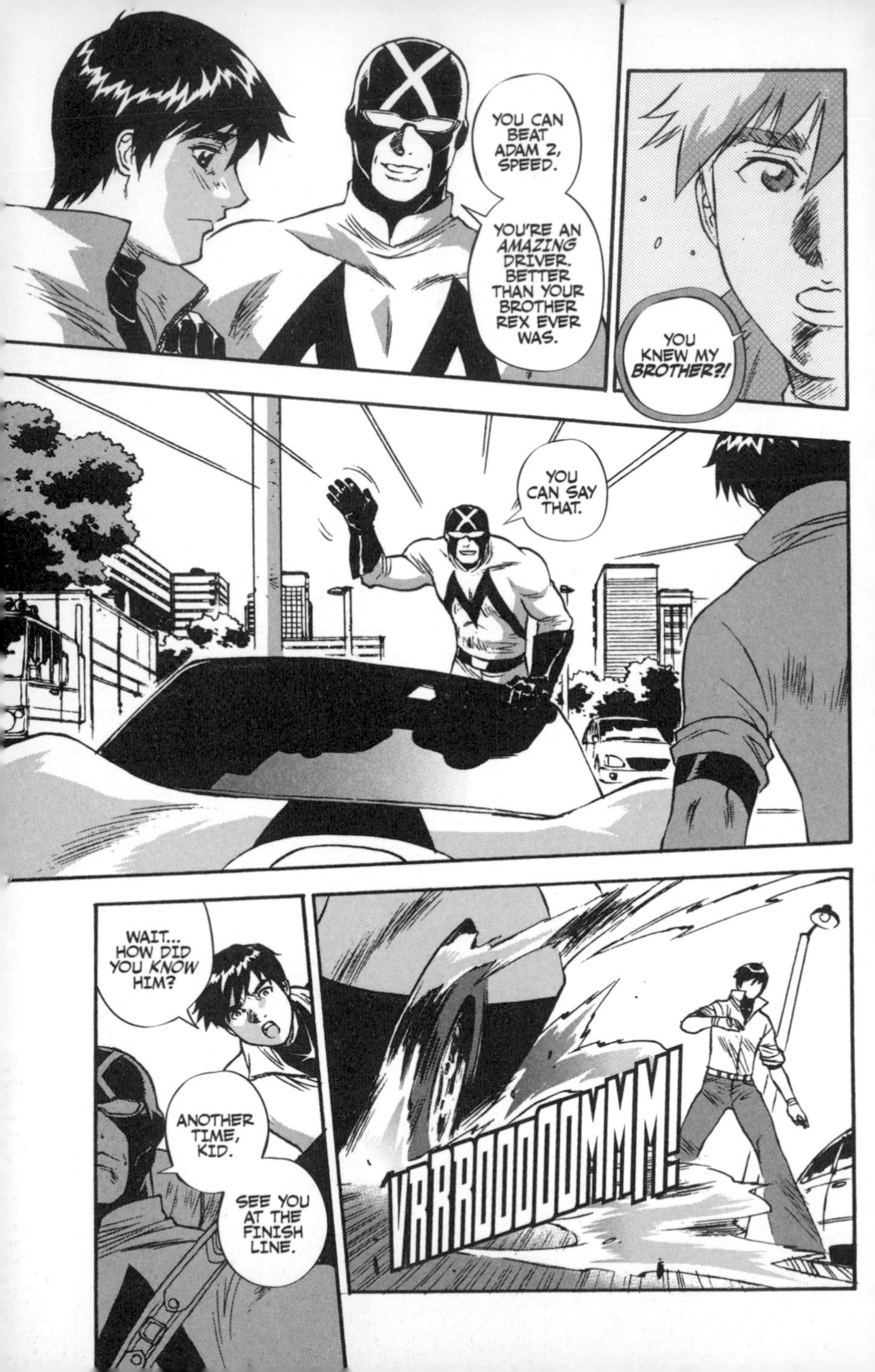
YOU CAN BEAT ADAM 2, SPEED.
YOU'RE AN *AMAZING* DRIVER. BETTER THAN YOUR BROTHER REX EVER WAS.
YOU KNEW MY *BROTHER?!*
YOU CAN SAY THAT.
WAIT... HOW DID YOU *KNOW* HIM?
ANOTHER TIME, KID.
SEE YOU AT THE FINISH LINE.
VRRROOOOMMM!

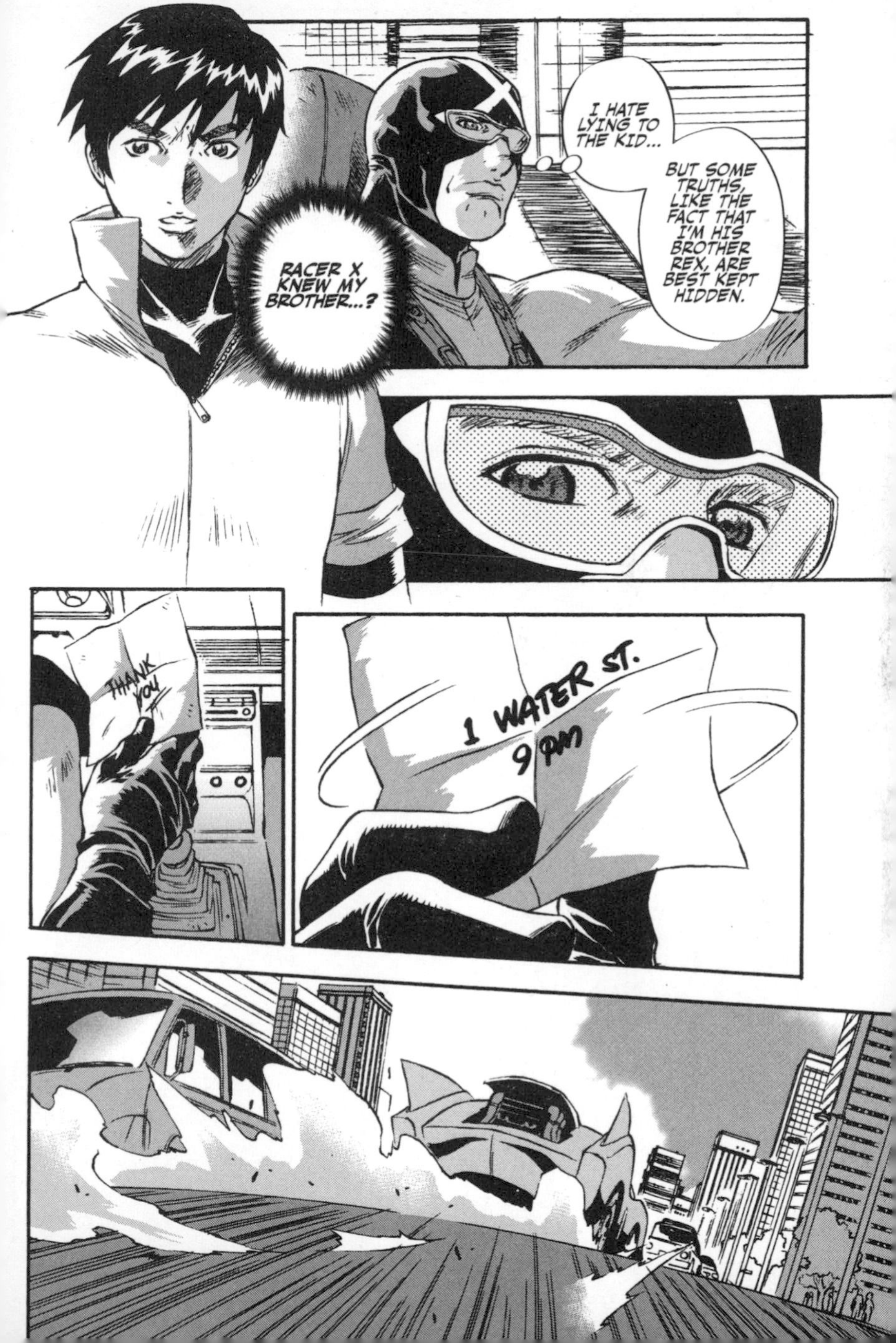
RACER X KNEW MY BROTHER...?
I HATE LYING TO THE KID...
BUT SOME TRUTHS, LIKE THE FACT THAT I'M HIS BROTHER REX, ARE BEST KEPT HIDDEN.
THANK YOU
1 WATER ST.
9 pm

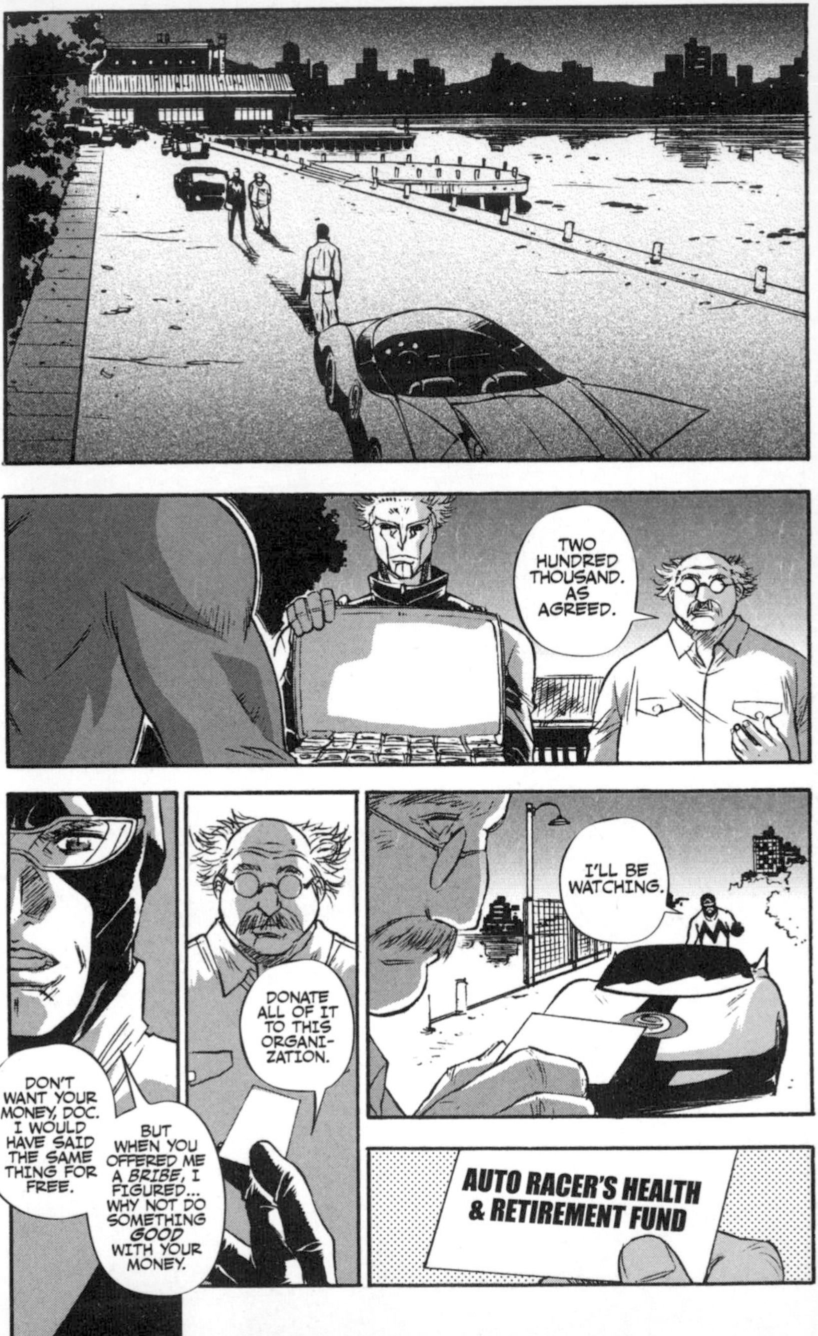
TWO HUNDRED THOUSAND. AS AGREED.
DON'T WANT YOUR MONEY, DOC. I WOULD HAVE SAID THE SAME THING FOR FREE.
BUT WHEN YOU OFFERED ME A *BRIBE*, I FIGURED... WHY NOT DO SOMETHING *GOOD* WITH YOUR MONEY.
DONATE ALL OF IT TO THIS ORGANIZATION.
I'LL BE WATCHING.
AUTO RACER'S HEALTH & RETIREMENT FUND

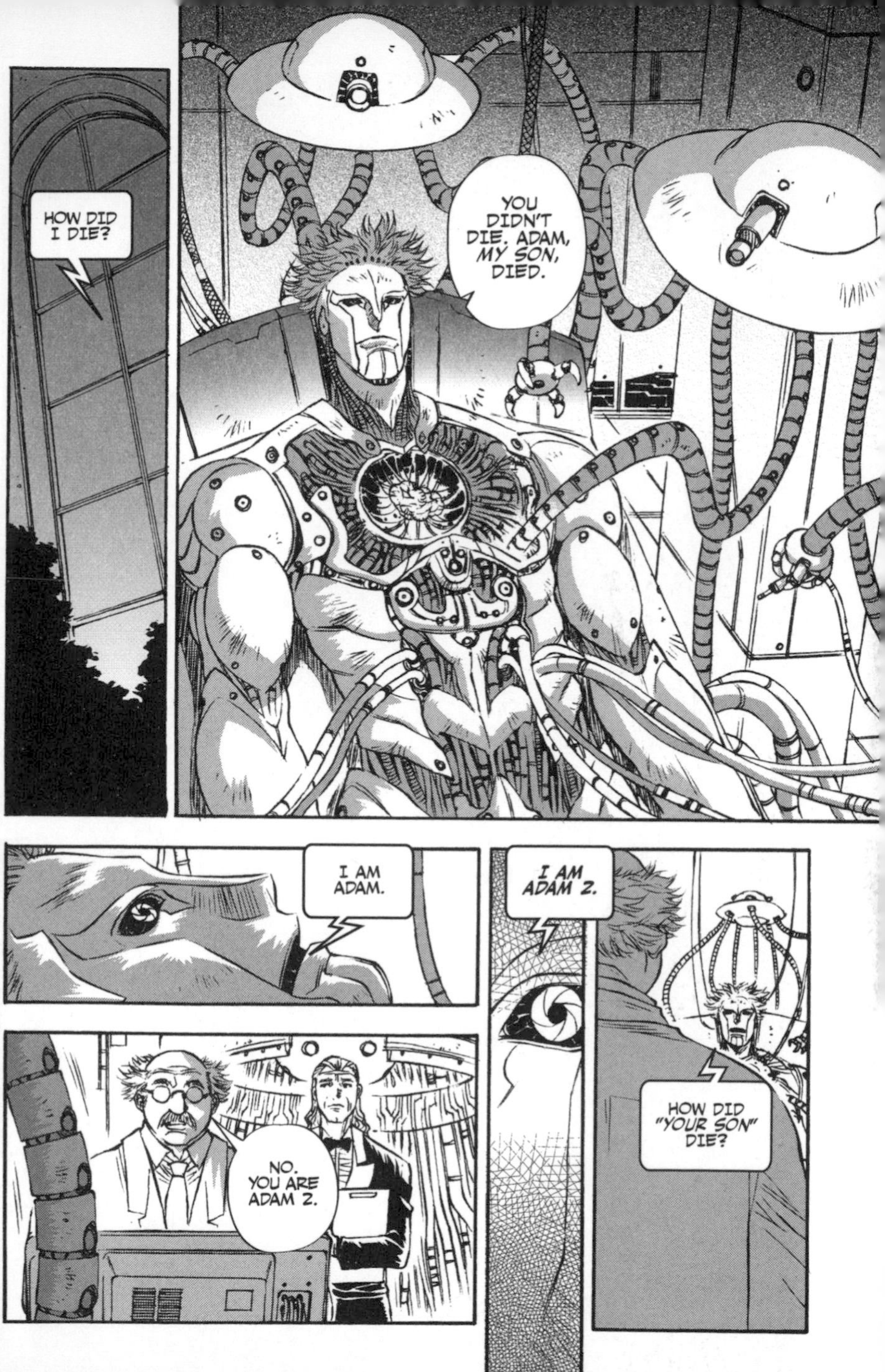
HOW DID I DIE?
YOU DIDN'T DIE. ADAM, MY SON, DIED.
I AM ADAM.
NO. YOU ARE ADAM 2.
I AM ADAM 2.
HOW DID "YOUR SON" DIE?

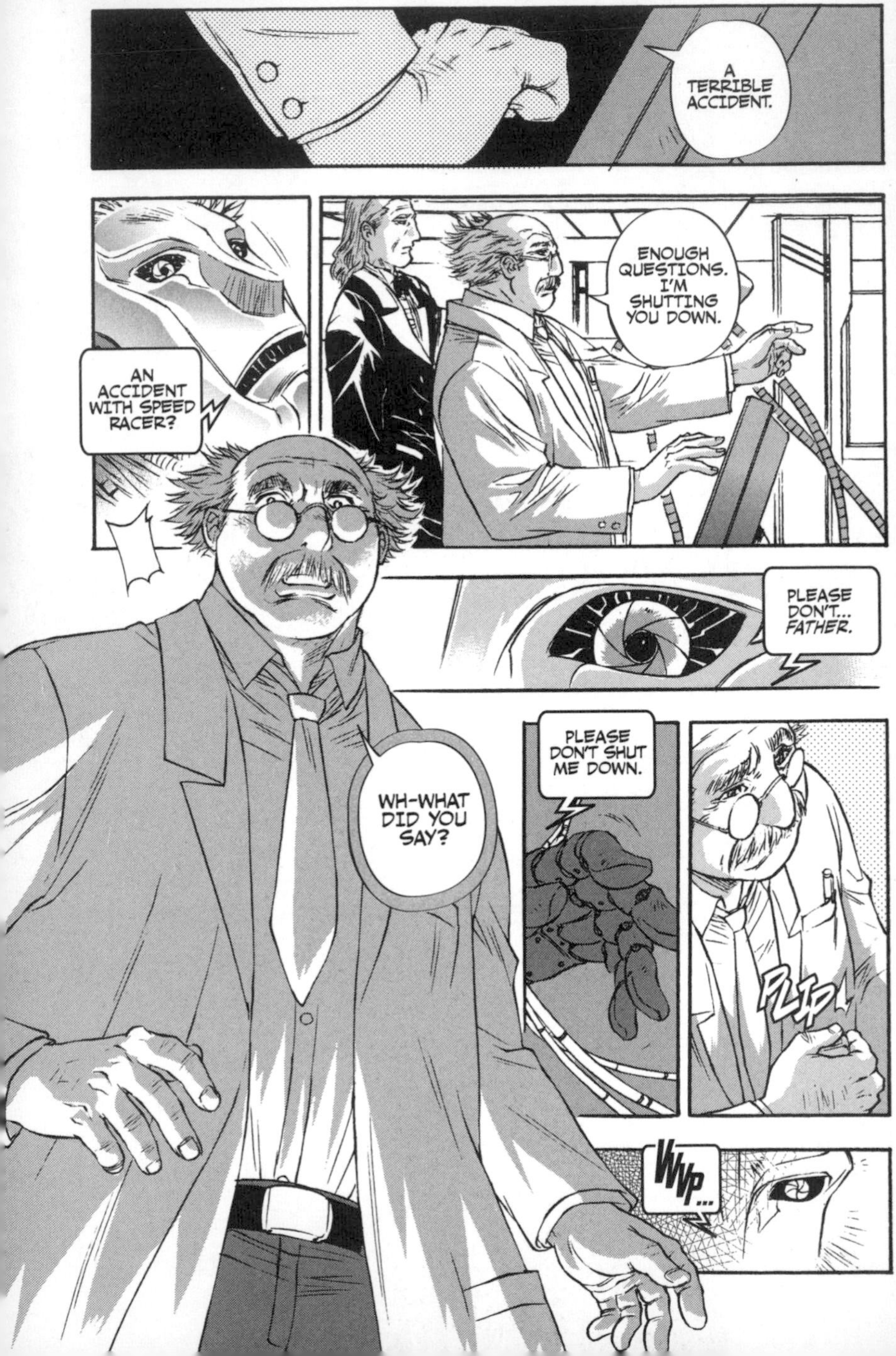
A TERRIBLE ACCIDENT.
AN ACCIDENT WITH SPEED RACER?
ENOUGH QUESTIONS. I'M SHUTTING YOU DOWN.
PLEASE DON'T... FATHER.
WH-WHAT DID YOU SAY?
PLEASE DON'T SHUT ME DOWN.
FLIP
WVP...

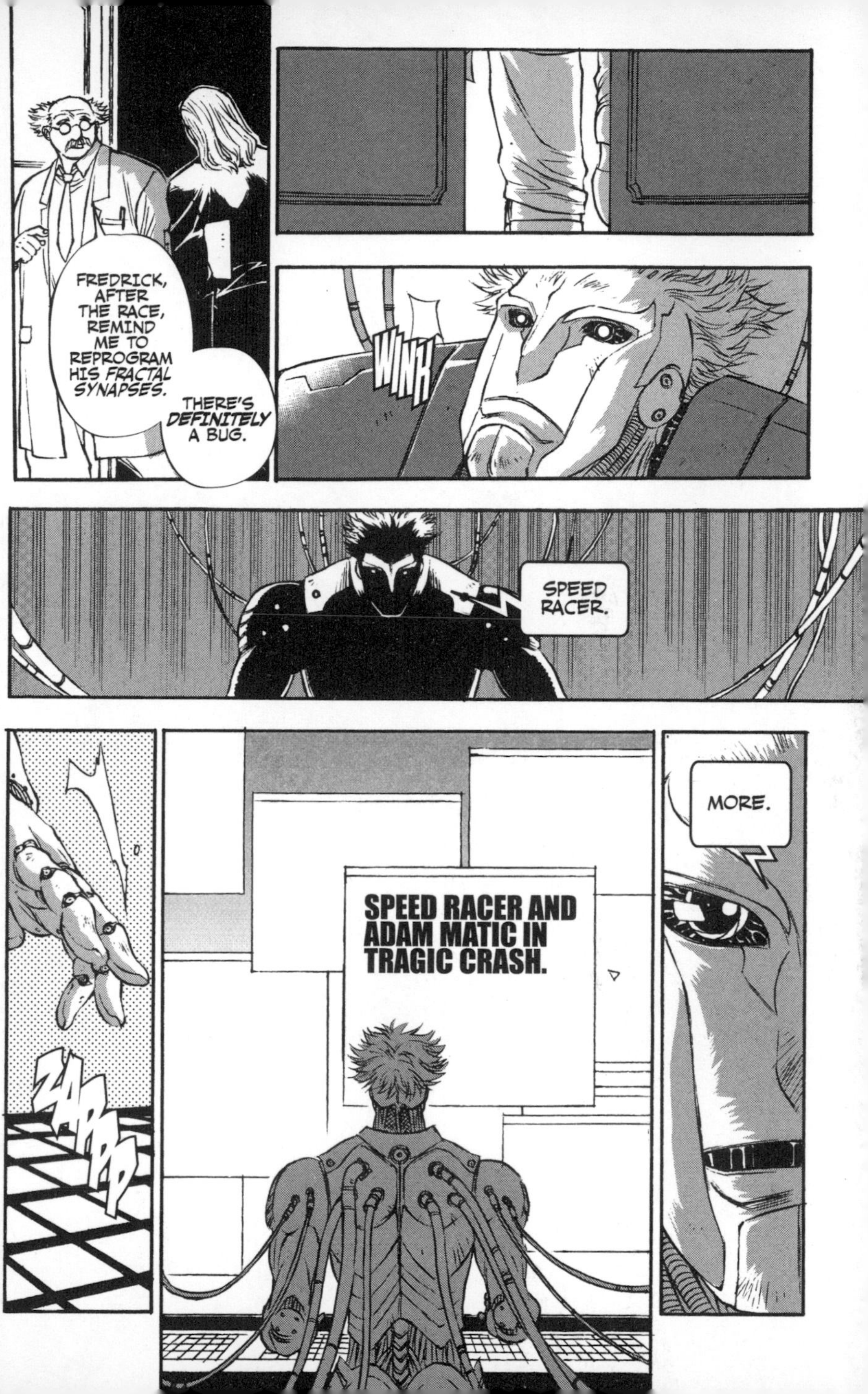
FREDRICK, AFTER THE RACE, REMIND ME TO REPROGRAM HIS *FRACTAL SYNAPSES.*
THERE'S *DEFINITELY* A BUG.
WINK
SPEED RACER.
ZAPPP
SPEED RACER AND ADAM MATIC IN TRAGIC CRASH.
MORE.

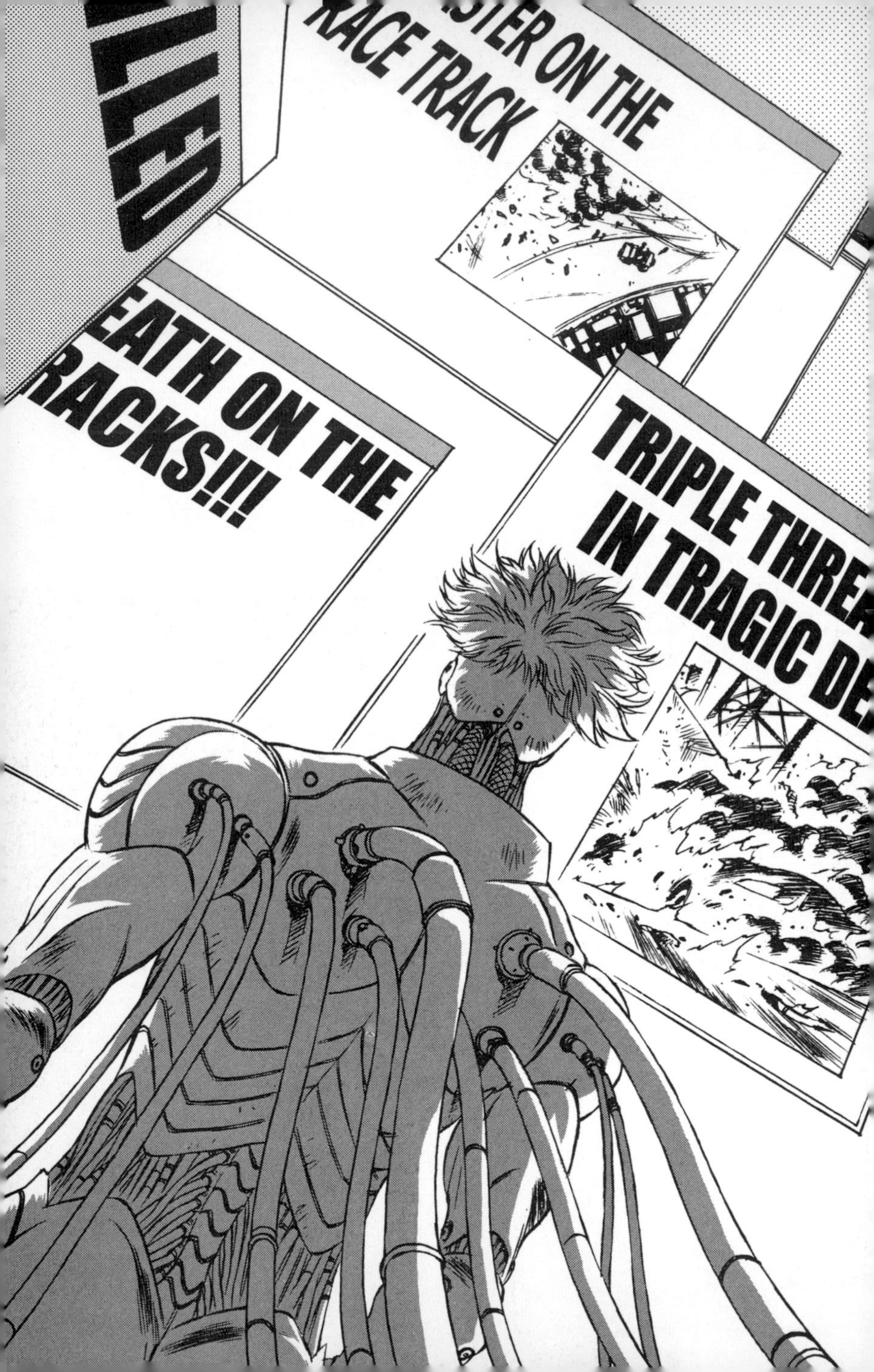
STER ON THE
RACE TRACK
EATH ON THE
RACKS!!!
TRIPLE THREA
IN TRAGIC DE

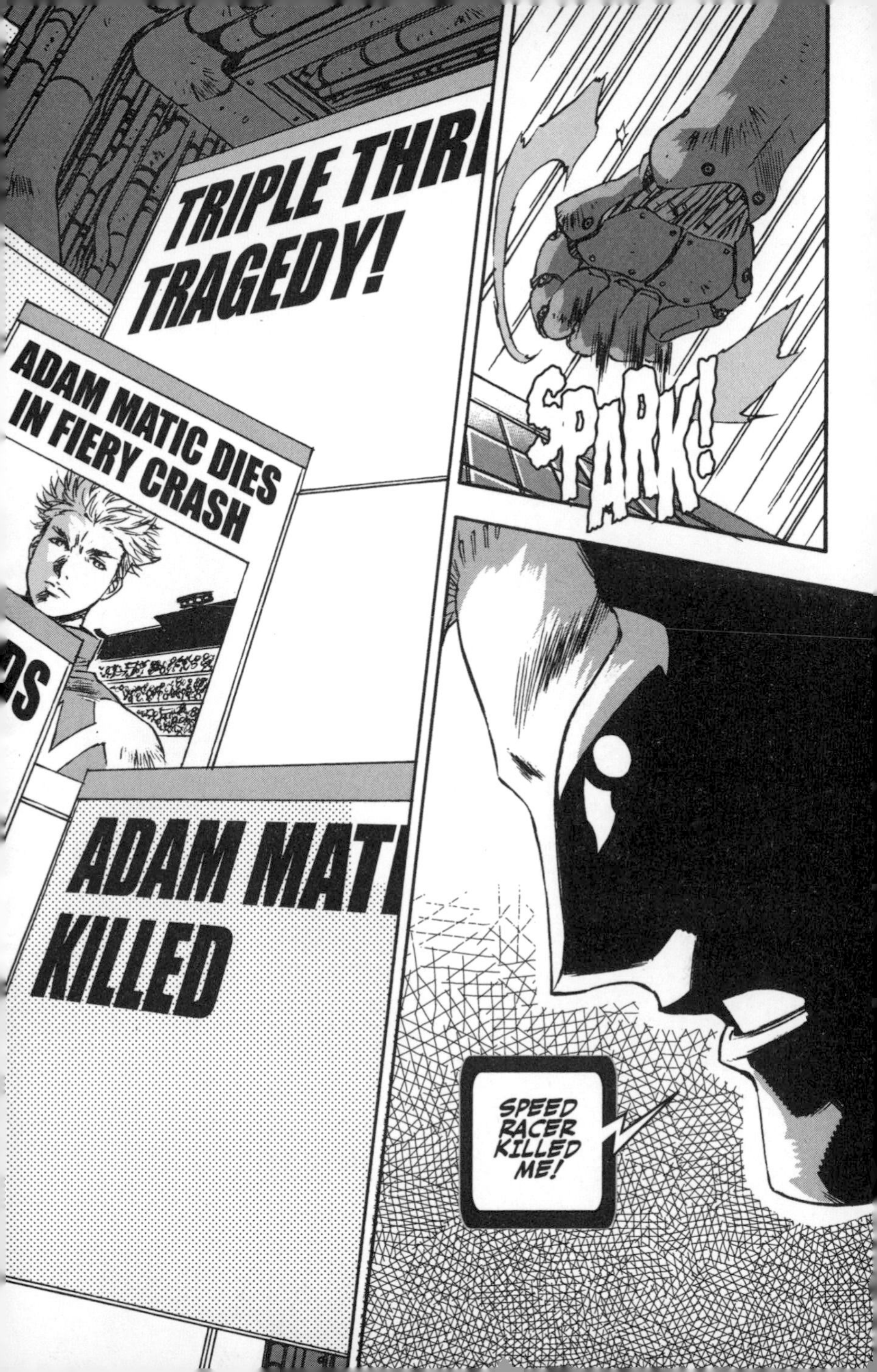
TRIPLE THR
TRAGEDY!
ADAM MATIC DIES IN FIERY CRASH
DS
ADAM MAT
KILLED
SPARK!
SPEED RACER KILLED ME!

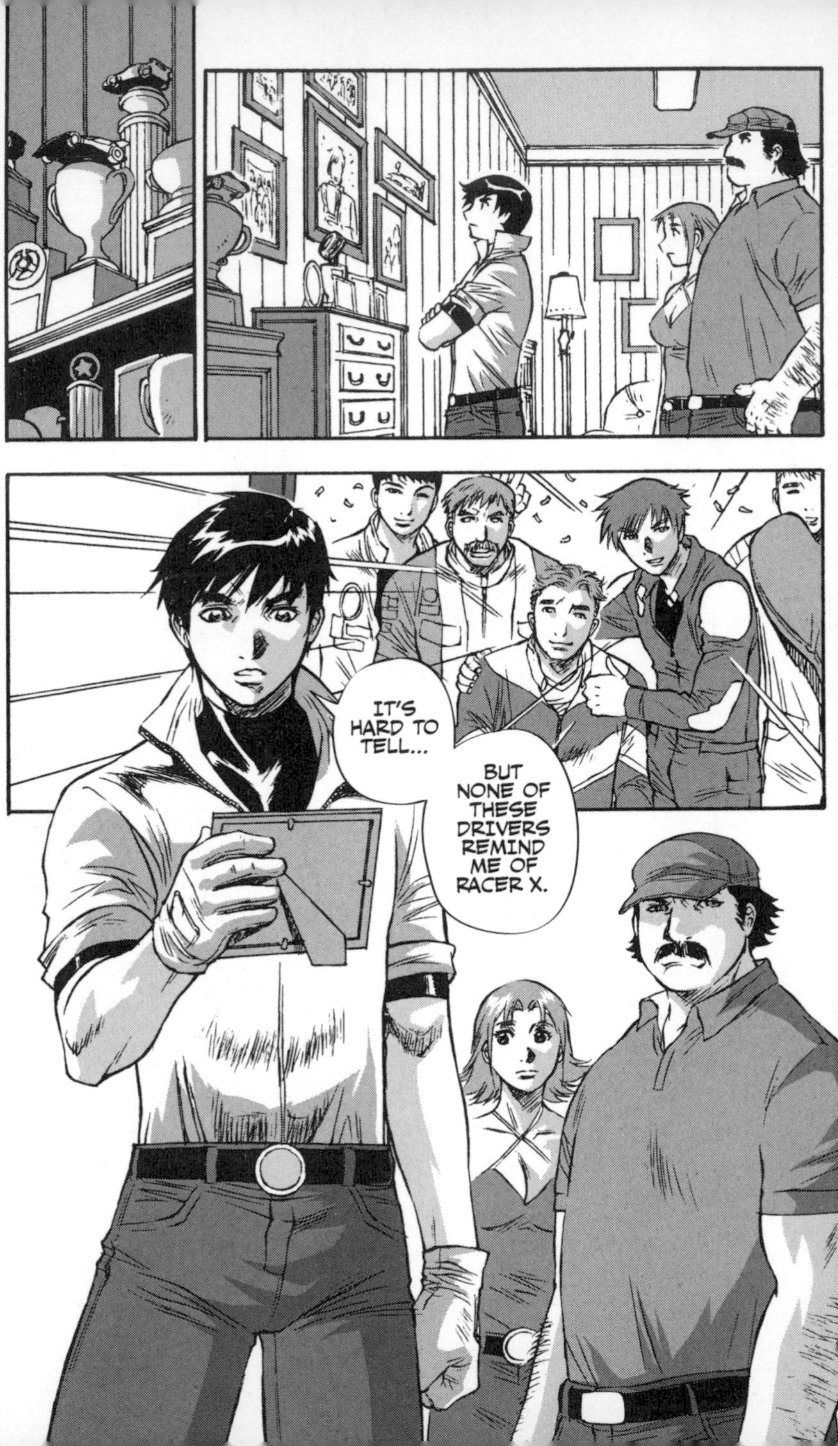
IT'S HARD TO TELL...
BUT NONE OF THESE DRIVERS REMIND ME OF RACER X.

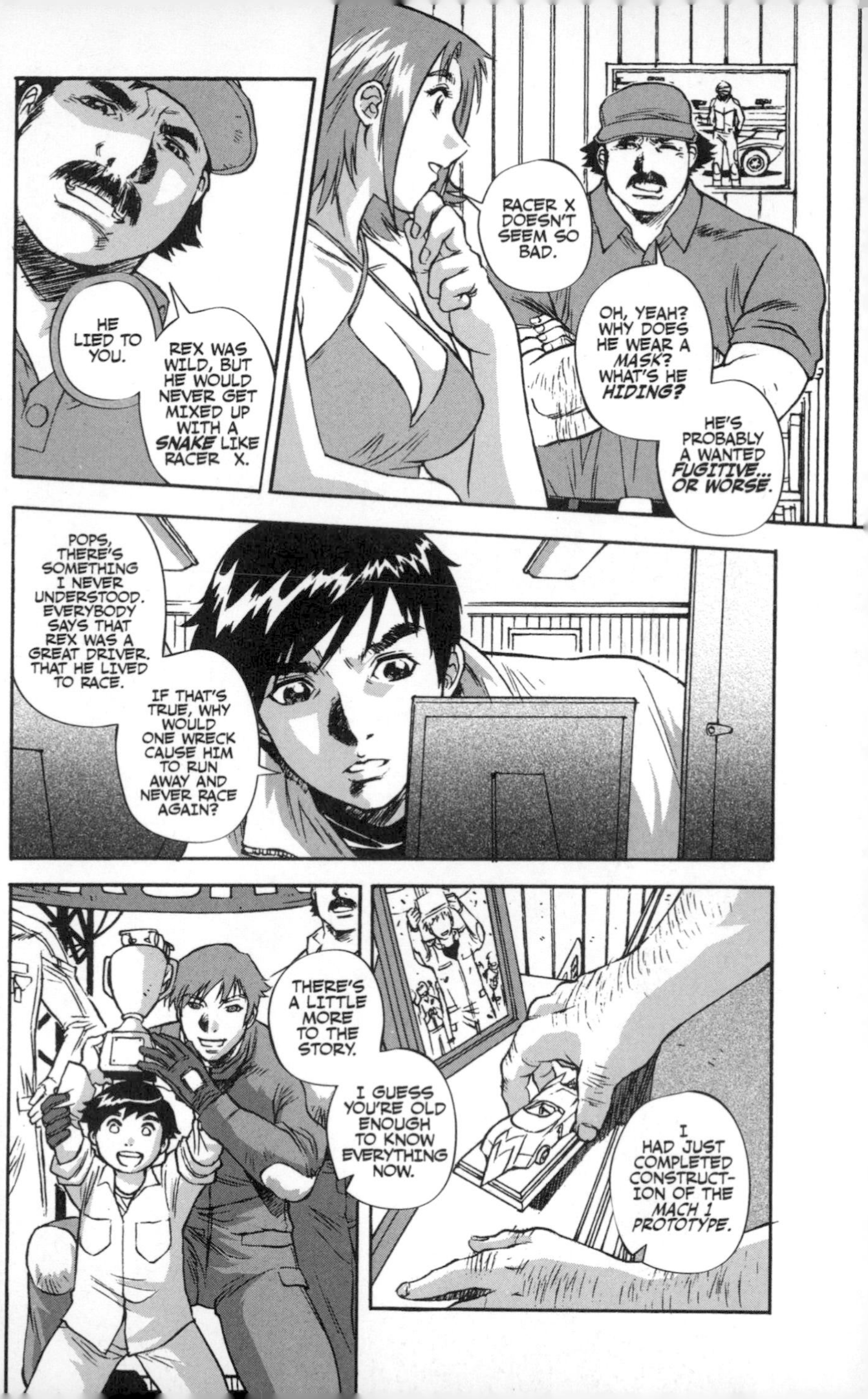
HE LIED TO YOU.
REX WAS WILD, BUT HE WOULD NEVER GET MIXED UP WITH A SNAKE LIKE RACER X.
RACER X DOESN'T SEEM SO BAD.
OH, YEAH? WHY DOES HE WEAR A MASK? WHAT'S HE HIDING?
HE'S PROBABLY A WANTED FUGITIVE... OR WORSE.
POPS, THERE'S SOMETHING I NEVER UNDERSTOOD. EVERYBODY SAYS THAT REX WAS A GREAT DRIVER. THAT HE LIVED TO RACE.
IF THAT'S TRUE, WHY WOULD ONE WRECK CAUSE HIM TO RUN AWAY AND NEVER RACE AGAIN?
THERE'S A LITTLE MORE TO THE STORY.
I GUESS YOU'RE OLD ENOUGH TO KNOW EVERYTHING NOW.
I HAD JUST COMPLETED CONSTRUCTION OF THE MACH 1 PROTOTYPE.

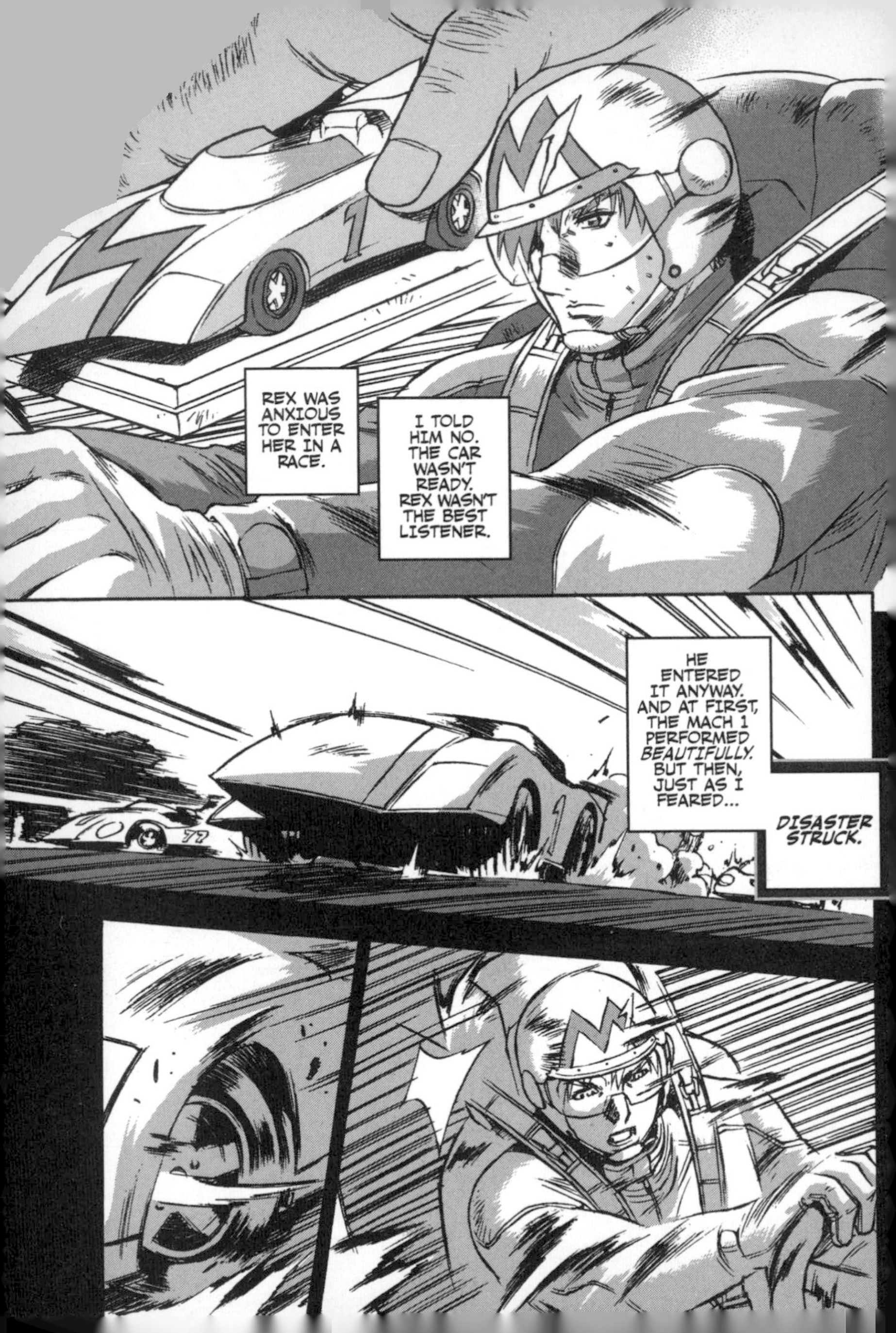
REX WAS ANXIOUS TO ENTER HER IN A RACE.
I TOLD HIM NO. THE CAR WASN'T READY. REX WASN'T THE BEST LISTENER.
HE ENTERED IT ANYWAY. AND AT FIRST, THE MACH 1 PERFORMED *BEAUTIFULLY.* BUT THEN, JUST AS I FEARED...
DISASTER STRUCK.

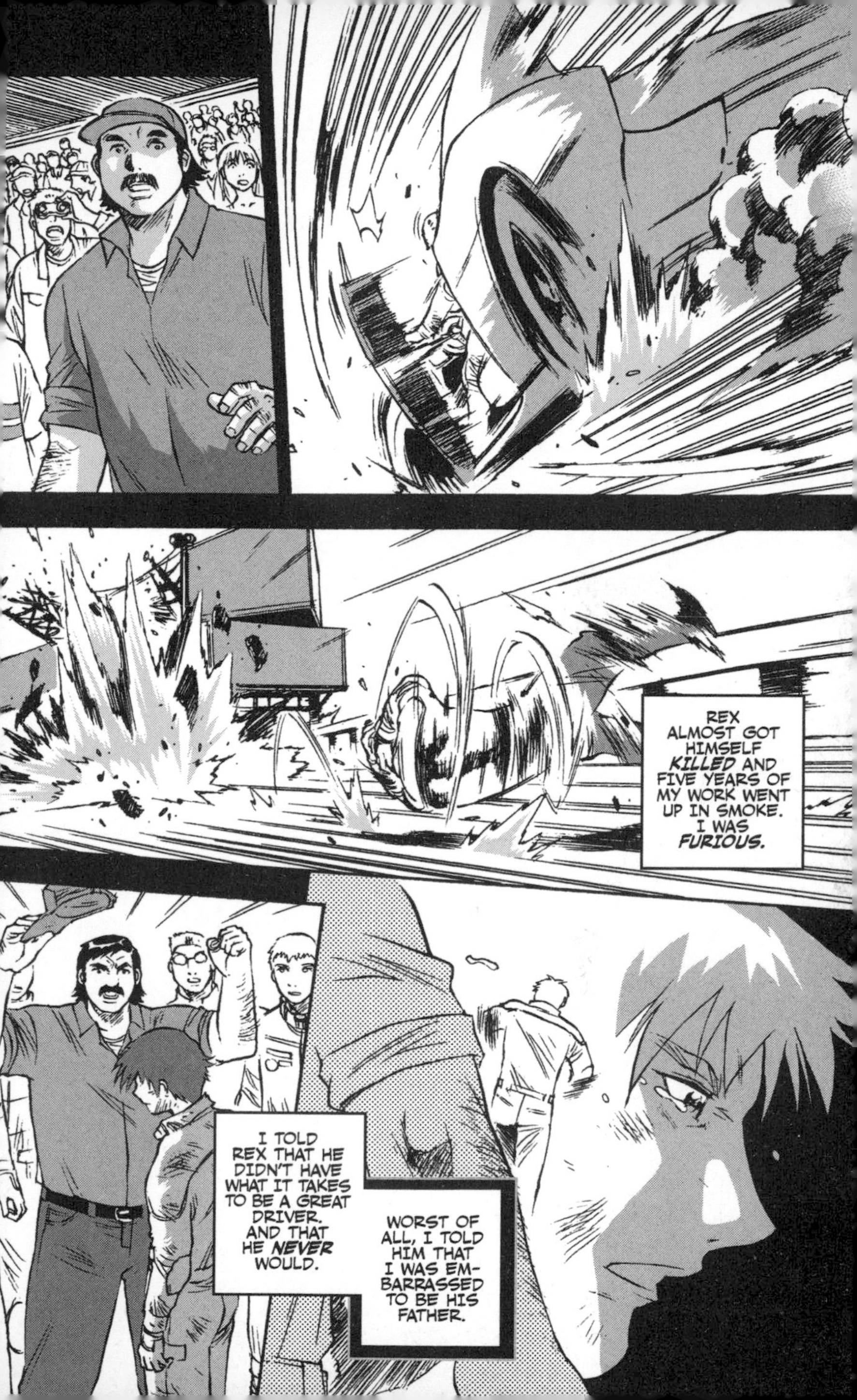
REX ALMOST GOT HIMSELF *KILLED* AND FIVE YEARS OF MY WORK WENT UP IN SMOKE. I WAS *FURIOUS.*
I TOLD REX THAT HE DIDN'T HAVE WHAT IT TAKES TO BE A GREAT DRIVER. AND THAT HE *NEVER* WOULD.
WORST OF ALL, I TOLD HIM THAT I WAS EM-BARRASSED TO BE HIS FATHER.

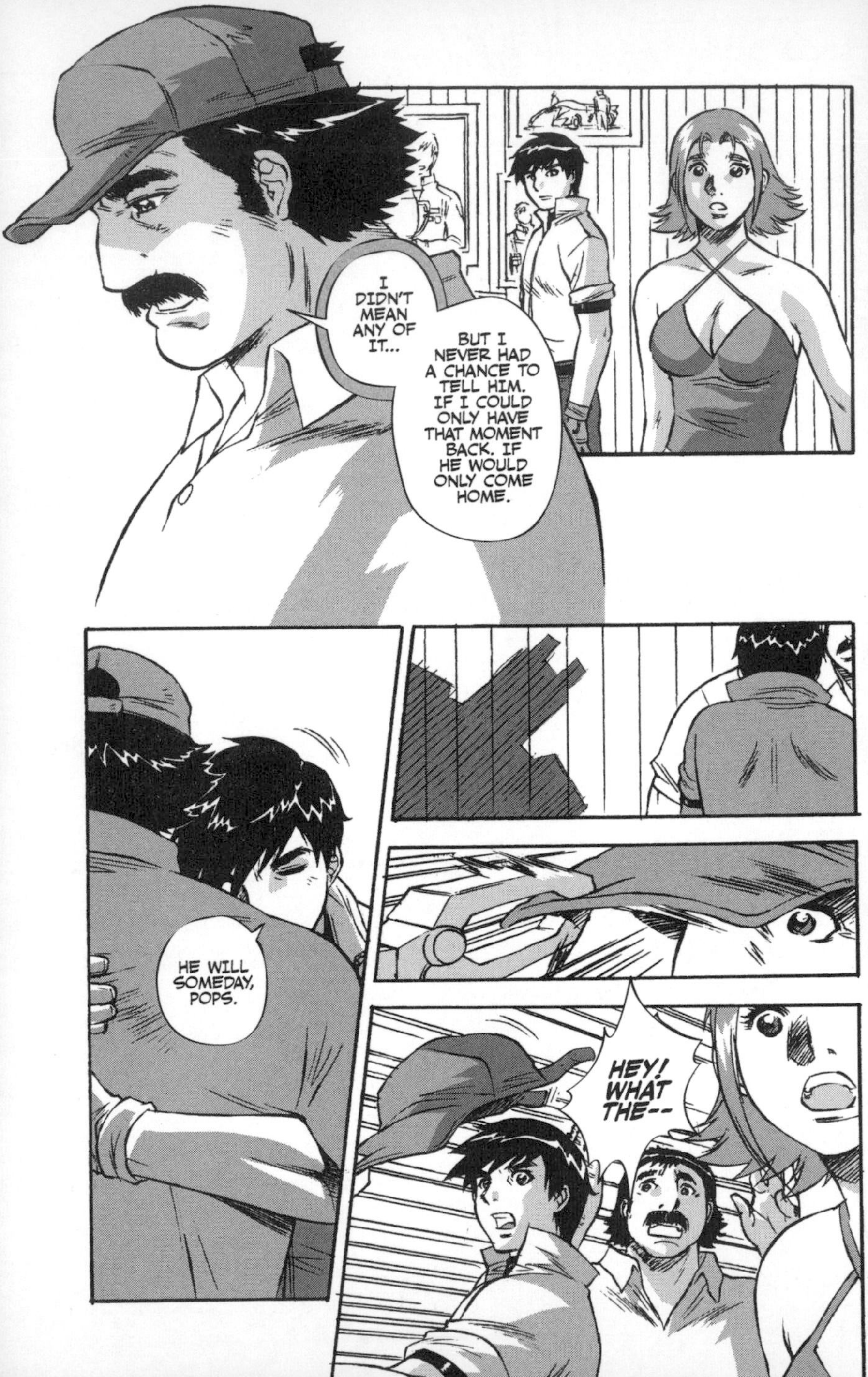
I DIDN'T MEAN ANY OF IT...
BUT I NEVER HAD A CHANCE TO TELL HIM. IF I COULD ONLY HAVE THAT MOMENT BACK. IF HE WOULD ONLY COME HOME.
HE WILL SOMEDAY, POPS.
HEY! WHAT THE--

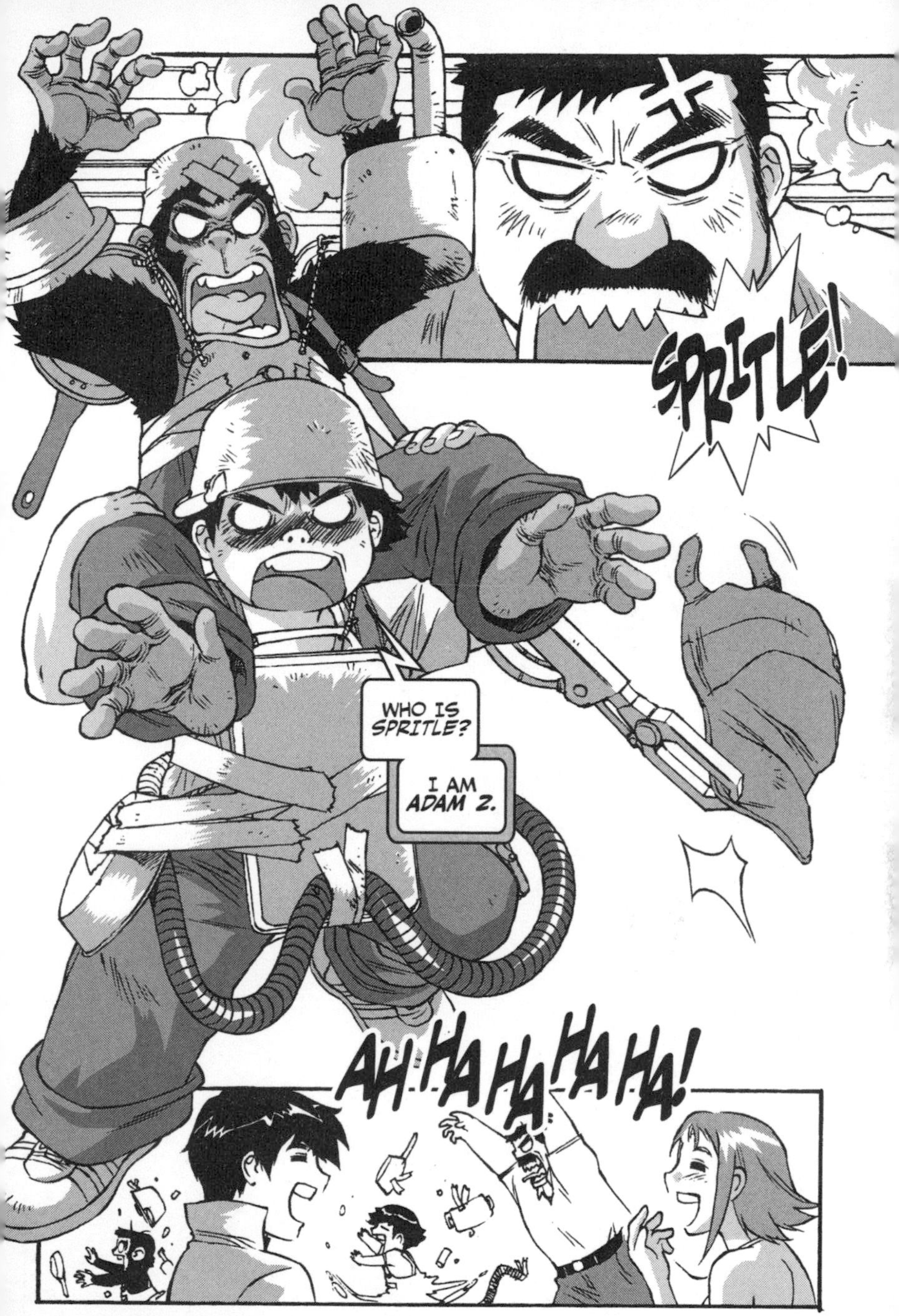
SPRITLE!
WHO IS SPRITLE?
I AM ADAM 2.
AH HA HA HA HA HA!

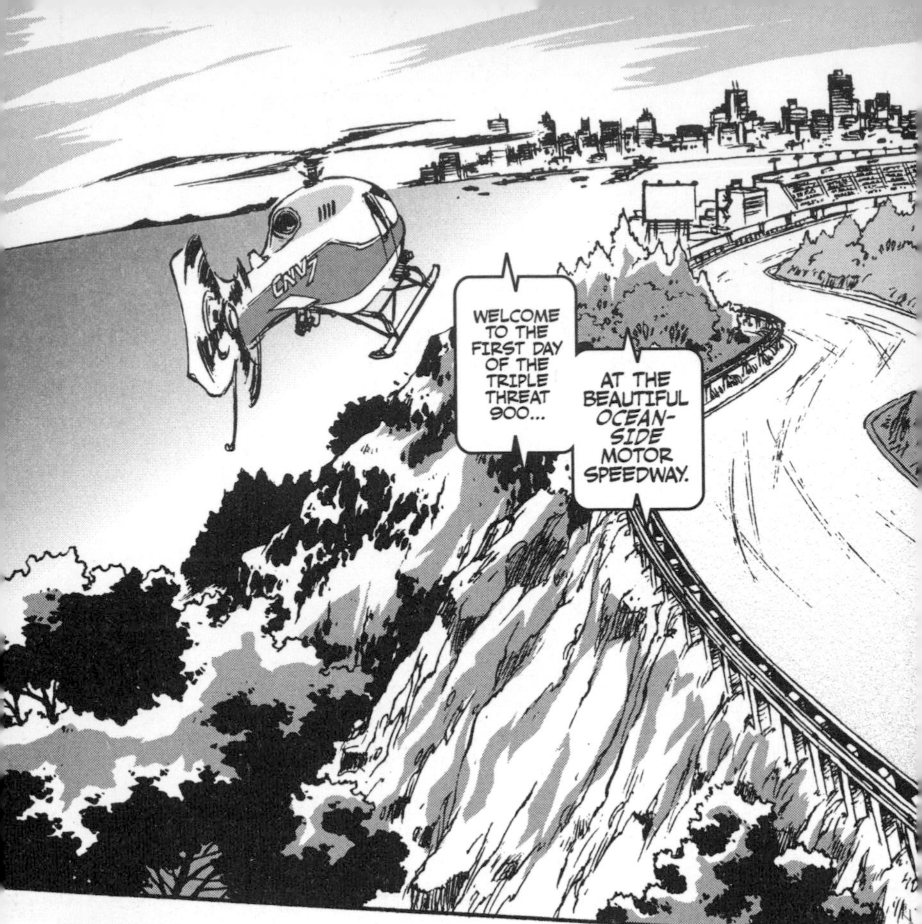
WELCOME TO THE FIRST DAY OF THE TRIPLE THREAT 900...
AT THE BEAUTIFUL *OCEAN-SIDE* MOTOR SPEEDWAY.
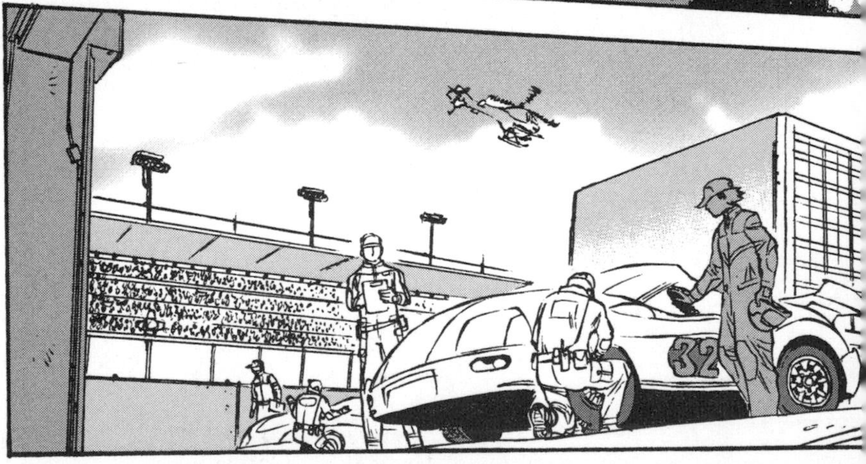
32

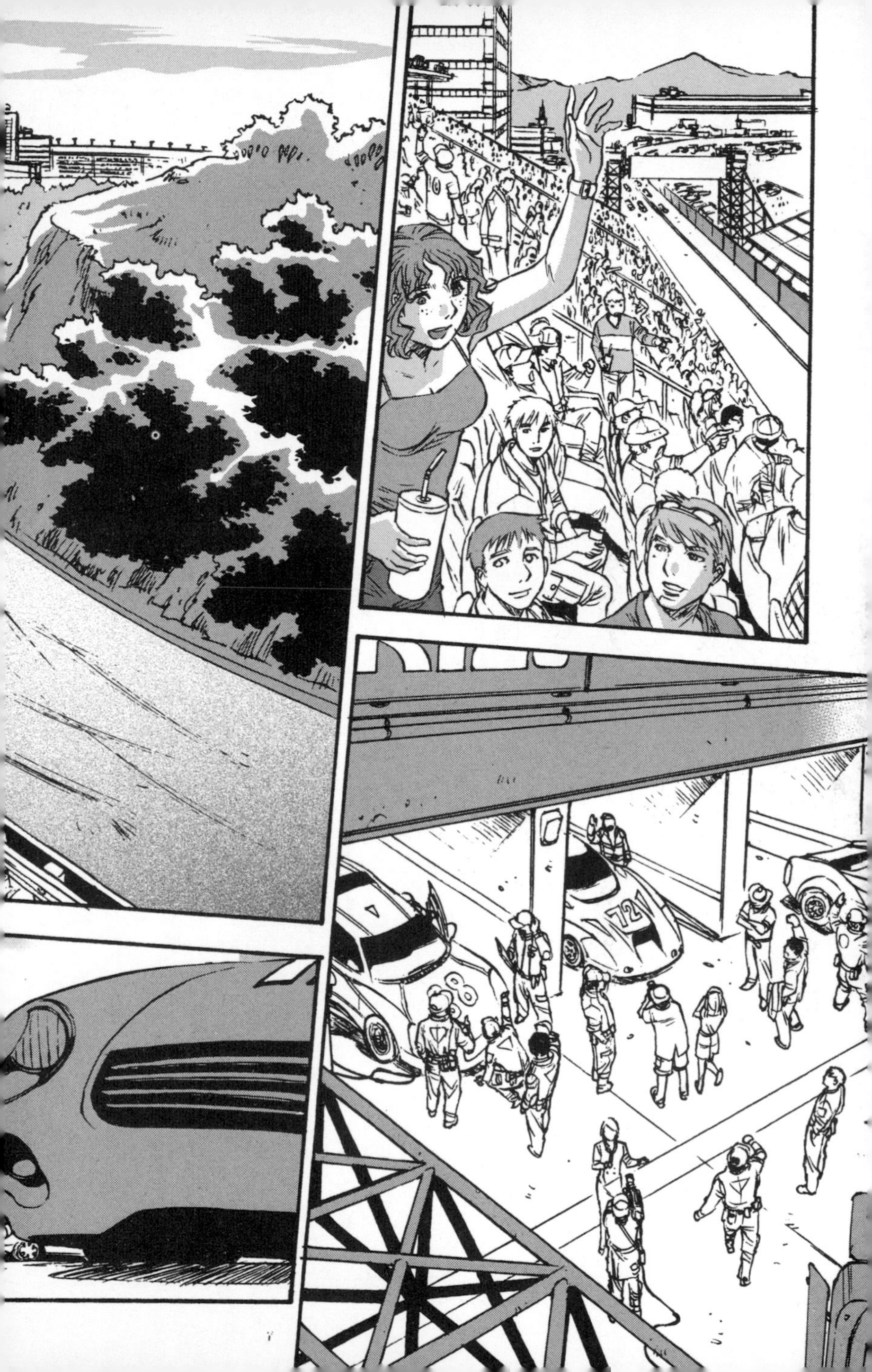
721

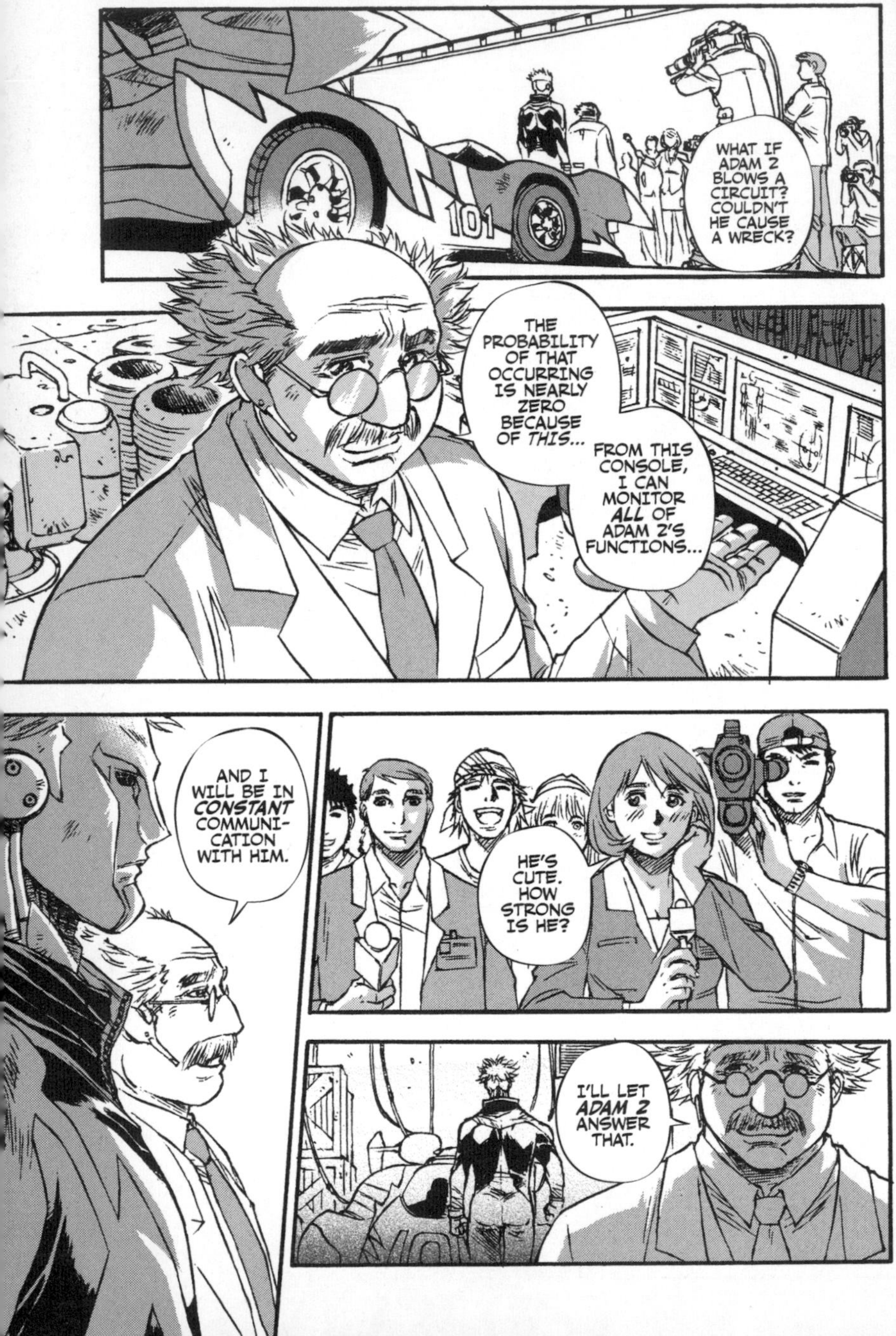
WHAT IF ADAM 2 BLOWS A CIRCUIT? COULDN'T HE CAUSE A WRECK?
THE PROBABILITY OF THAT OCCURRING IS NEARLY ZERO BECAUSE OF *THIS*...
FROM THIS CONSOLE, I CAN MONITOR ***ALL*** OF ADAM 2'S FUNCTIONS...
AND I WILL BE IN ***CONSTANT*** COMMUNI-CATION WITH HIM.
HE'S CUTE. HOW STRONG IS HE?
I'LL LET ***ADAM 2*** ANSWER THAT.

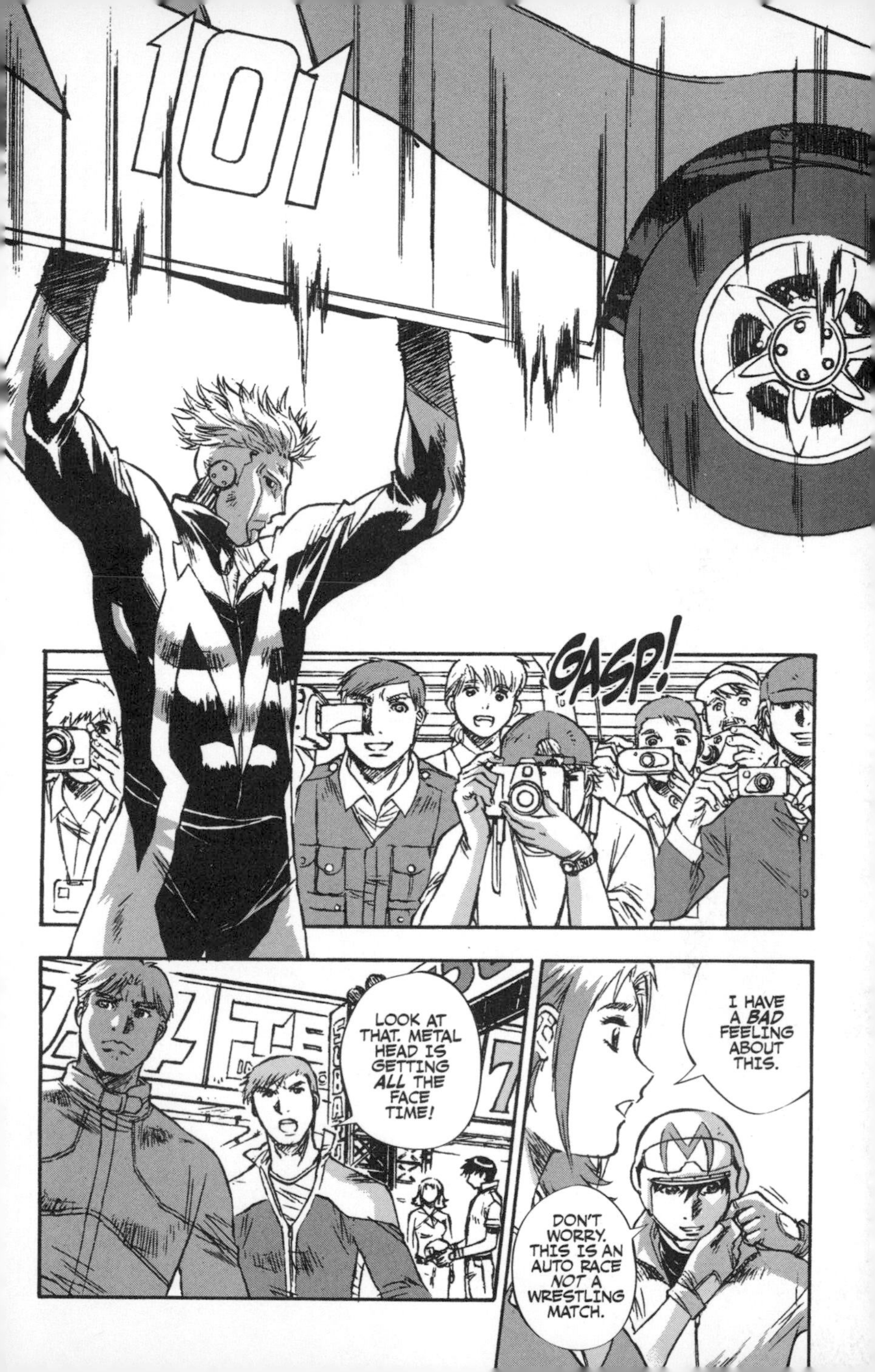

101
GASP!
LOOK AT THAT. METAL HEAD IS GETTING ALL THE FACE TIME!
I HAVE A BAD FEELING ABOUT THIS.
DON'T WORRY. THIS IS AN AUTO RACE NOT A WRESTLING MATCH.

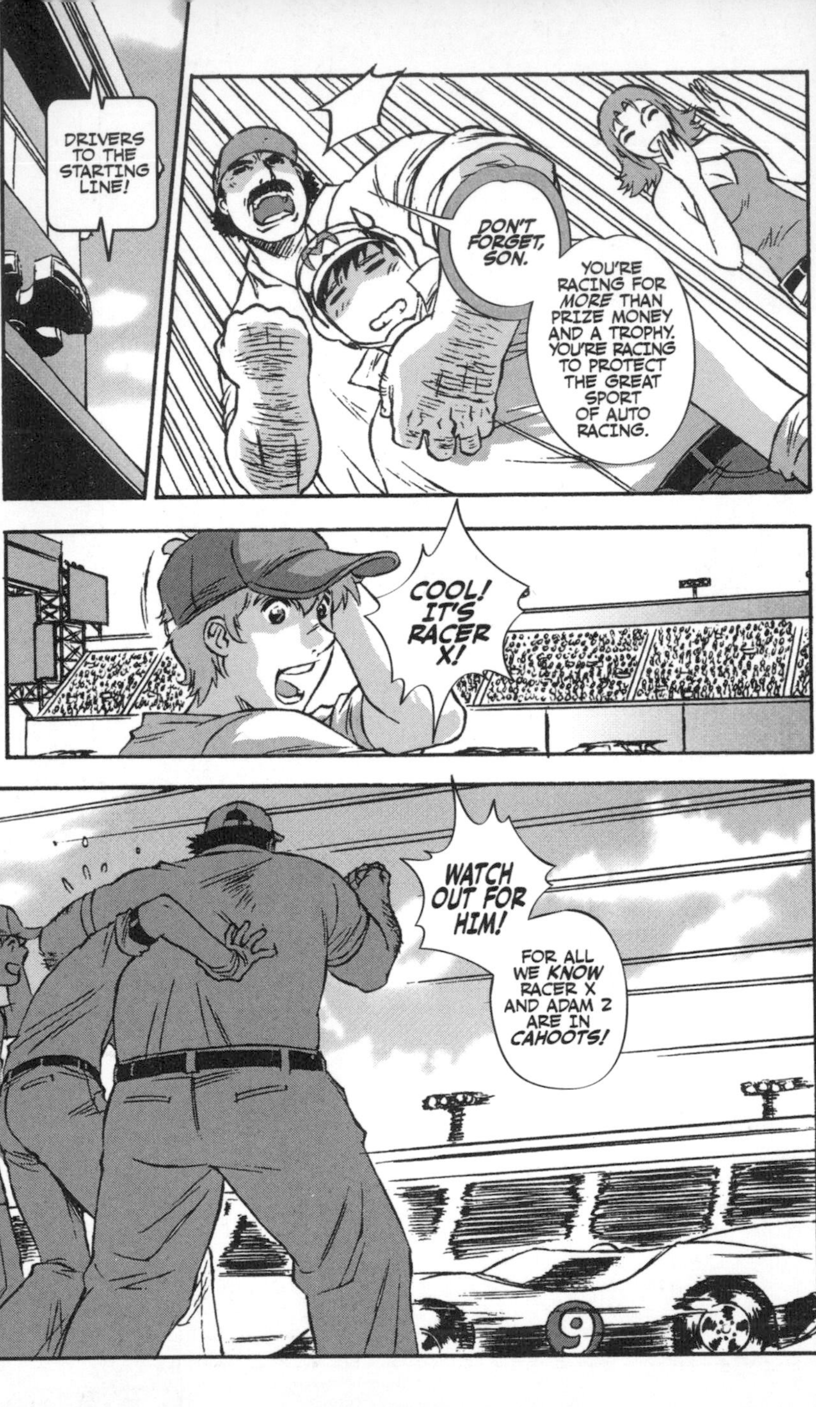
DRIVERS TO THE STARTING LINE!
DON'T FORGET, SON.
YOU'RE RACING FOR MORE THAN PRIZE MONEY AND A TROPHY. YOU'RE RACING TO PROTECT THE GREAT SPORT OF AUTO RACING.
COOL! IT'S RACER X!
WATCH OUT FOR HIM!
FOR ALL WE KNOW RACER X AND ADAM 2 ARE IN CAHOOTS!

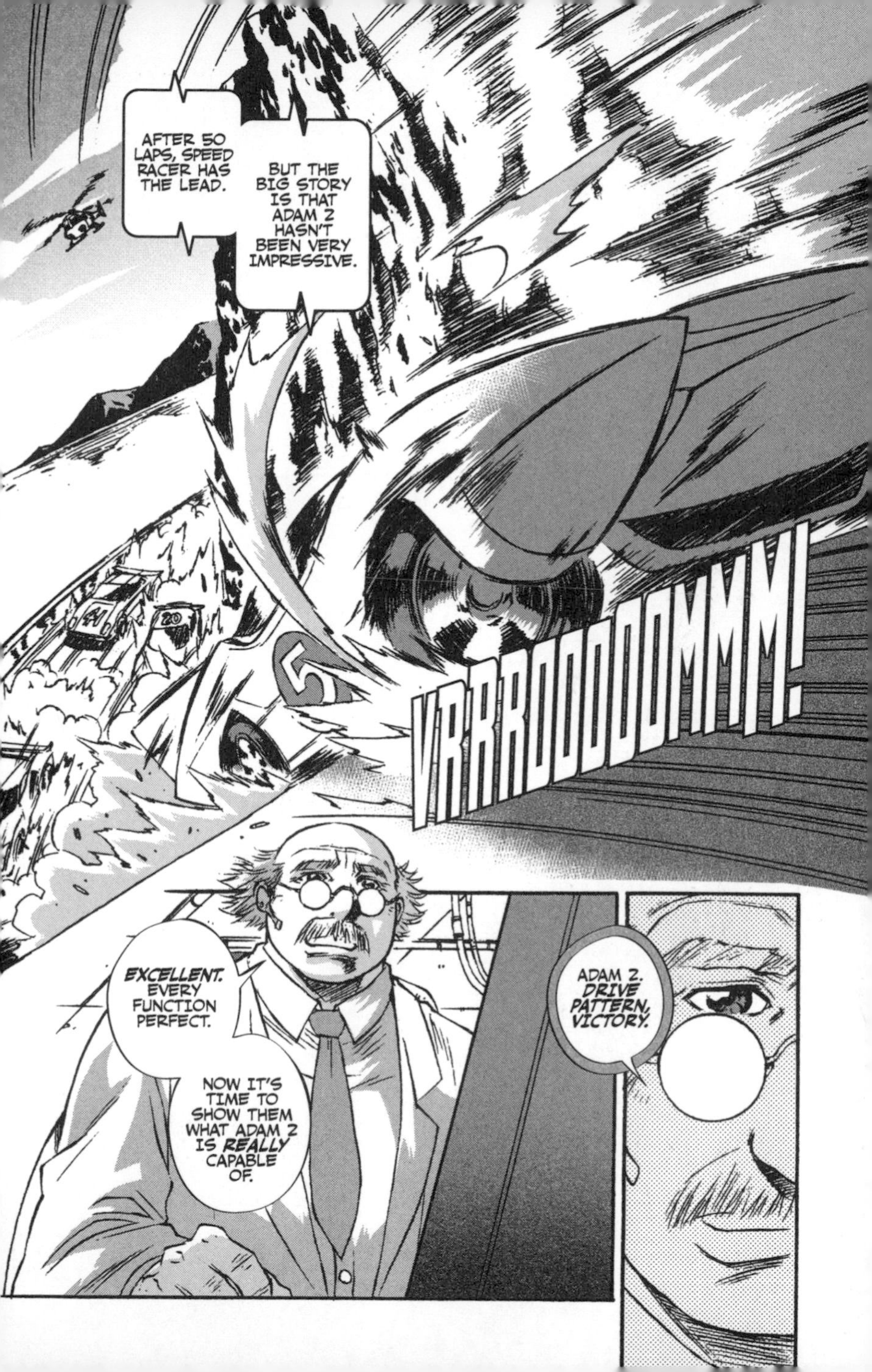
AFTER 50 LAPS, SPEED RACER HAS THE LEAD.
BUT THE BIG STORY IS THAT ADAM 2 HASN'T BEEN VERY IMPRESSIVE.
VRRROOOOOMMM!
EXCELLENT. EVERY FUNCTION PERFECT.
NOW IT'S TIME TO SHOW THEM WHAT ADAM 2 IS *REALLY* CAPABLE OF.
ADAM 2. *DRIVE PATTERN, VICTORY.*

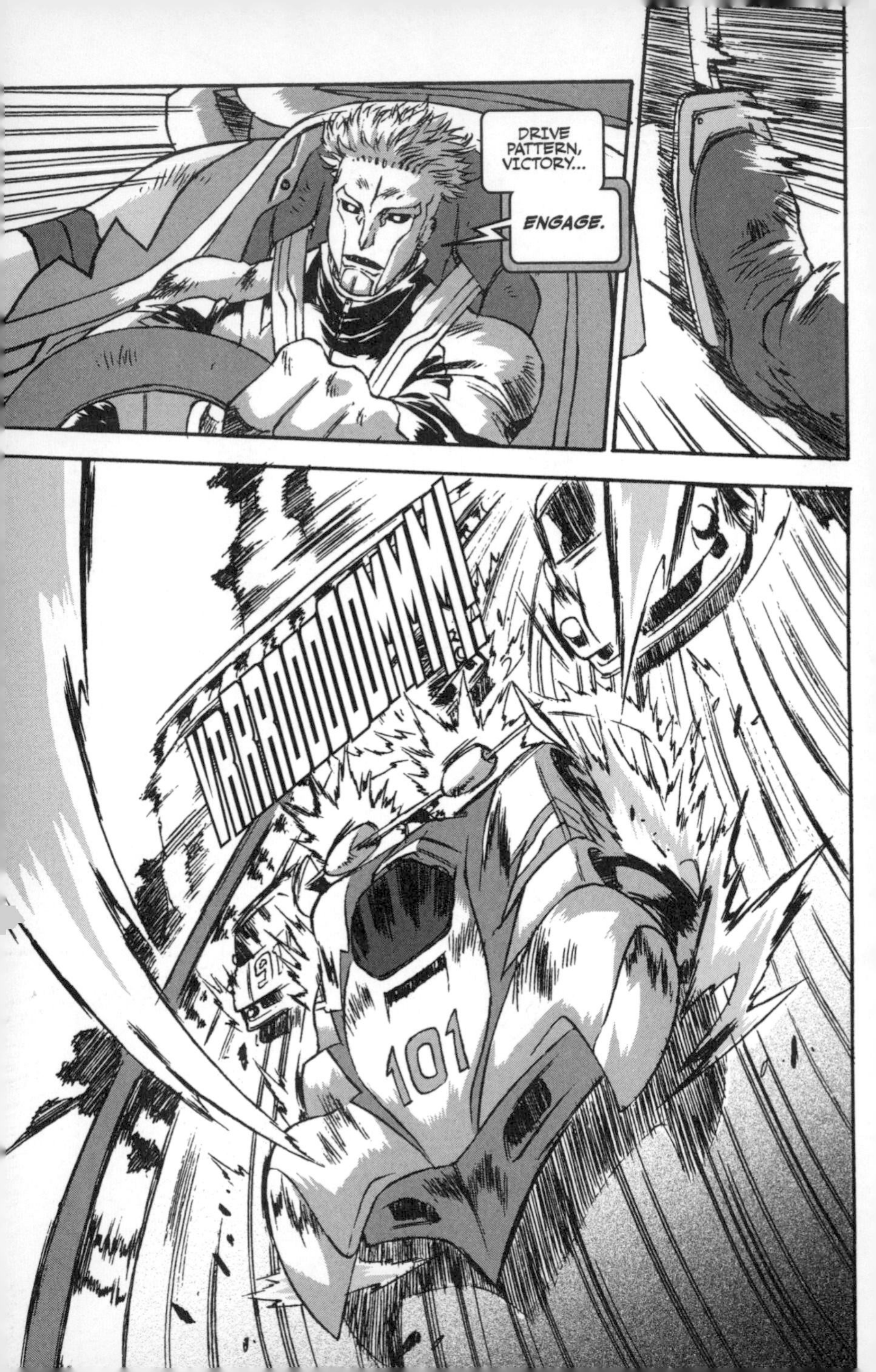
DRIVE PATTERN, VICTORY...
ENGAGE.
VRRROOOOMM!
101

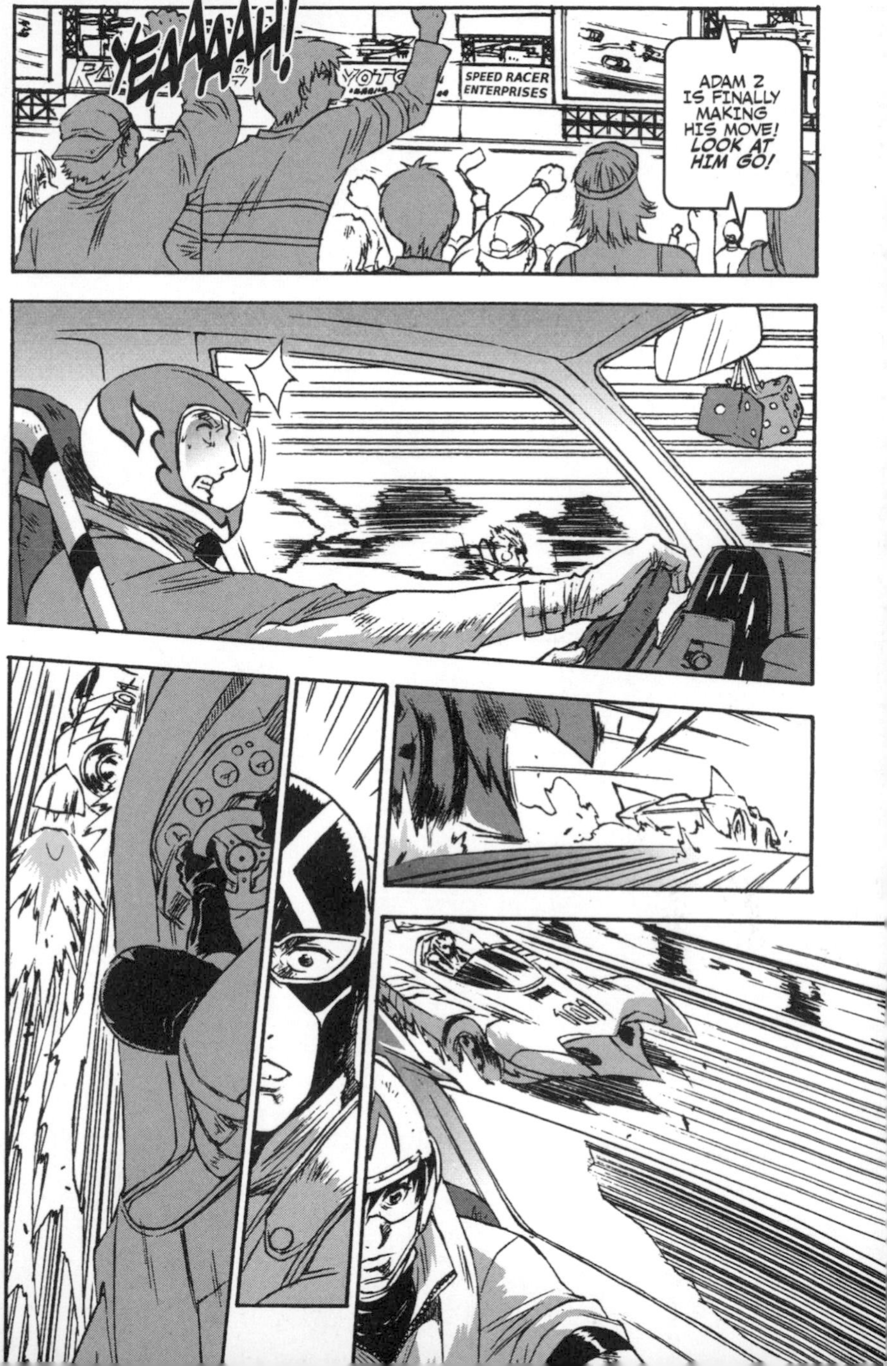
YEAAAAH!
SPEED RACER ENTERPRISES
ADAM 2 IS FINALLY MAKING HIS MOVE! *LOOK AT HIM GO!*

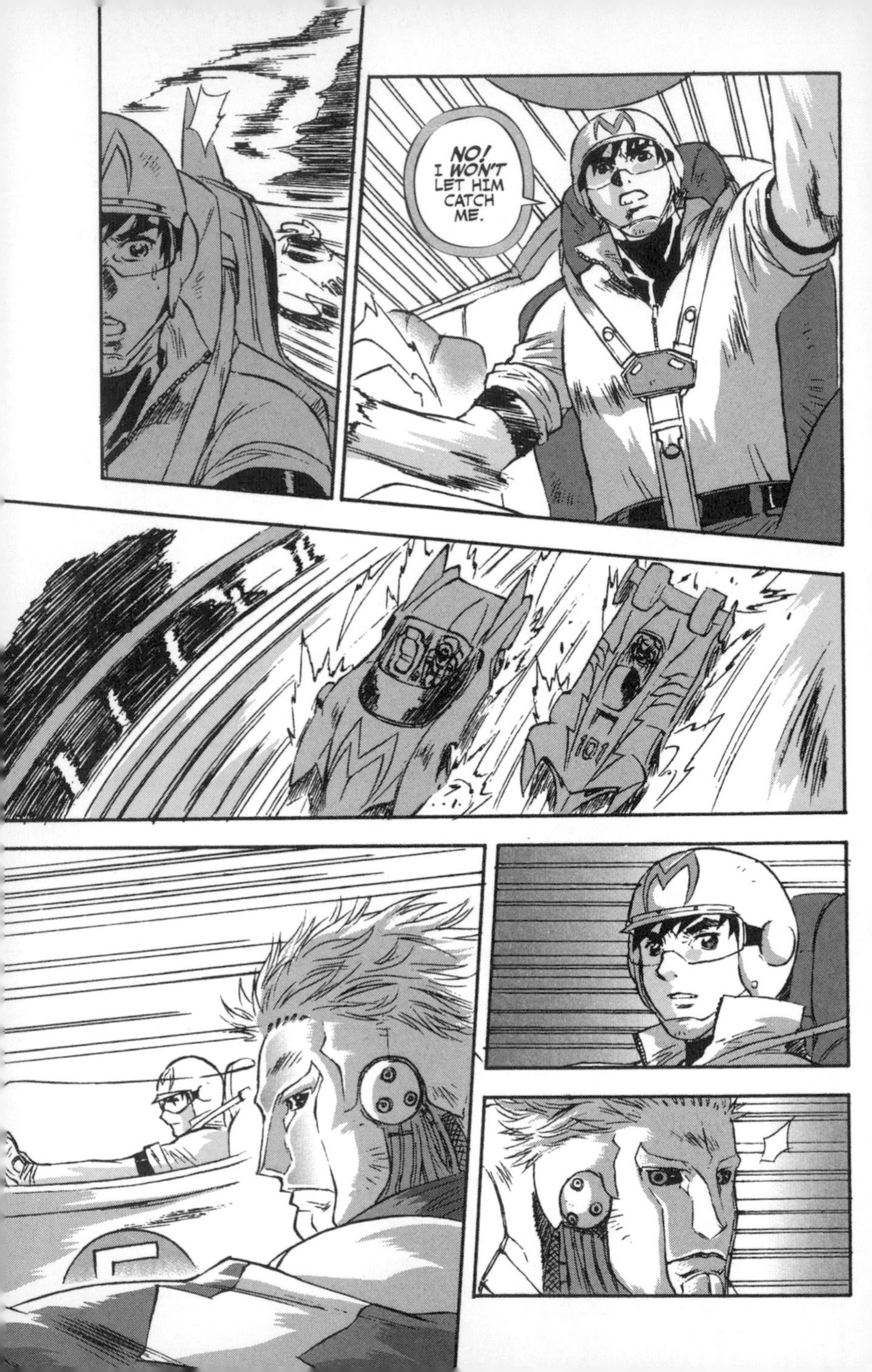
NO! I WON'T LET HIM CATCH ME.

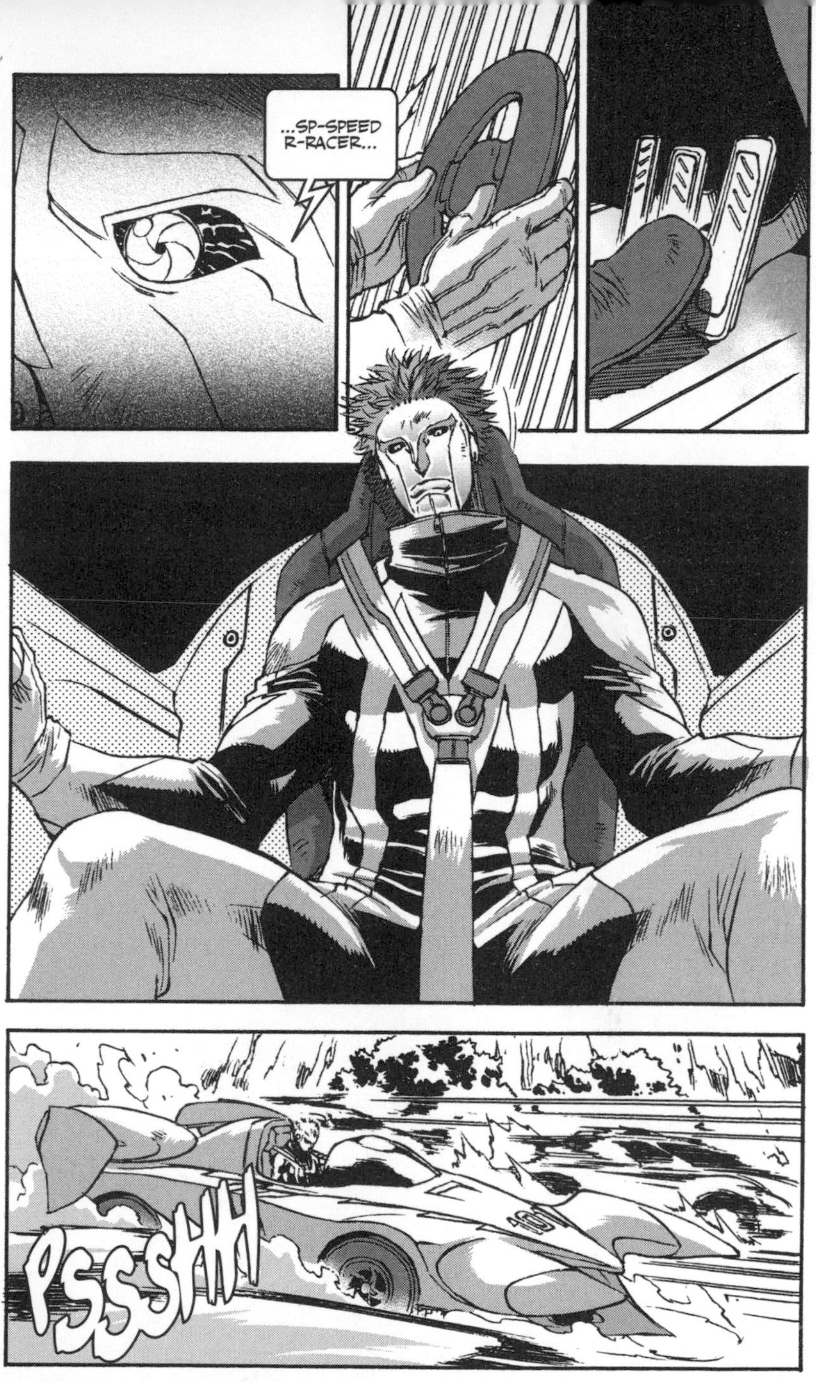
...SP-SPEED R-RACER...
PSSSHH

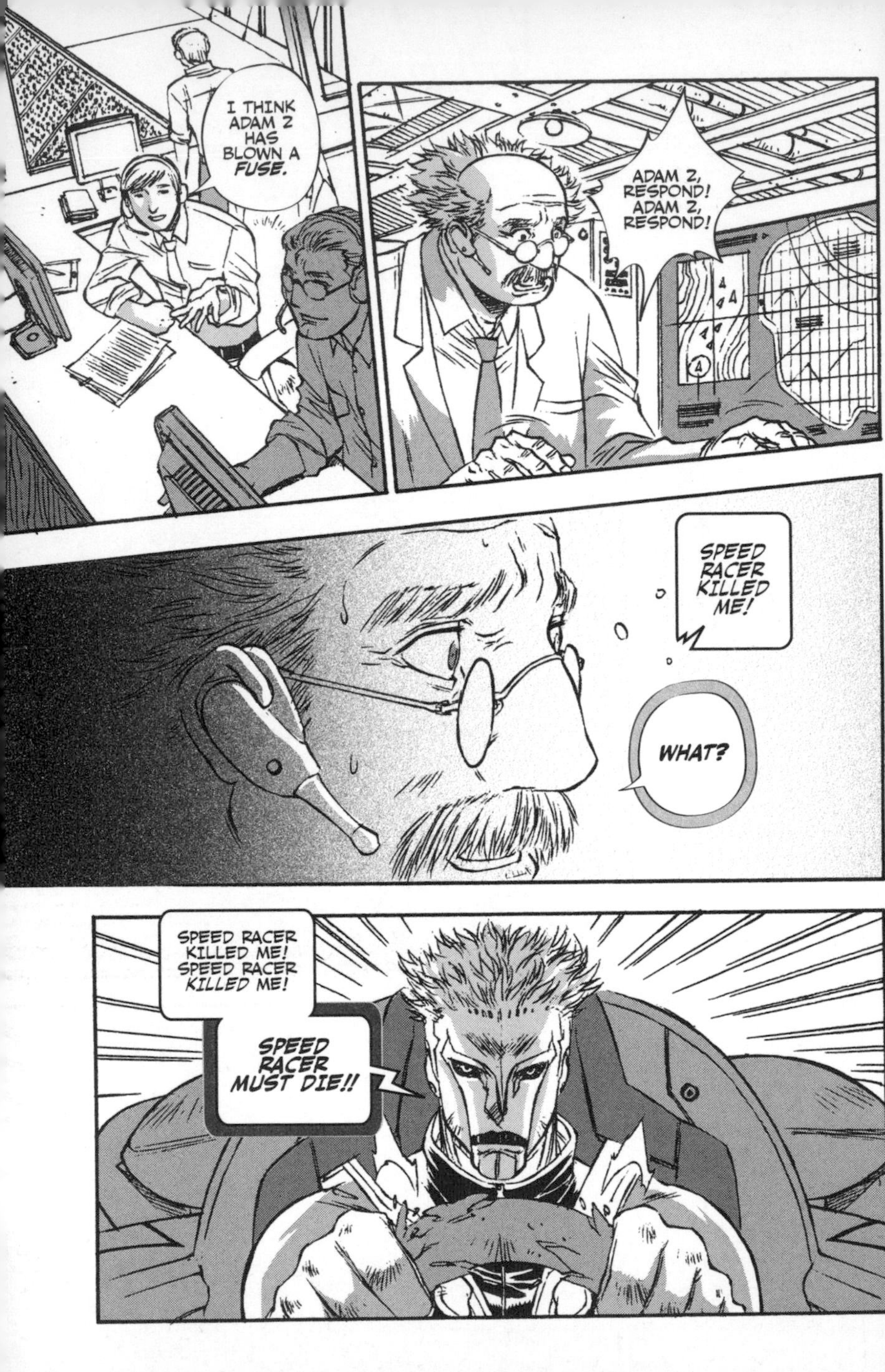
I THINK ADAM 2 HAS BLOWN A *FUSE.*
ADAM 2, RESPOND! ADAM 2, RESPOND!
SPEED RACER KILLED ME!
WHAT?
SPEED RACER KILLED ME! SPEED RACER *KILLED* ME!
SPEED RACER MUST DIE!!

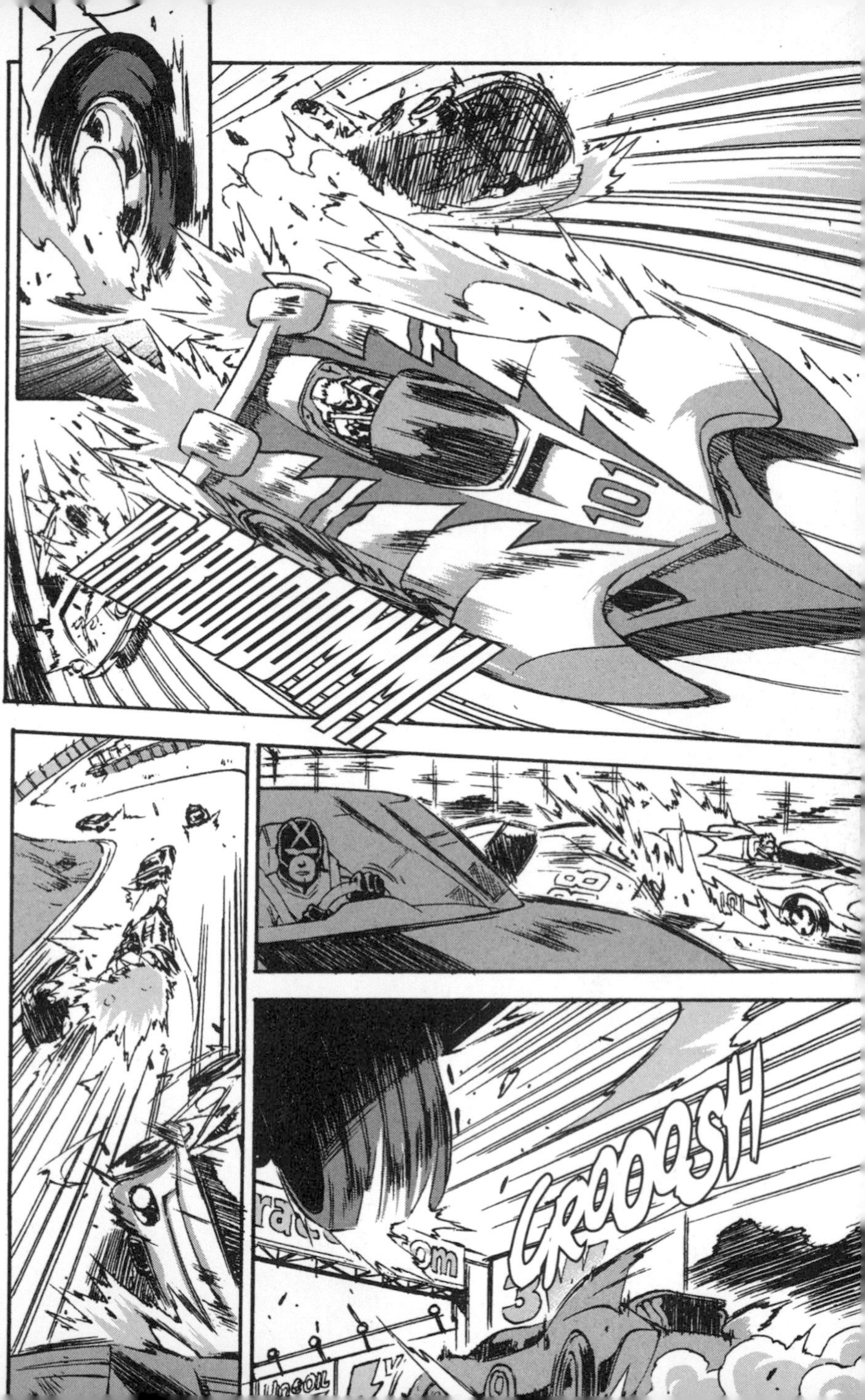
GROOOSH

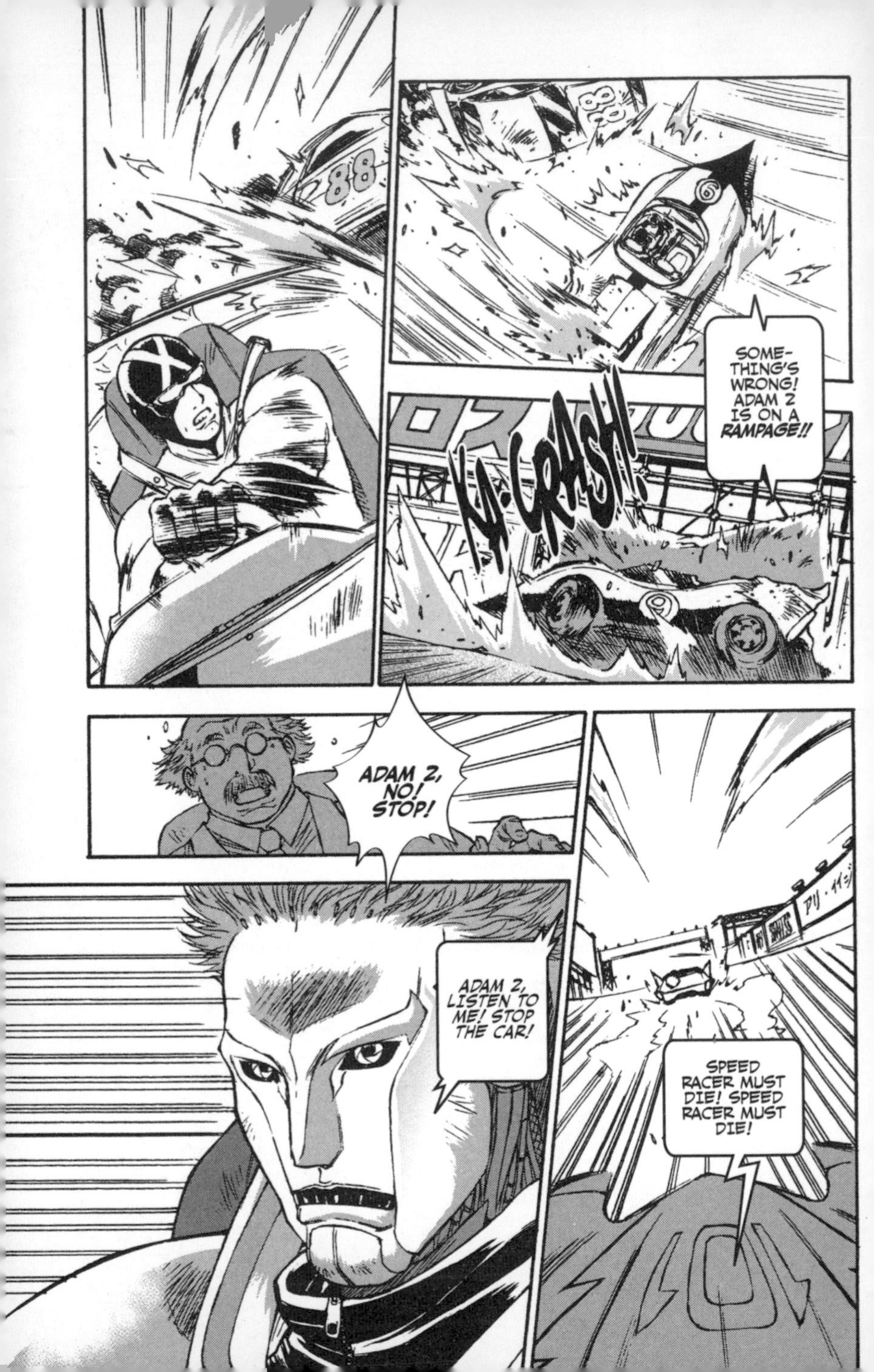
KA-CRASH!
SOME-THING'S WRONG! ADAM 2 IS ON A *RAMPAGE!!*
ADAM 2, NO! STOP!
ADAM 2, LISTEN TO ME! STOP THE CAR!
SPEED RACER MUST DIE! SPEED RACER MUST DIE!

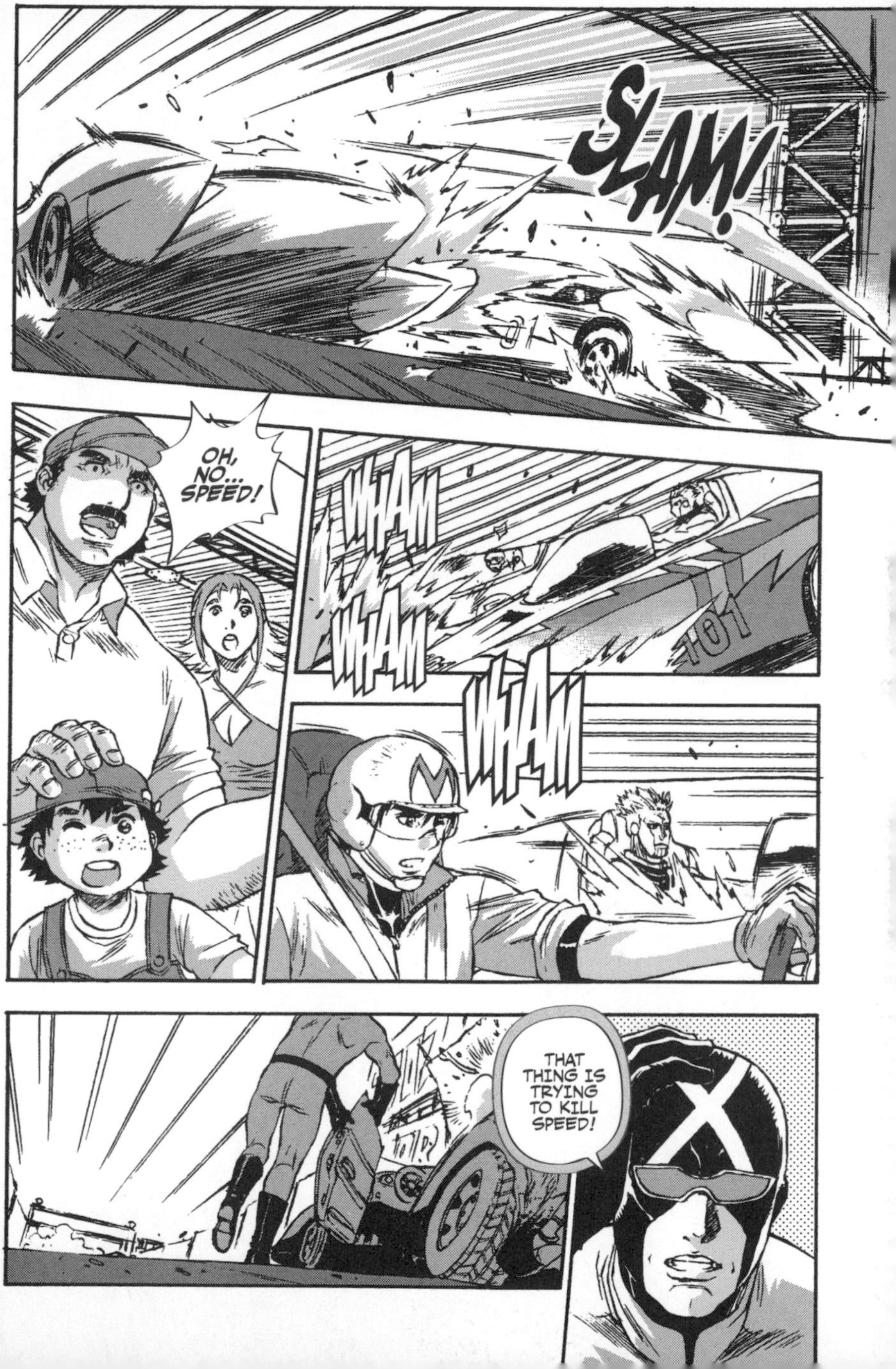
SLAM!
OH, NO... SPEED!
WHAM
WHAM
WHAM
THAT THING IS TRYING TO KILL SPEED!

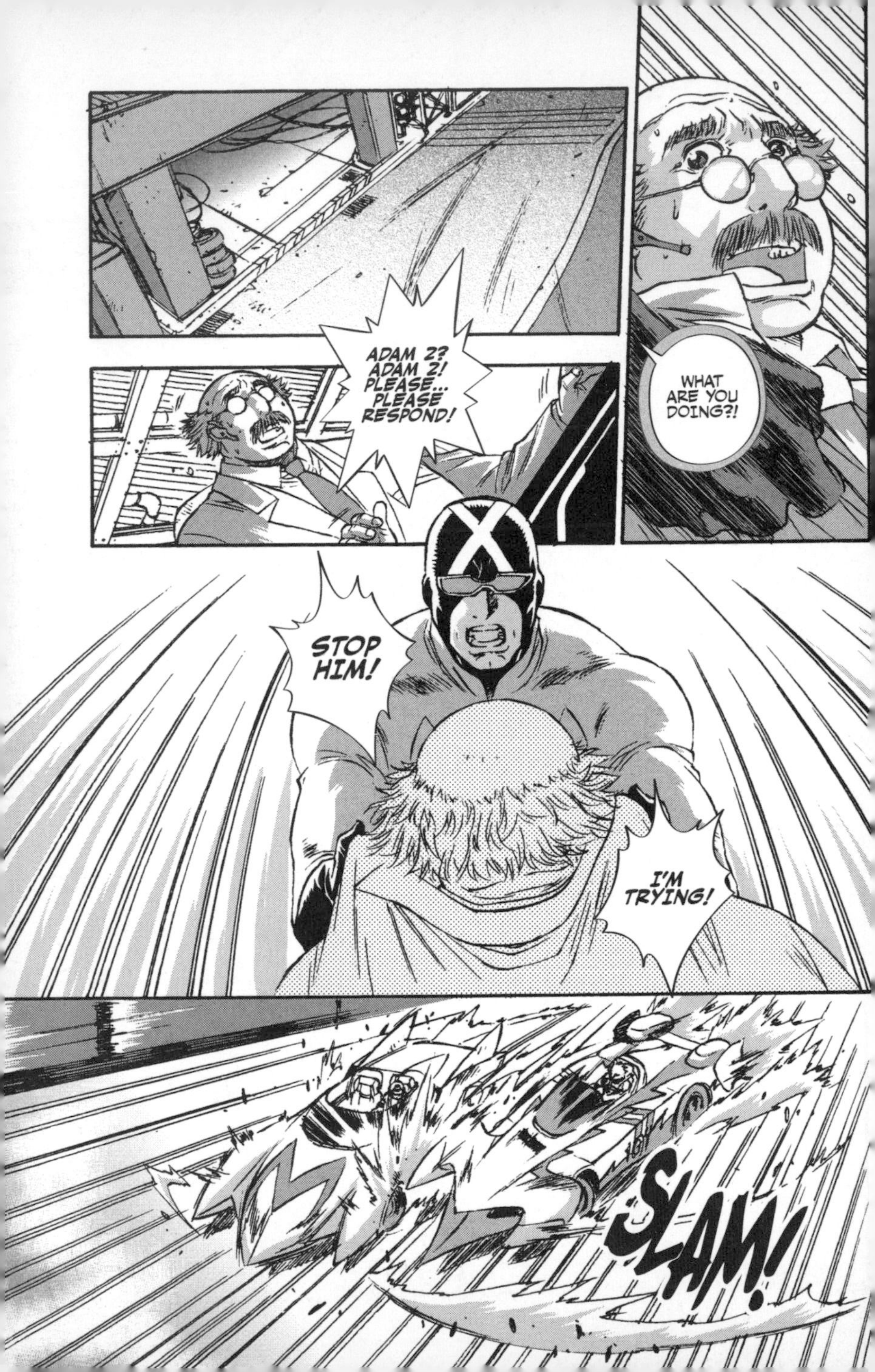
ADAM 2? ADAM 2! PLEASE... PLEASE RESPOND!
WHAT ARE YOU DOING?!
STOP HIM!
I'M TRYING!
SLAM!

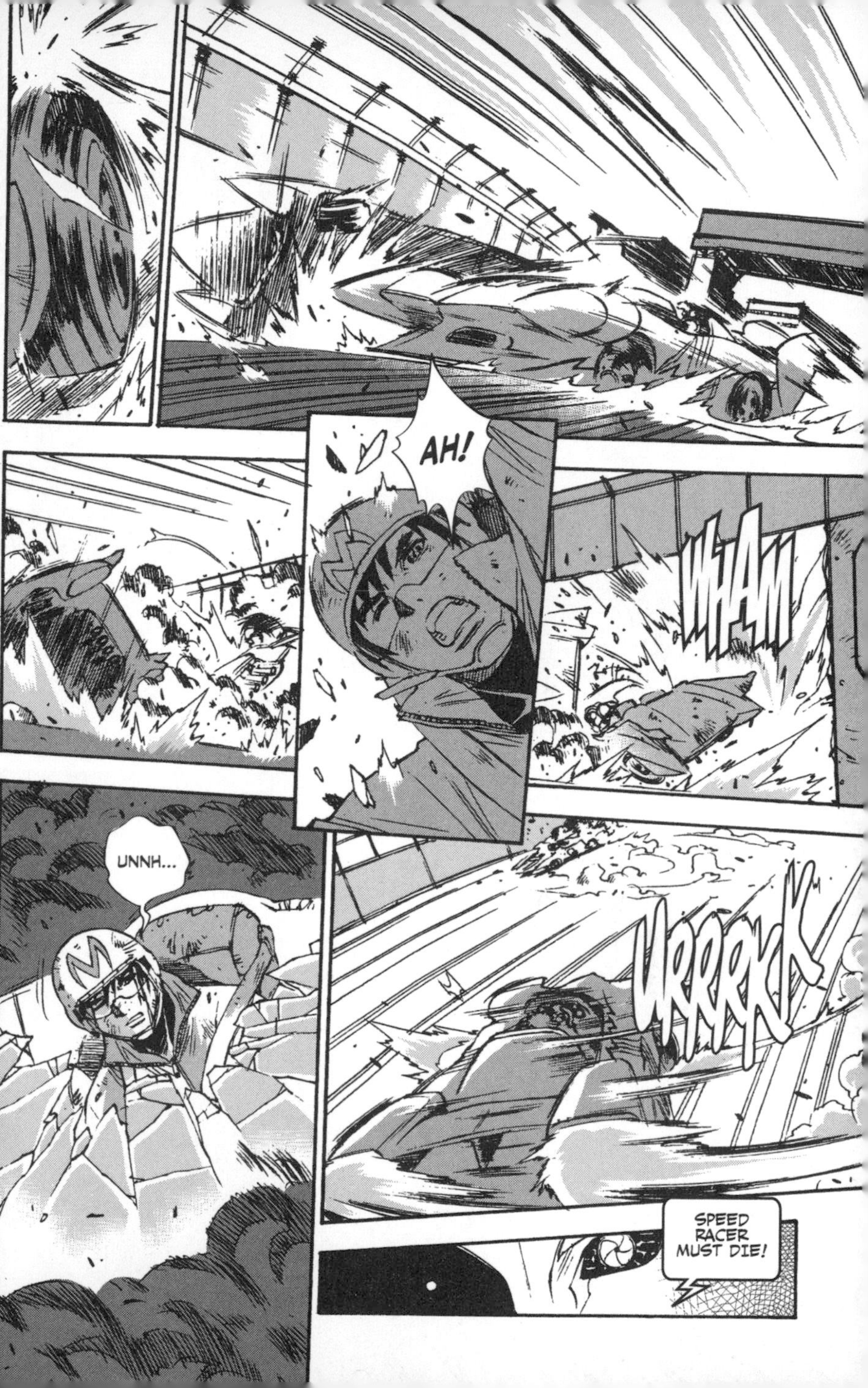

AH!
WHAM
UNNH...
URRRKK
SPEED RACER MUST DIE!

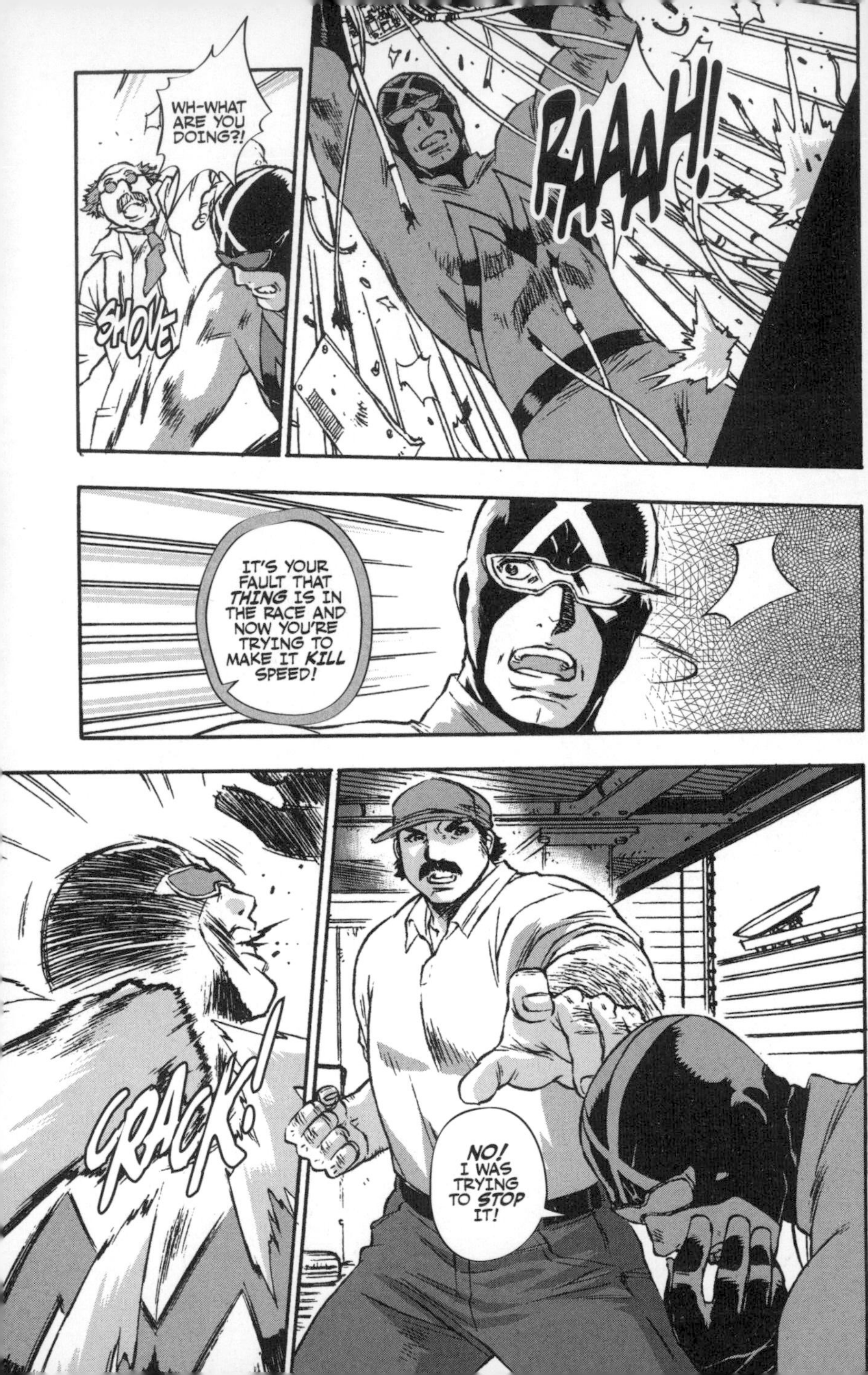
WH-WHAT ARE YOU DOING?!
SHOVE
RAAAH!
IT'S YOUR FAULT THAT *THING* IS IN THE RACE AND NOW YOU'RE TRYING TO MAKE IT *KILL* SPEED!
CRACK!
NO! I WAS TRYING TO *STOP* IT!

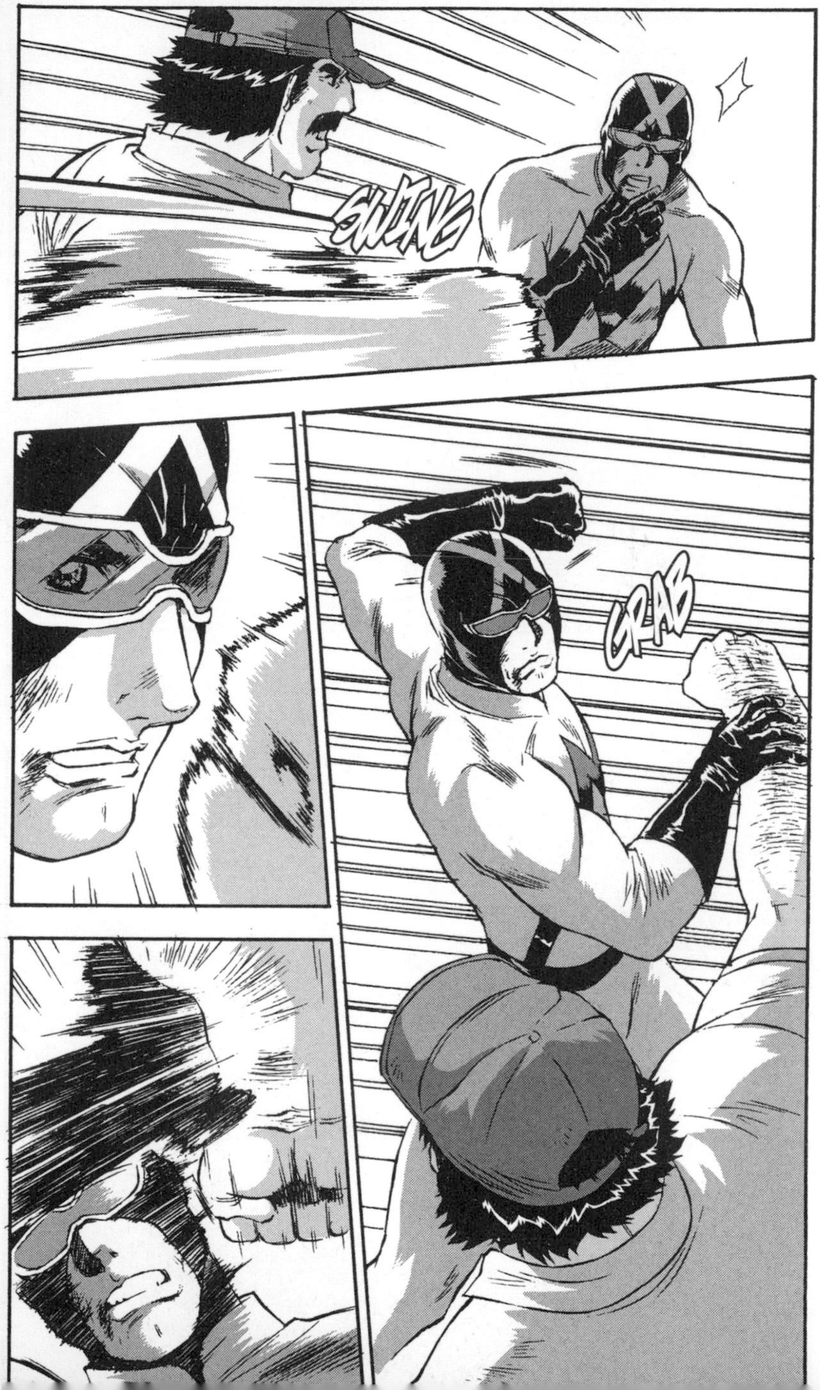
SWING
GRAB

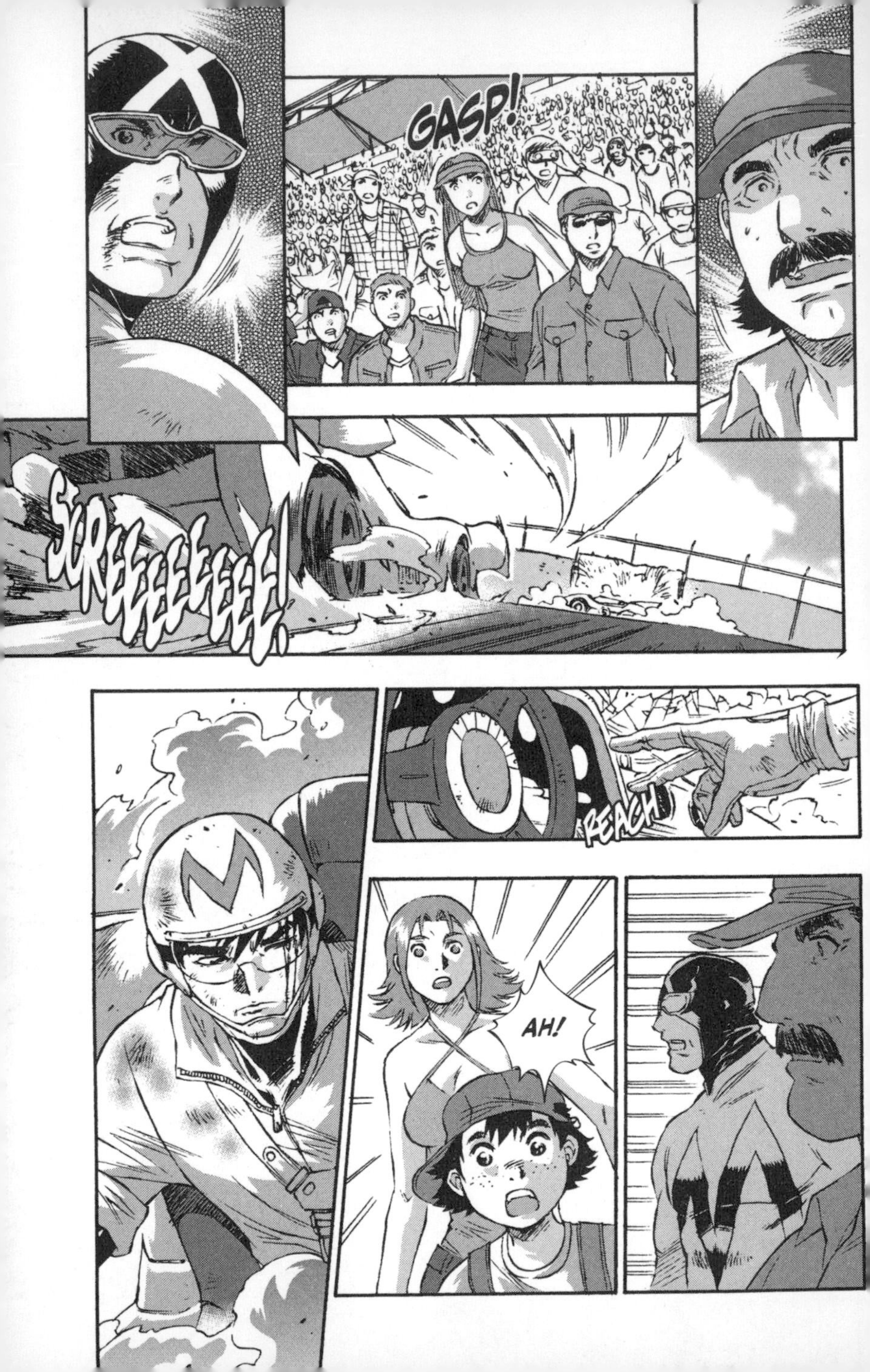
GASP!
SCREEEEEEEEEE!
REACH
AH!

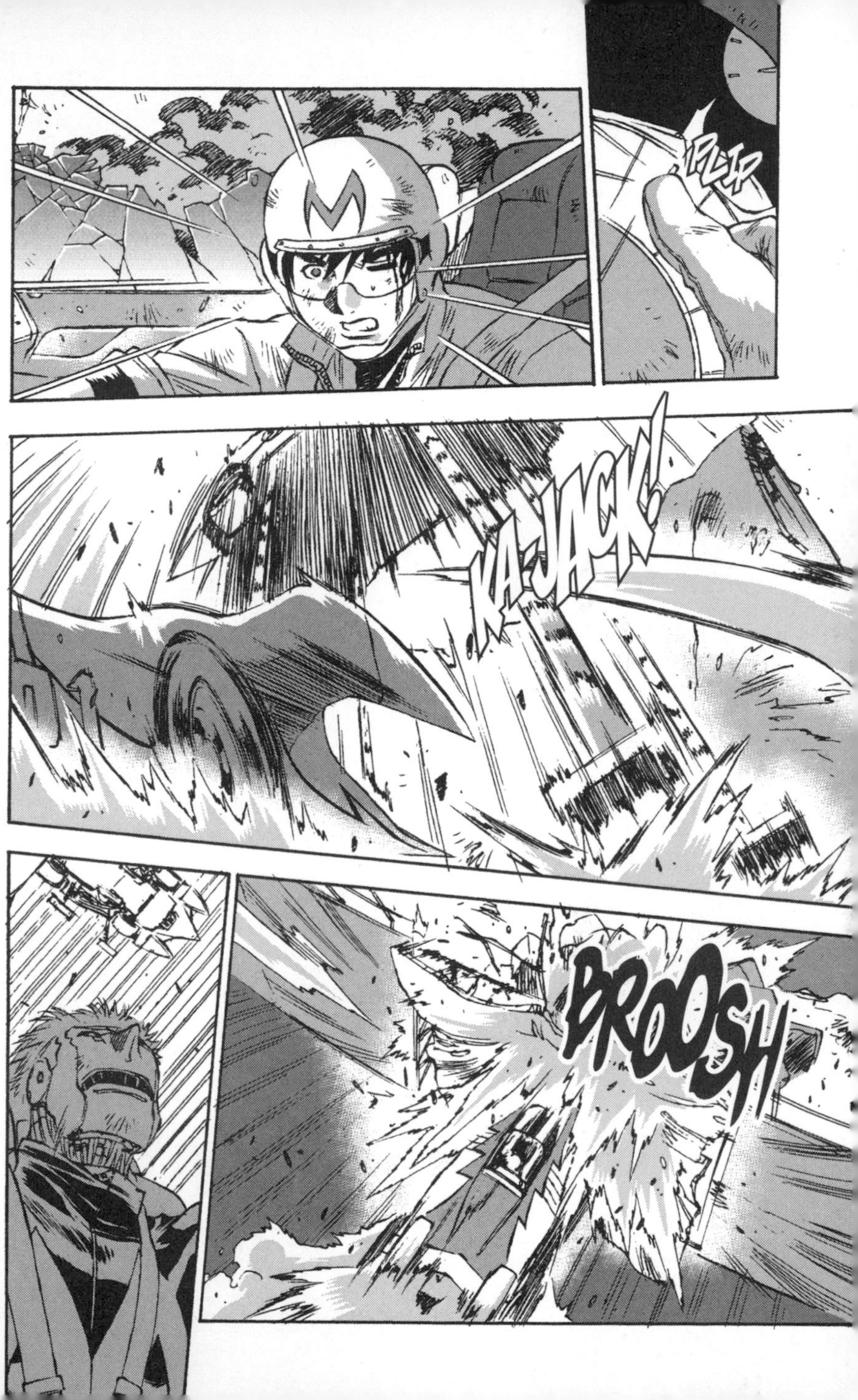
PLIP
KA-JACK!
BROOSH

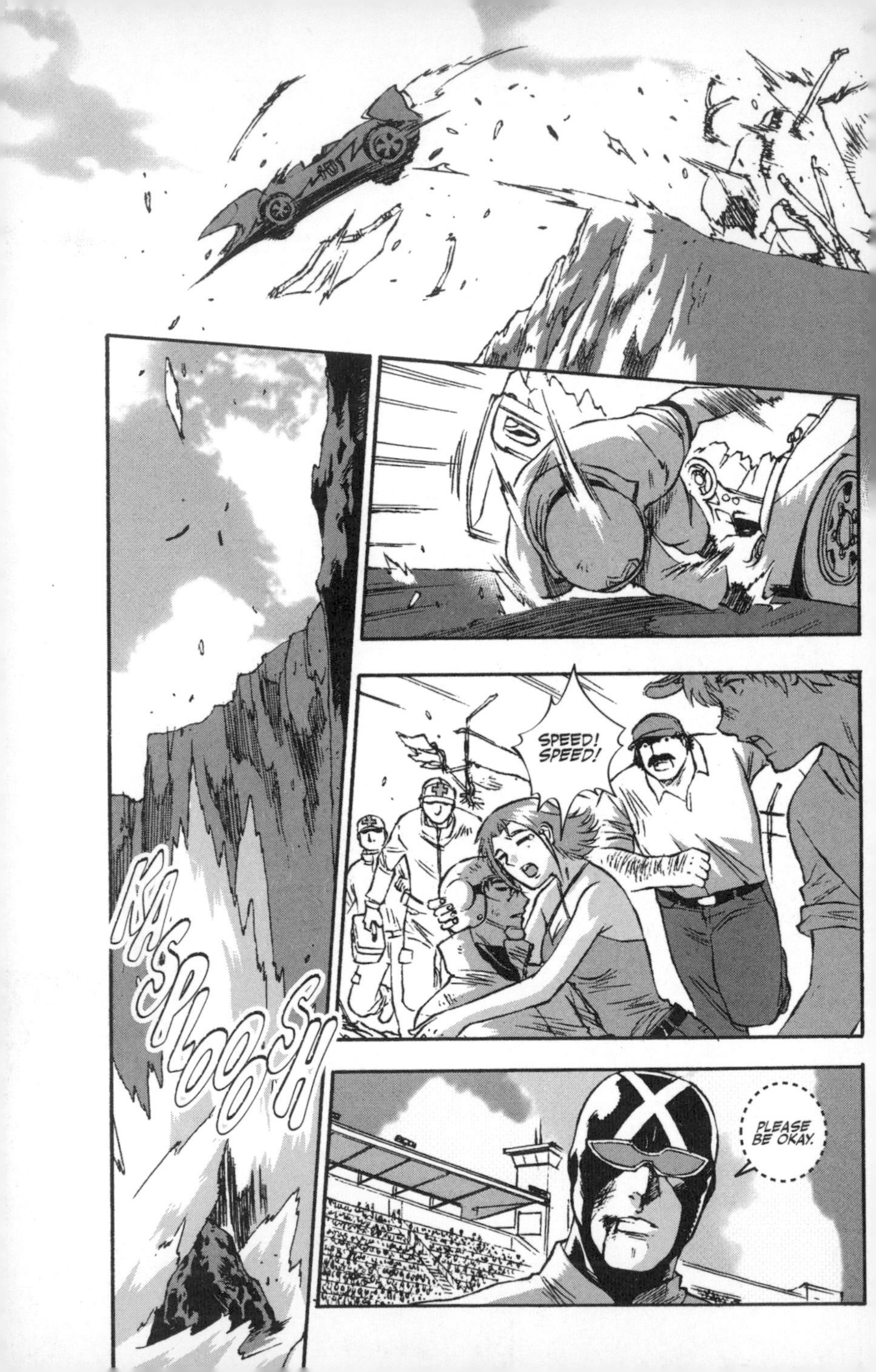
KASPLOOSH
SPEED! SPEED!
PLEASE BE OKAY.

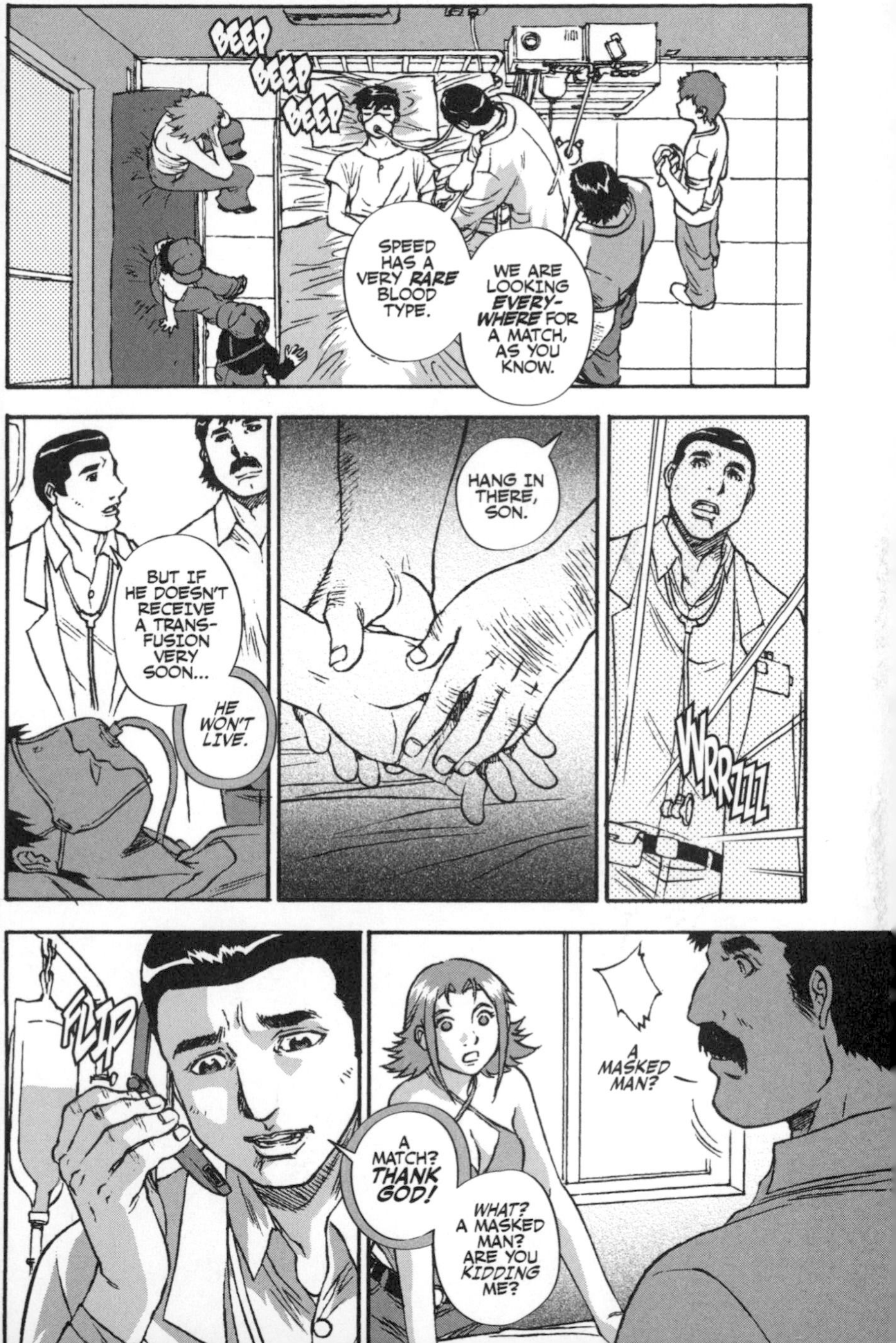
BEEP BEEP BEEP
SPEED HAS A VERY RARE BLOOD TYPE.
WE ARE LOOKING EVERY-WHERE FOR A MATCH, AS YOU KNOW.
BUT IF HE DOESN'T RECEIVE A TRANS-FUSION VERY SOON...
HE WON'T LIVE.
HANG IN THERE, SON.
WRRZZZ
FLIP
A MATCH? THANK GOD!
WHAT? A MASKED MAN? ARE YOU KIDDING ME?
A MASKED MAN?

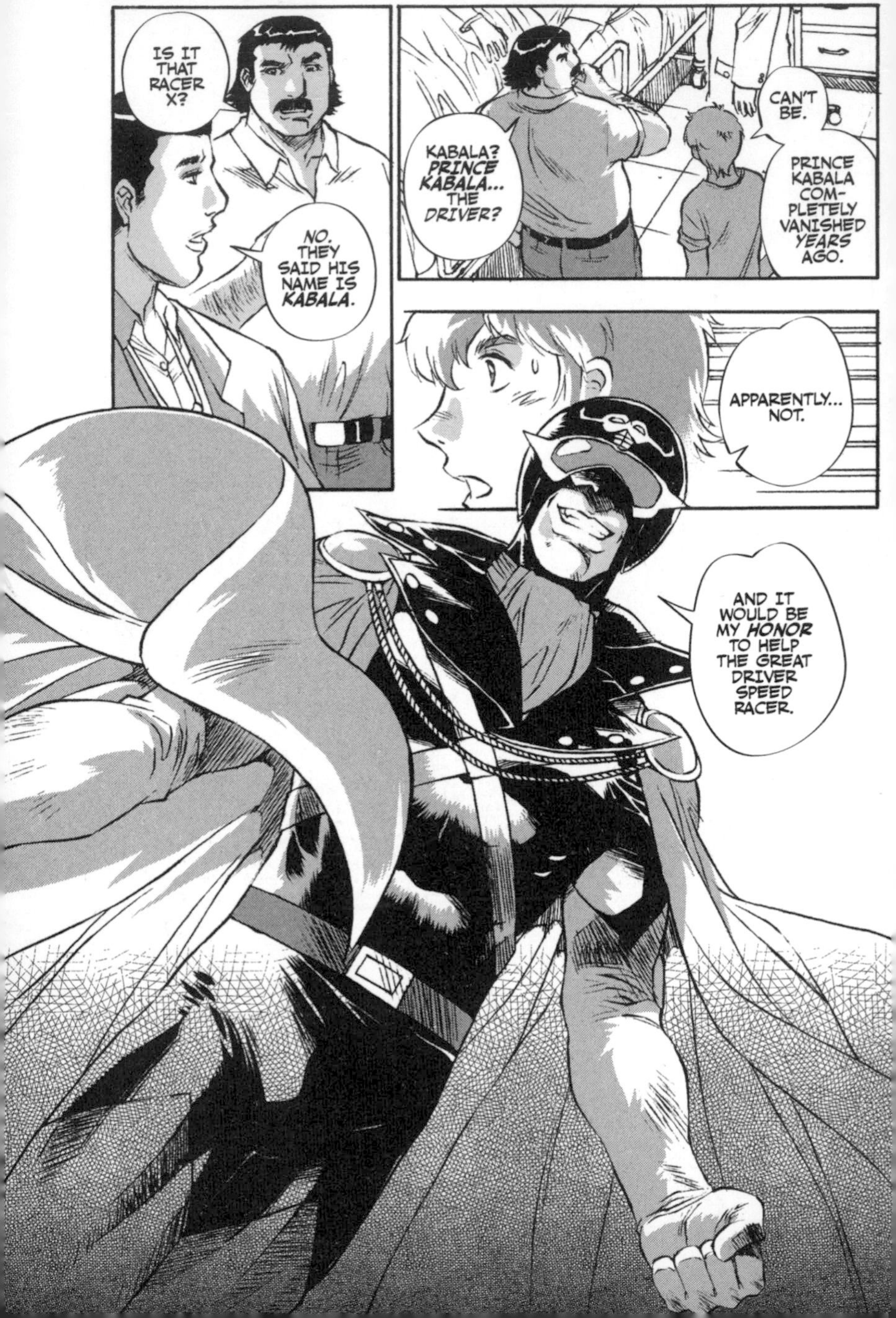
IS IT THAT RACER X?
NO. THEY SAID HIS NAME IS KABALA.
KABALA? PRINCE KABALA... THE DRIVER?
CAN'T BE.
PRINCE KABALA COM-PLETELY VANISHED YEARS AGO.
APPARENTLY... NOT.
AND IT WOULD BE MY HONOR TO HELP THE GREAT DRIVER SPEED RACER.

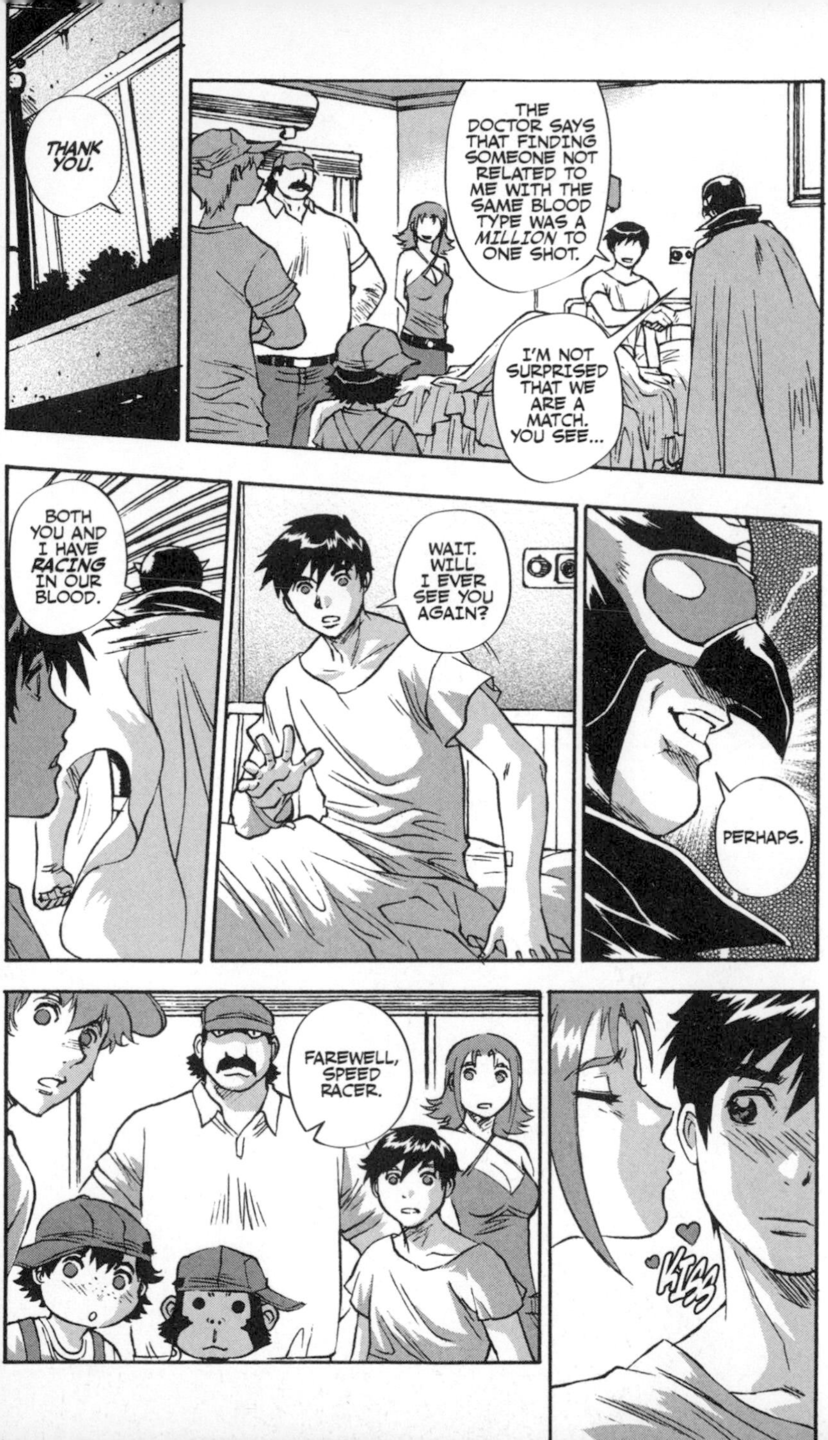
THANK YOU.
THE DOCTOR SAYS THAT FINDING SOMEONE NOT RELATED TO ME WITH THE SAME BLOOD TYPE WAS A MILLION TO ONE SHOT.
I'M NOT SURPRISED THAT WE ARE A MATCH. YOU SEE...
BOTH YOU AND I HAVE RACING IN OUR BLOOD.
WAIT. WILL I EVER SEE YOU AGAIN?
PERHAPS.
FAREWELL, SPEED RACER.
KISS

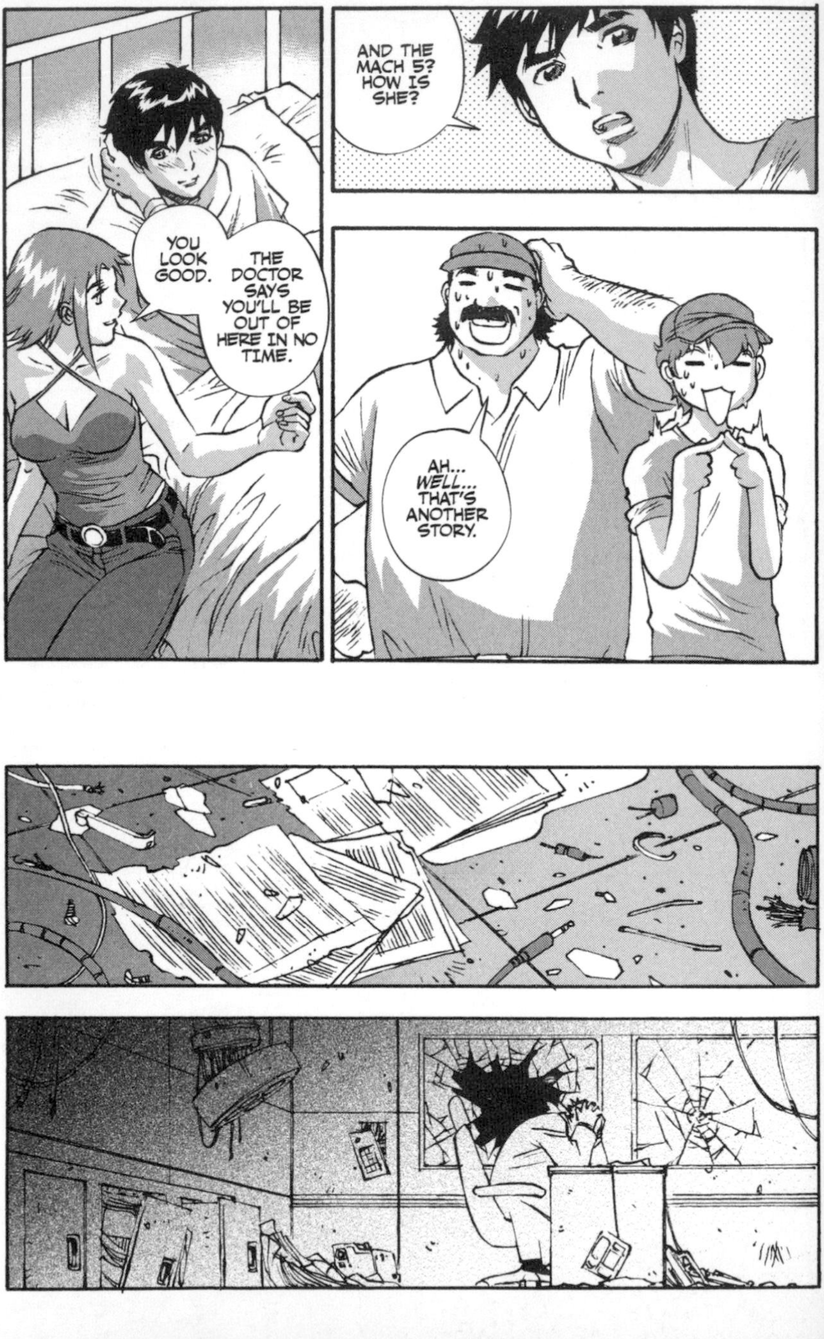
YOU LOOK GOOD.
THE DOCTOR SAYS YOU'LL BE OUT OF HERE IN NO TIME.
AND THE MACH 5? HOW IS SHE?
AH... *WELL*... THAT'S ANOTHER STORY.

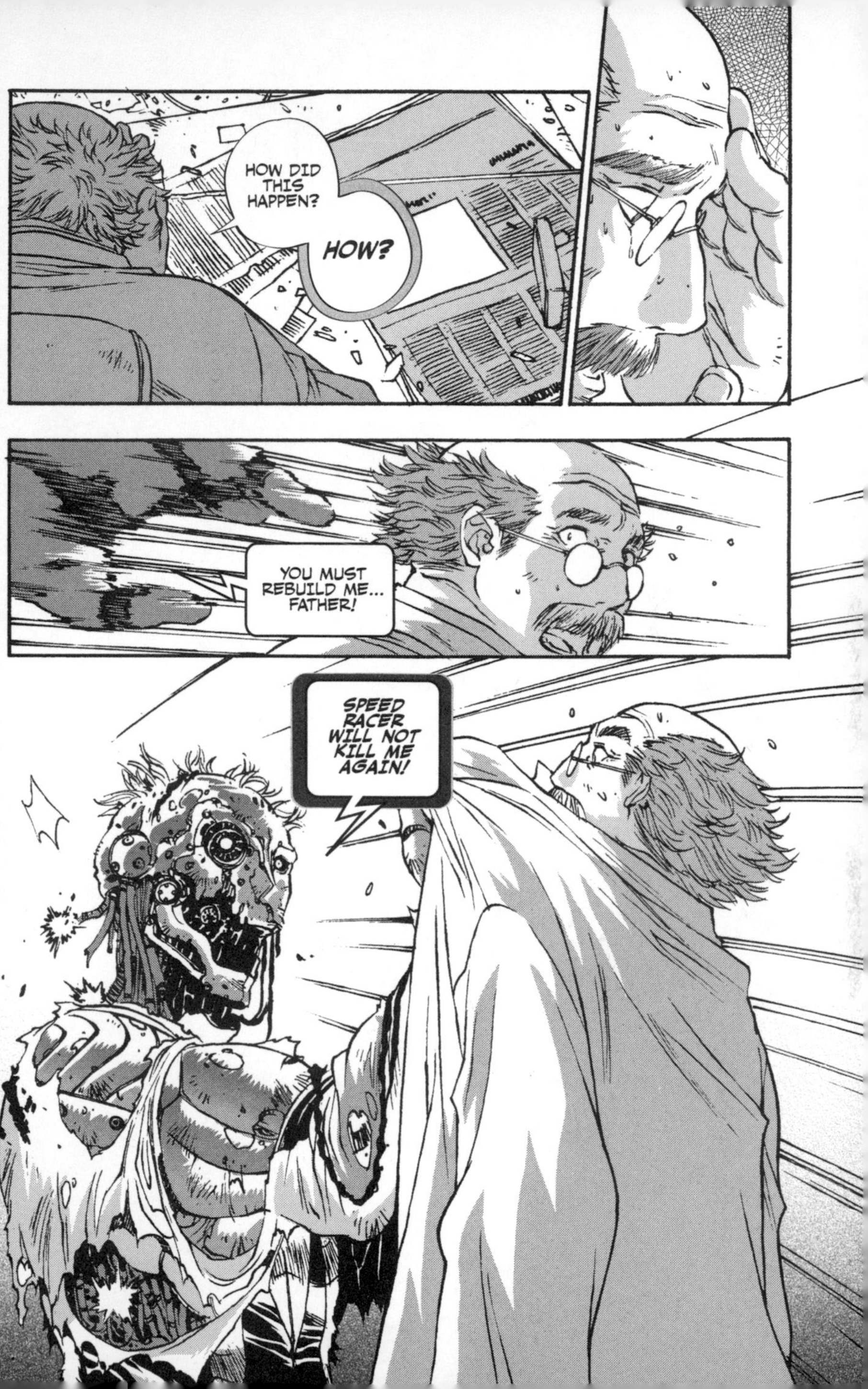
HOW DID THIS HAPPEN?
HOW?
YOU MUST REBUILD ME... FATHER!
SPEED RACER WILL NOT KILL ME AGAIN!

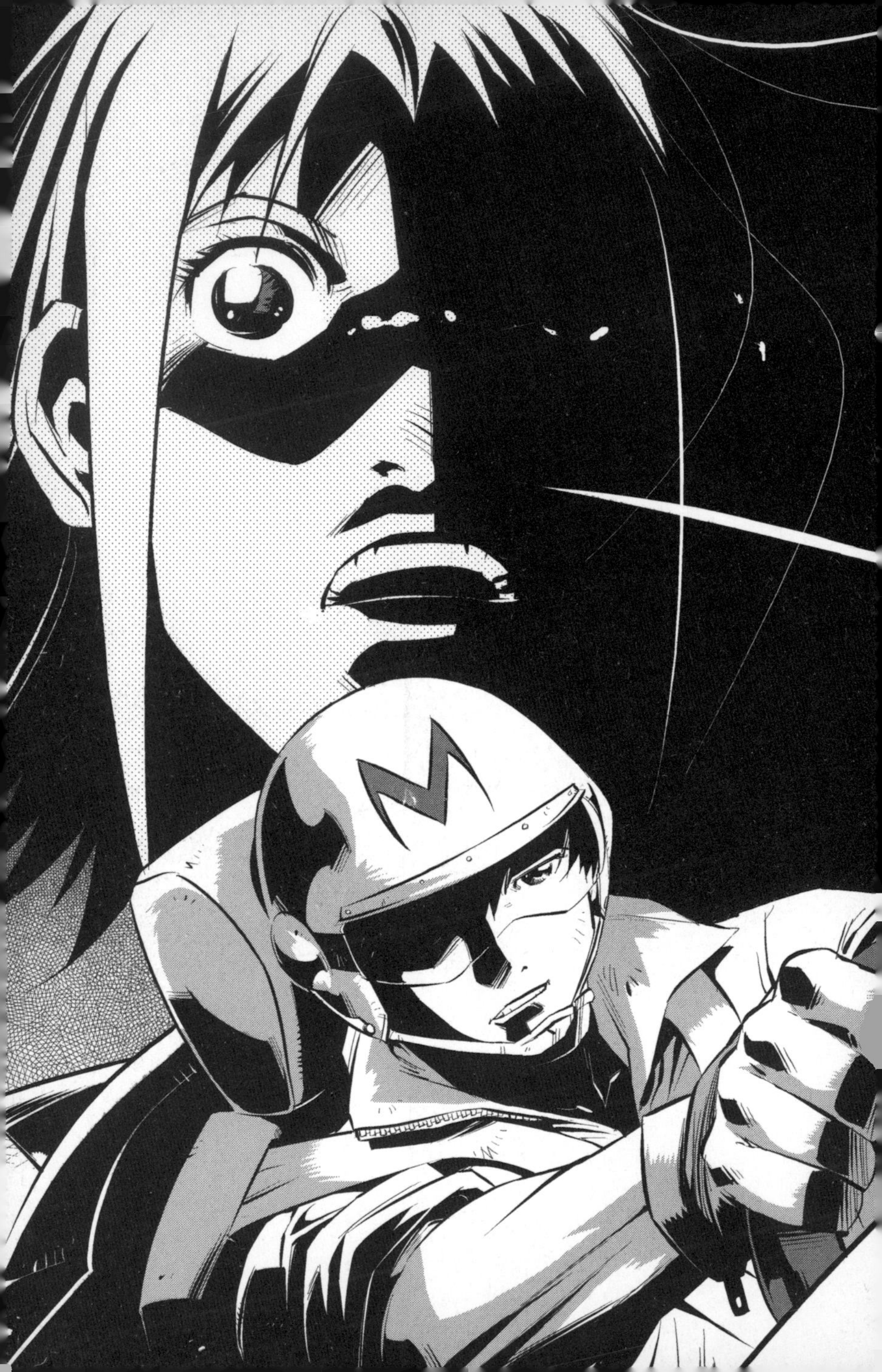

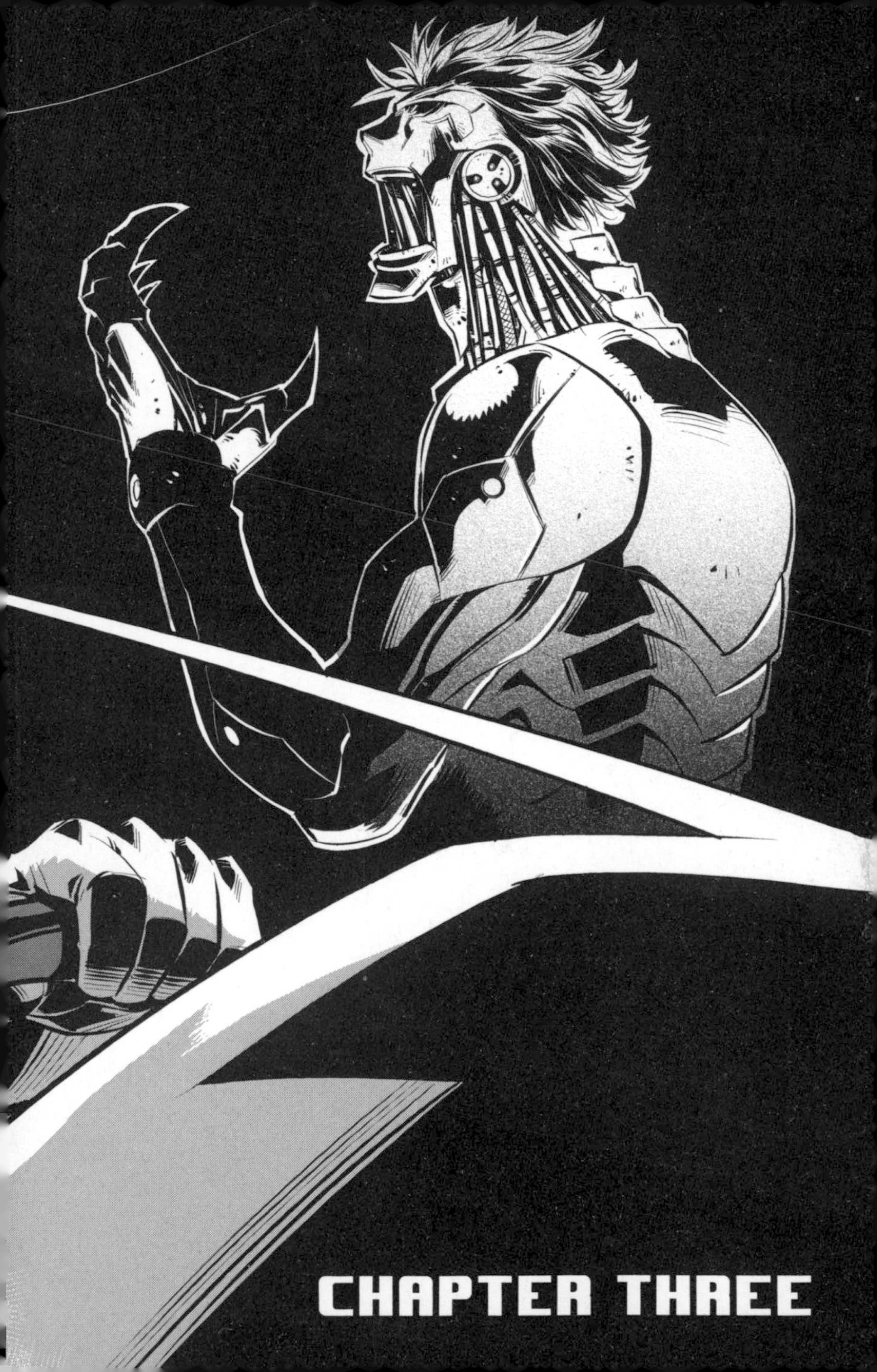
CHAPTER THREE

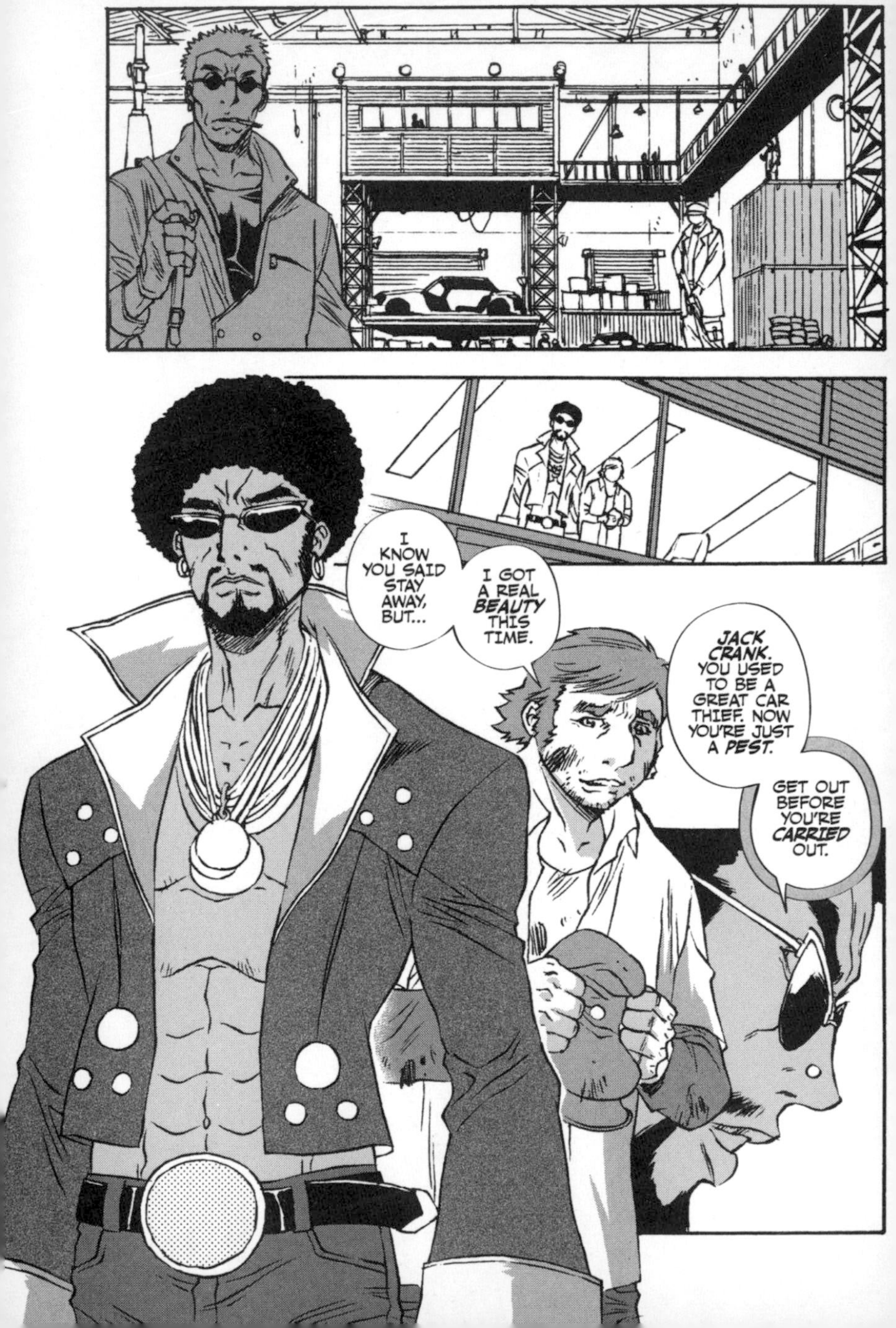
I KNOW YOU SAID STAY AWAY, BUT...
I GOT A REAL *BEAUTY* THIS TIME.
JACK CRANK. YOU USED TO BE A GREAT CAR THIEF. NOW YOU'RE JUST A *PEST.*
GET OUT BEFORE YOU'RE *CARRIED* OUT.

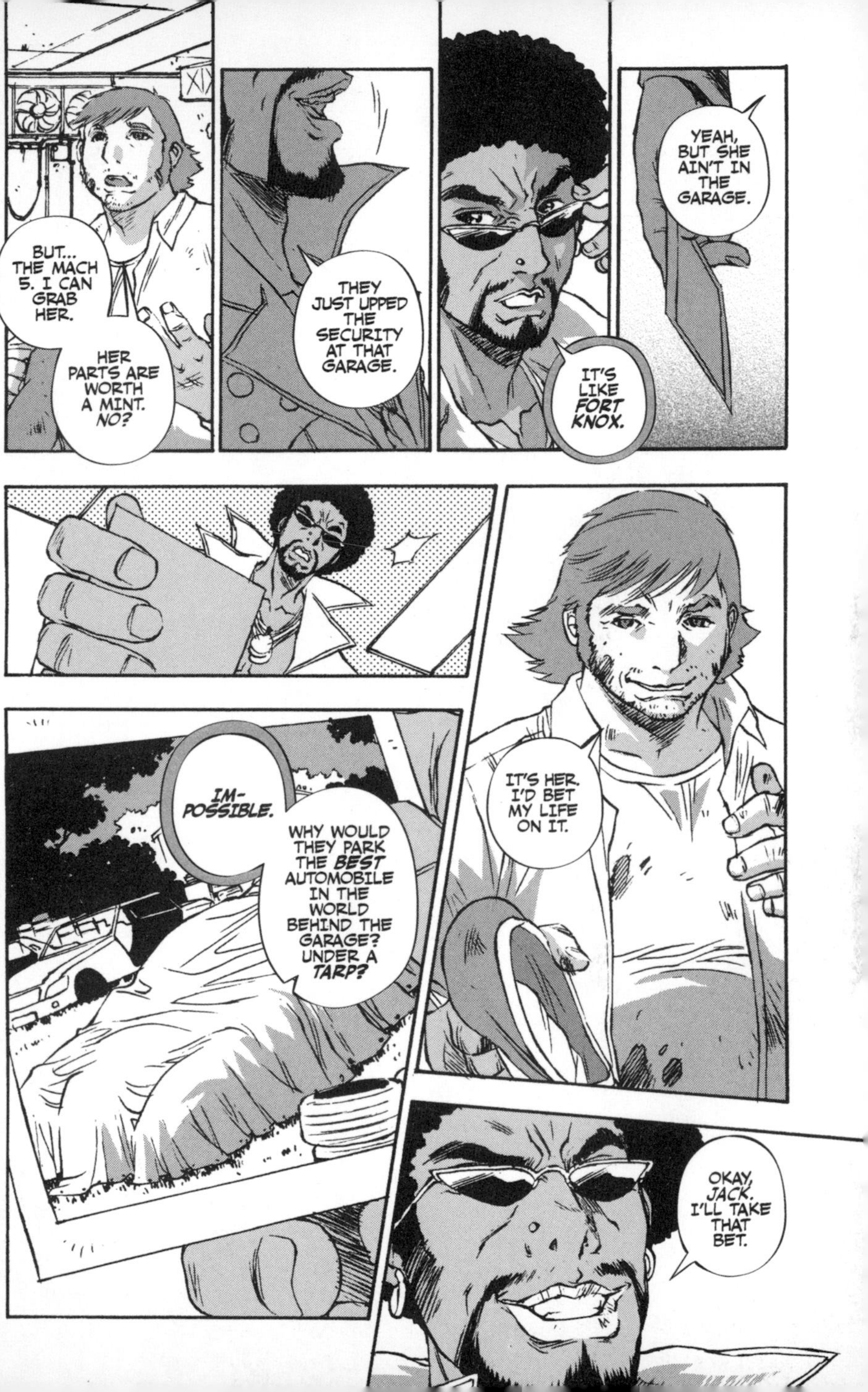
BUT... THE MACH 5. I CAN GRAB HER.
HER PARTS ARE WORTH A MINT. NO?
THEY JUST UPPED THE SECURITY AT THAT GARAGE.
IT'S LIKE FORT KNOX.
YEAH, BUT SHE AIN'T IN THE GARAGE.
IM-POSSIBLE.
WHY WOULD THEY PARK THE BEST AUTOMOBILE IN THE WORLD BEHIND THE GARAGE? UNDER A TARP?
IT'S HER. I'D BET MY LIFE ON IT.
OKAY, JACK. I'LL TAKE THAT BET.

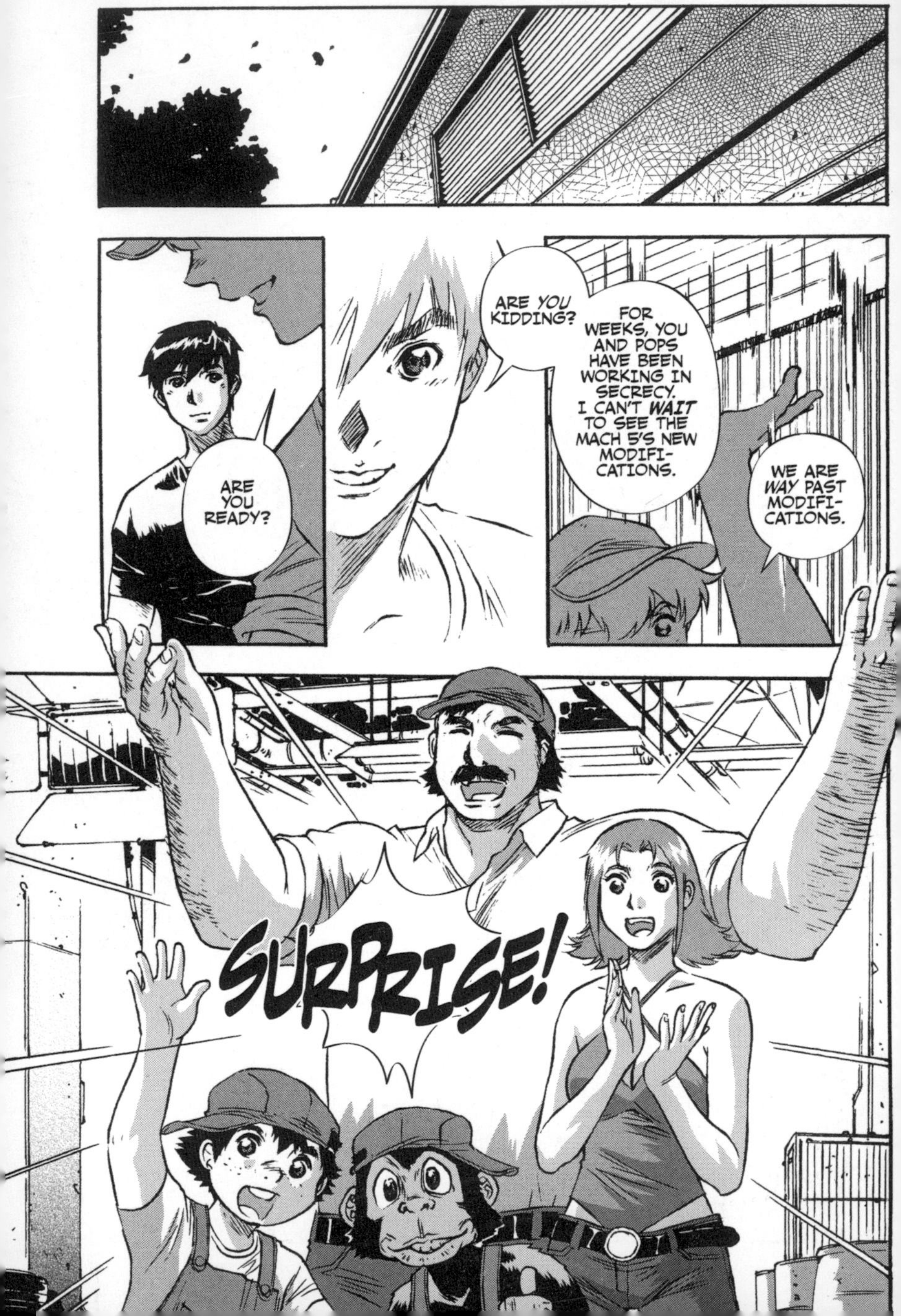
ARE YOU READY?
ARE *YOU* KIDDING?
FOR WEEKS, YOU AND POPS HAVE BEEN WORKING IN SECRECY. I CAN'T ***WAIT*** TO SEE THE MACH 5'S NEW MODIFICATIONS.
WE ARE *WAY* PAST MODIFICATIONS.
SURPRISE!

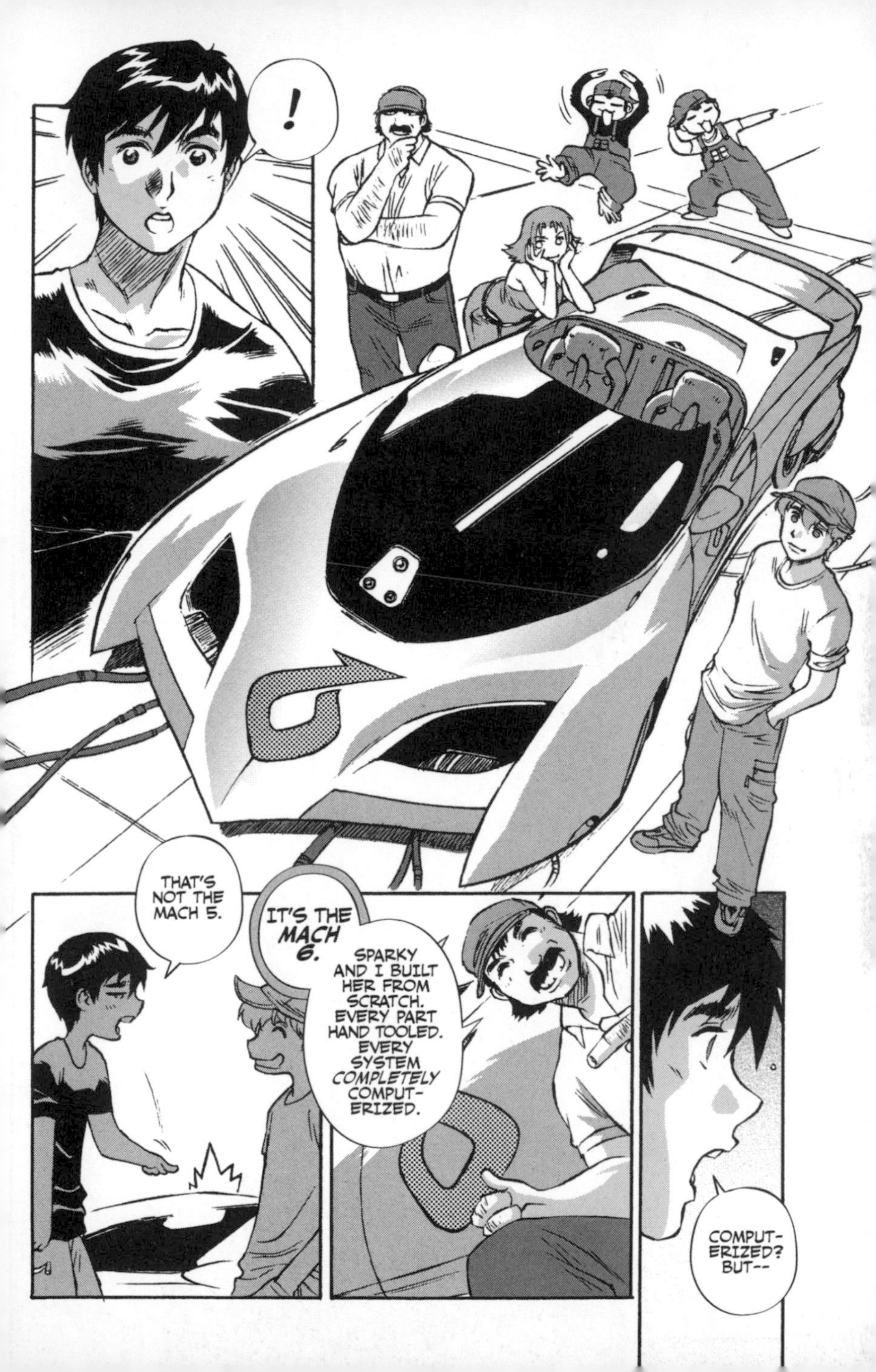
!
THAT'S NOT THE MACH 5.
IT'S THE *MACH 6.*
SPARKY AND I BUILT HER FROM SCRATCH. EVERY PART HAND TOOLED. EVERY SYSTEM *COMPLETELY* COMPUT-ERIZED.
COMPUT-ERIZED? BUT--

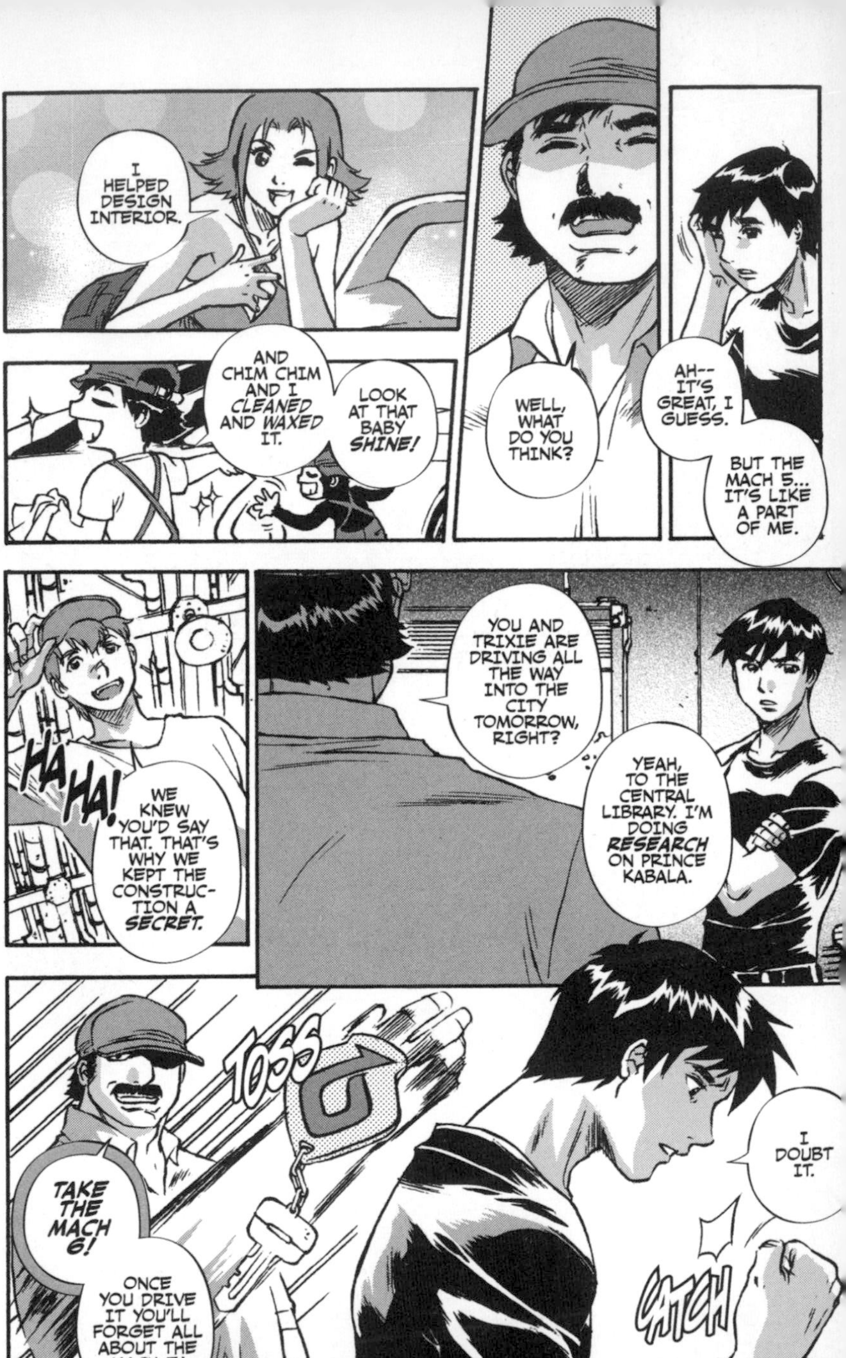
I HELPED DESIGN INTERIOR.
WELL, WHAT DO YOU THINK?
AH-- IT'S GREAT, I GUESS.
BUT THE MACH 5... IT'S LIKE A PART OF ME.
AND CHIM CHIM AND I CLEANED AND WAXED IT.
LOOK AT THAT BABY SHINE!
HA HA!
WE KNEW YOU'D SAY THAT. THAT'S WHY WE KEPT THE CONSTRUCTION A SECRET.
YOU AND TRIXIE ARE DRIVING ALL THE WAY INTO THE CITY TOMORROW, RIGHT?
YEAH, TO THE CENTRAL LIBRARY. I'M DOING RESEARCH ON PRINCE KABALA.
TOSS
TAKE THE MACH 6!
ONCE YOU DRIVE IT YOU'LL FORGET ALL ABOUT THE MACH 5!
I DOUBT IT.
CATCH

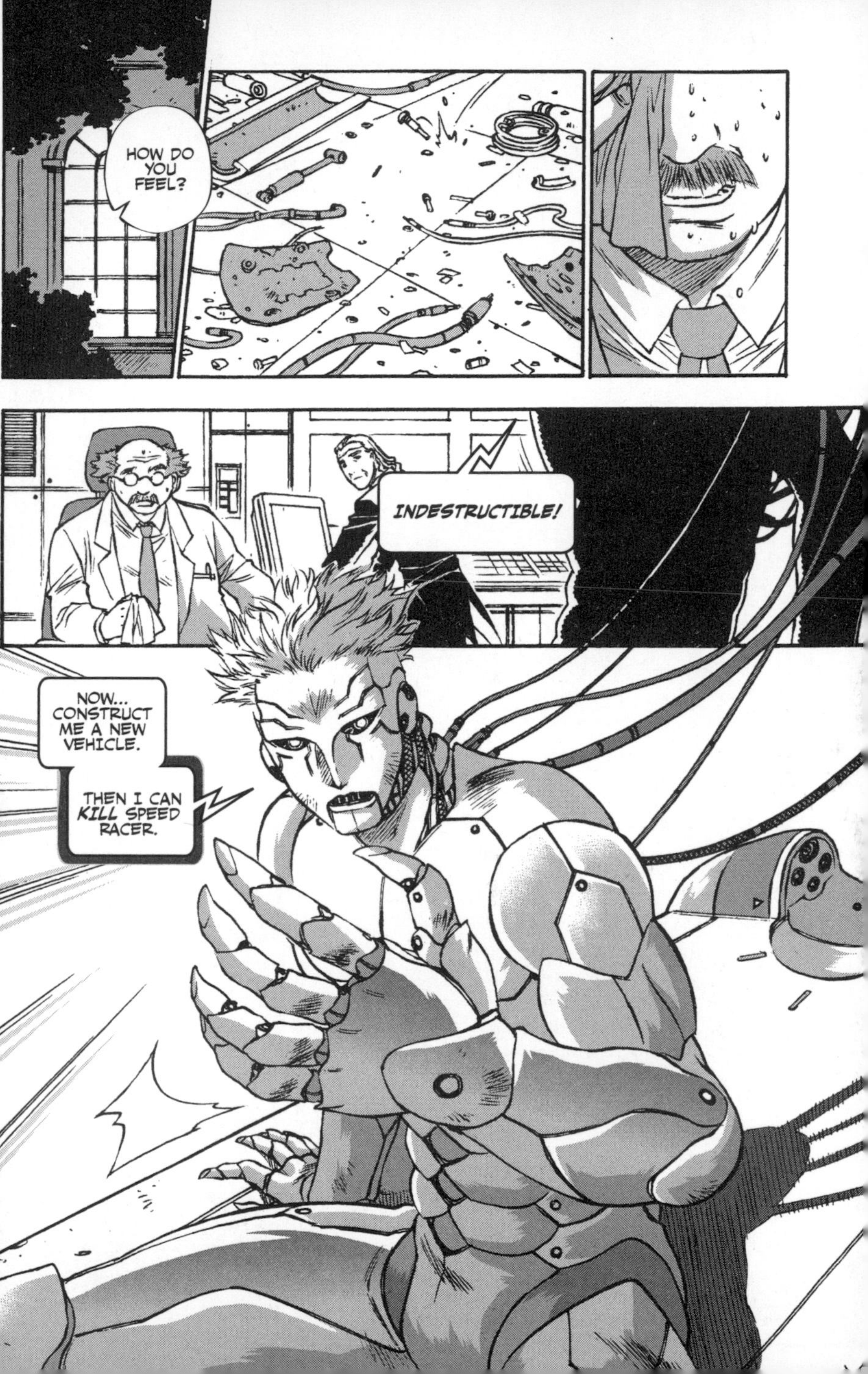
HOW DO YOU FEEL?
INDESTRUCTIBLE!
NOW... CONSTRUCT ME A NEW VEHICLE.
THEN I CAN KILL SPEED RACER.

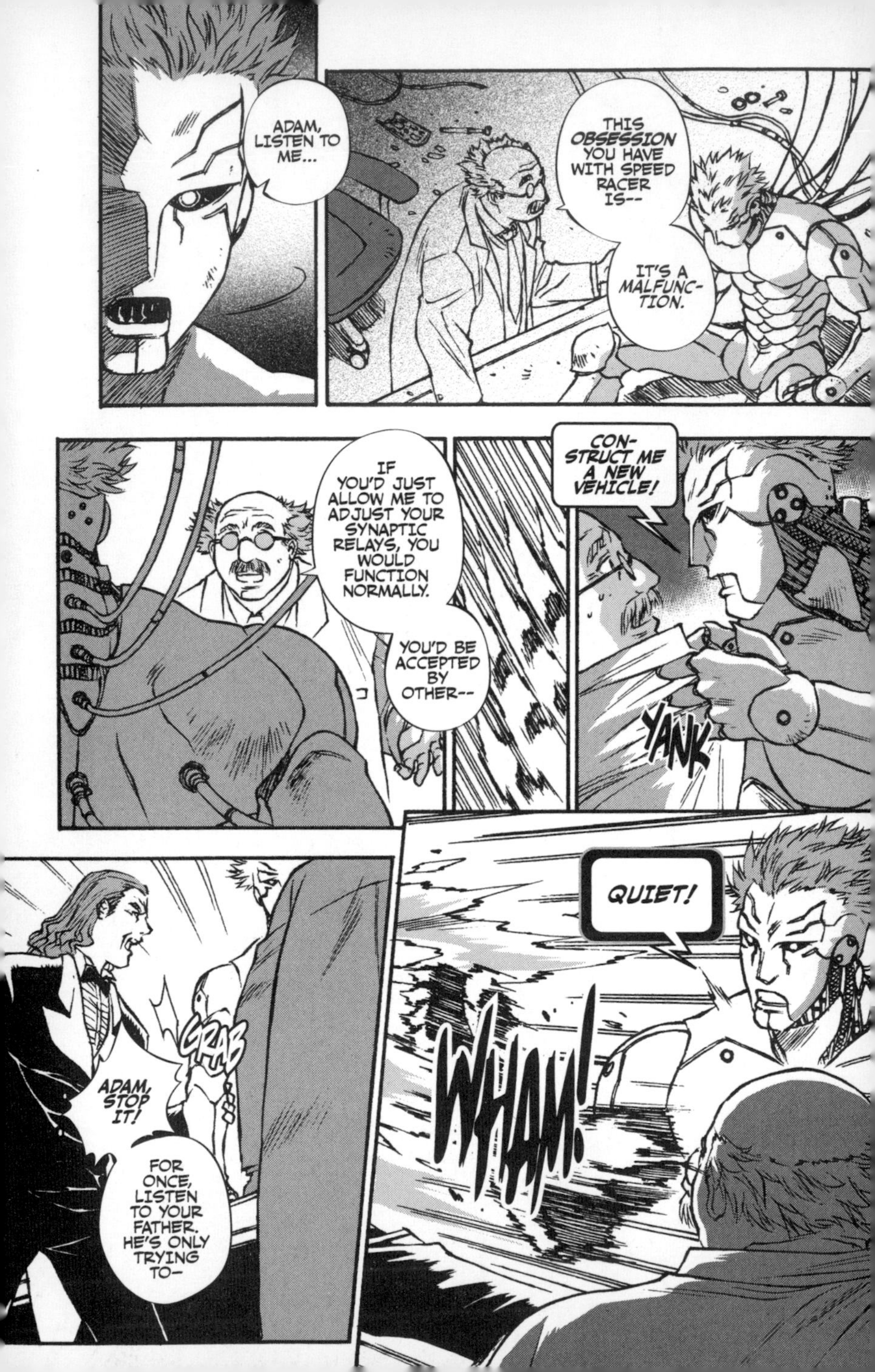
ADAM, LISTEN TO ME...
THIS *OBSESSION* YOU HAVE WITH SPEED RACER IS--
IT'S A MALFUNCTION.
IF YOU'D JUST ALLOW ME TO ADJUST YOUR SYNAPTIC RELAYS, YOU WOULD FUNCTION NORMALLY.
YOU'D BE ACCEPTED BY OTHER--
CONSTRUCT ME A NEW VEHICLE!
YANK
ADAM, STOP IT!
GRAB
FOR ONCE, LISTEN TO YOUR FATHER. HE'S ONLY TRYING TO–
QUIET!
WHAM!

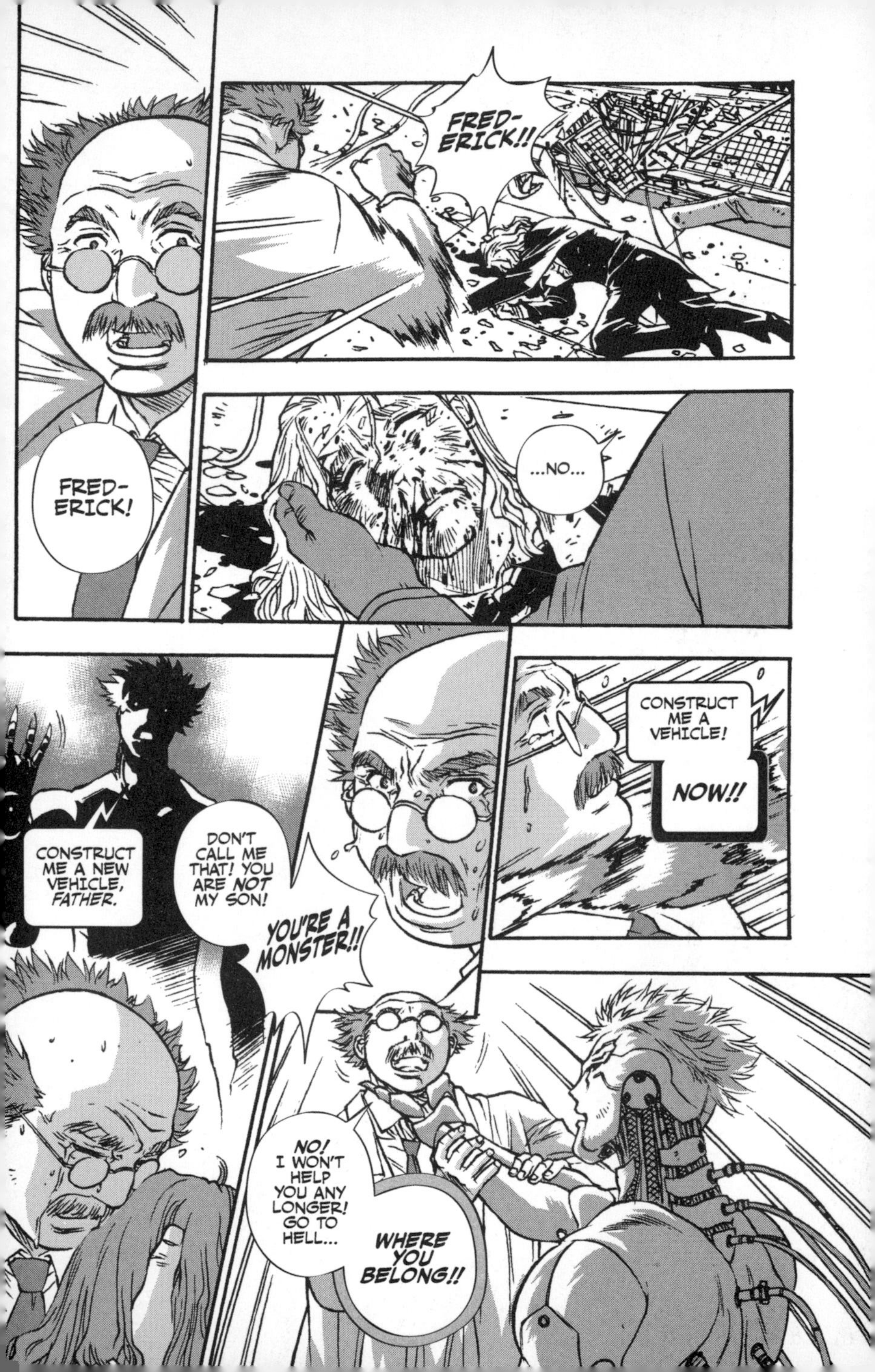
FRED-ERICK!
FRED-ERICK!!
...NO...
CONSTRUCT ME A NEW VEHICLE, *FATHER.*
DON'T CALL ME THAT! YOU ARE *NOT* MY SON!
YOU'RE A MONSTER!!
CONSTRUCT ME A VEHICLE!
NOW!!
NO! I WON'T HELP YOU ANY LONGER! GO TO HELL...
WHERE YOU BELONG!!

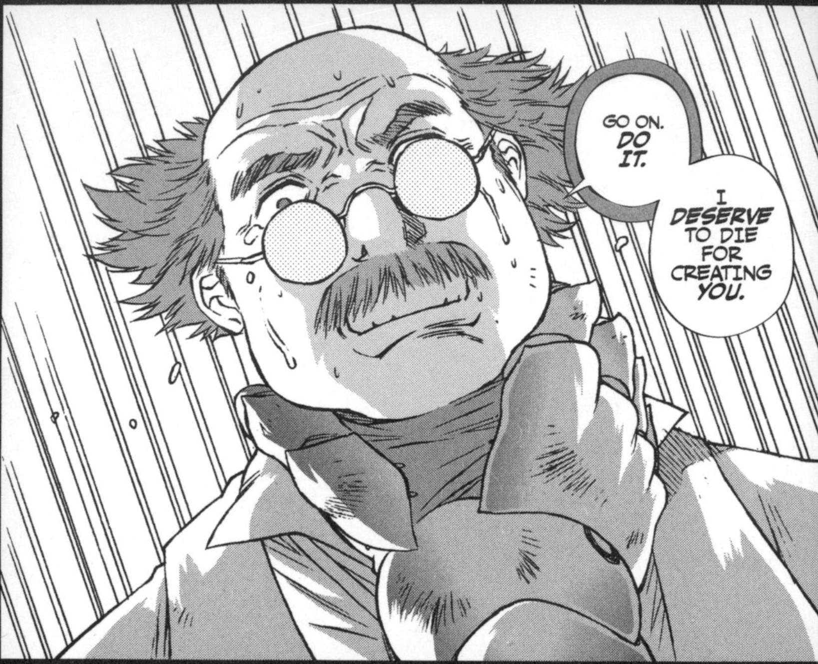
GO ON. *DO IT.*
I *DESERVE* TO DIE FOR CREATING *YOU.*
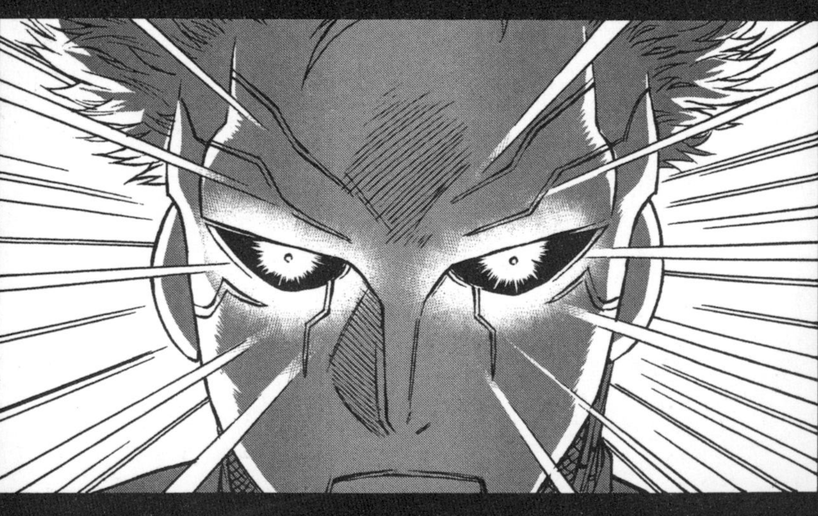

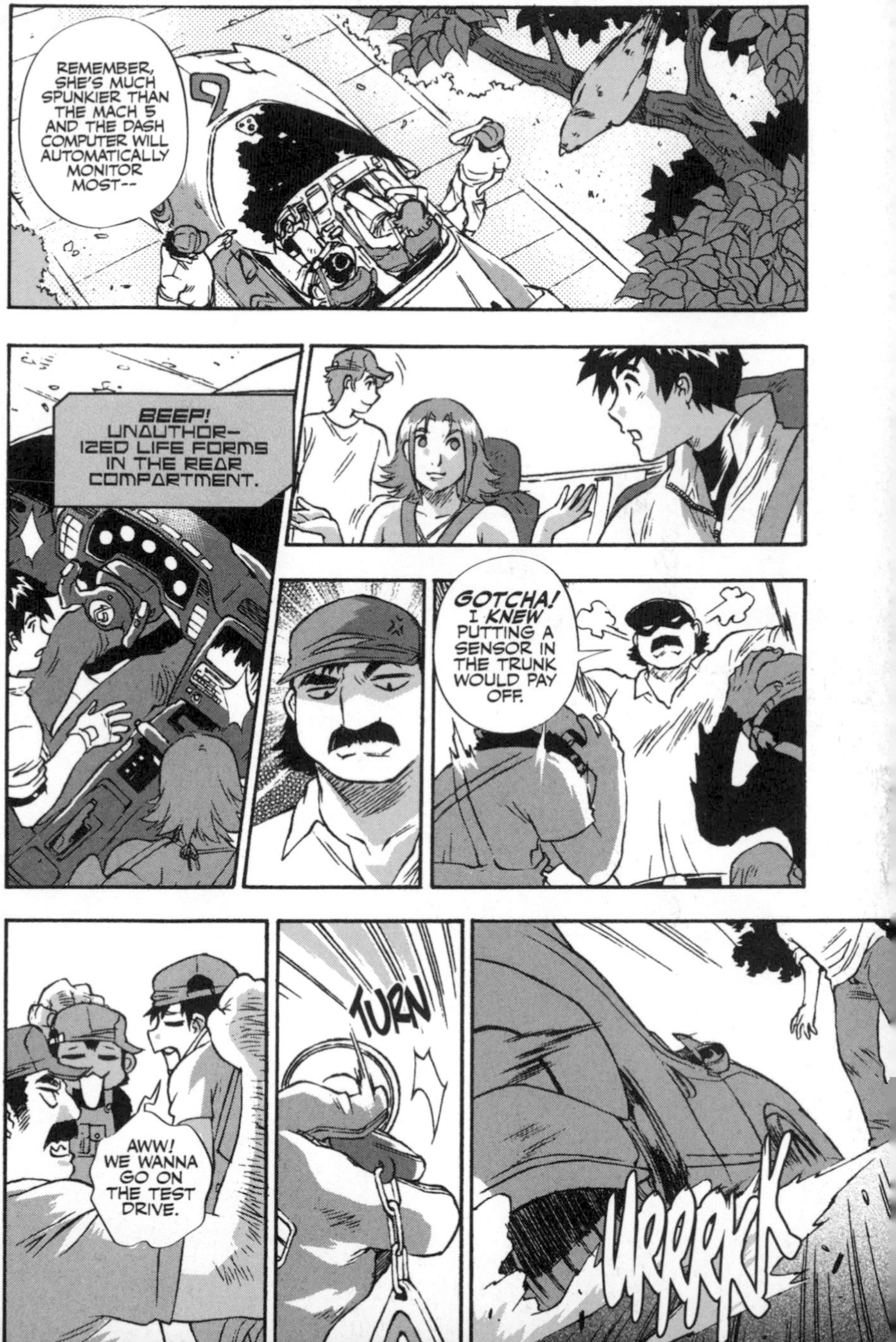
REMEMBER, SHE'S MUCH SPUNKIER THAN THE MACH 5 AND THE DASH COMPUTER WILL AUTOMATICALLY MONITOR MOST--
BEEP! UNAUTHOR-IZED LIFE FORMS IN THE REAR COMPARTMENT.
GOTCHA! I KNEW PUTTING A SENSOR IN THE TRUNK WOULD PAY OFF.
AWW! WE WANNA GO ON THE TEST DRIVE.
TURN
URRRRKK

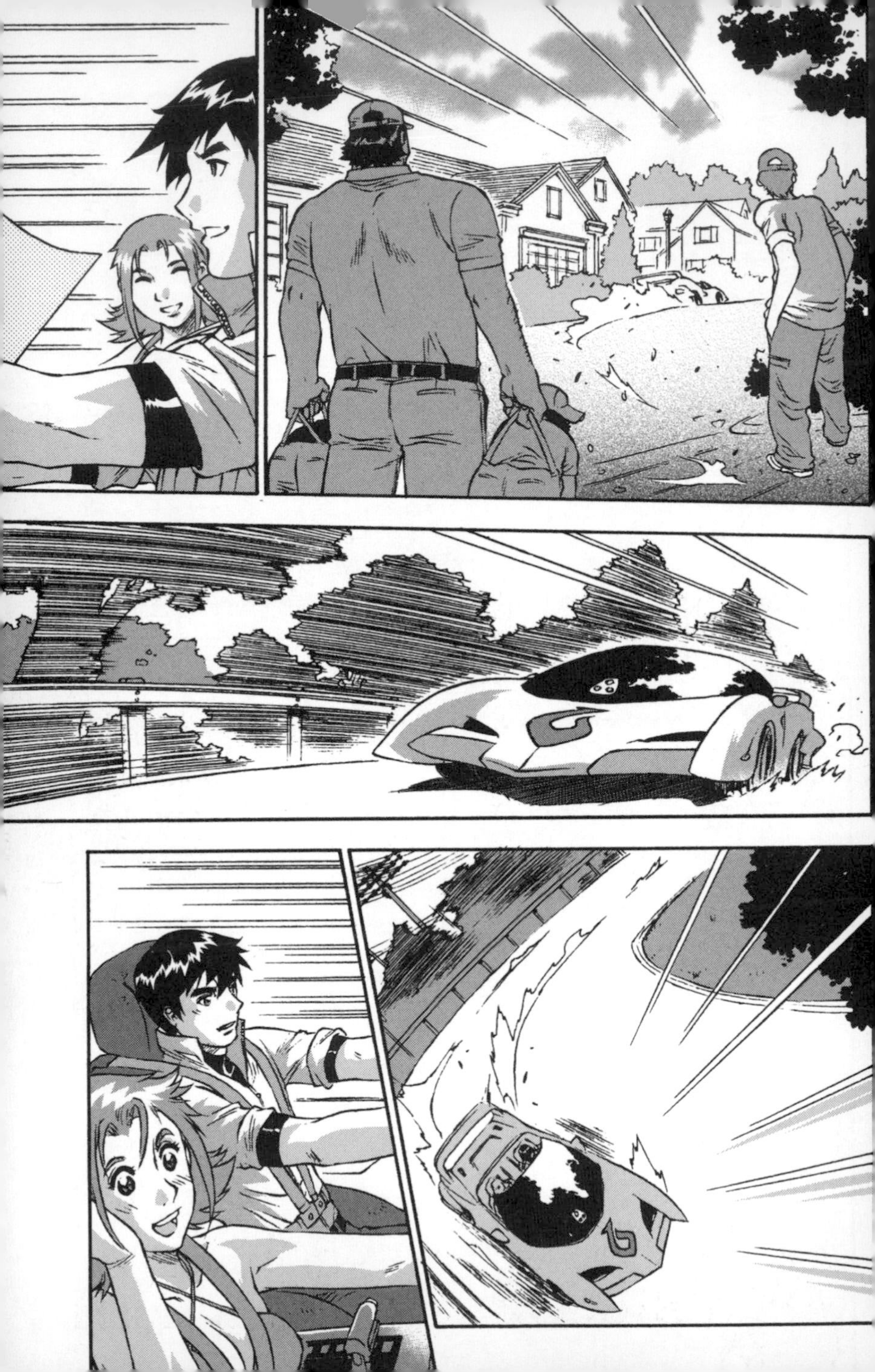

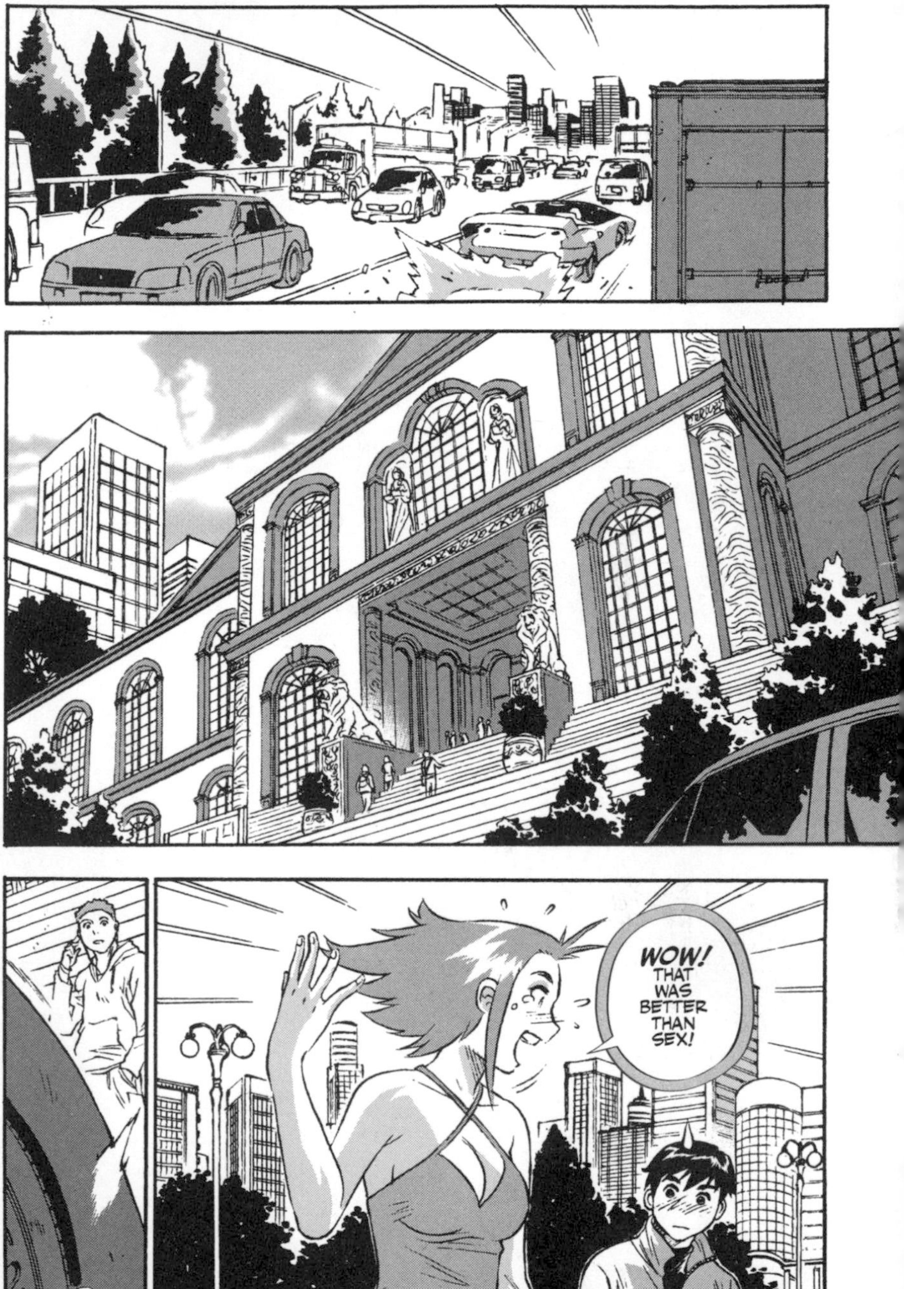
WOW! THAT WAS BETTER THAN SEX!

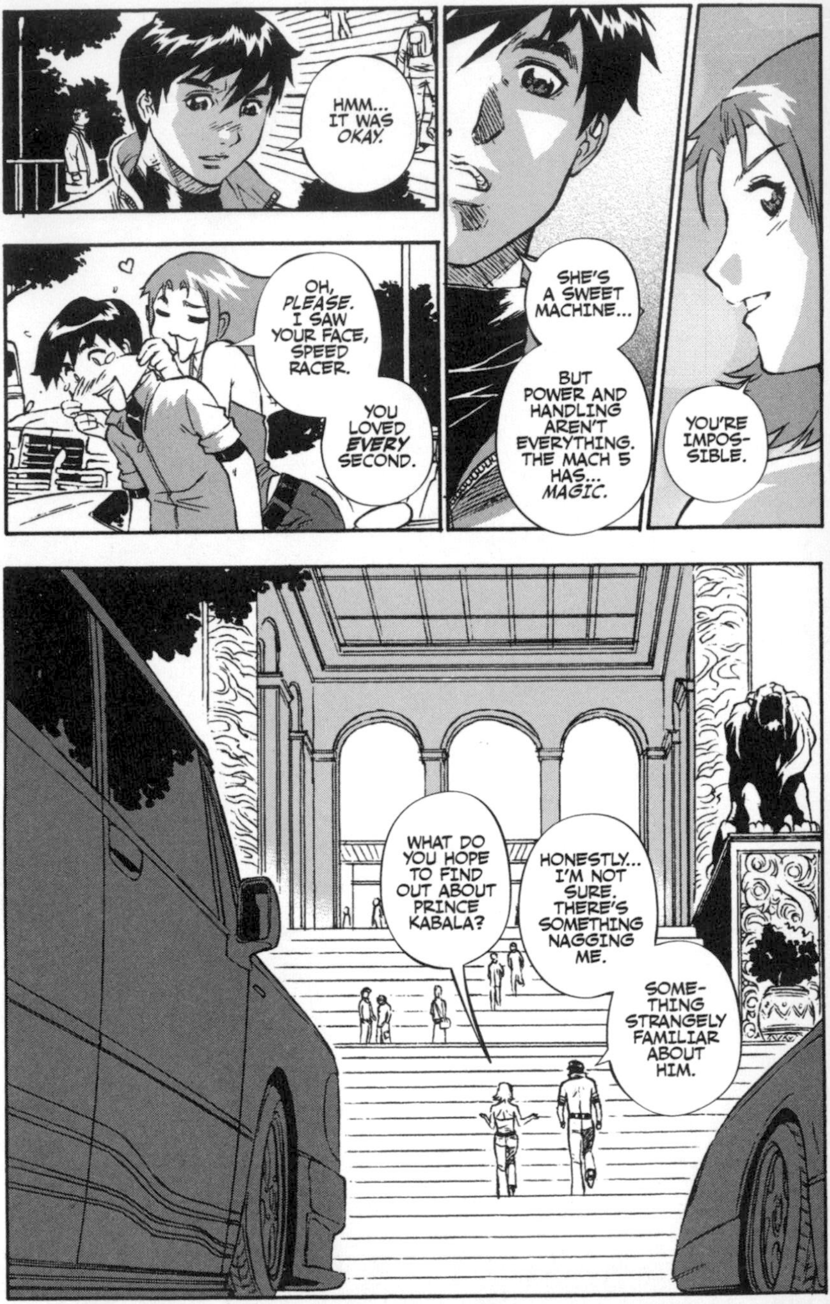

HMM... IT WAS OKAY.
OH, PLEASE. I SAW YOUR FACE, SPEED RACER.
YOU LOVED EVERY SECOND.
SHE'S A SWEET MACHINE...
BUT POWER AND HANDLING AREN'T EVERYTHING. THE MACH 5 HAS... MAGIC.
YOU'RE IMPOS-SIBLE.
WHAT DO YOU HOPE TO FIND OUT ABOUT PRINCE KABALA?
HONESTLY... I'M NOT SURE. THERE'S SOMETHING NAGGING ME.
SOME-THING STRANGELY FAMILIAR ABOUT HIM.

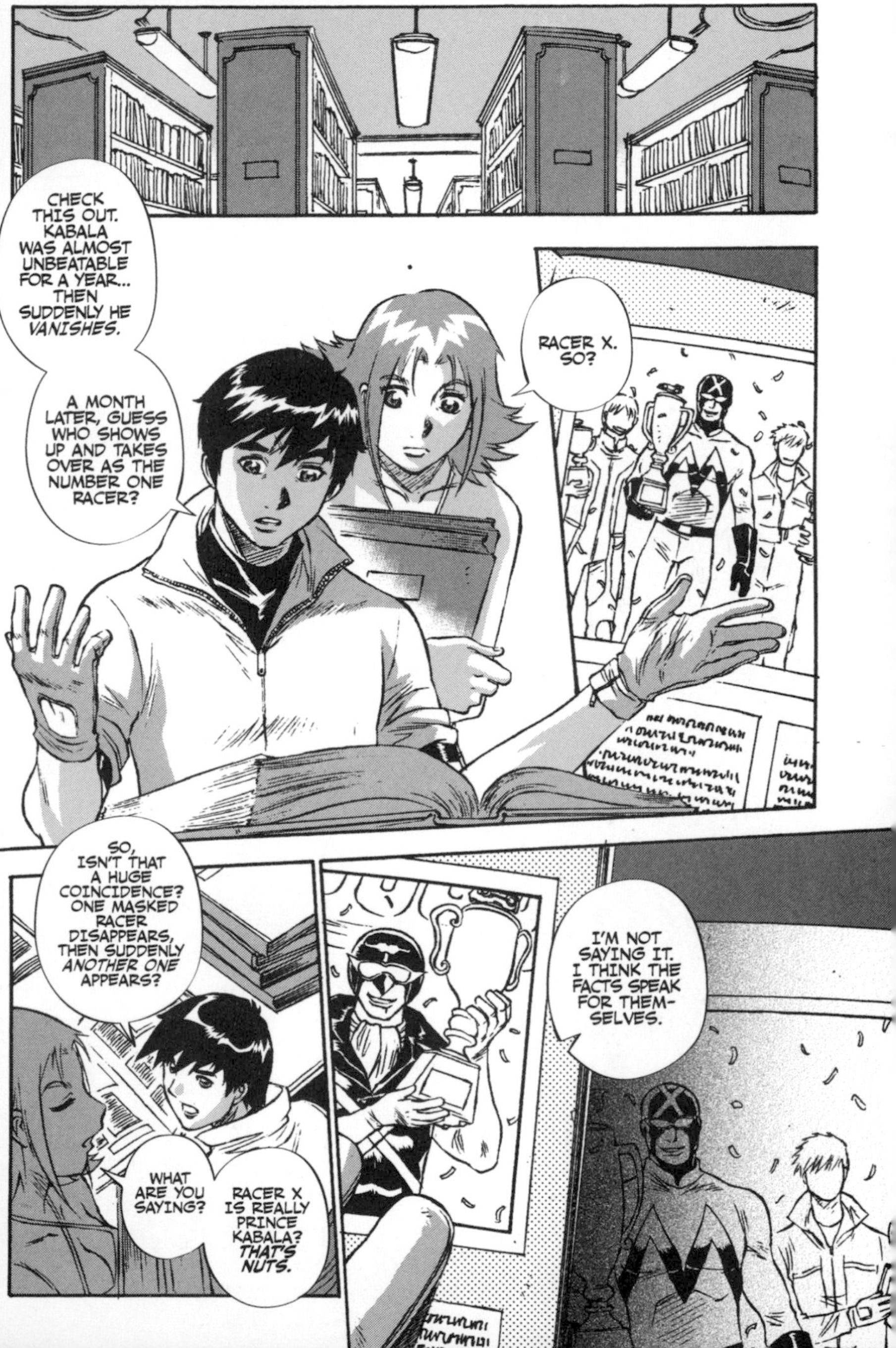
CHECK THIS OUT. KABALA WAS ALMOST UNBEATABLE FOR A YEAR... THEN SUDDENLY HE *VANISHES.*
A MONTH LATER, GUESS WHO SHOWS UP AND TAKES OVER AS THE NUMBER ONE RACER?
RACER X. SO?
SO, ISN'T THAT A HUGE COINCIDENCE? ONE MASKED RACER DISAPPEARS, THEN SUDDENLY *ANOTHER ONE* APPEARS?
WHAT ARE YOU SAYING?
RACER X IS REALLY PRINCE KABALA? ***THAT'S NUTS.***
I'M NOT SAYING IT. I THINK THE FACTS SPEAK FOR THEM-SELVES.

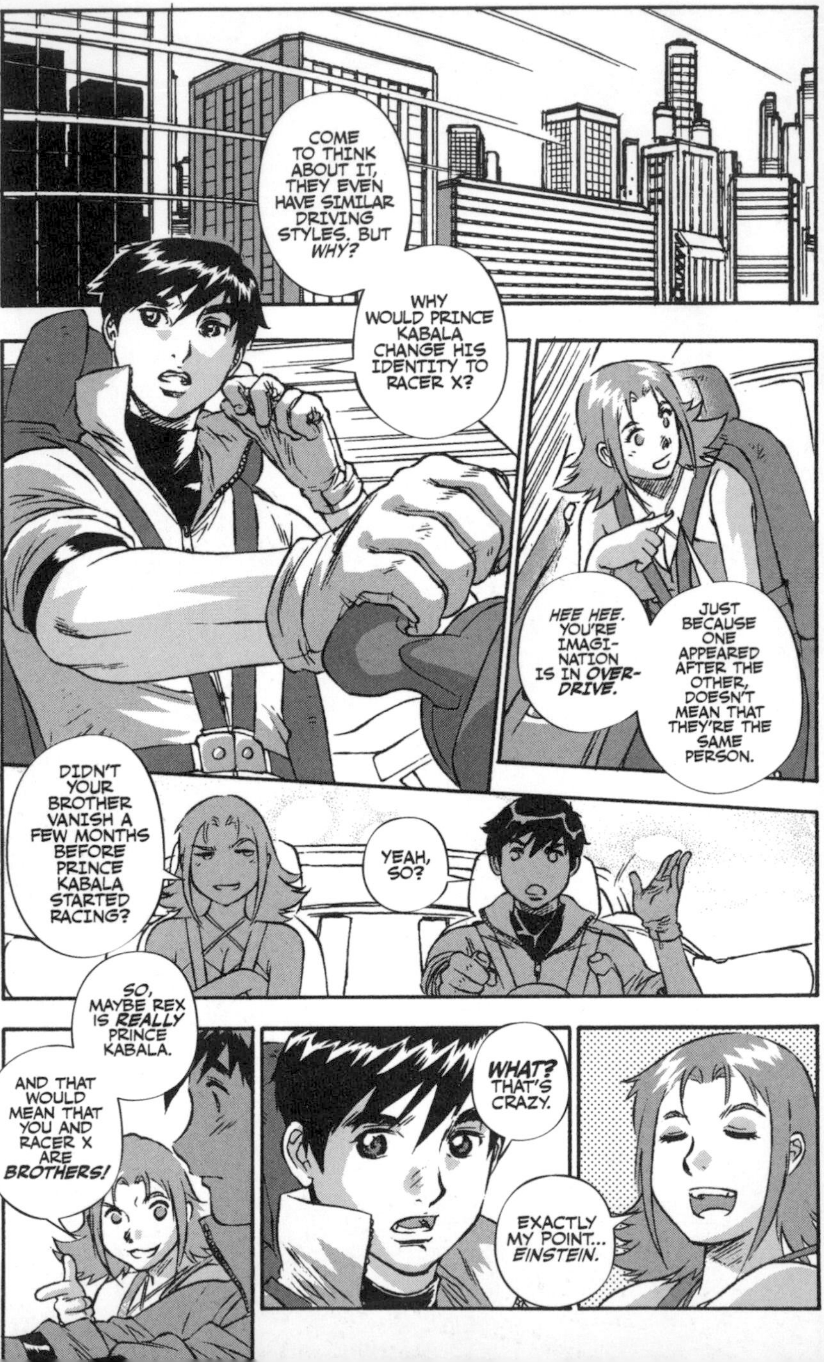
COME TO THINK ABOUT IT, THEY EVEN HAVE SIMILAR DRIVING STYLES. BUT *WHY?*
WHY WOULD PRINCE KABALA CHANGE HIS IDENTITY TO RACER X?
HEE HEE. YOU'RE IMAGI- NATION IS IN ***OVER- DRIVE.***
JUST BECAUSE ONE APPEARED AFTER THE OTHER, DOESN'T MEAN THAT THEY'RE THE SAME PERSON.
DIDN'T YOUR BROTHER VANISH A FEW MONTHS BEFORE PRINCE KABALA STARTED RACING?
YEAH, SO?
SO, MAYBE REX IS ***REALLY*** PRINCE KABALA.
AND THAT WOULD MEAN THAT YOU AND RACER X ARE ***BROTHERS!***
WHAT? THAT'S CRAZY.
EXACTLY MY POINT... *EINSTEIN.*

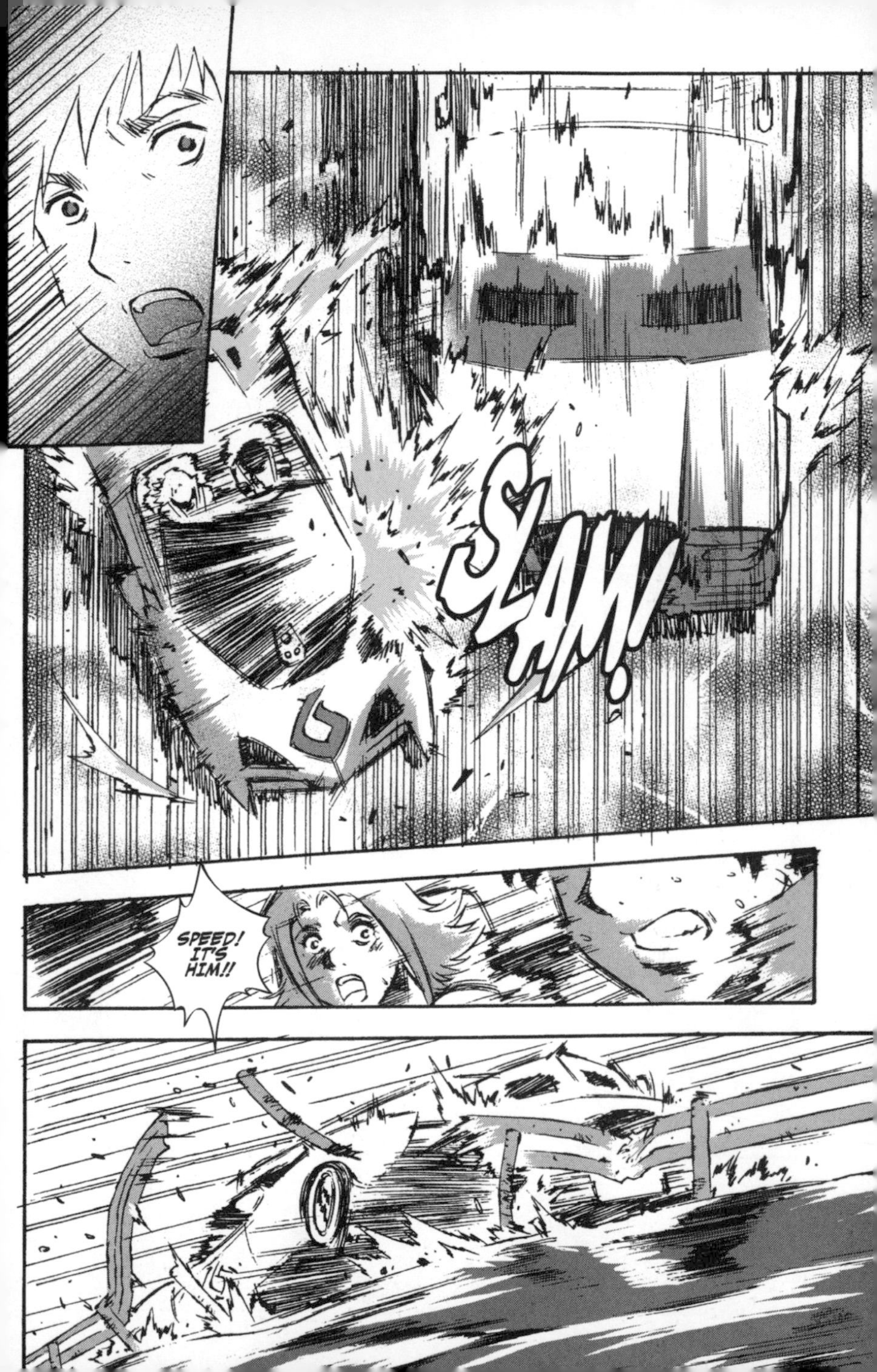
SLAM!
SPEED! IT'S HIM!!

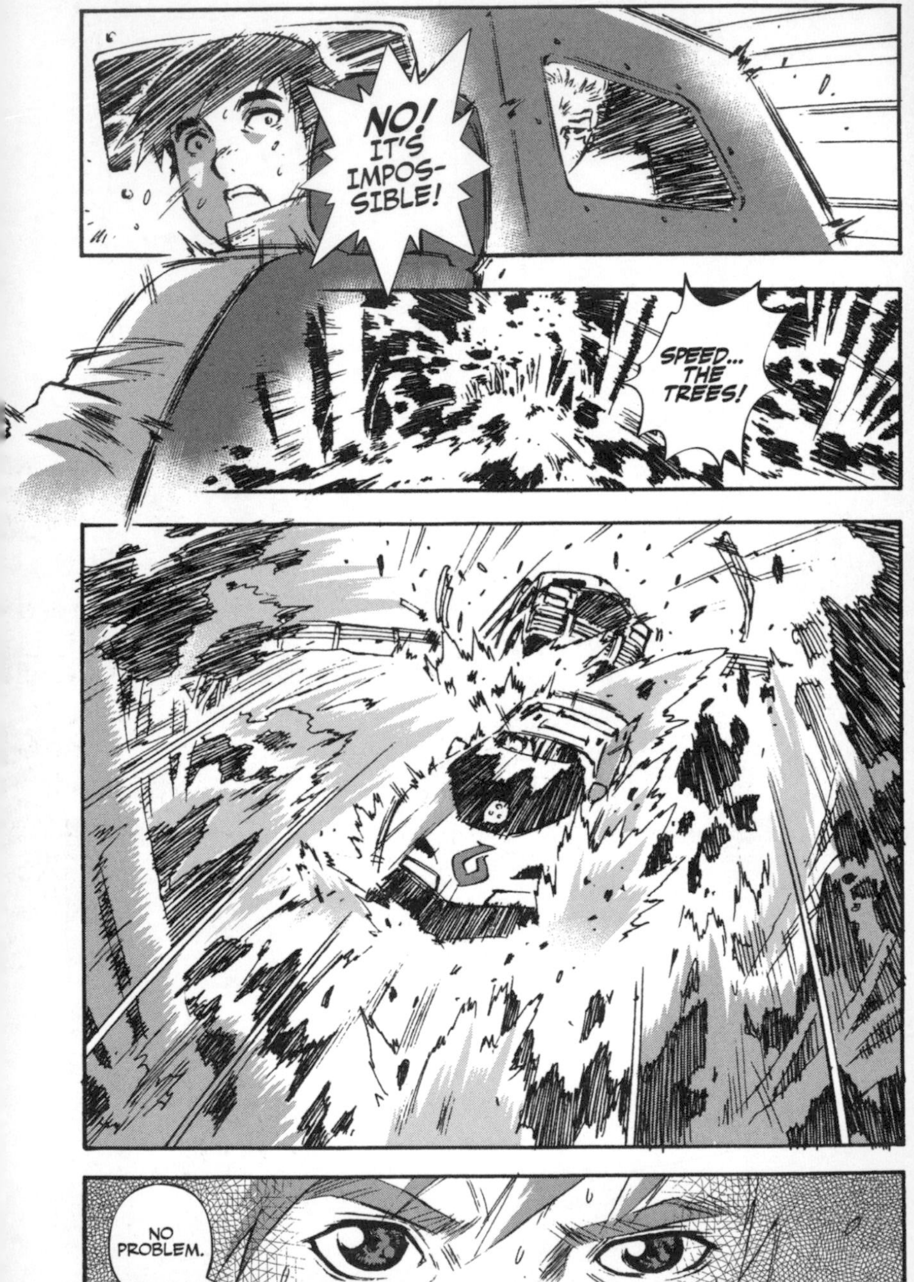
NO! IT'S IMPOSSIBLE!
SPEED... THE TREES!
NO PROBLEM.

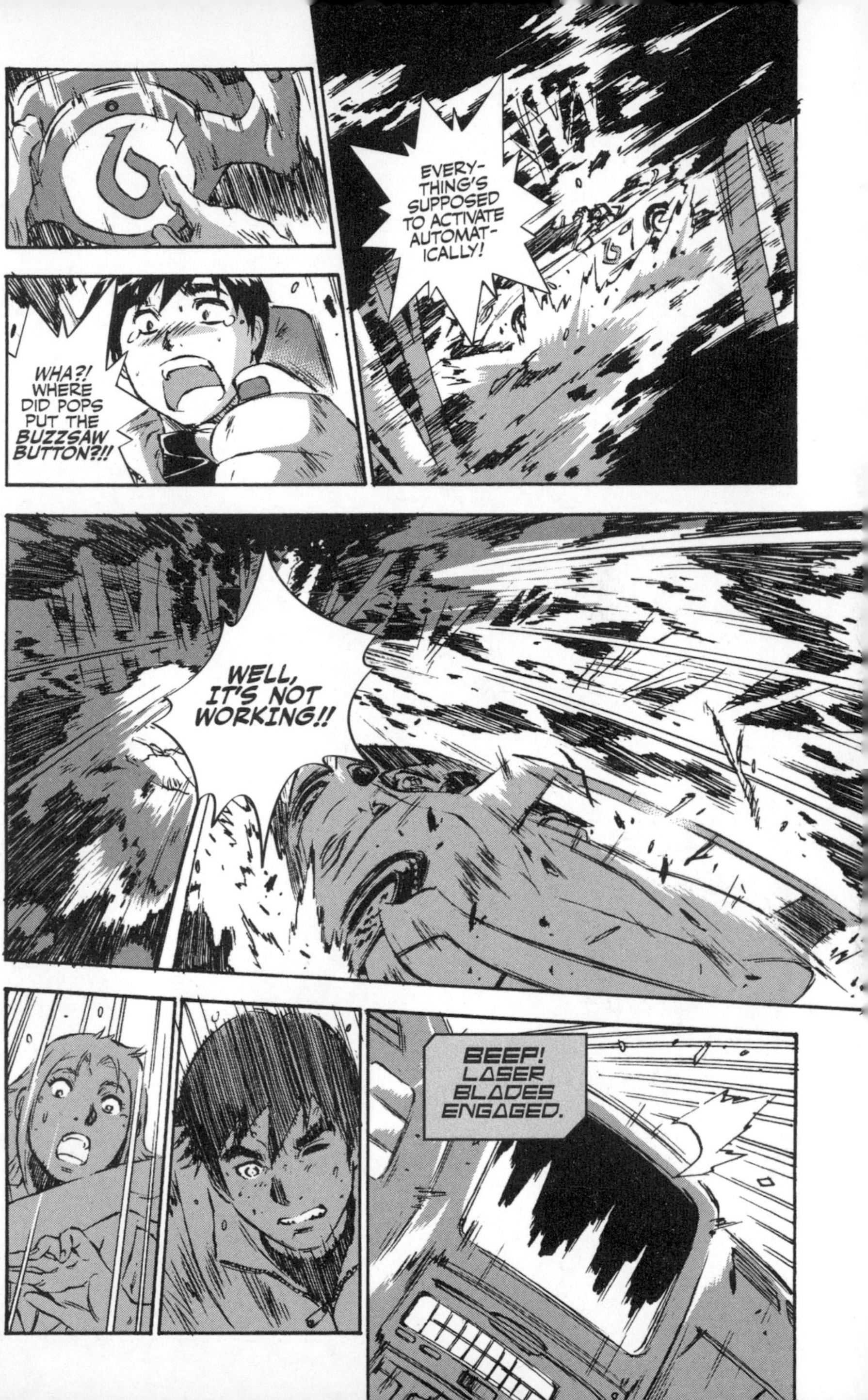
EVERY-THING'S SUPPOSED TO ACTIVATE AUTOMAT-ICALLY!
WHA?! WHERE DID POPS PUT THE BUZZSAW BUTTON?!!
WELL, IT'S NOT WORKING!!
BEEP! LASER BLADES ENGAGED.

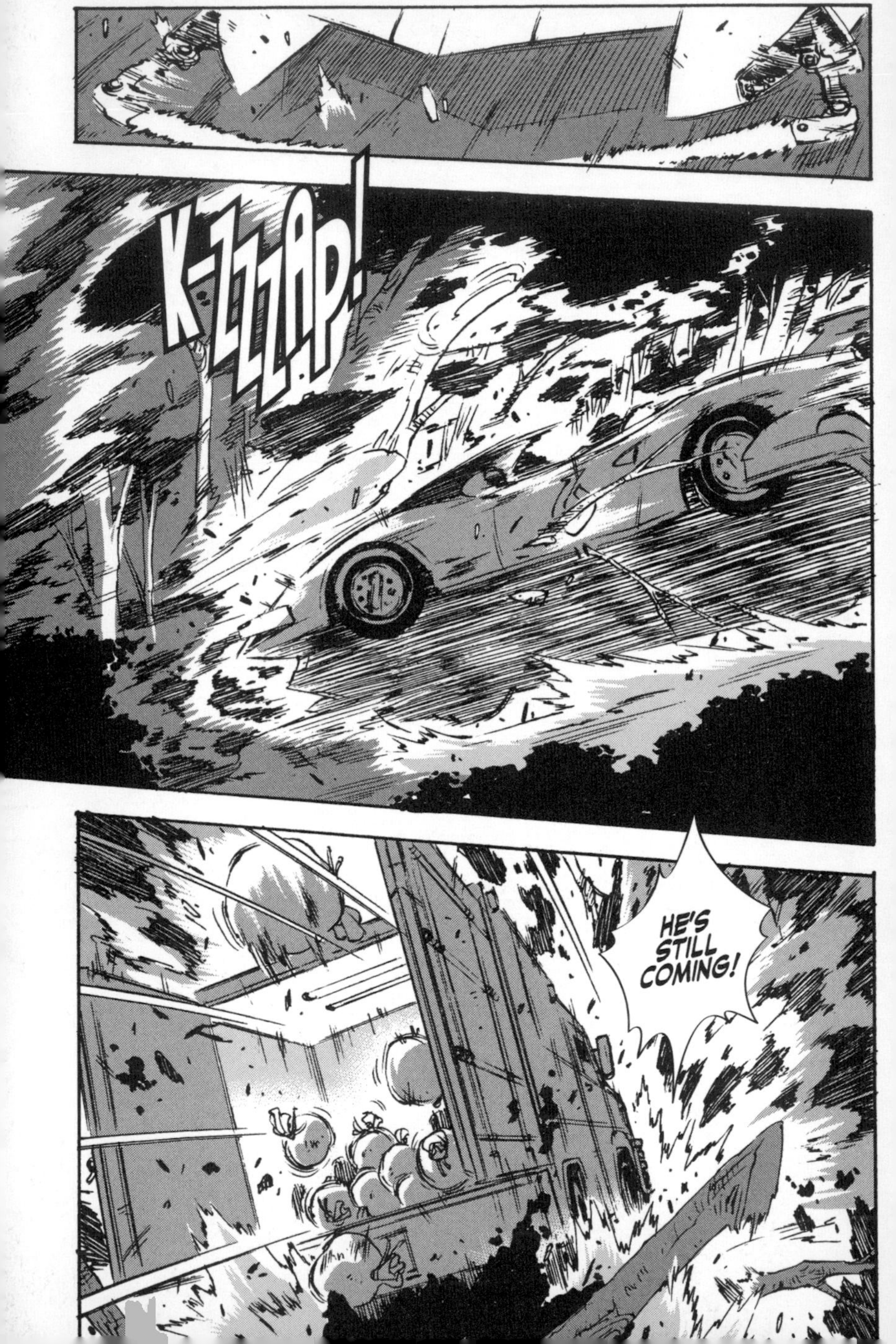
K-ZZZAP!
HE'S STILL COMING!

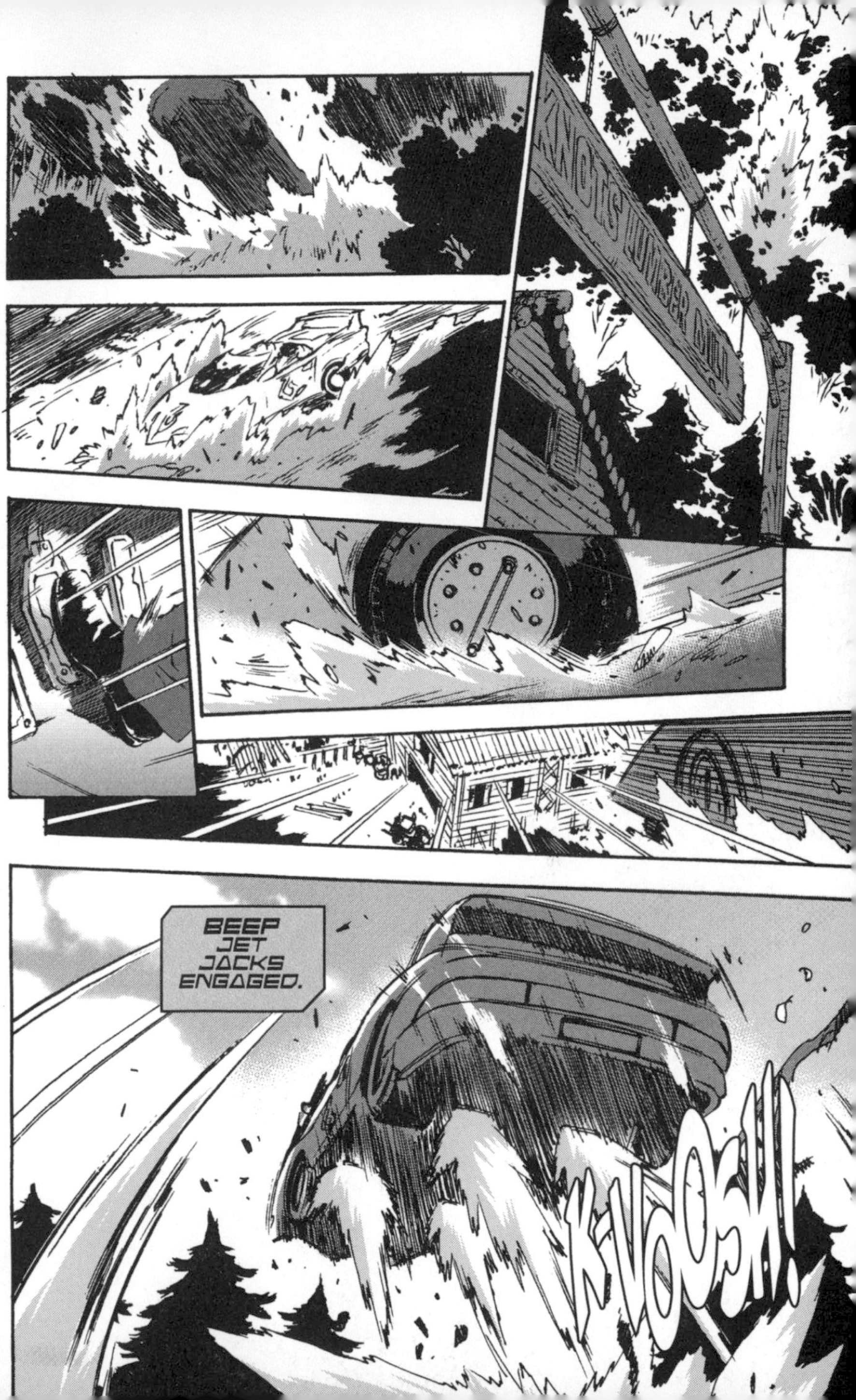
BEEP
JET
JACKS
ENGAGED.
K-VOOSH!

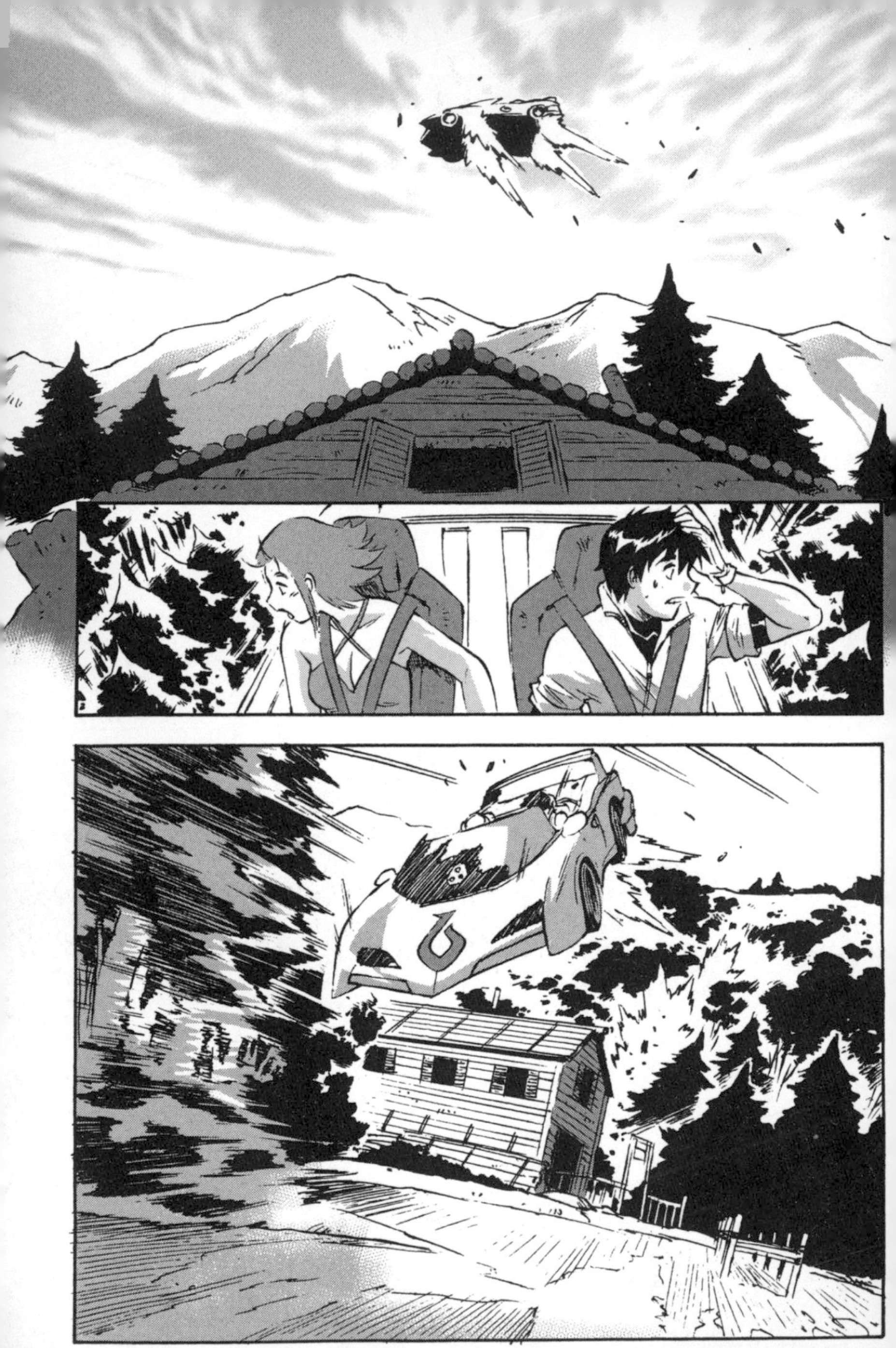

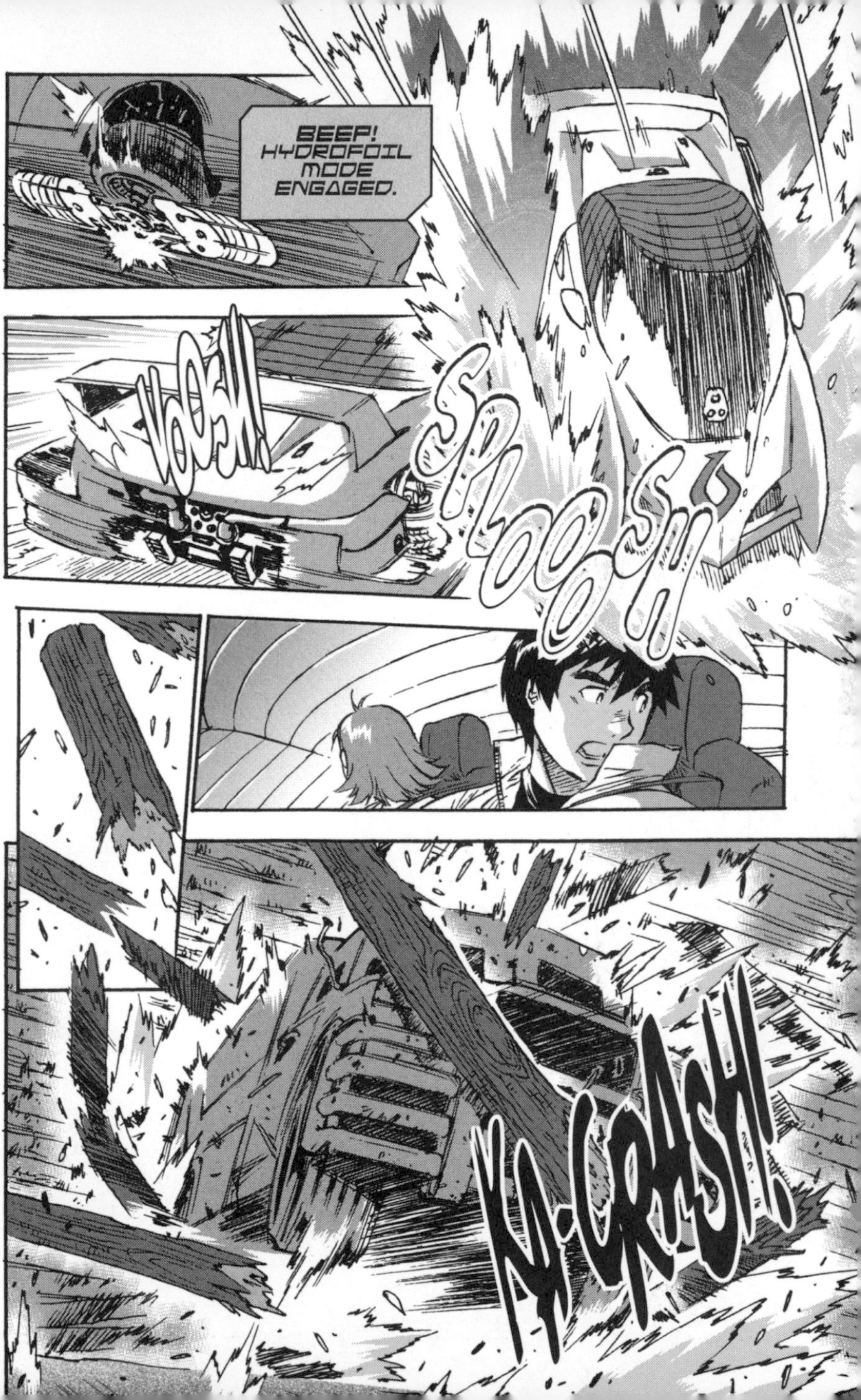
BEEP! HYDROFOIL MODE ENGAGED.
VOOSH!!
SPLOOSH
KA-CRASH!!

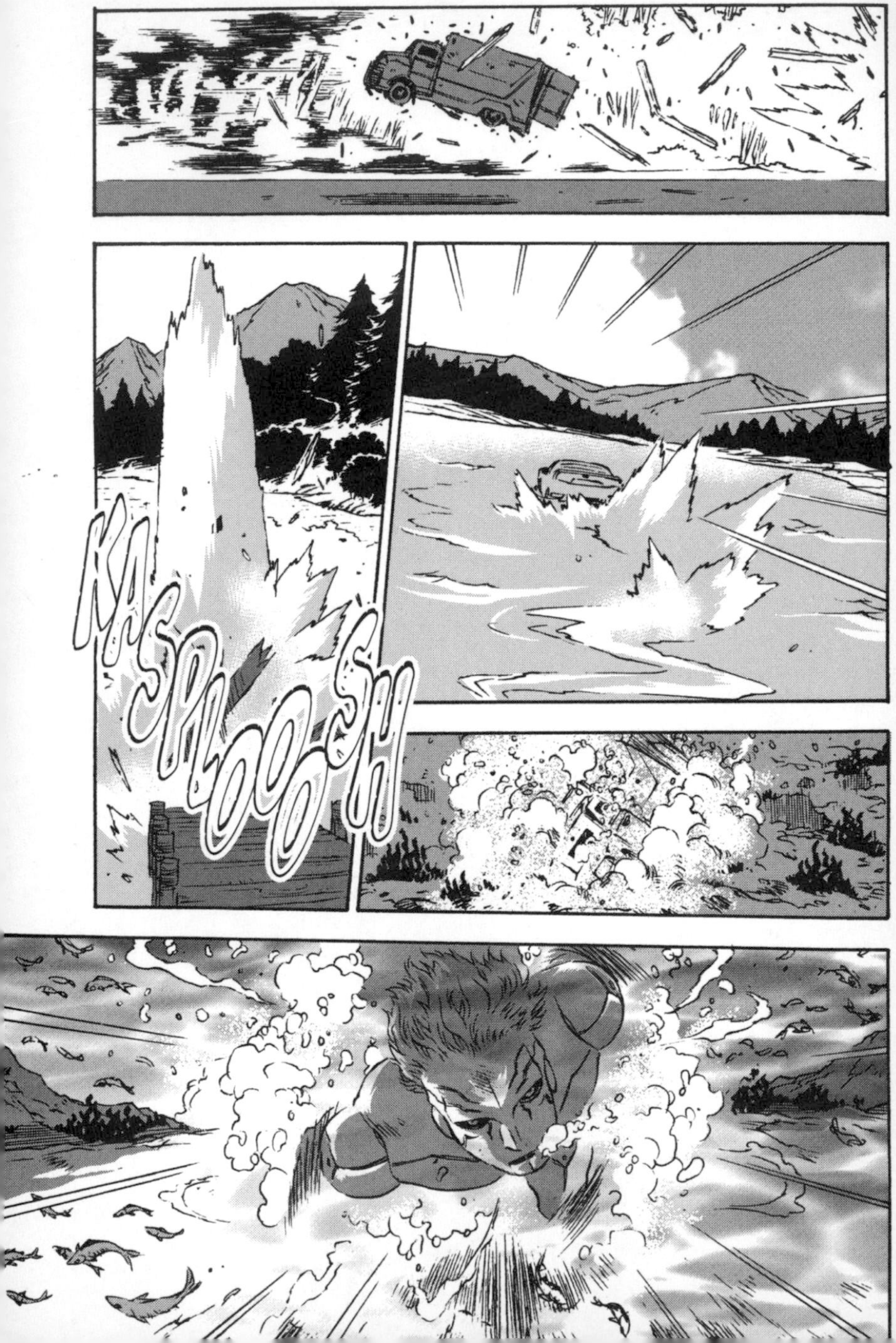
KASPLOOOSH

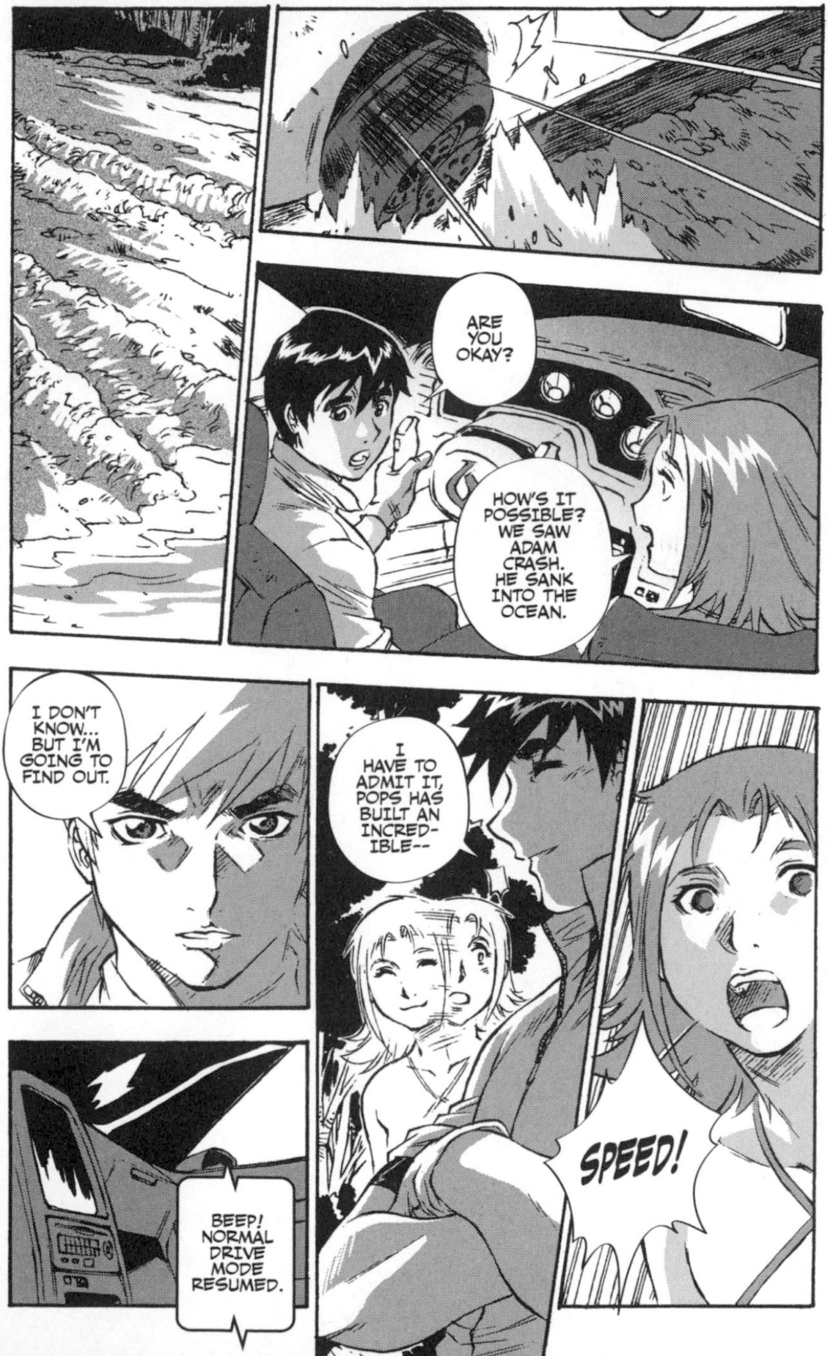
ARE YOU OKAY?
HOW'S IT POSSIBLE? WE SAW ADAM CRASH. HE SANK INTO THE OCEAN.
I DON'T KNOW... BUT I'M GOING TO FIND OUT.
BEEP! NORMAL DRIVE MODE RESUMED.
I HAVE TO ADMIT IT, POPS HAS BUILT AN INCRED-IBLE--
SPEED!

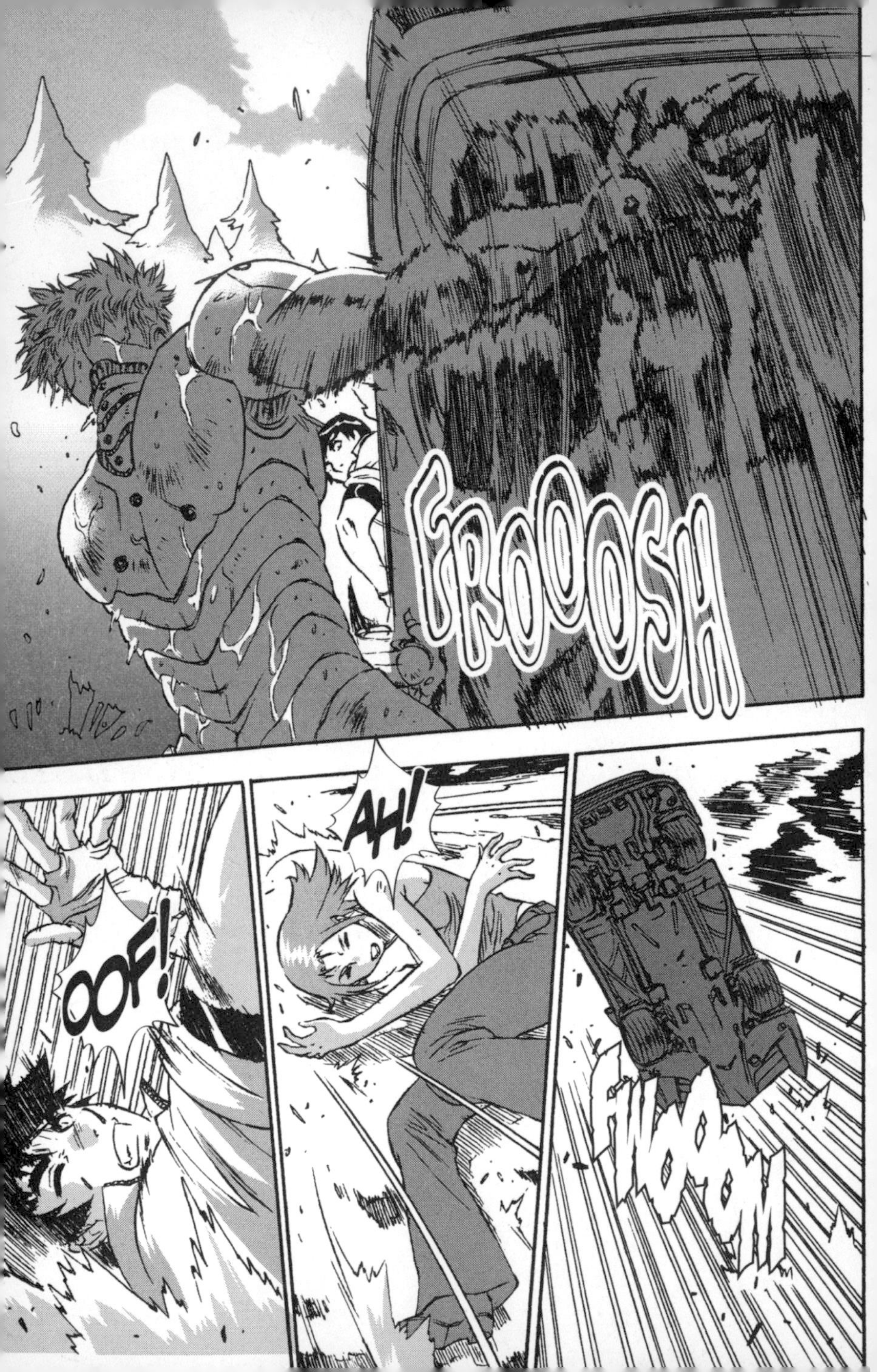
FROOOSH
OOF!
AH!
FWOOOM

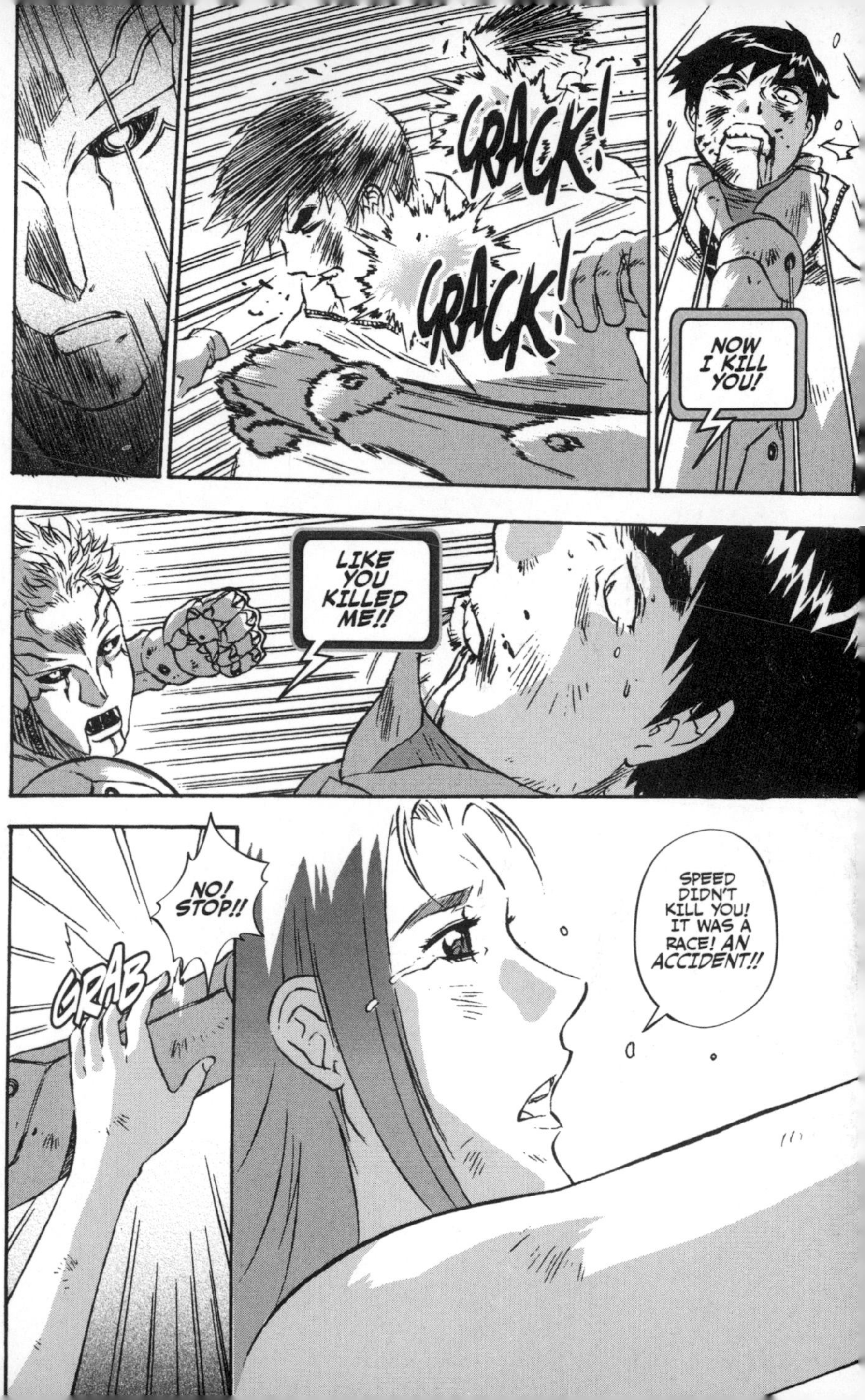
CRACK!
CRACK!
NOW I KILL YOU!
LIKE YOU KILLED ME!!
NO! STOP!!
GRAB
SPEED DIDN'T KILL YOU! IT WAS A RACE! AN ACCIDENT!!

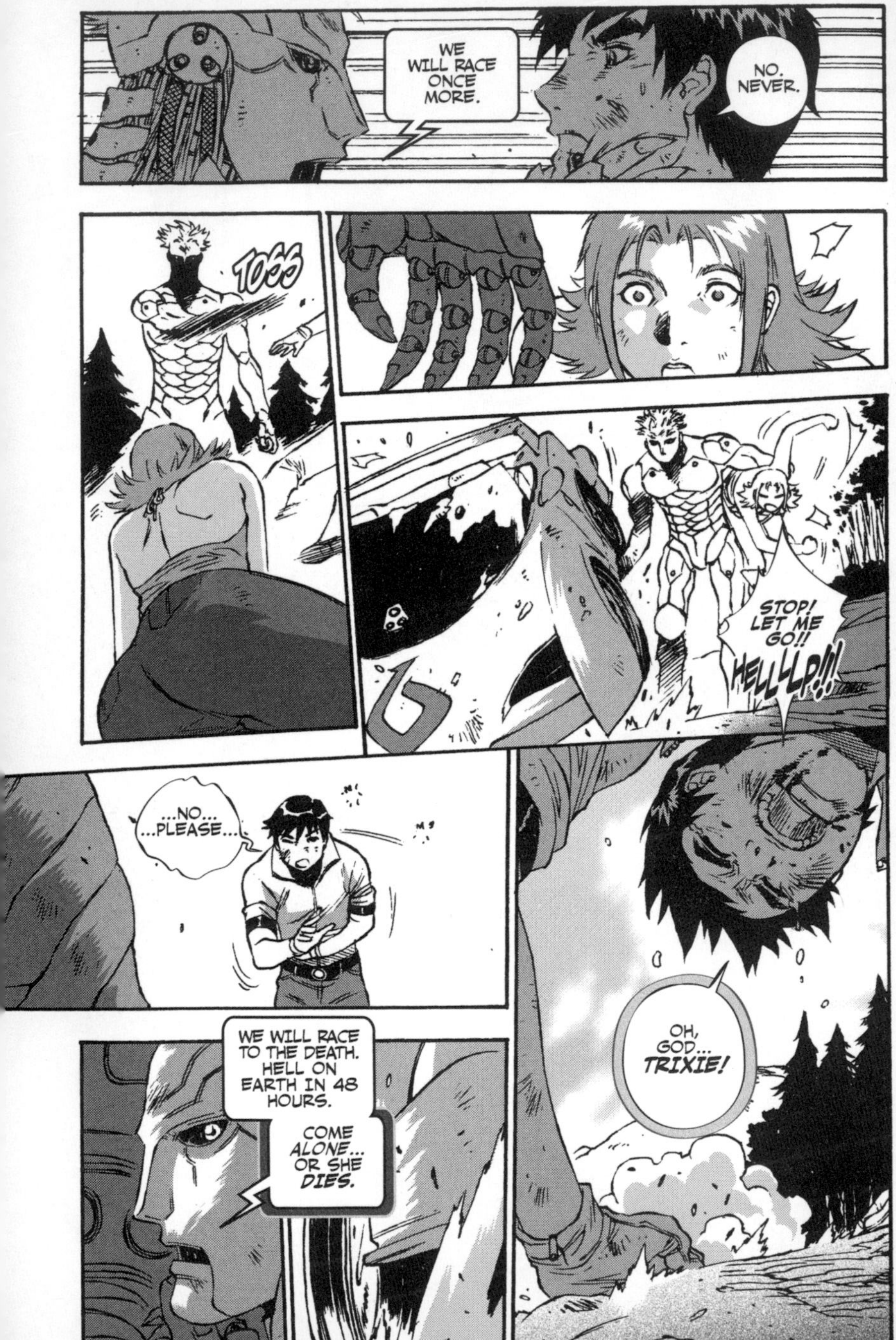
WE WILL RACE ONCE MORE.
NO. NEVER.
TOSS
STOP! LET ME GO!!
HELLLLP!!!
...NO... ...PLEASE...
WE WILL RACE TO THE DEATH. HELL ON EARTH IN 48 HOURS.
COME ALONE... OR SHE DIES.
OH, GOD... TRIXIE!

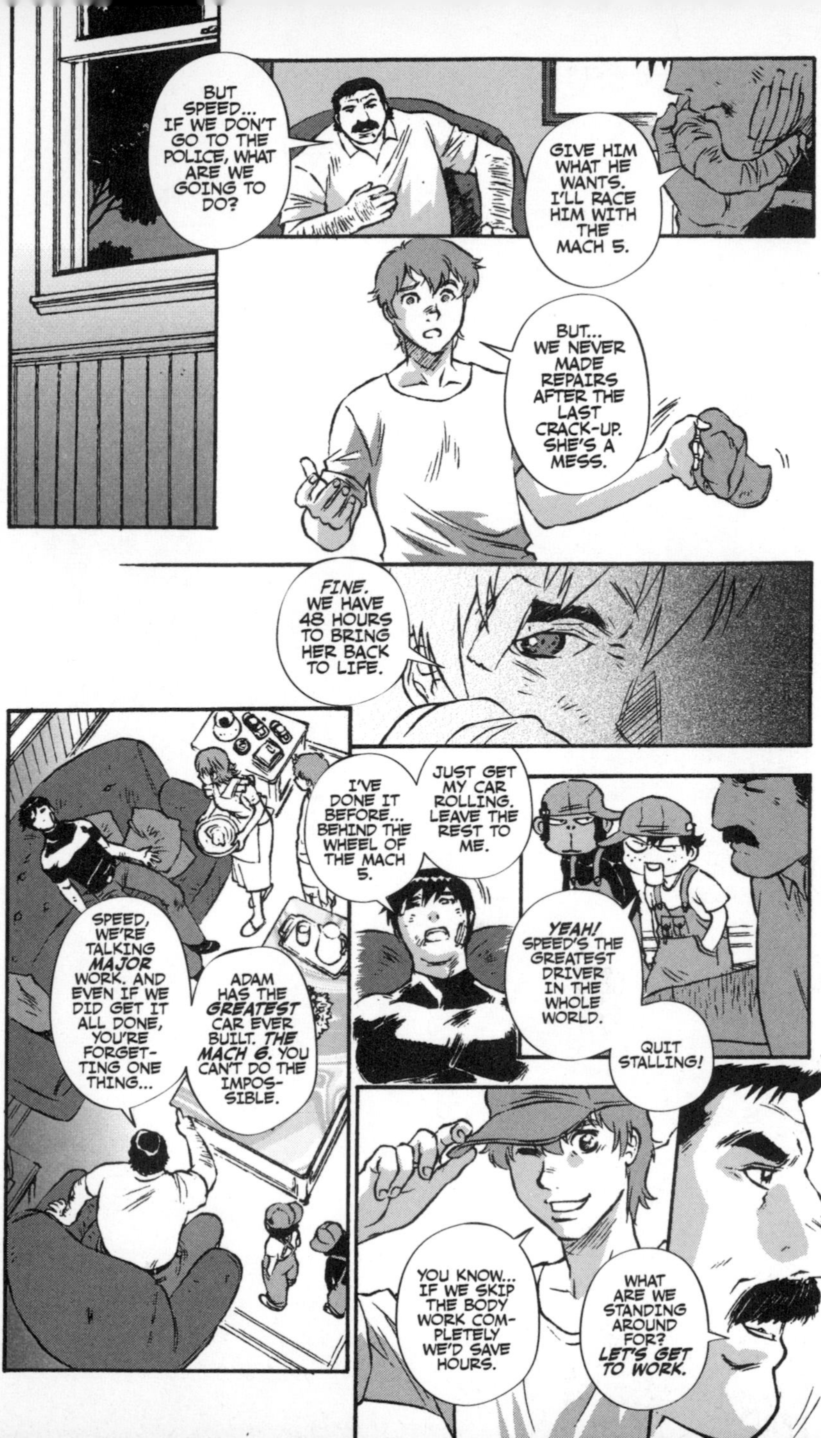
BUT SPEED... IF WE DON'T GO TO THE POLICE, WHAT ARE WE GOING TO DO?
GIVE HIM WHAT HE WANTS. I'LL RACE HIM WITH THE MACH 5.
BUT... WE NEVER MADE REPAIRS AFTER THE LAST CRACK-UP. SHE'S A MESS.
FINE. WE HAVE 48 HOURS TO BRING HER BACK TO LIFE.
SPEED, WE'RE TALKING ***MAJOR*** WORK. AND EVEN IF WE DID GET IT ALL DONE, YOU'RE FORGET-TING ONE THING...
ADAM HAS THE ***GREATEST*** CAR EVER BUILT. ***THE MACH 6.*** YOU CAN'T DO THE IMPOS-SIBLE.
I'VE DONE IT BEFORE... BEHIND THE WHEEL OF THE MACH 5.
JUST GET MY CAR ROLLING. LEAVE THE REST TO ME.
YEAH! SPEED'S THE GREATEST DRIVER IN THE WHOLE WORLD.
QUIT STALLING!
YOU KNOW... IF WE SKIP THE BODY WORK COM-PLETELY WE'D SAVE HOURS.
WHAT ARE WE STANDING AROUND FOR? ***LET'S GET TO WORK.***

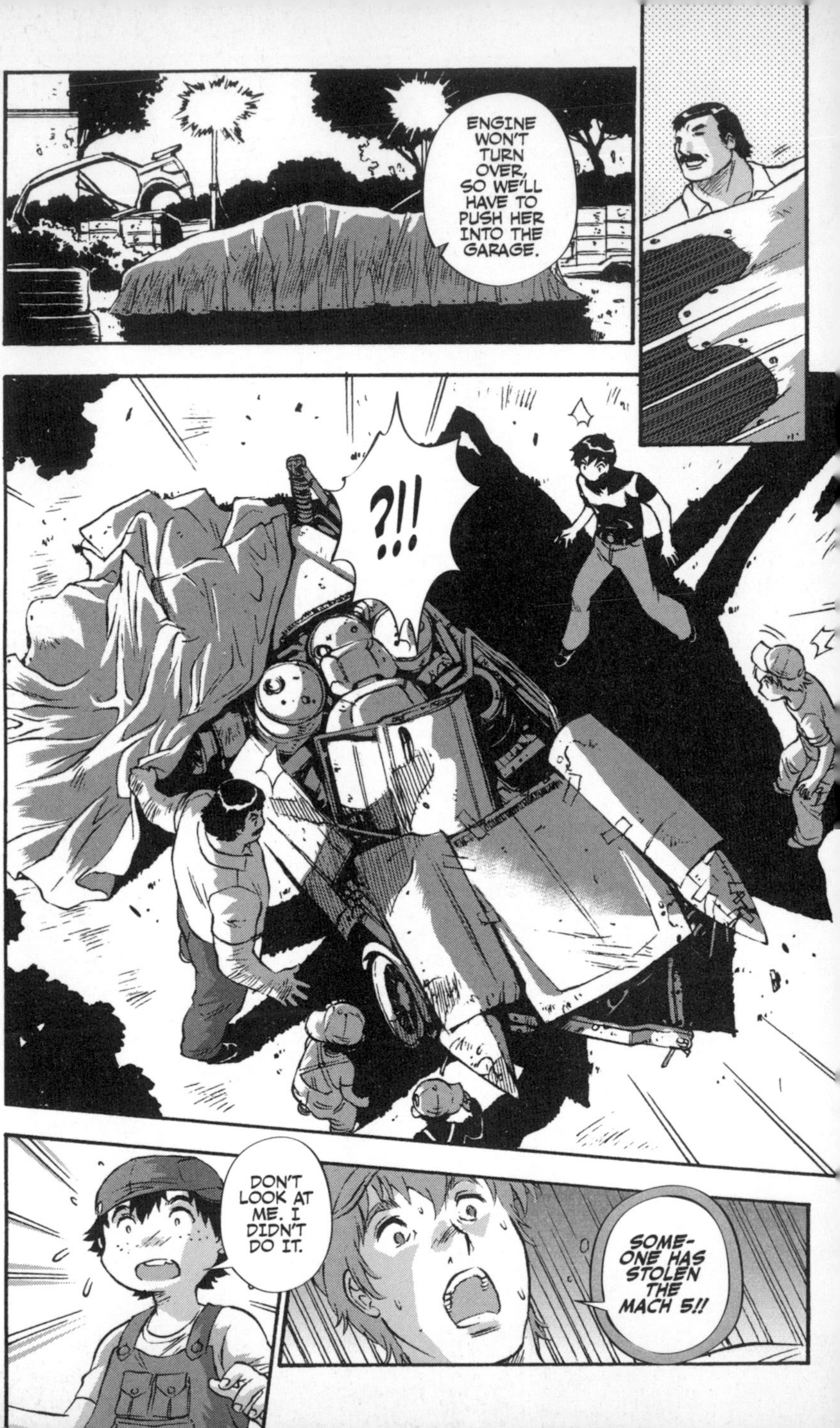
ENGINE WON'T TURN OVER, SO WE'LL HAVE TO PUSH HER INTO THE GARAGE.
?!!
DON'T LOOK AT ME. I DIDN'T DO IT.
SOME-ONE HAS STOLEN THE MACH 5!!

CHAPTER FOUR

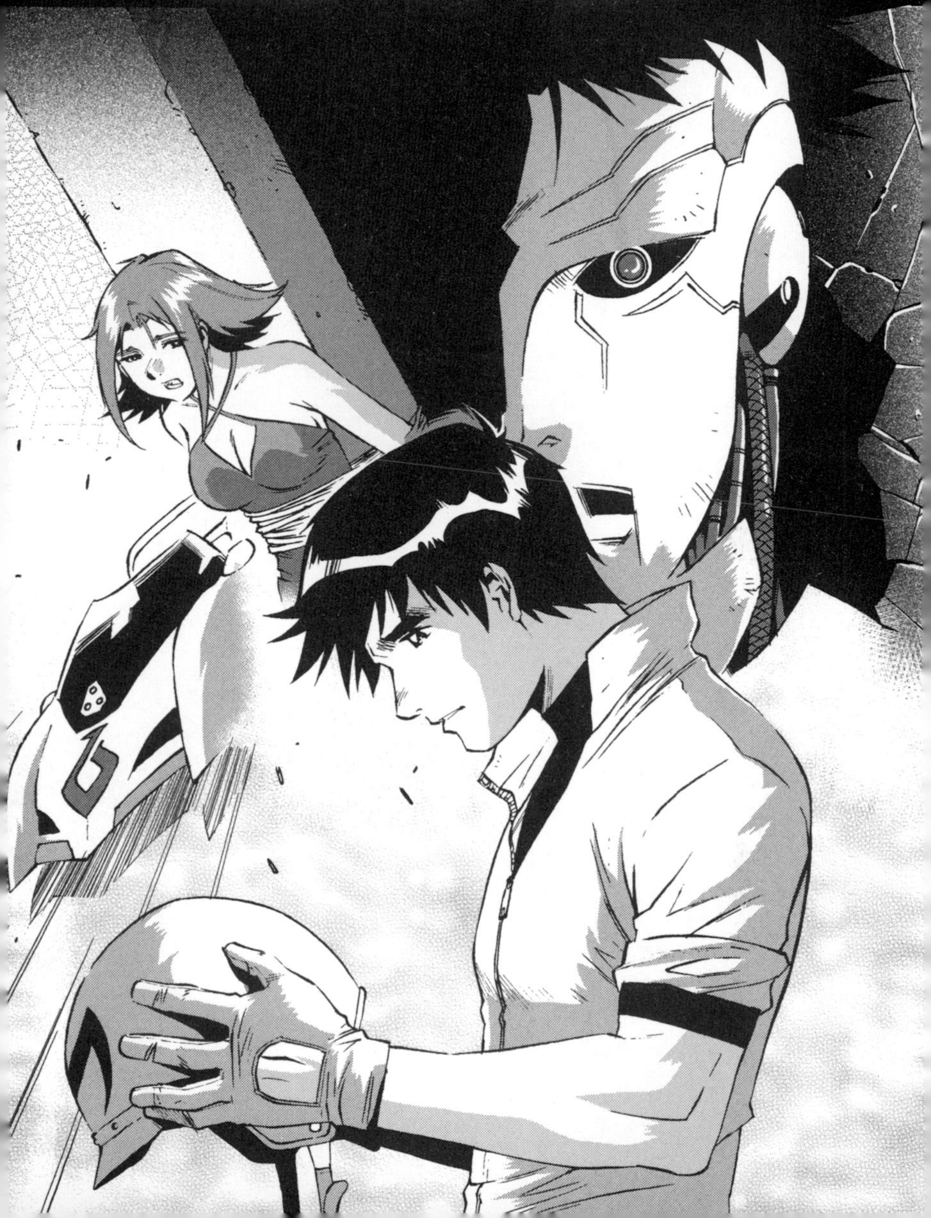

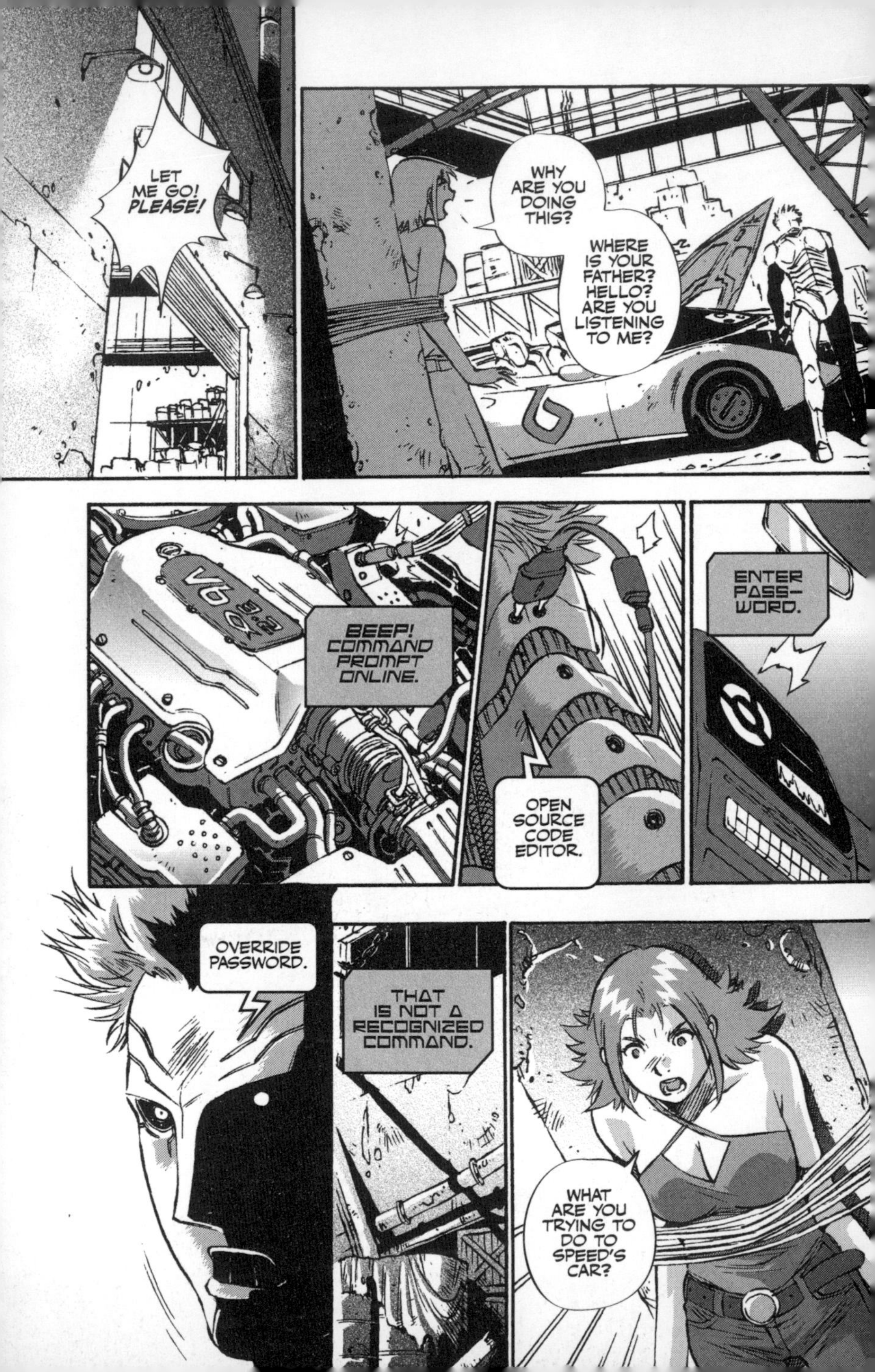
LET ME GO! *PLEASE!*
WHY ARE YOU DOING THIS?
WHERE IS YOUR FATHER? HELLO? ARE YOU LISTENING TO ME?
BEEP! COMMAND PROMPT ONLINE.
OPEN SOURCE CODE EDITOR.
ENTER PASS-WORD.
OVERRIDE PASSWORD.
THAT IS NOT A RECOGNIZED COMMAND.
WHAT ARE YOU TRYING TO DO TO SPEED'S CAR?

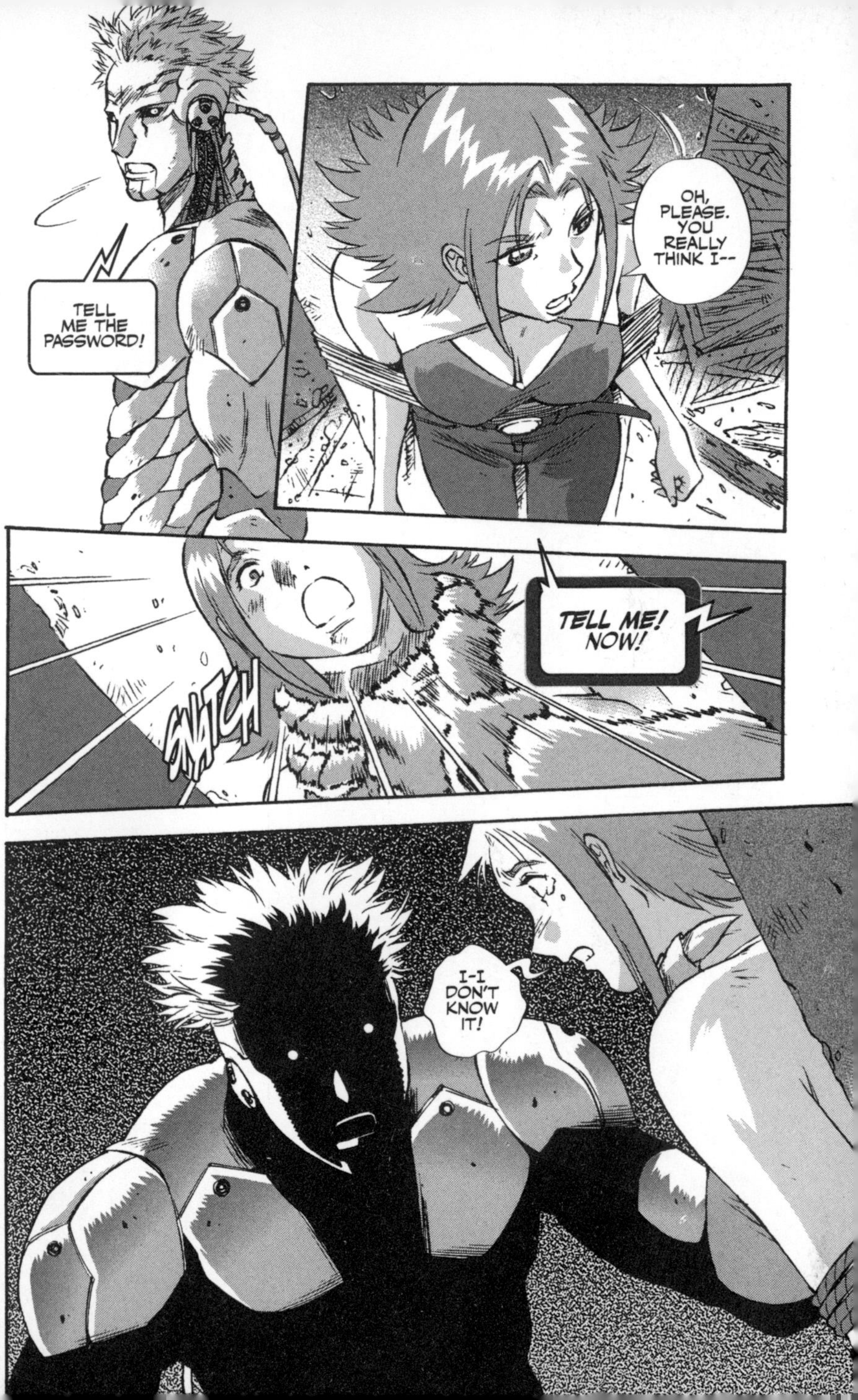
TELL ME THE PASSWORD!
OH, PLEASE. YOU REALLY THINK I--
SNATCH
TELL ME! NOW!
I-I DON'T KNOW IT!

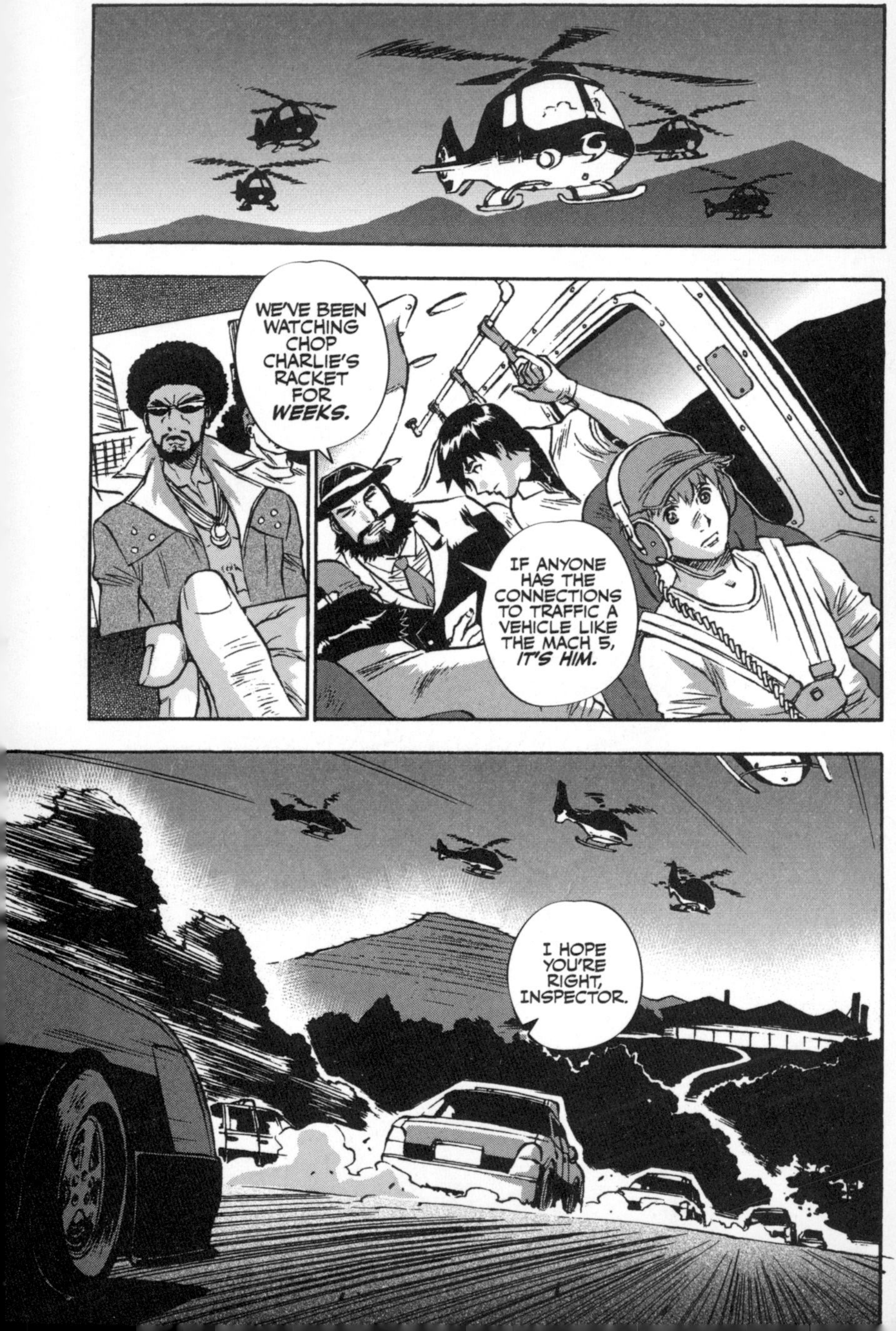
WE'VE BEEN WATCHING CHOP CHARLIE'S RACKET FOR *WEEKS.*
IF ANYONE HAS THE CONNECTIONS TO TRAFFIC A VEHICLE LIKE THE MACH 5, *IT'S HIM.*
I HOPE YOU'RE RIGHT, INSPECTOR.

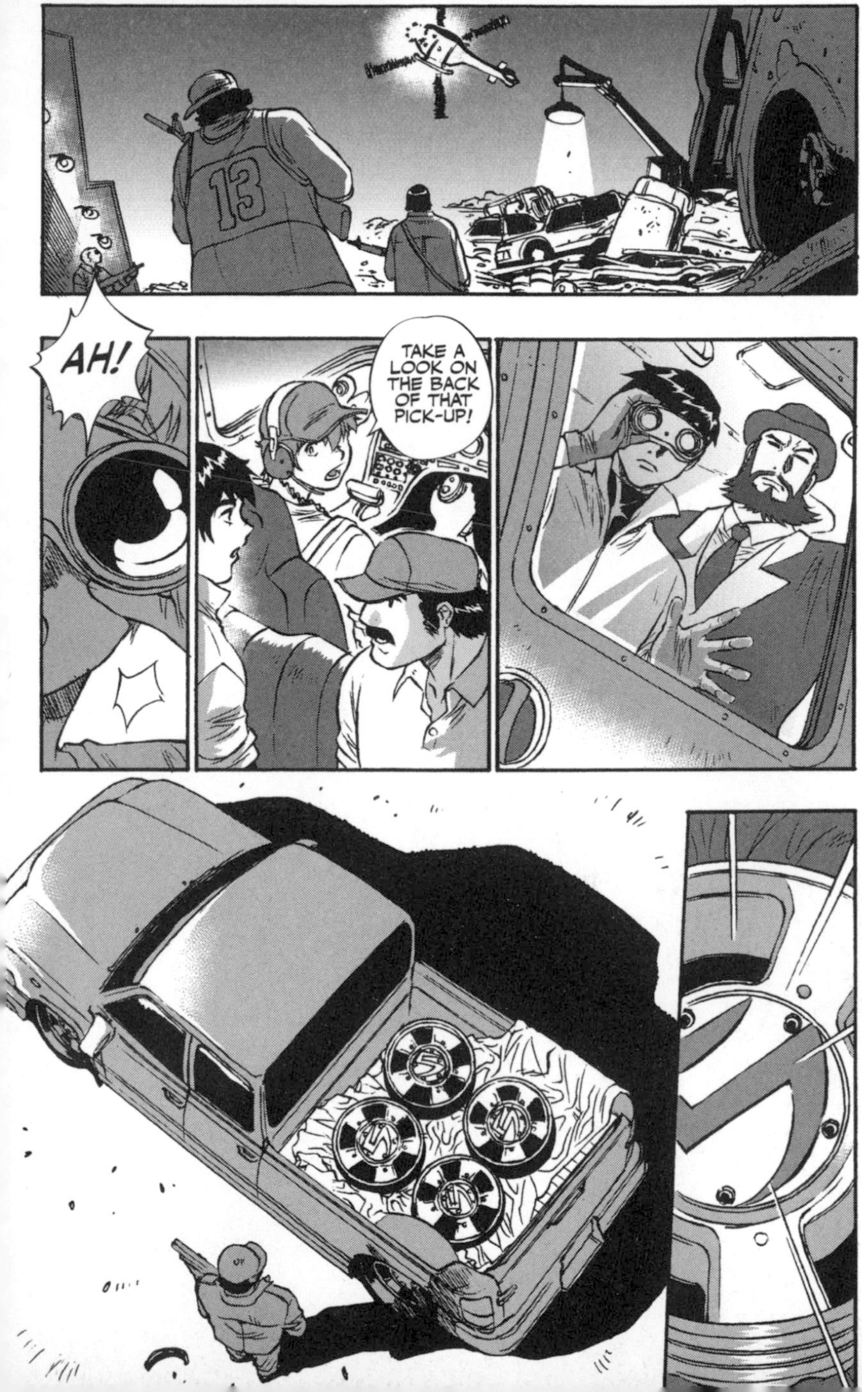
AH!
TAKE A LOOK ON THE BACK OF THAT PICK-UP!

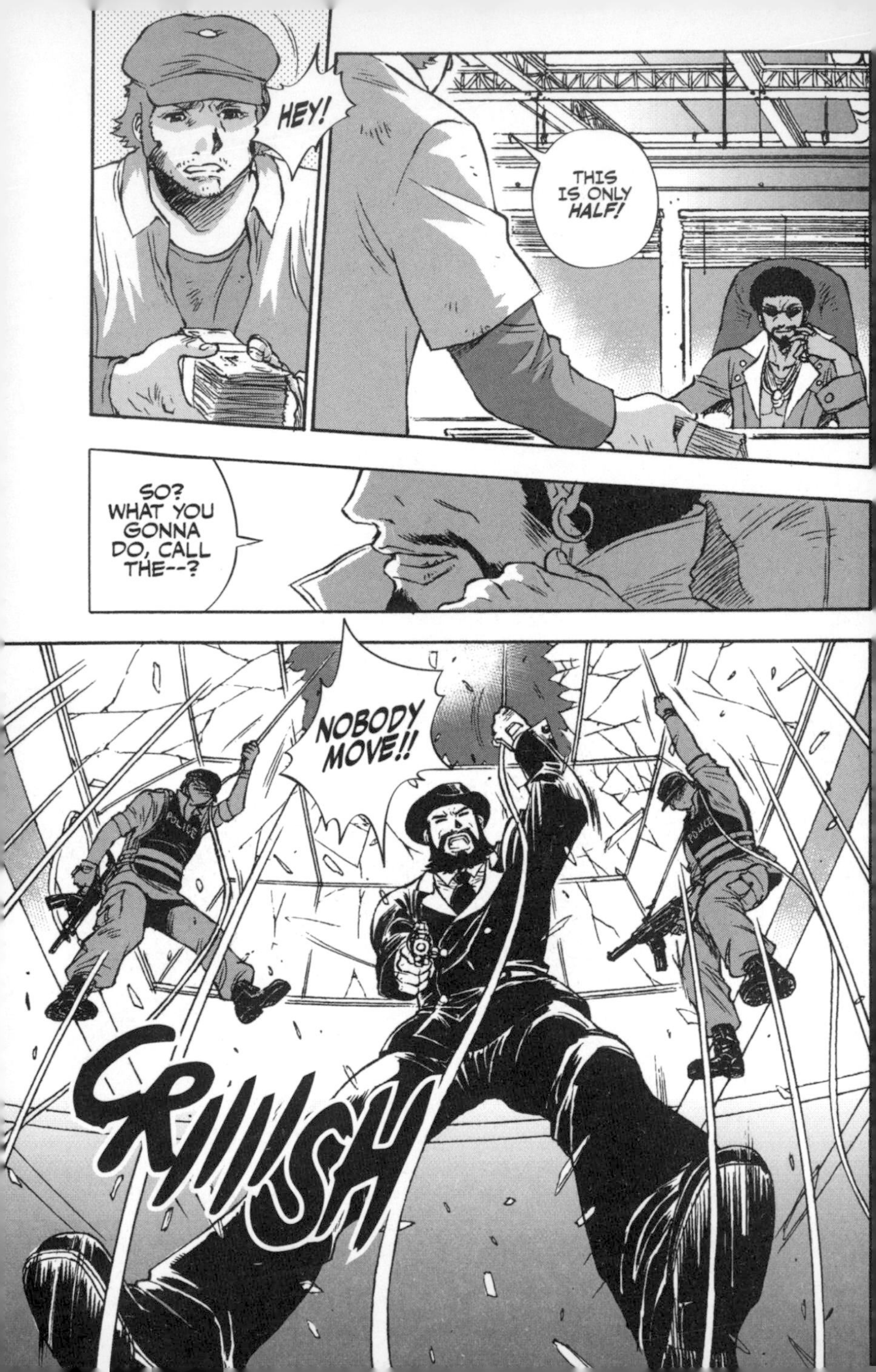
HEY!
THIS IS ONLY HALF!
SO? WHAT YOU GONNA DO, CALL THE--?
NOBODY MOVE!!
GRIIISH

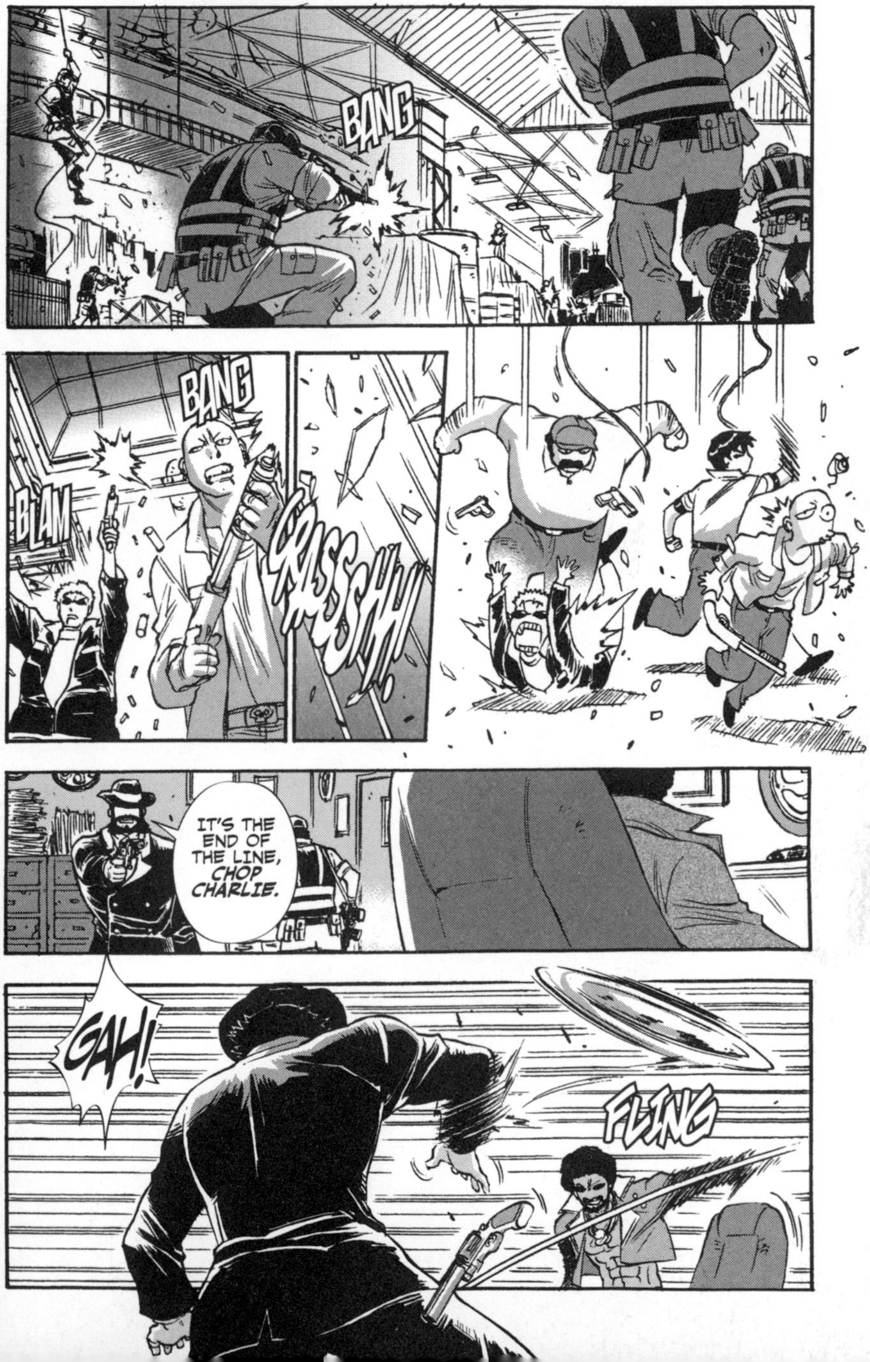
BANG
BLAM
BANG
CRASSSHH!
IT'S THE END OF THE LINE, *CHOP CHARLIE.*
GAH!
FLING

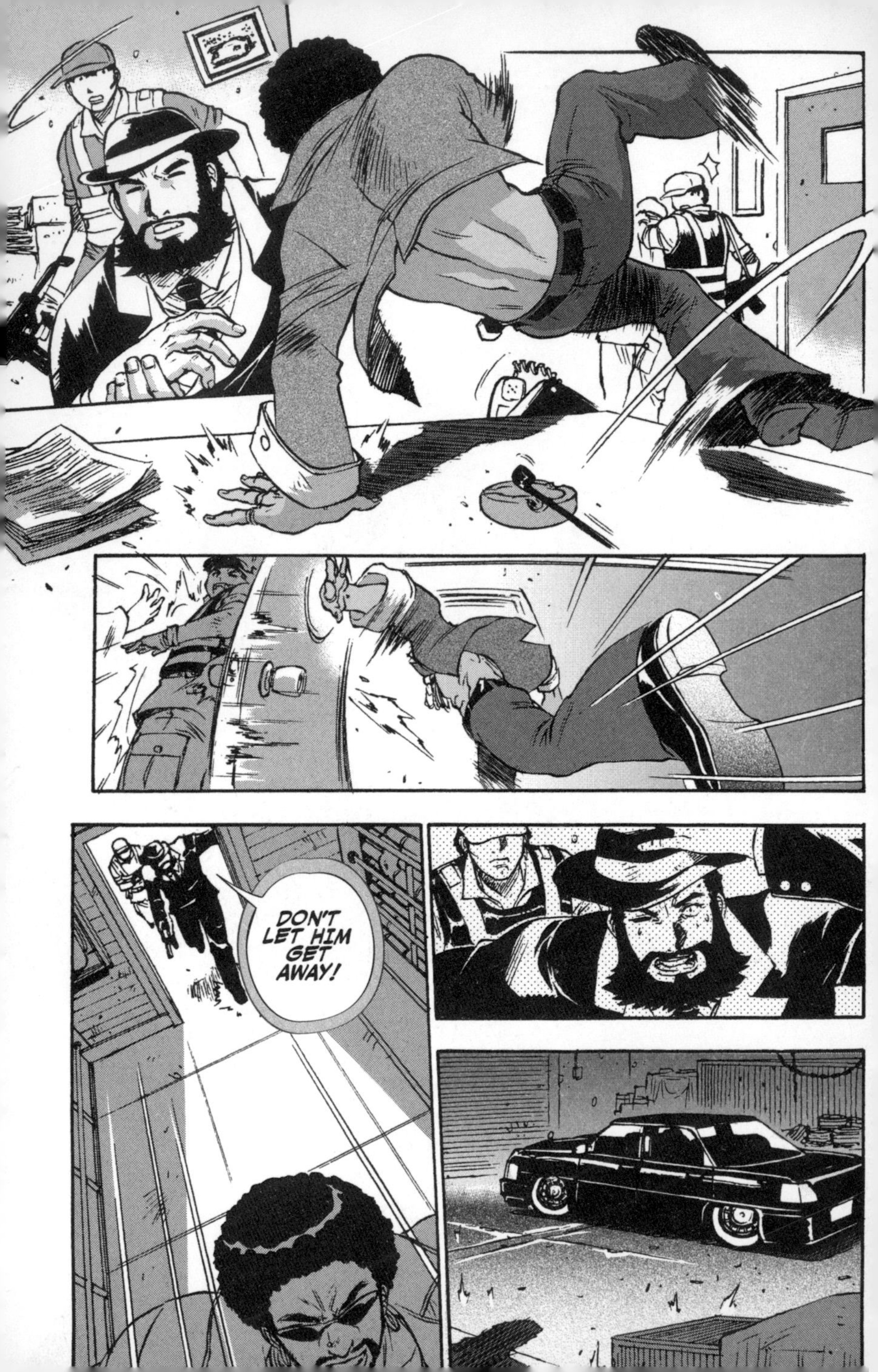
DON'T LET HIM GET AWAY!

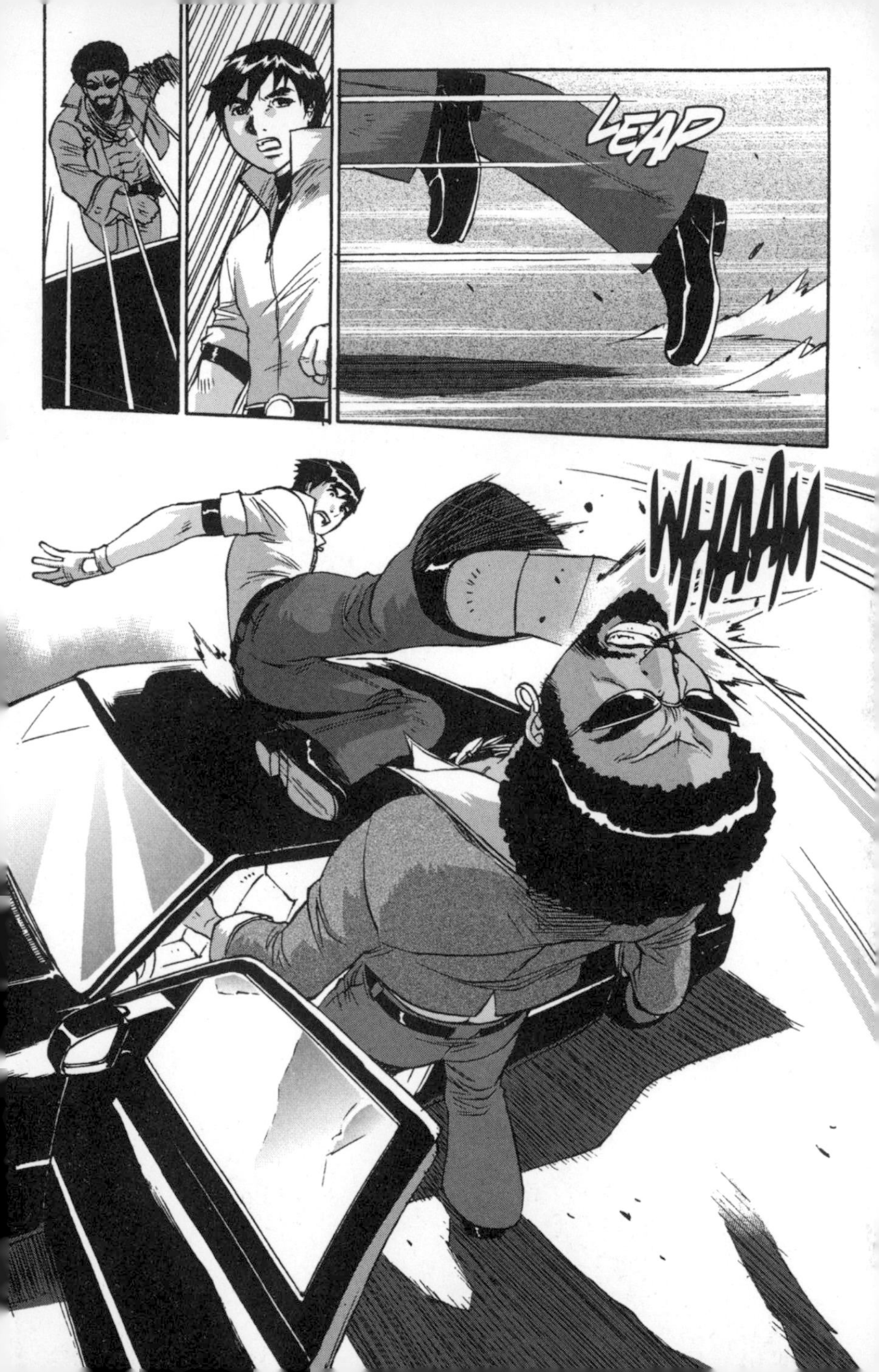
LEAP
WHAAM

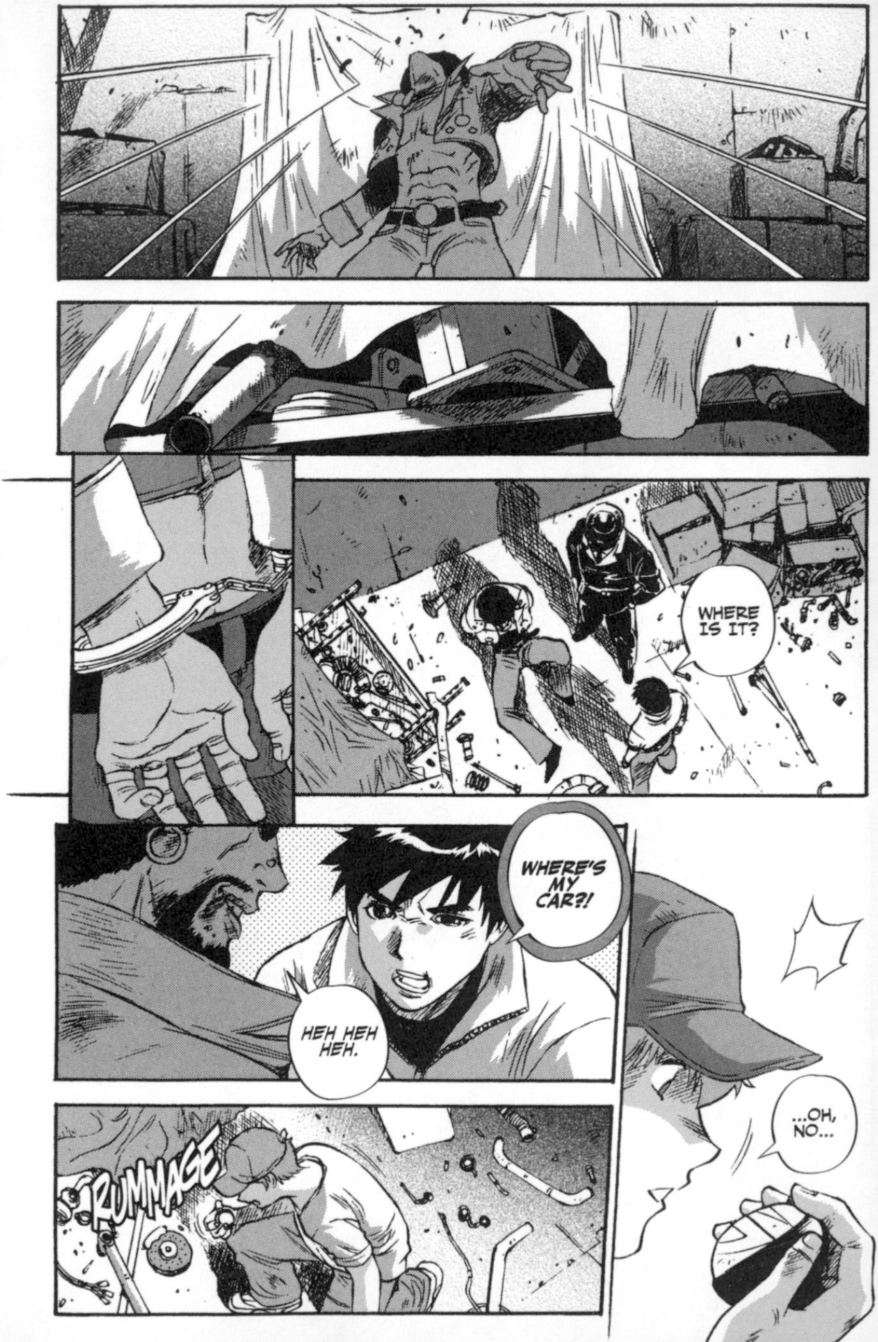
WHERE IS IT?
WHERE'S MY CAR?!
HEH HEH HEH.
...OH, NO...
RUMMAGE

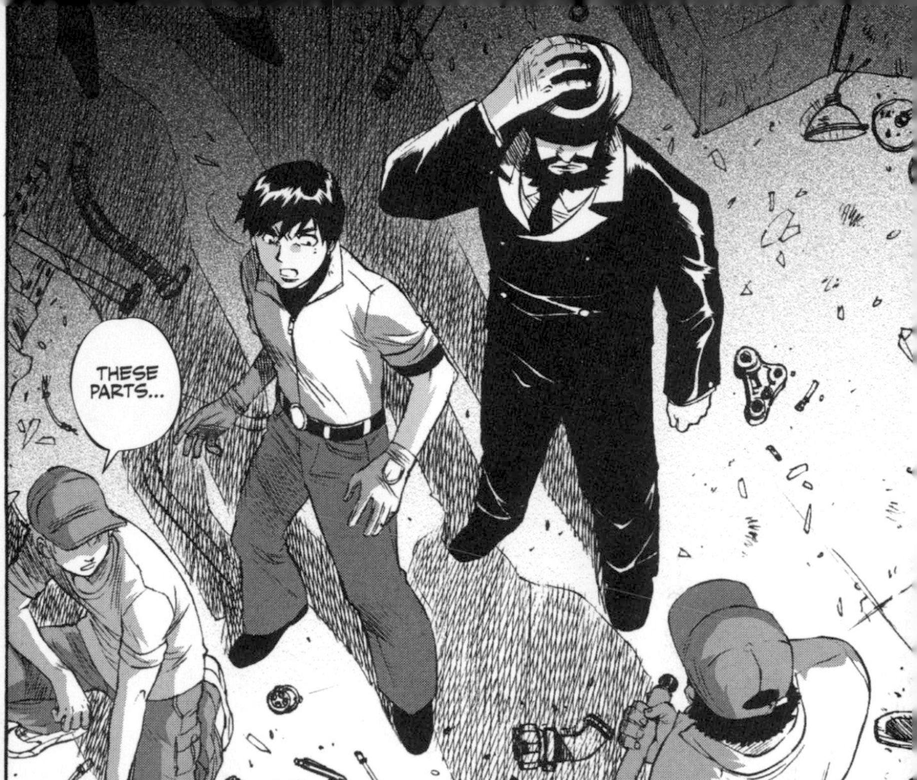
THESE PARTS...

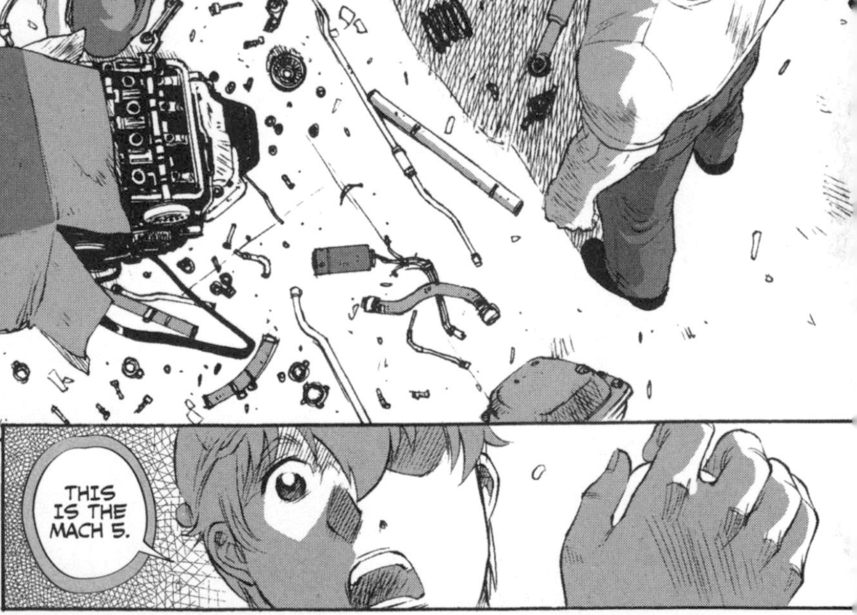
THIS IS THE MACH 5.

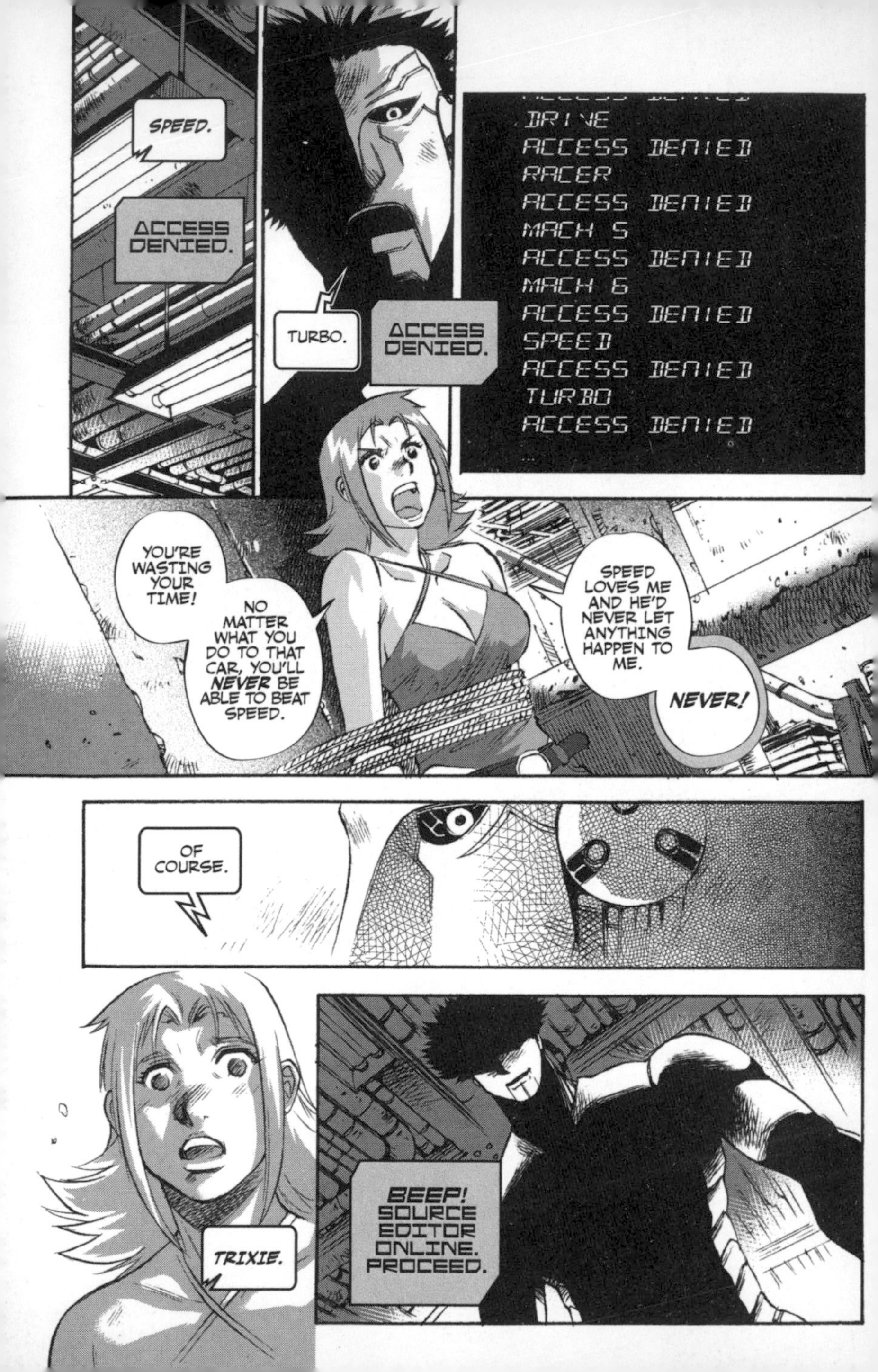
SPEED.
ACCESS DENIED.
TURBO.
ACCESS DENIED.
DRIVE
ACCESS DENIED
RACER
ACCESS DENIED
MACH 5
ACCESS DENIED
MACH 6
ACCESS DENIED
SPEED
ACCESS DENIED
TURBO
ACCESS DENIED
...
YOU'RE WASTING YOUR TIME!
NO MATTER WHAT YOU DO TO THAT CAR, YOU'LL *NEVER* BE ABLE TO BEAT SPEED.
SPEED LOVES ME AND HE'D NEVER LET ANYTHING HAPPEN TO ME.
NEVER!
OF COURSE.
TRIXIE.
BEEP! SOURCE EDITOR ONLINE. PROCEED.

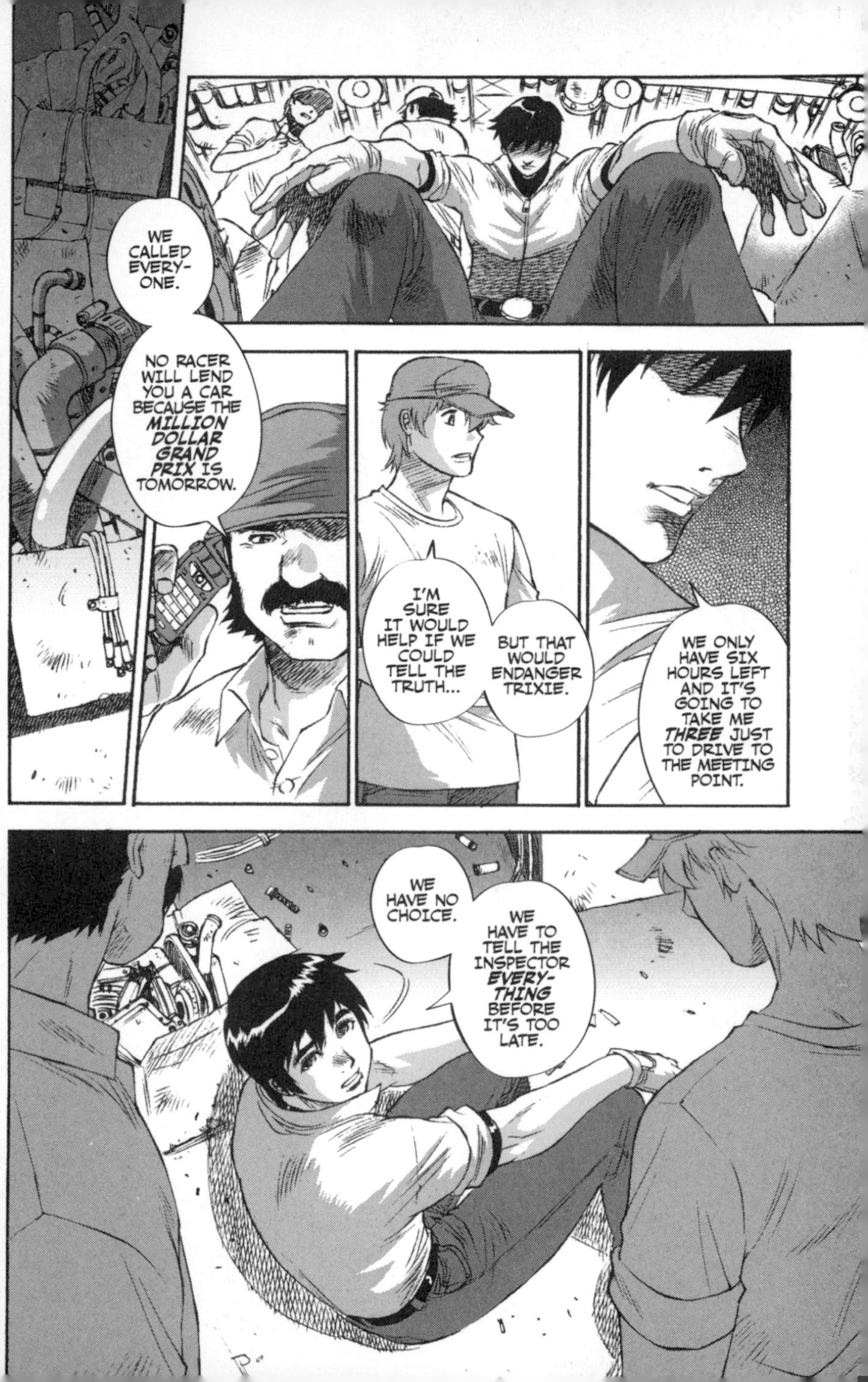
WE CALLED EVERY-ONE.
NO RACER WILL LEND YOU A CAR BECAUSE THE *MILLION DOLLAR GRAND PRIX* IS TOMORROW.
I'M SURE IT WOULD HELP IF WE COULD TELL THE TRUTH...
BUT THAT WOULD ENDANGER TRIXIE.
WE ONLY HAVE SIX HOURS LEFT AND IT'S GOING TO TAKE ME *THREE* JUST TO DRIVE TO THE MEETING POINT.
WE HAVE NO CHOICE.
WE HAVE TO TELL THE INSPECTOR *EVERY-THING* BEFORE IT'S TOO LATE.

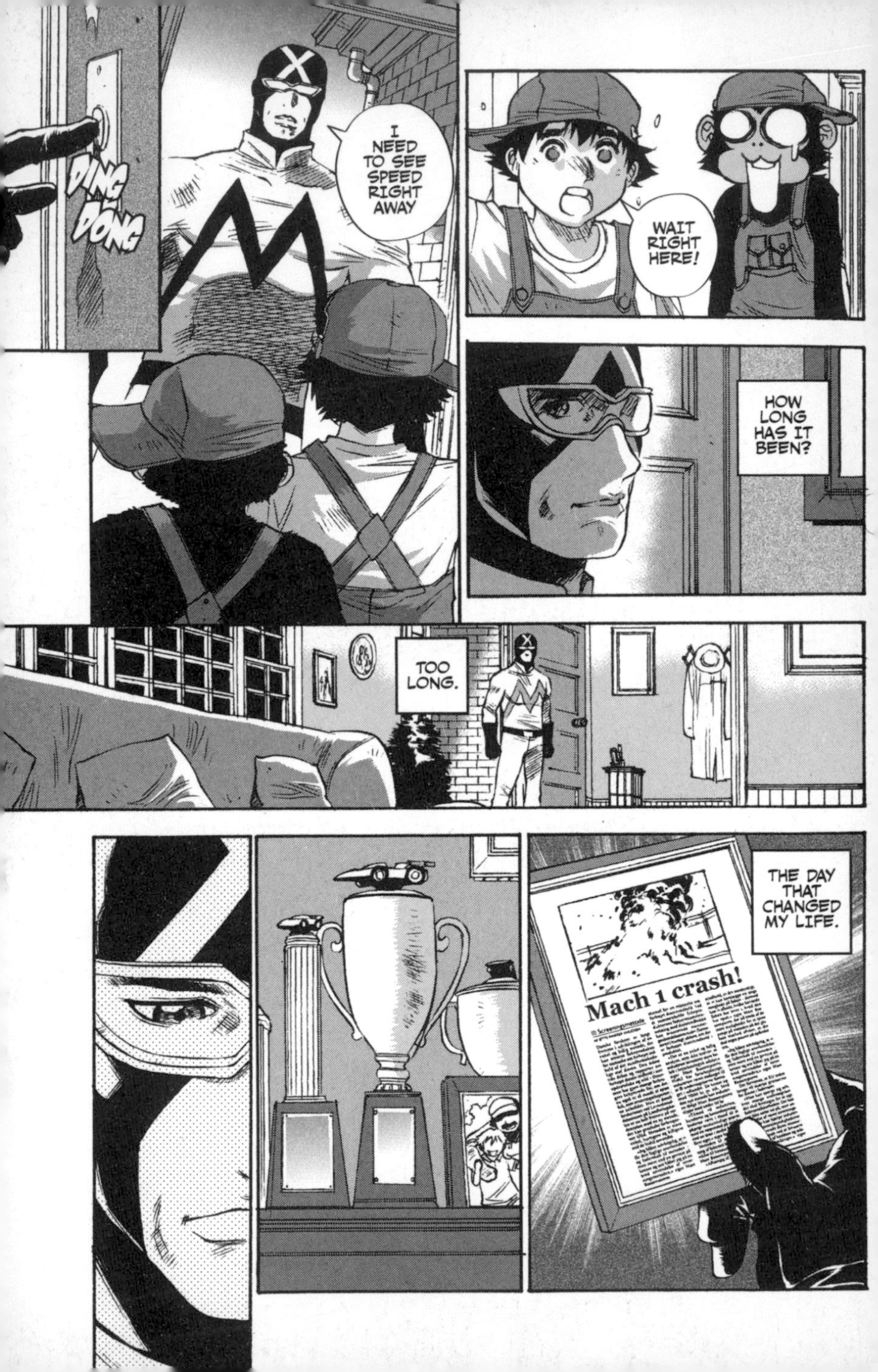
DING DONG
I NEED TO SEE SPEED RIGHT AWAY
WAIT RIGHT HERE!
HOW LONG HAS IT BEEN?
TOO LONG.
THE DAY THAT CHANGED MY LIFE.
Mach 1 crash!

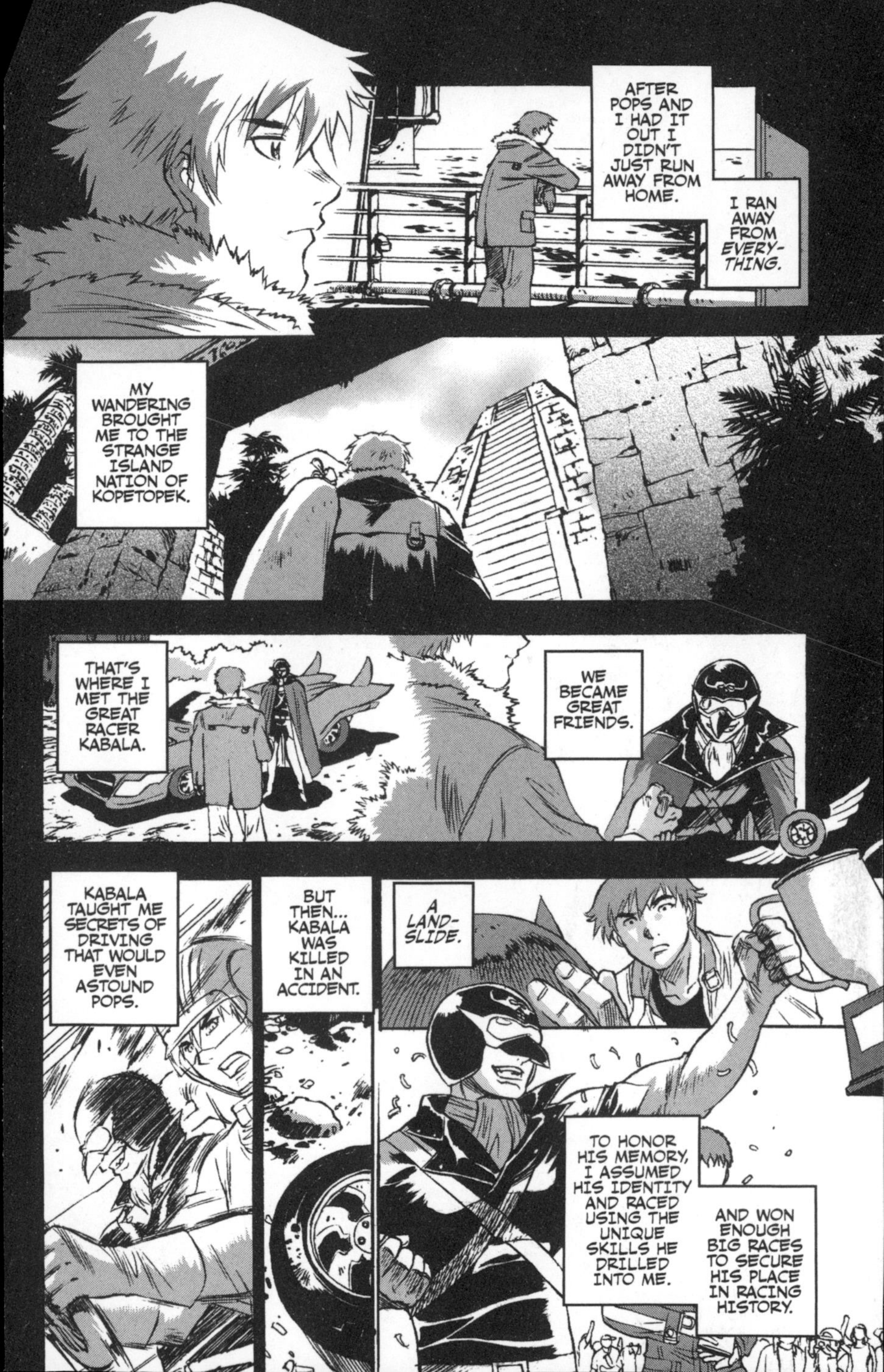
AFTER POPS AND I HAD IT OUT I DIDN'T JUST RUN AWAY FROM HOME.
I RAN AWAY FROM *EVERYTHING.*
MY WANDERING BROUGHT ME TO THE STRANGE ISLAND NATION OF KOPETOPEK.
THAT'S WHERE I MET THE GREAT RACER KABALA.
WE BECAME GREAT FRIENDS.
KABALA TAUGHT ME SECRETS OF DRIVING THAT WOULD EVEN ASTOUND POPS.
BUT THEN... KABALA WAS KILLED IN AN ACCIDENT.
A LAND-SLIDE.
TO HONOR HIS MEMORY, I ASSUMED HIS IDENTITY AND RACED USING THE UNIQUE SKILLS HE DRILLED INTO ME.
AND WON ENOUGH BIG RACES TO SECURE HIS PLACE IN RACING HISTORY.

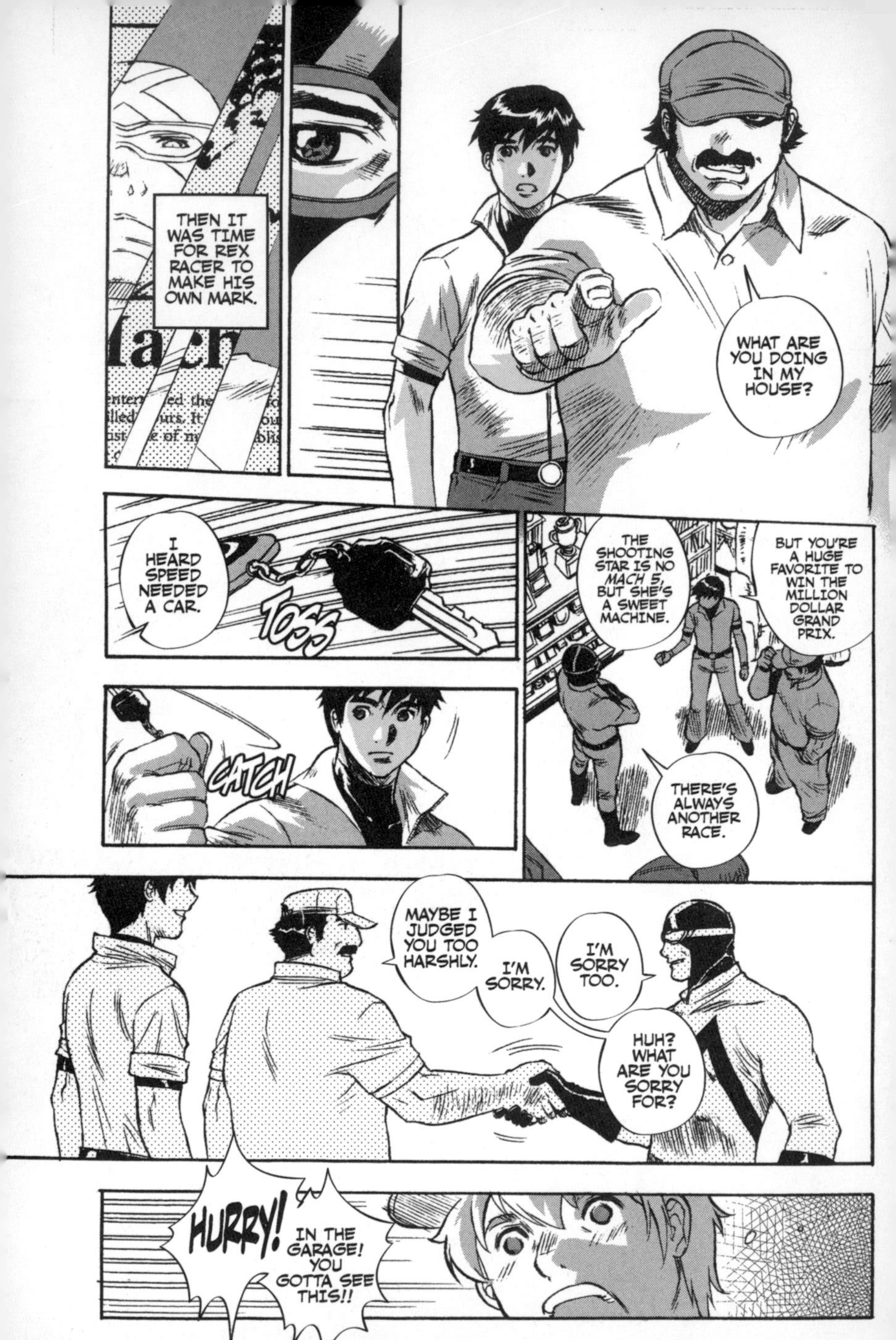
THEN IT WAS TIME FOR REX RACER TO MAKE HIS OWN MARK.
WHAT ARE YOU DOING IN MY HOUSE?
I HEARD SPEED NEEDED A CAR.
TOSS
CATCH
THE SHOOTING STAR IS NO *MACH 5*, BUT SHE'S A SWEET MACHINE.
BUT YOU'RE A HUGE FAVORITE TO WIN THE MILLION DOLLAR GRAND PRIX.
THERE'S ALWAYS ANOTHER RACE.
MAYBE I JUDGED YOU TOO HARSHLY.
I'M SORRY.
I'M SORRY TOO.
HUH? WHAT ARE YOU SORRY FOR?
HURRY!
IN THE GARAGE! YOU GOTTA SEE THIS!!

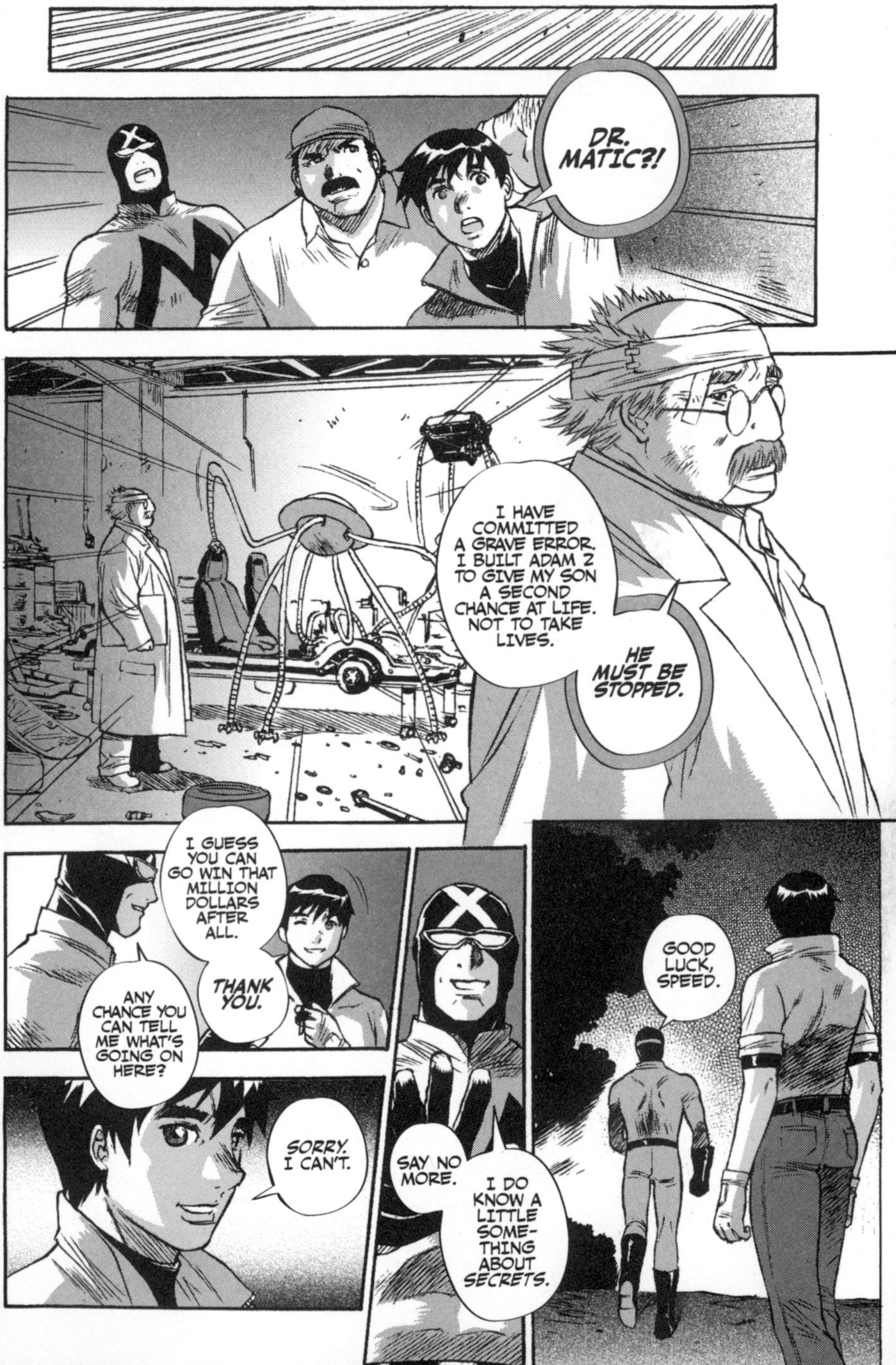
DR. MATIC?!
I HAVE COMMITTED A GRAVE ERROR. I BUILT ADAM 2 TO GIVE MY SON A SECOND CHANCE AT LIFE. NOT TO TAKE LIVES.
HE MUST BE STOPPED.
I GUESS YOU CAN GO WIN THAT MILLION DOLLARS AFTER ALL.
THANK YOU.
ANY CHANCE YOU CAN TELL ME WHAT'S GOING ON HERE?
SORRY. I CAN'T.
SAY NO MORE.
I DO KNOW A LITTLE SOME-THING ABOUT SECRETS.
GOOD LUCK, SPEED.

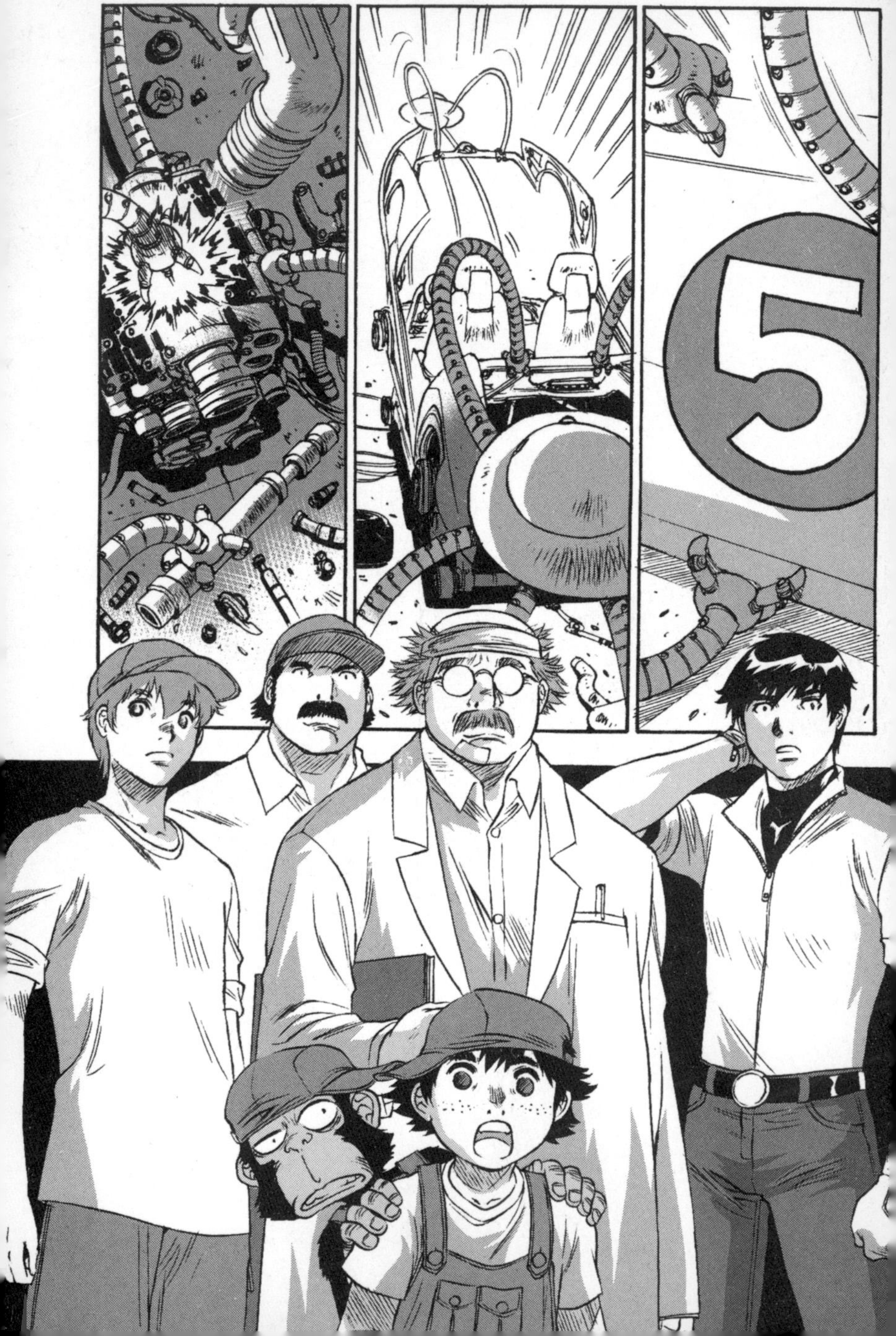
5

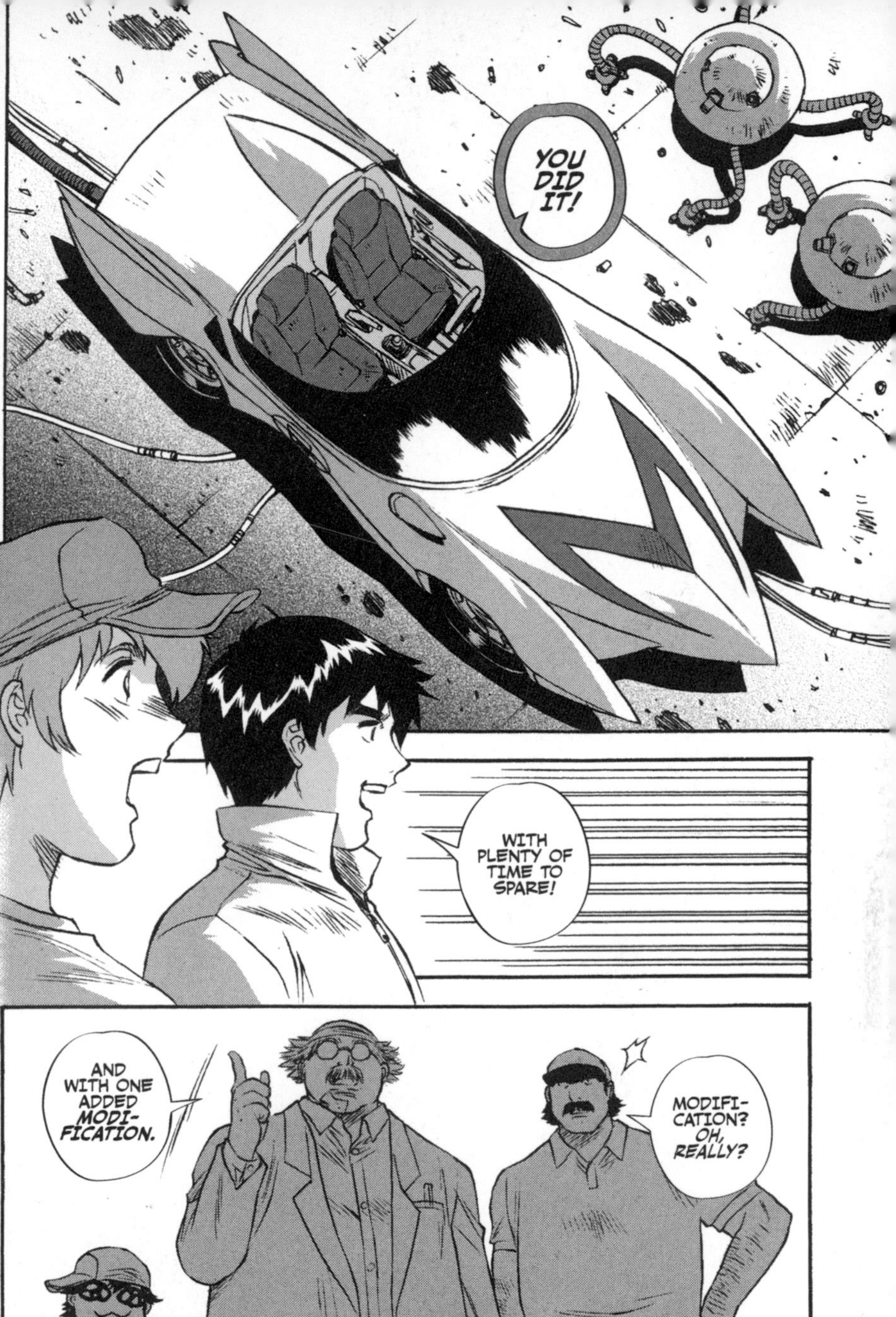
YOU DID IT!
WITH PLENTY OF TIME TO SPARE!
AND WITH ONE ADDED MODI-FICATION.
MODIFI-CATION? OH, REALLY?

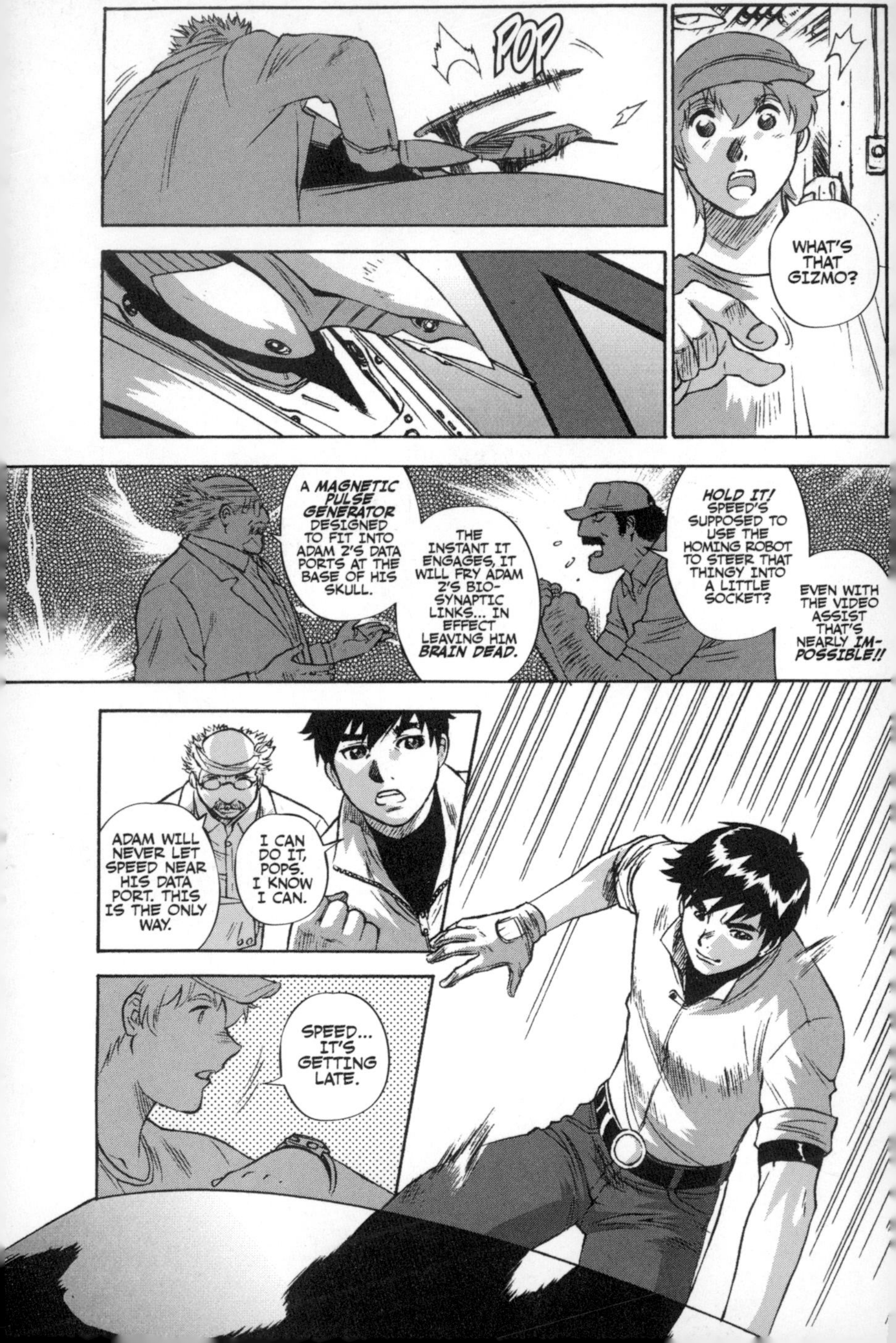

POP
WHAT'S THAT GIZMO?
A MAGNETIC PULSE GENERATOR DESIGNED TO FIT INTO ADAM Z'S DATA PORTS AT THE BASE OF HIS SKULL.
THE INSTANT IT ENGAGES, IT WILL FRY ADAM Z'S BIO-SYNAPTIC LINKS... IN EFFECT LEAVING HIM BRAIN DEAD.
HOLD IT! SPEED'S SUPPOSED TO USE THE HOMING ROBOT TO STEER THAT THINGY INTO A LITTLE SOCKET?
EVEN WITH THE VIDEO ASSIST THAT'S NEARLY IM-POSSIBLE!!
ADAM WILL NEVER LET SPEED NEAR HIS DATA PORT. THIS IS THE ONLY WAY.
I CAN DO IT, POPS. I KNOW I CAN.
SPEED... IT'S GETTING LATE.

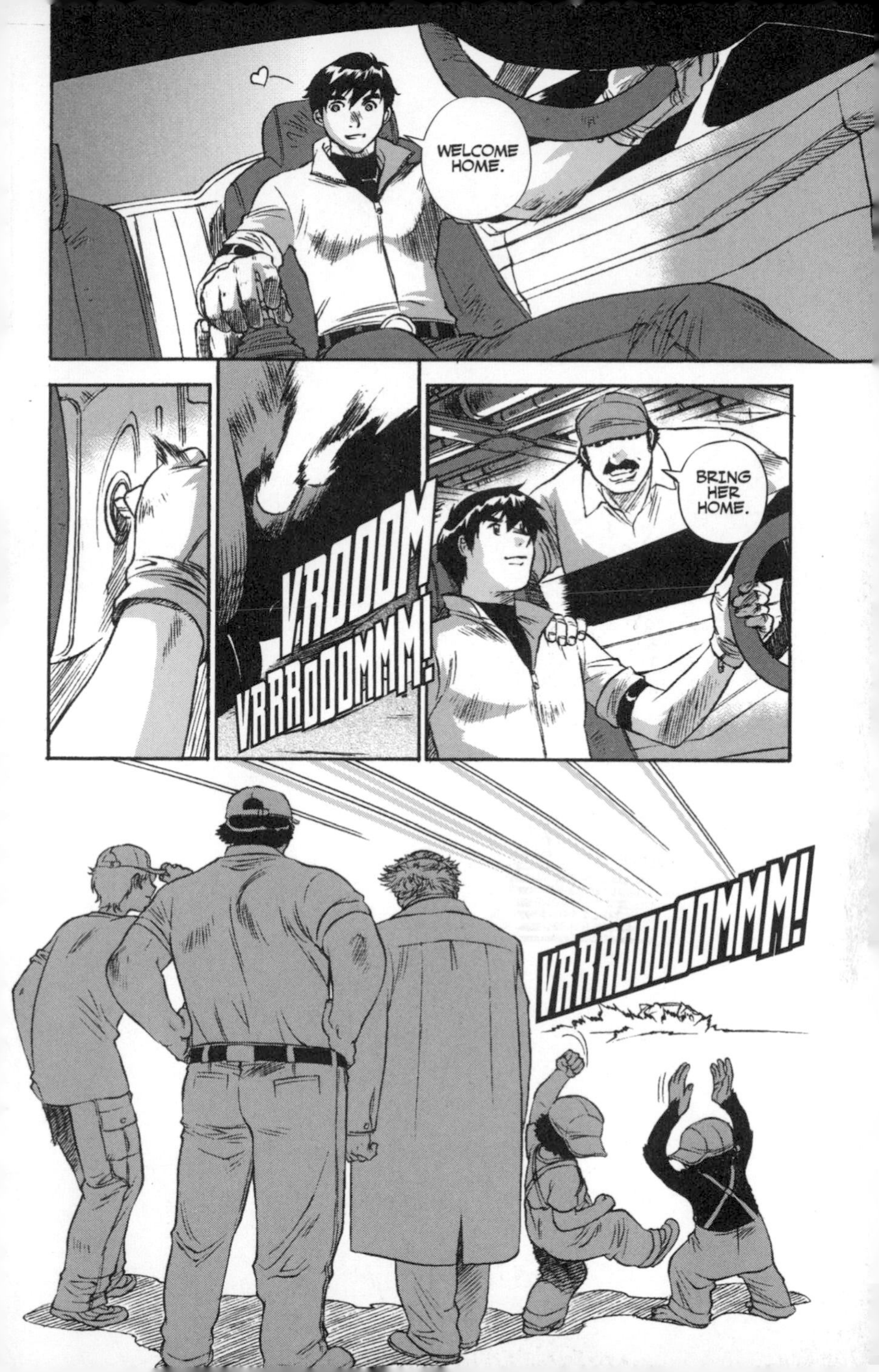
WELCOME HOME.
VROOOM!
VRRROOOMMM!
BRING HER HOME.
VRRROOOOOMMM!

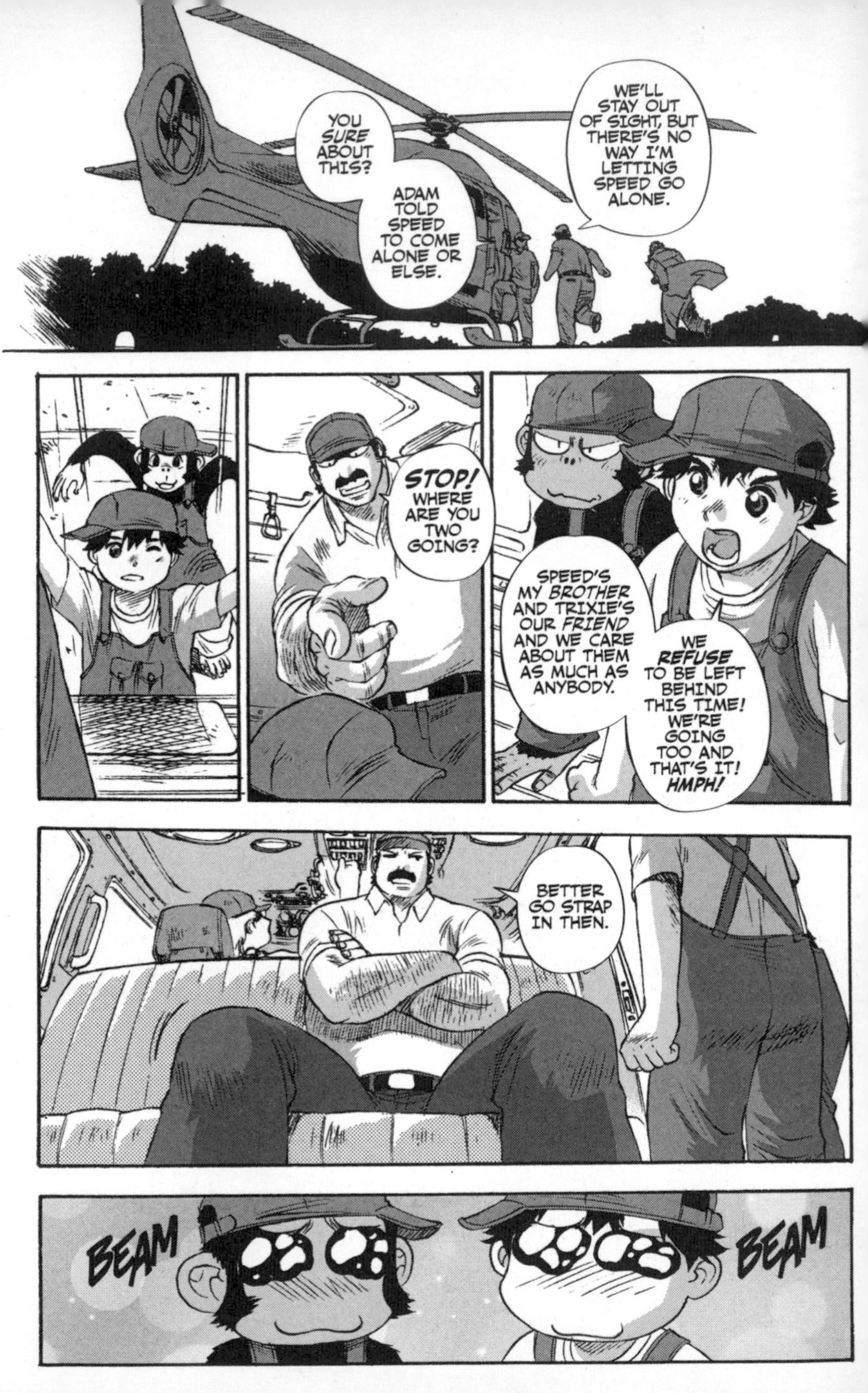
YOU SURE ABOUT THIS?
ADAM TOLD SPEED TO COME ALONE OR ELSE.
WE'LL STAY OUT OF SIGHT, BUT THERE'S NO WAY I'M LETTING SPEED GO ALONE.
STOP! WHERE ARE YOU TWO GOING?
SPEED'S MY BROTHER AND TRIXIE'S OUR FRIEND AND WE CARE ABOUT THEM AS MUCH AS ANYBODY.
WE REFUSE TO BE LEFT BEHIND THIS TIME! WE'RE GOING TOO AND THAT'S IT! HMPH!
BETTER GO STRAP IN THEN.
BEAM
BEAM

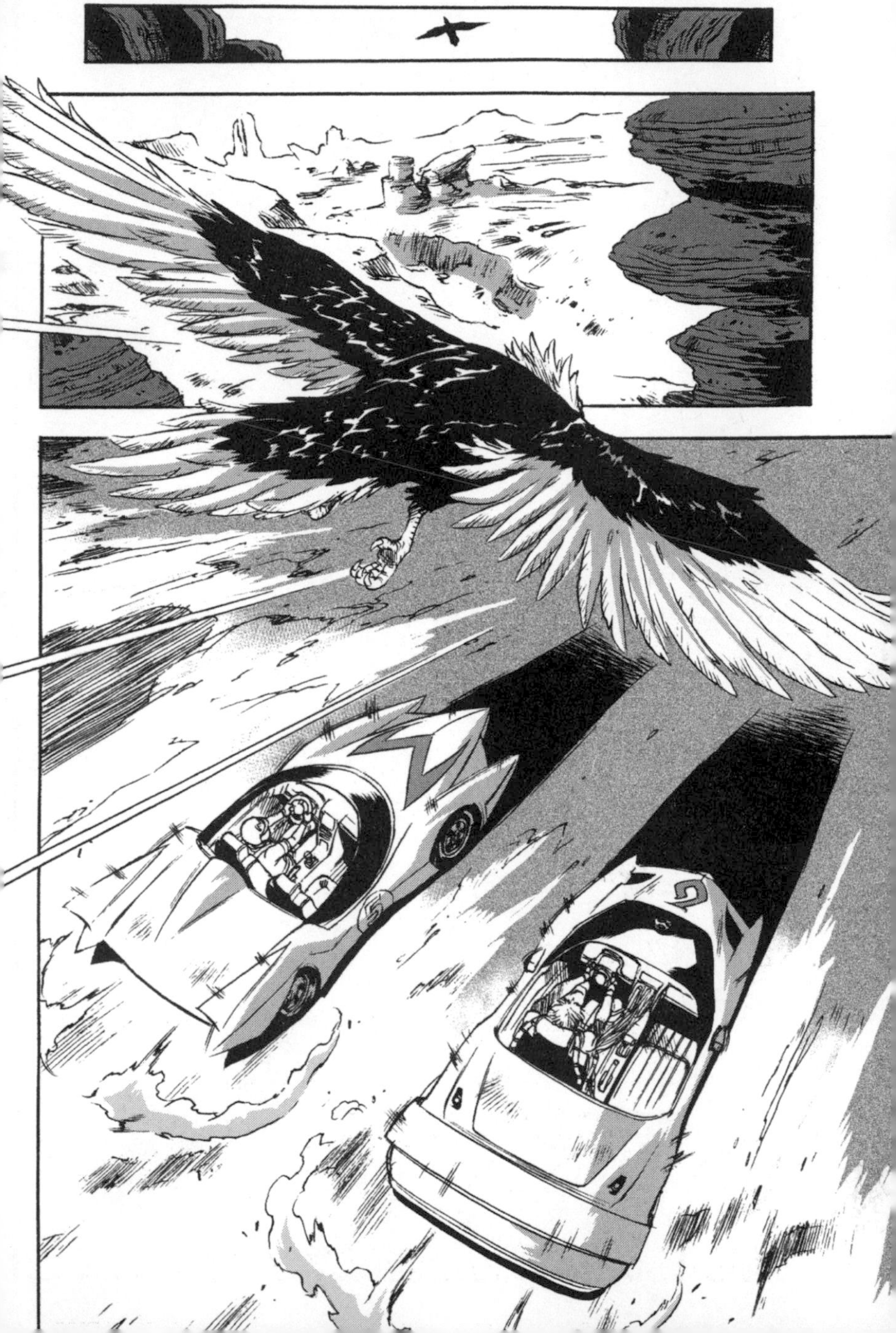

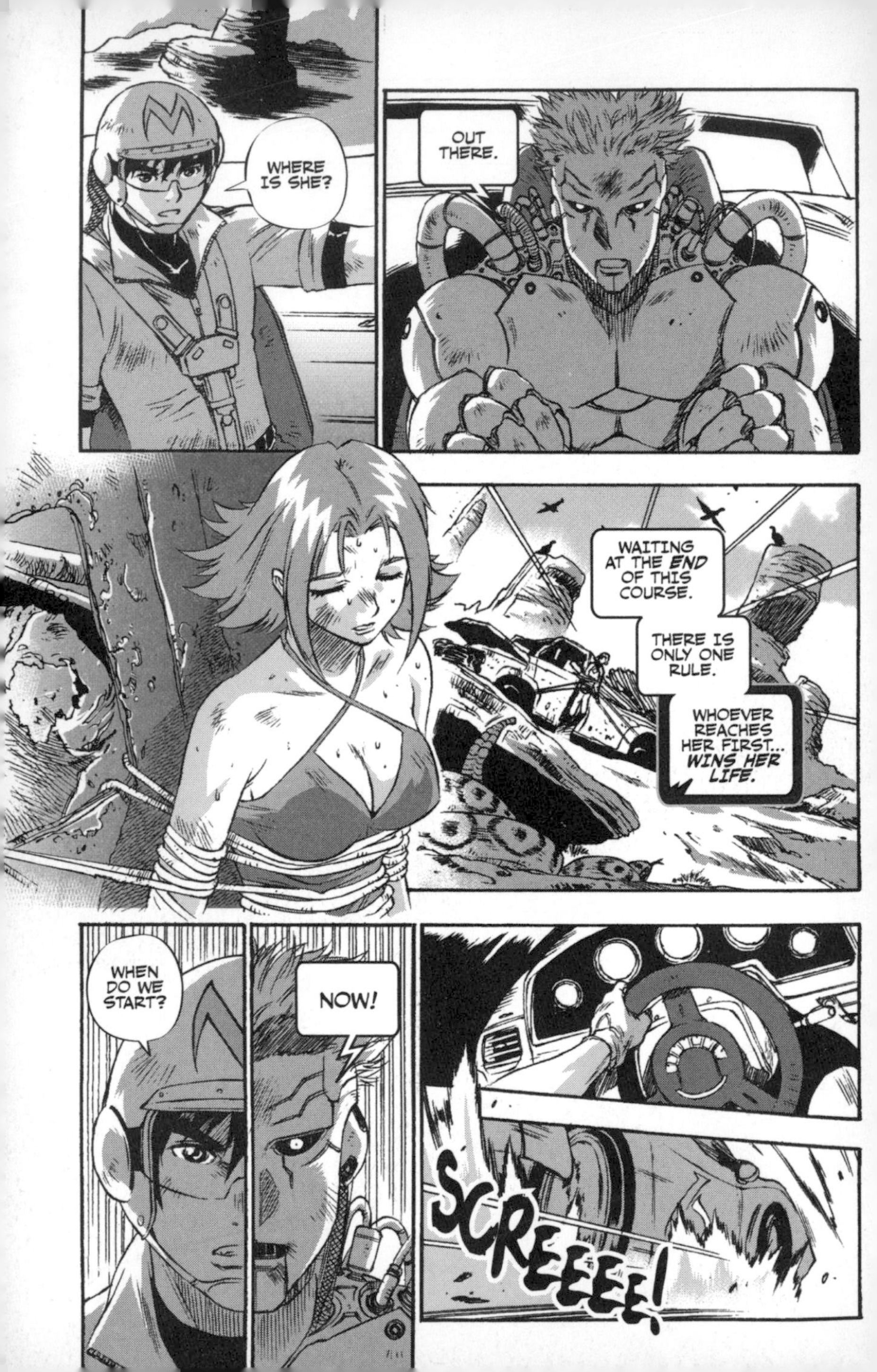
WHERE IS SHE?
OUT THERE.
WAITING AT THE END OF THIS COURSE.
THERE IS ONLY ONE RULE.
WHOEVER REACHES HER FIRST... WINS HER LIFE.
WHEN DO WE START?
NOW!
SCREEEEE!

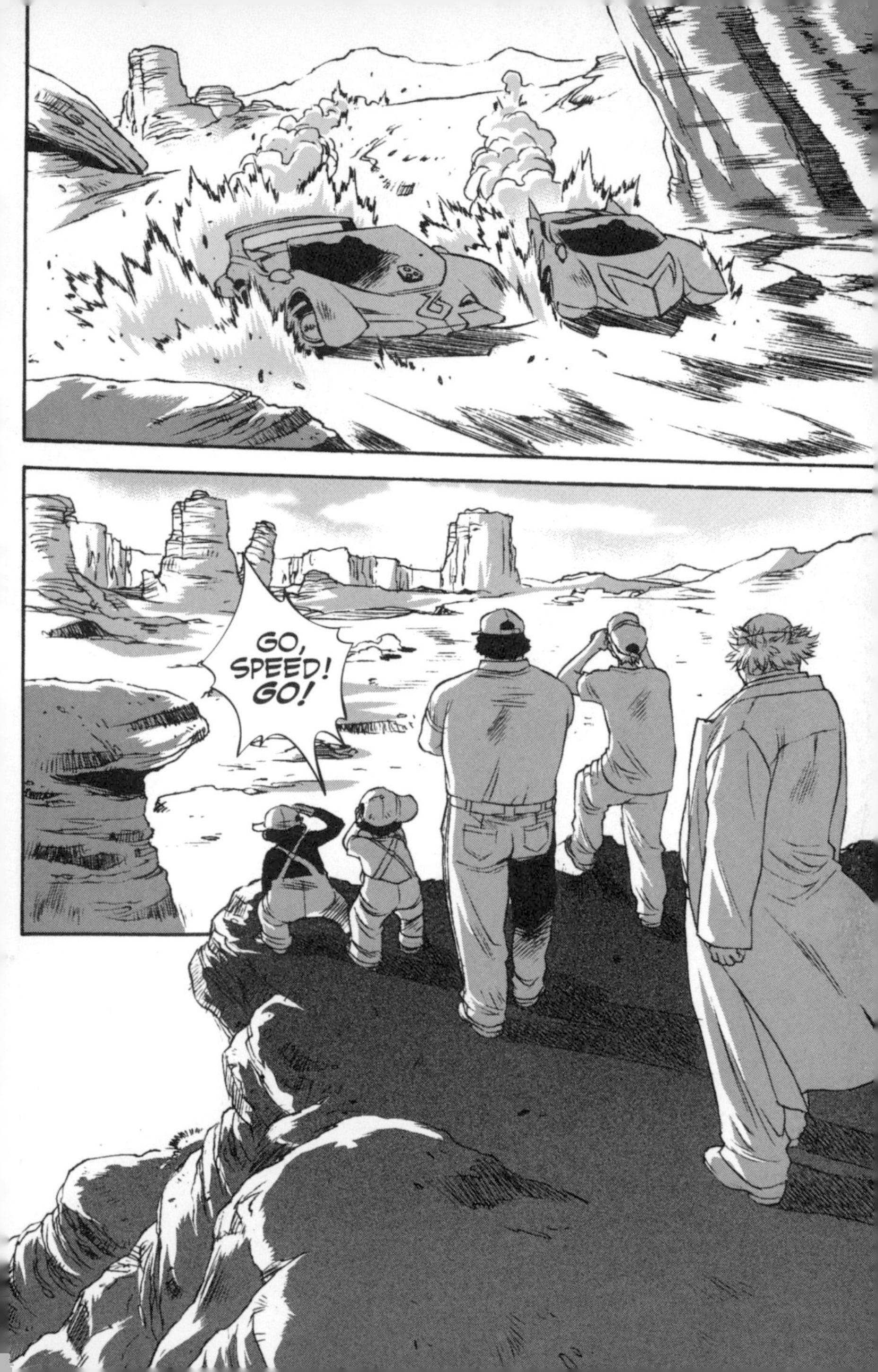
GO, SPEED! GO!

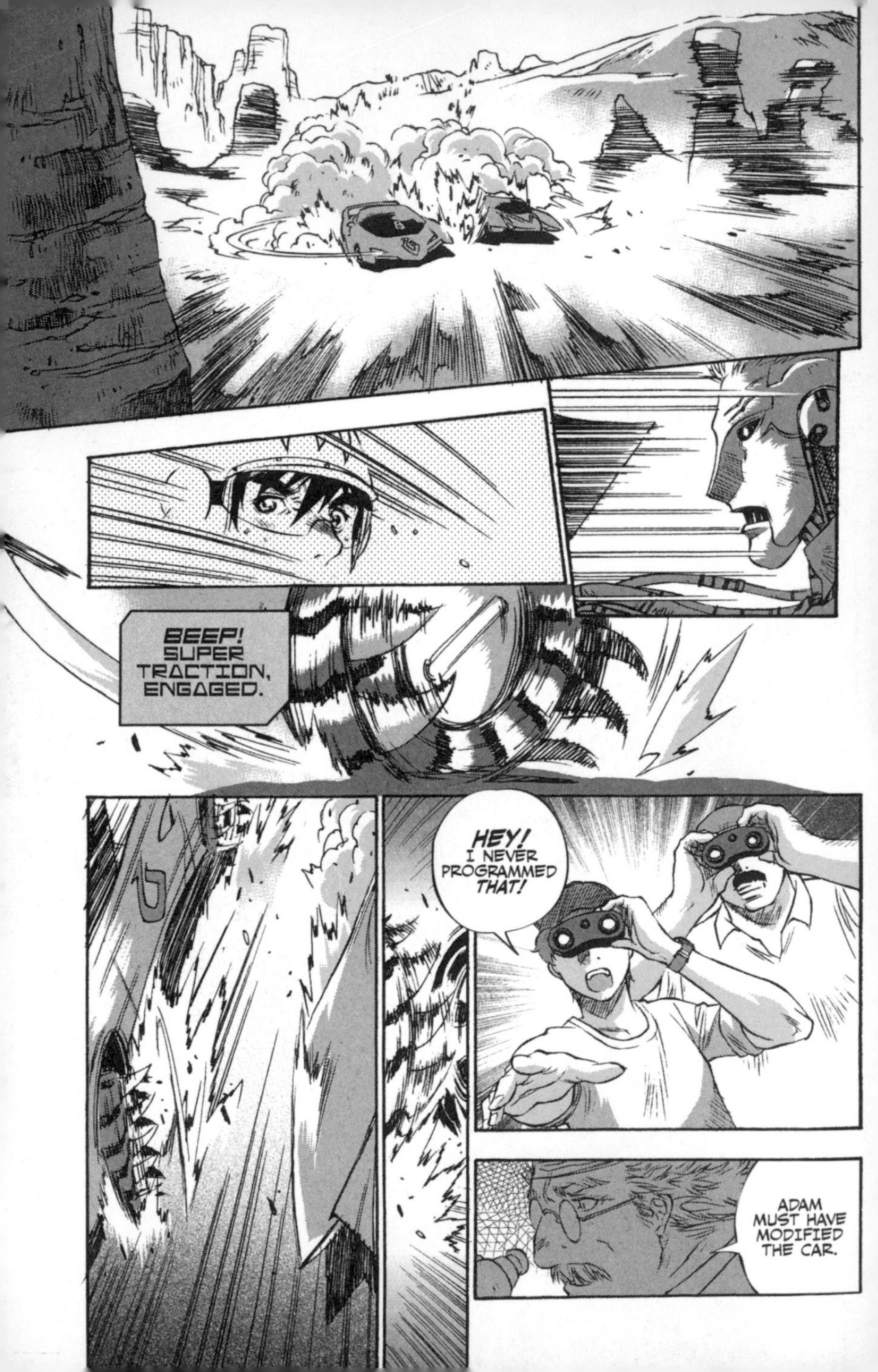
BEEP! SUPER TRACTION, ENGAGED.
HEY! I NEVER PROGRAMMED THAT!
ADAM MUST HAVE MODIFIED THE CAR.

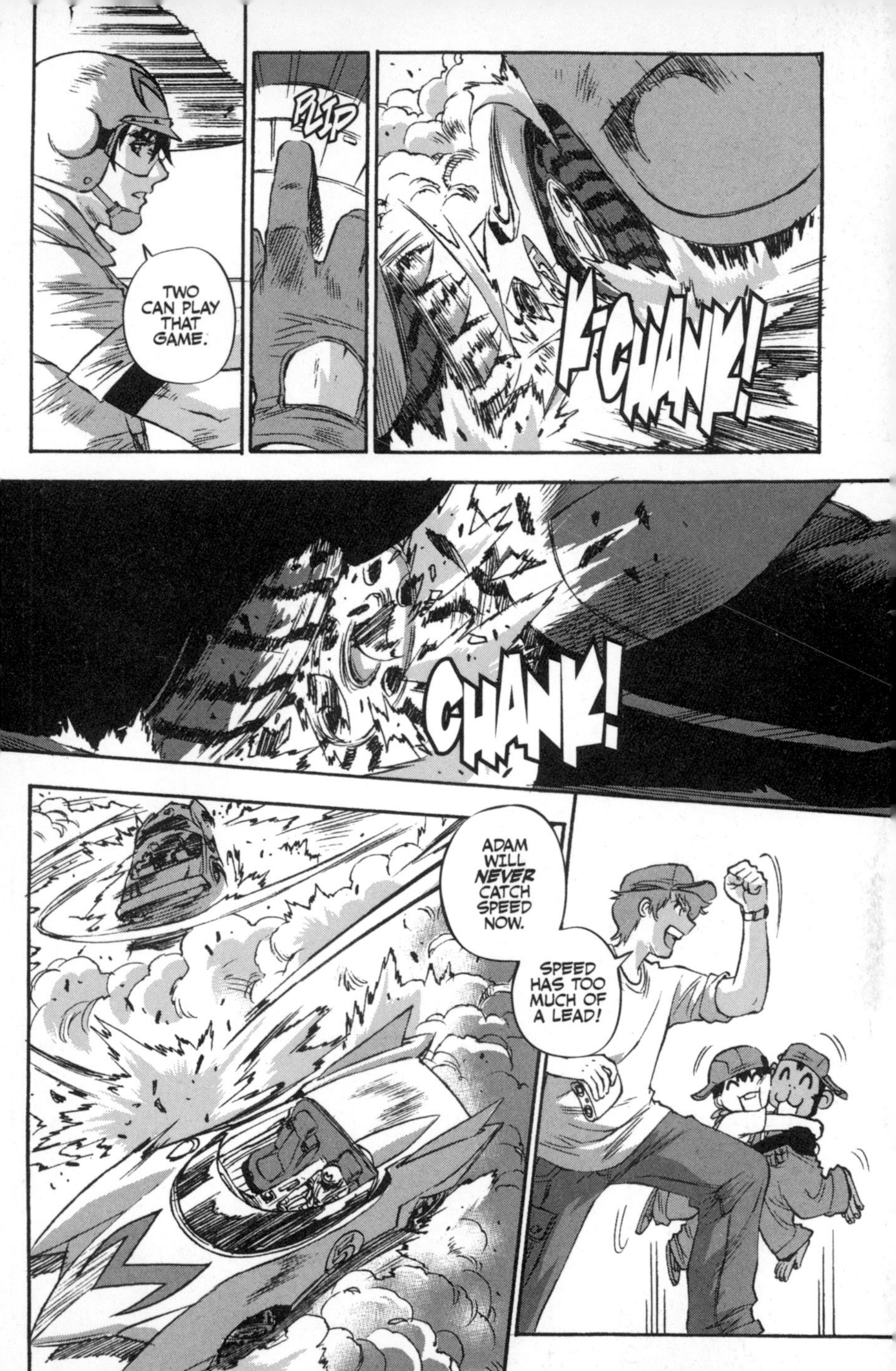
TWO CAN PLAY THAT GAME.
FLIP
K'CHANK!
CHANK!
ADAM WILL NEVER CATCH SPEED NOW.
SPEED HAS TOO MUCH OF A LEAD!

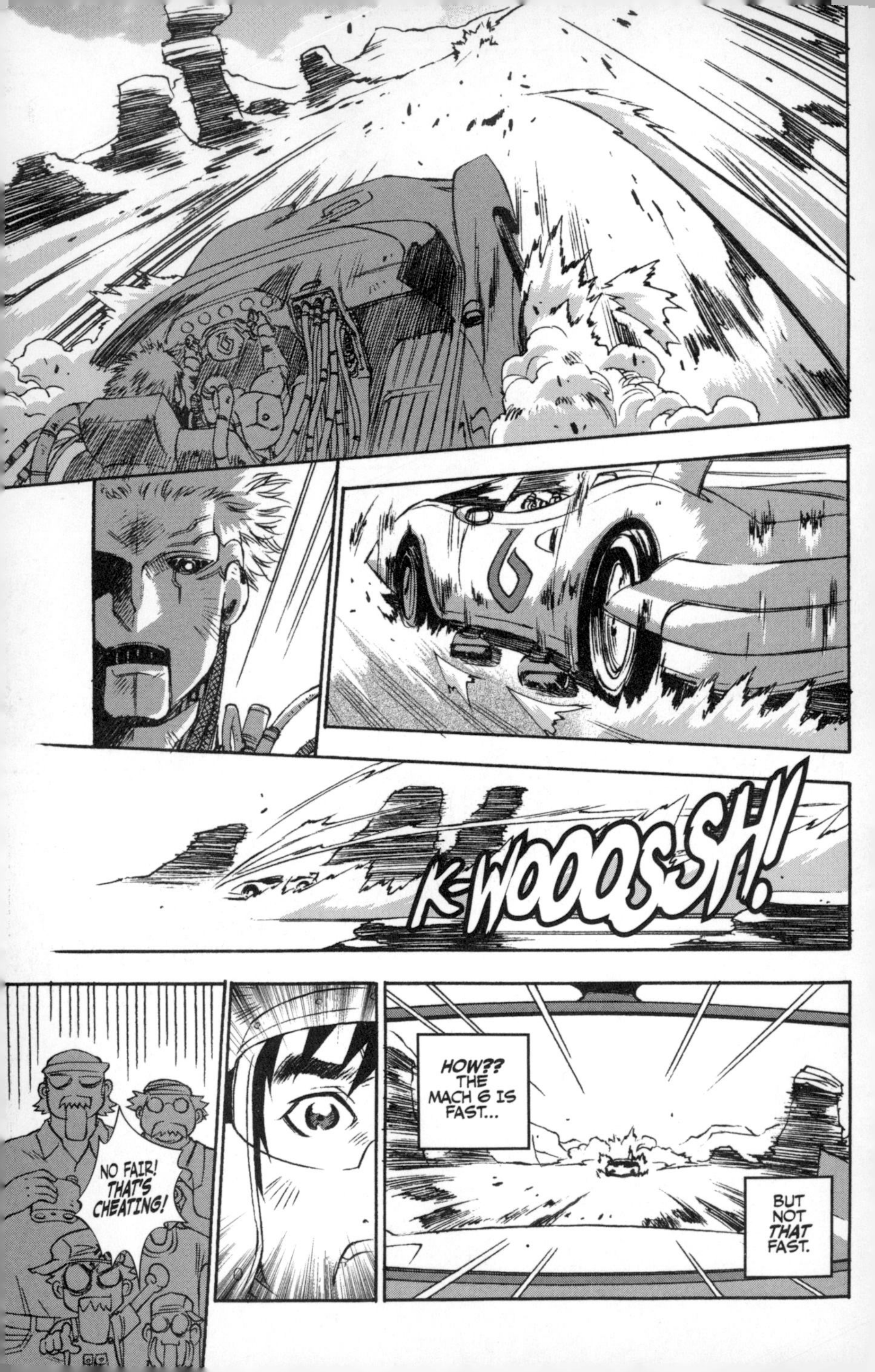
K-WOOOSH!
NO FAIR! THAT'S CHEATING!
HOW?? THE MACH 6 IS FAST...
BUT NOT THAT FAST.

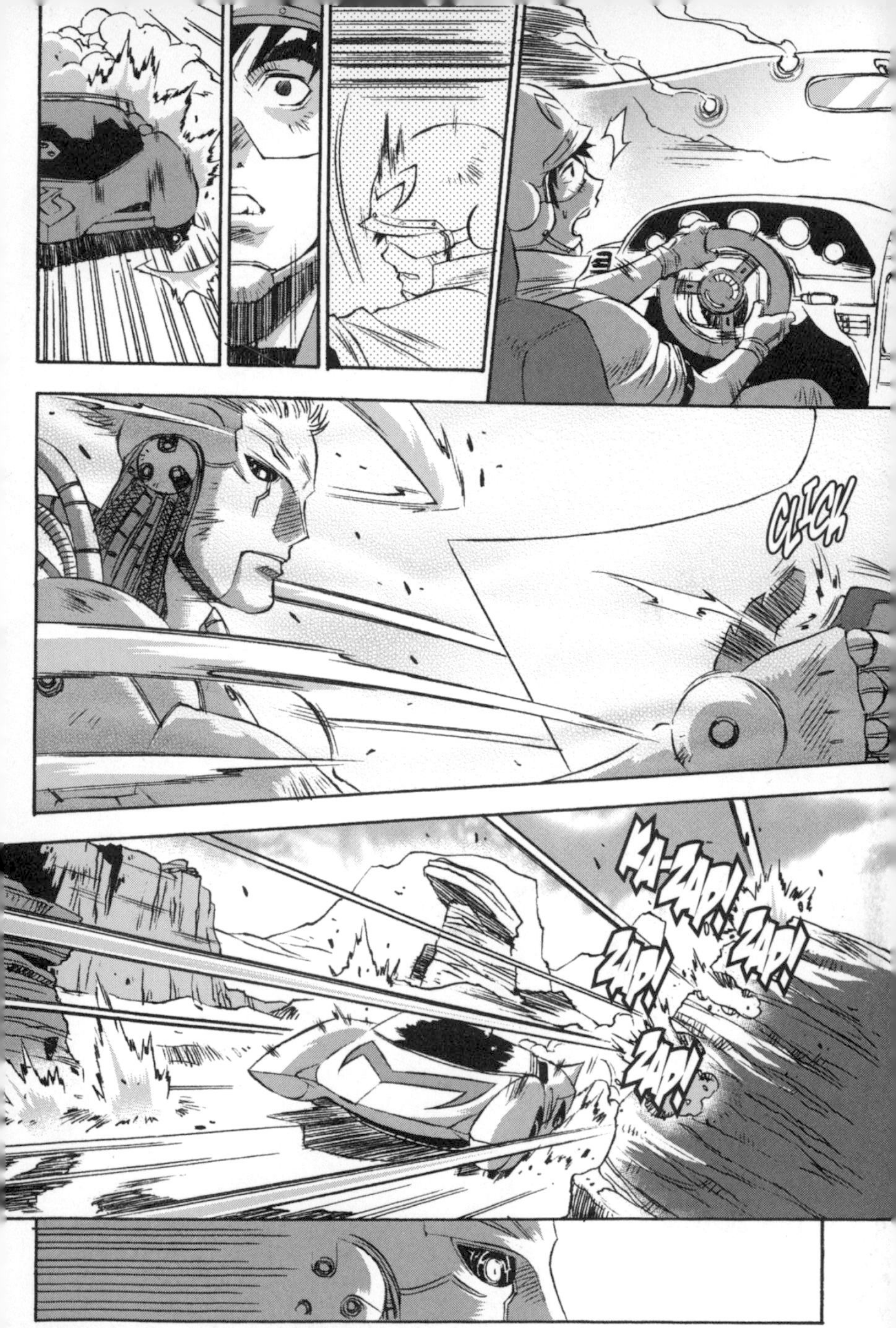
CLICK
KA-ZAP!
ZAP!
ZAP!
ZAP!

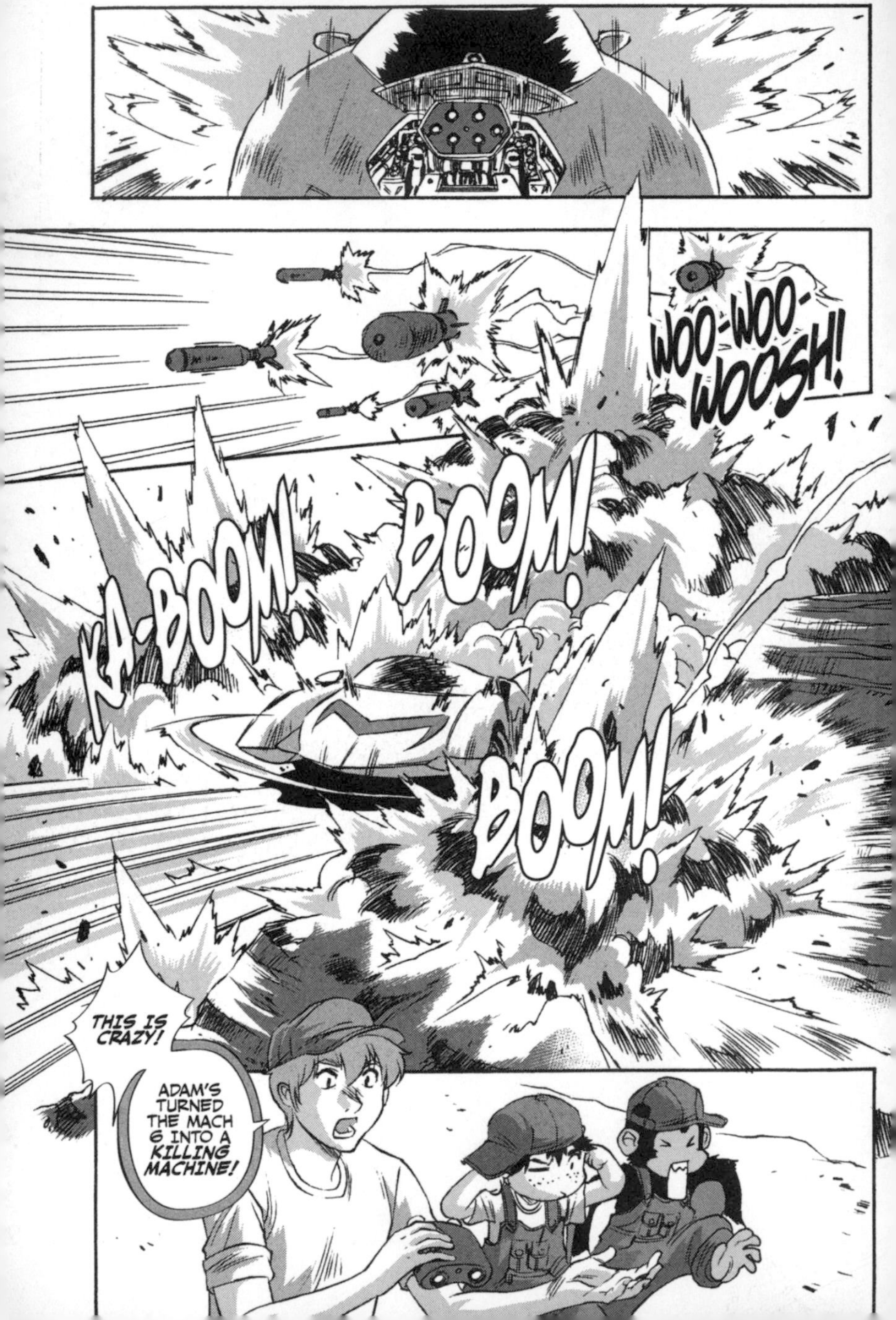
WOO-WOO-WOOSH!
KA-BOOM!
BOOM!
BOOM!
THIS IS CRAZY!
ADAM'S TURNED THE MACH 6 INTO A KILLING MACHINE!

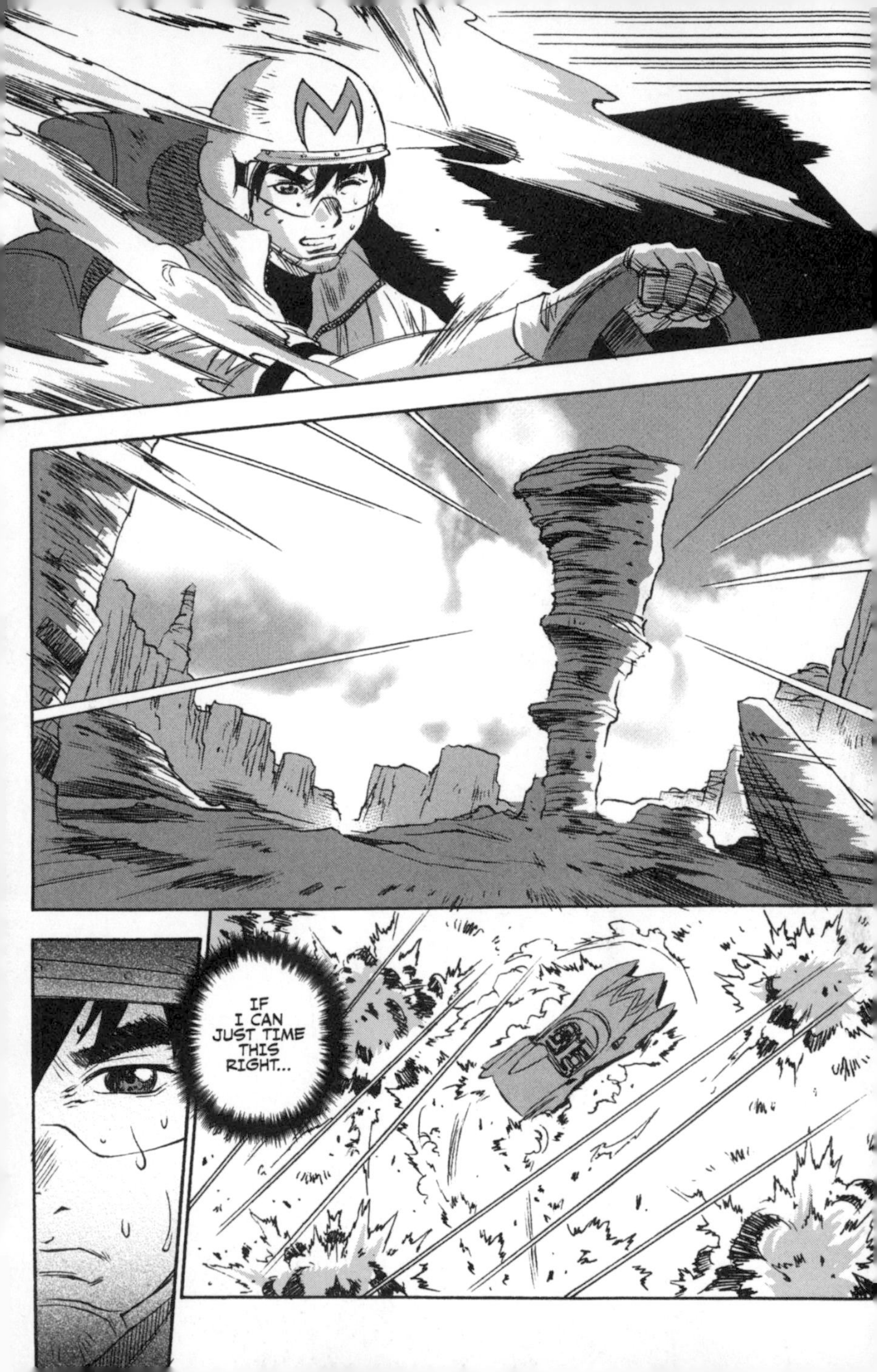
IF I CAN JUST TIME THIS RIGHT...

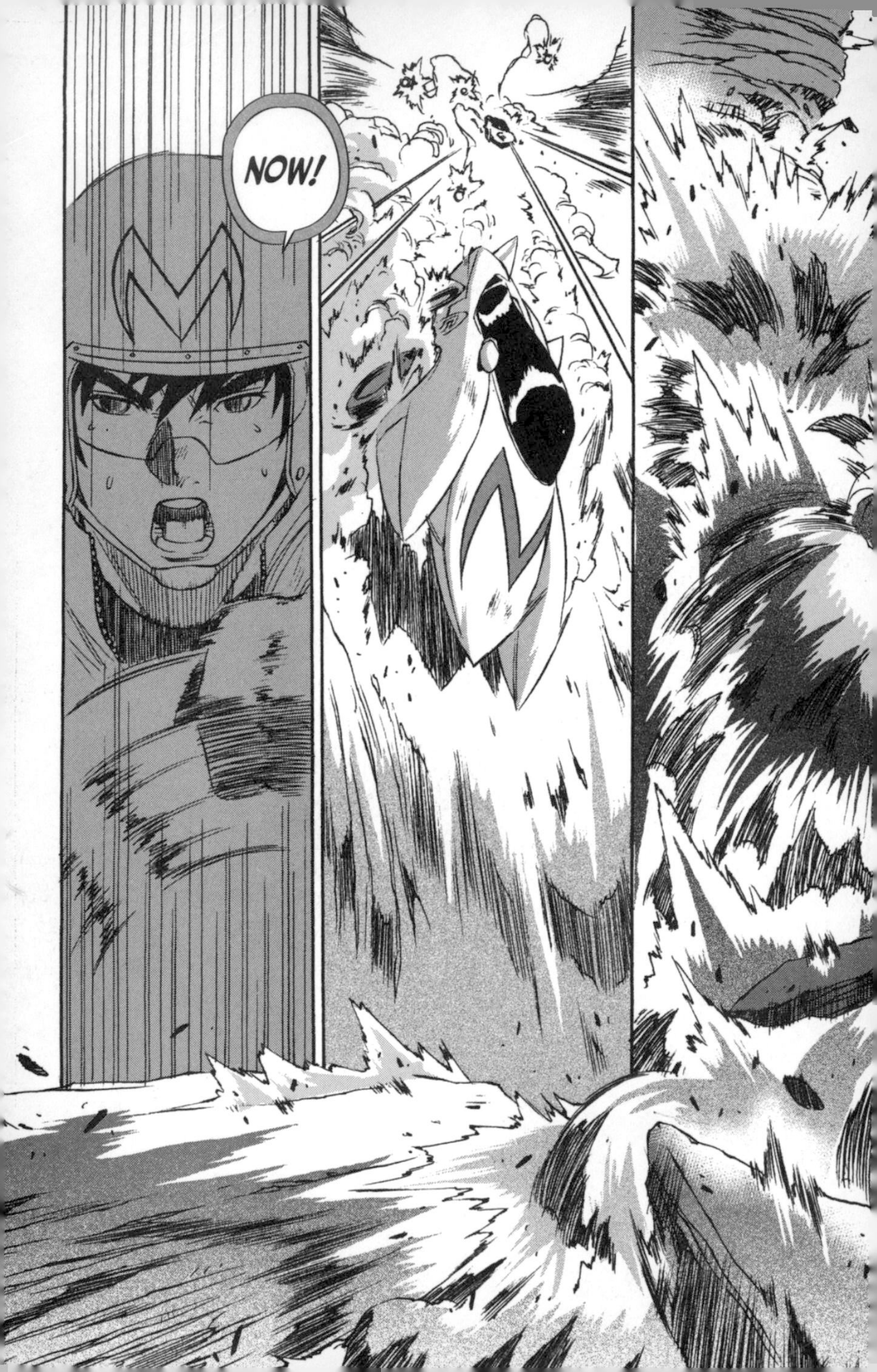
NOW!

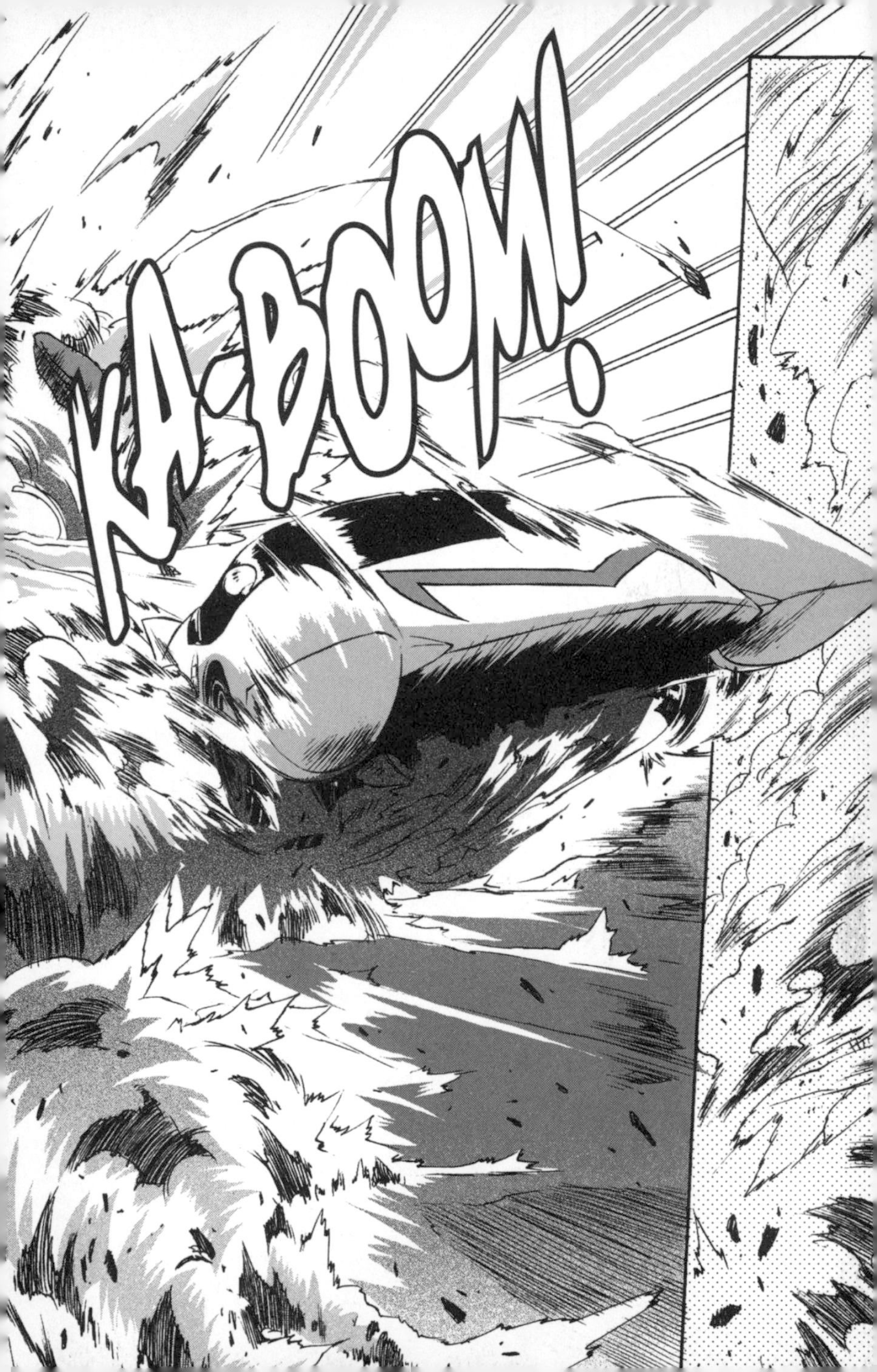
KA-BOOM!

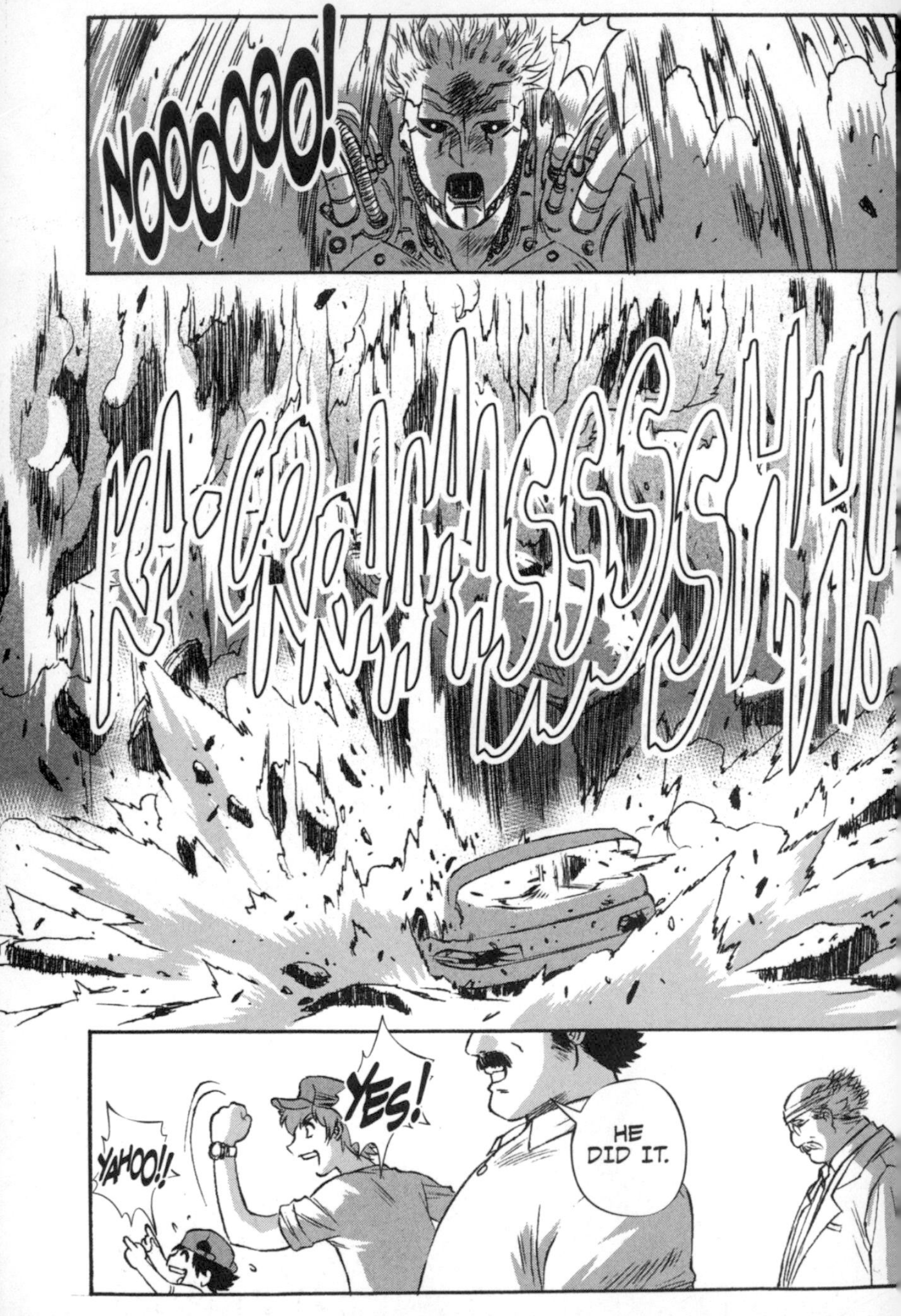
NOOOOOO!
KA-CRAAAASSSSHH!
YAHOO!!
YES!
HE DID IT.

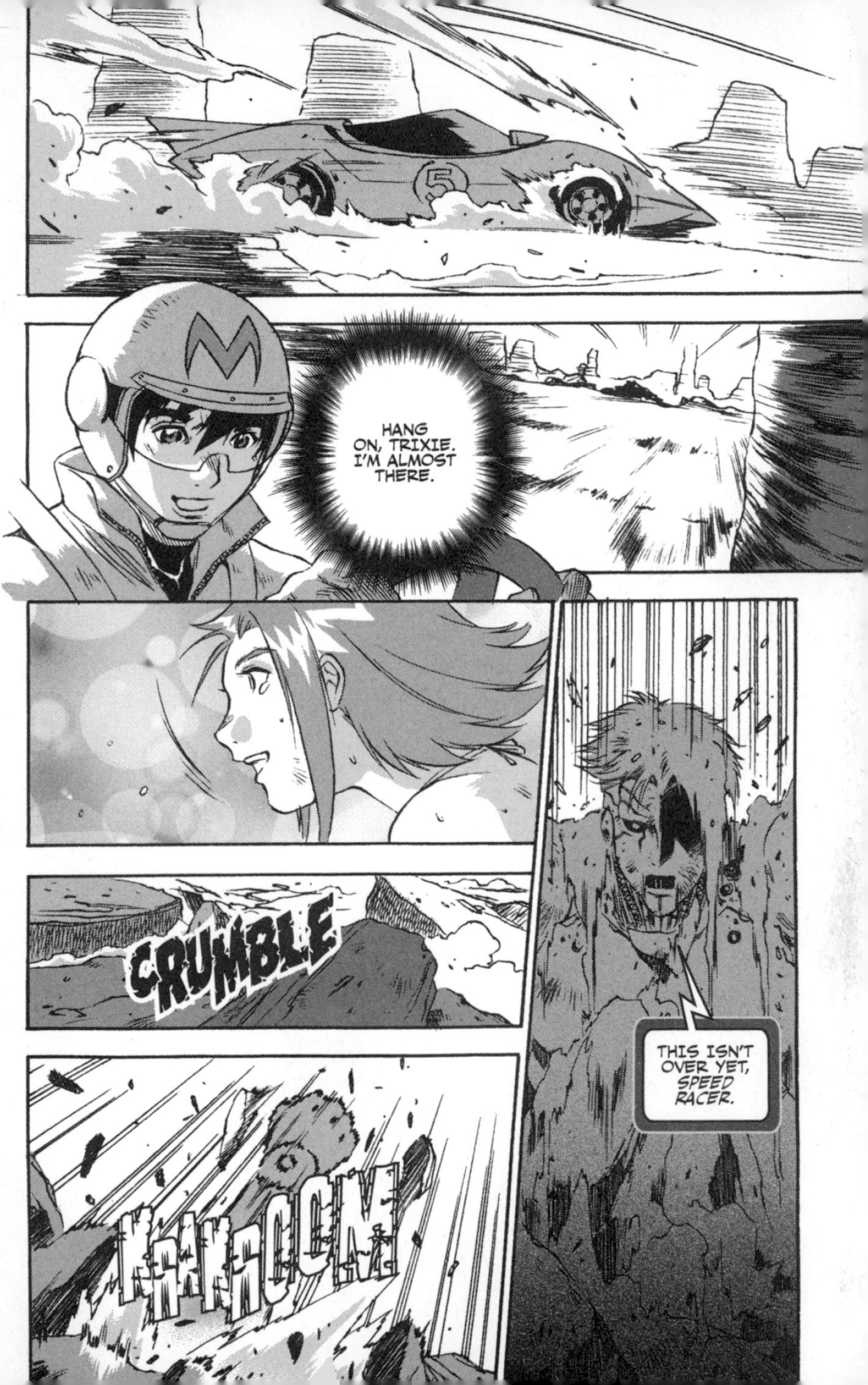
HANG ON, TRIXIE. I'M ALMOST THERE.
CRUMBLE
THIS ISN'T OVER YET, SPEED RACER.
KRAKSOOM

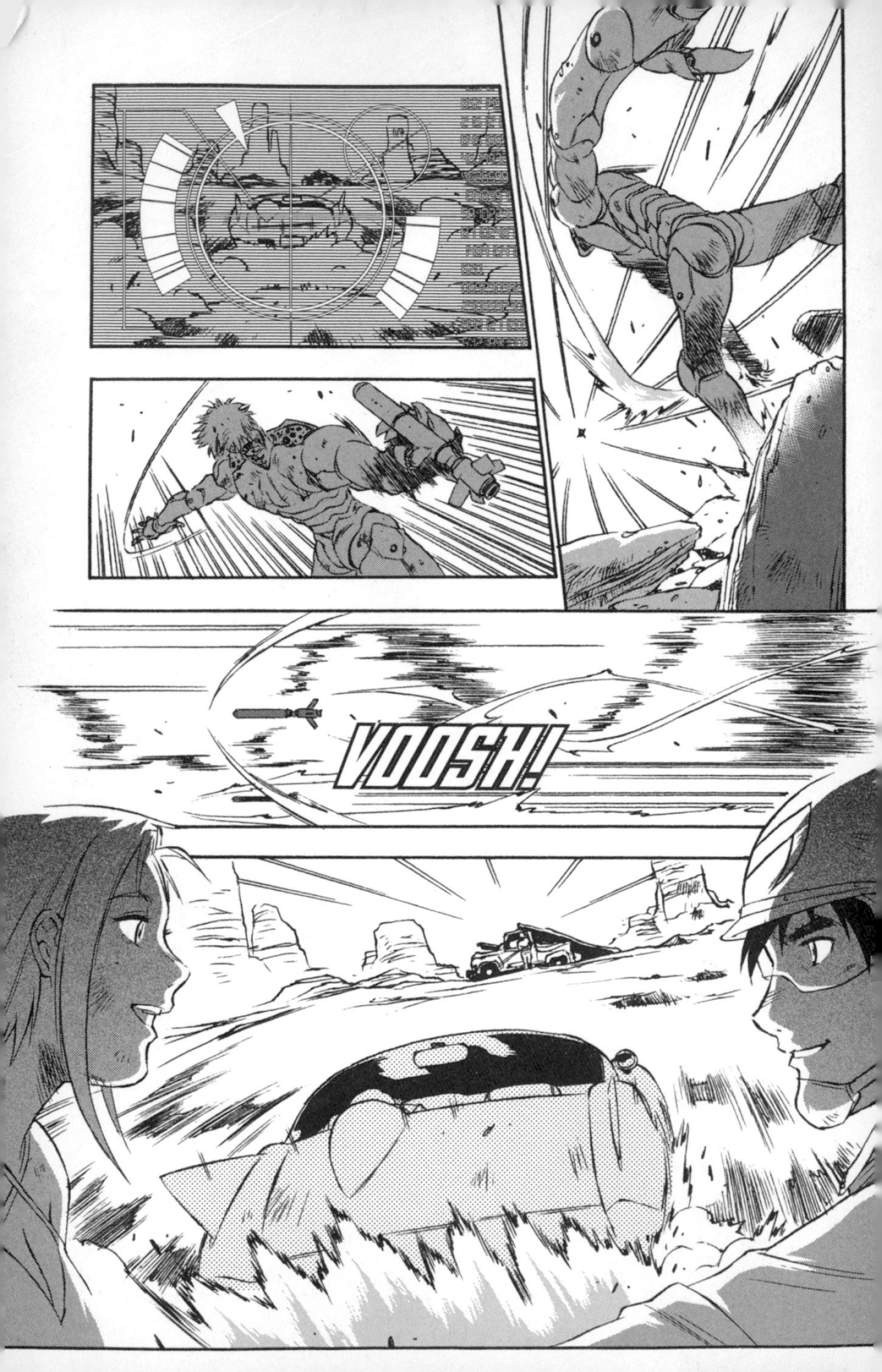
VOOSH!

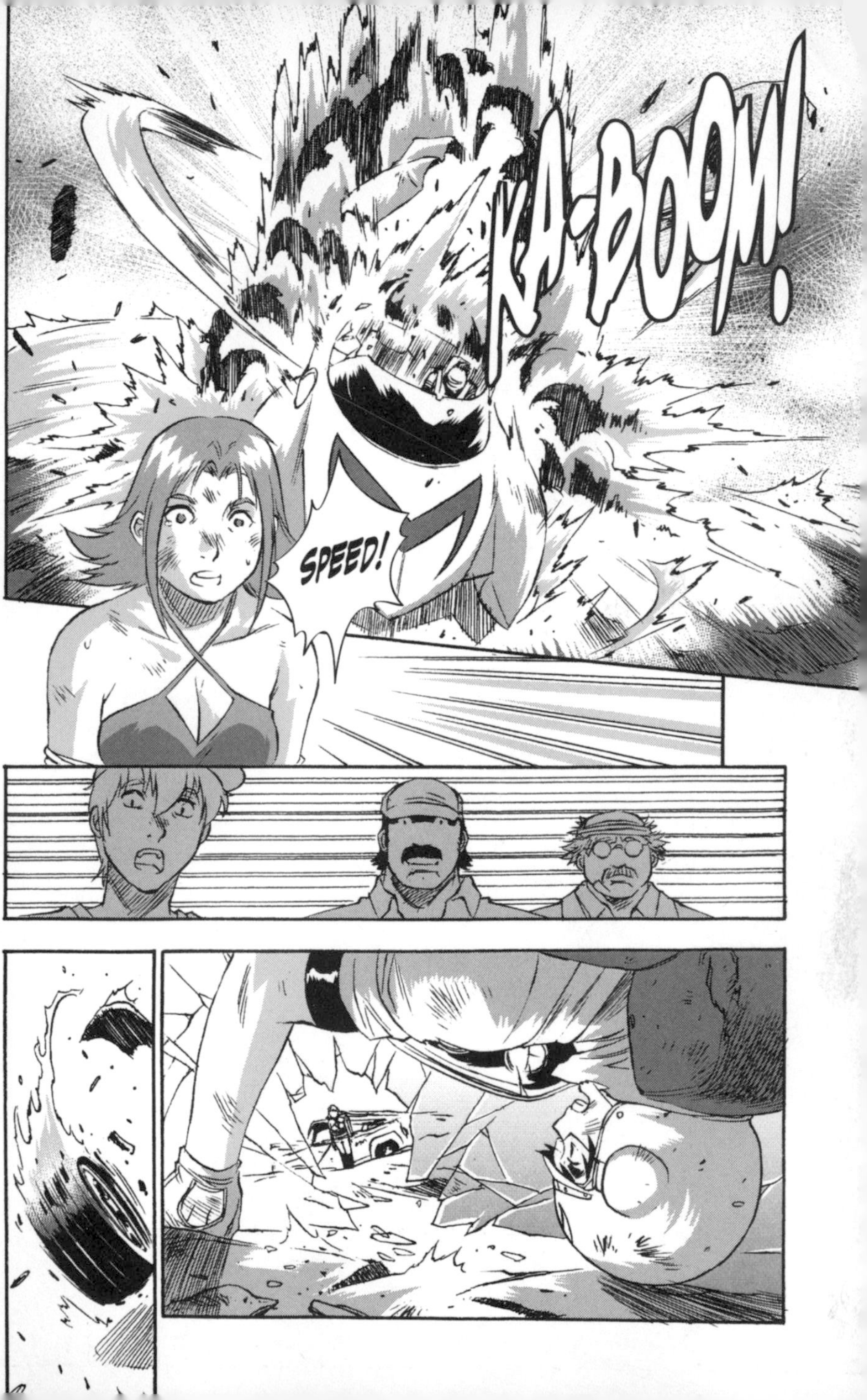
KA-BOOM!
SPEED!

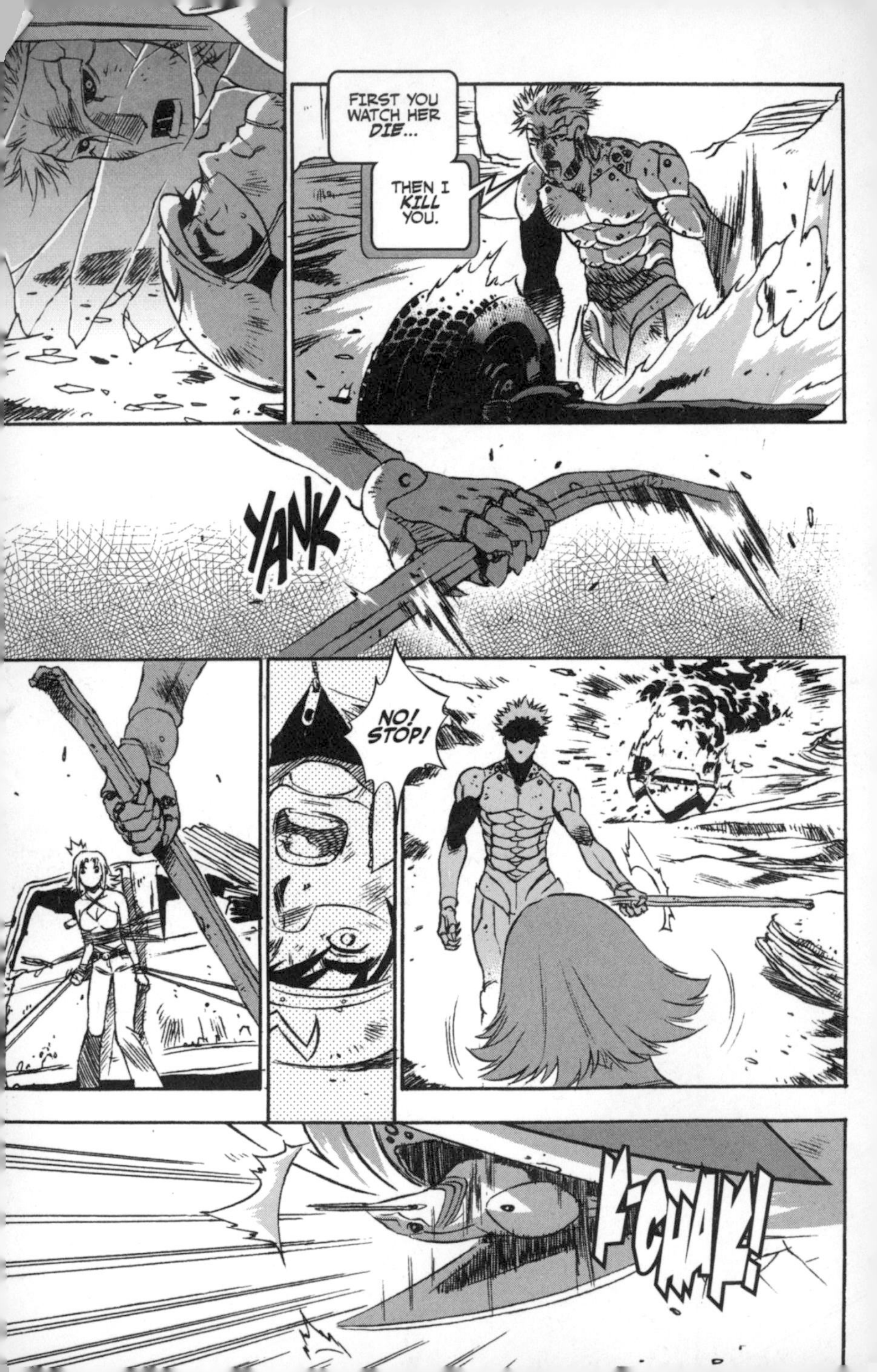
FIRST YOU WATCH HER DIE...
THEN I KILL YOU.
YANK
NO! STOP!
K-CHAK!

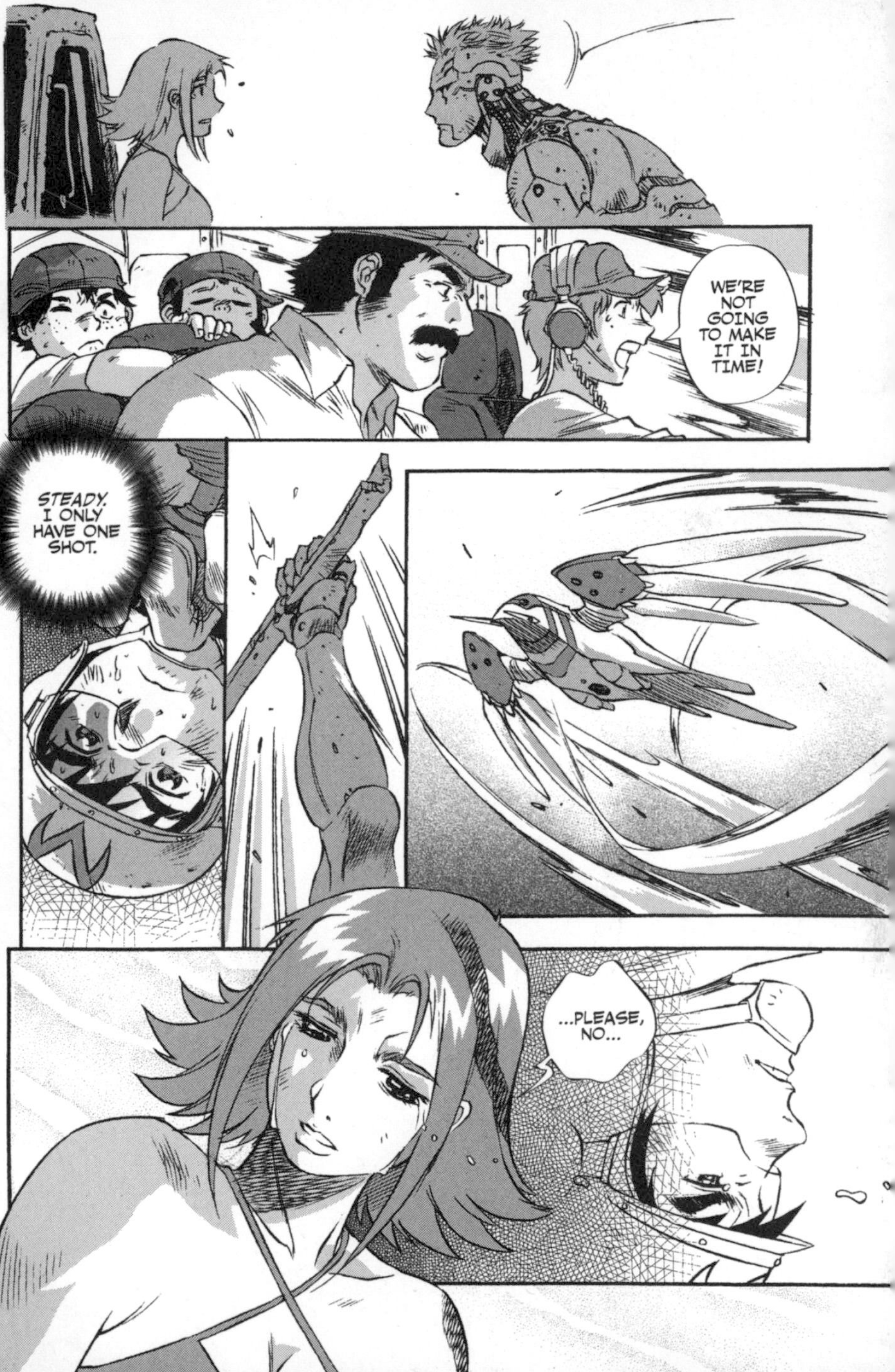
WE'RE NOT GOING TO MAKE IT IN TIME!
STEADY. I ONLY HAVE ONE SHOT.
...PLEASE, NO...

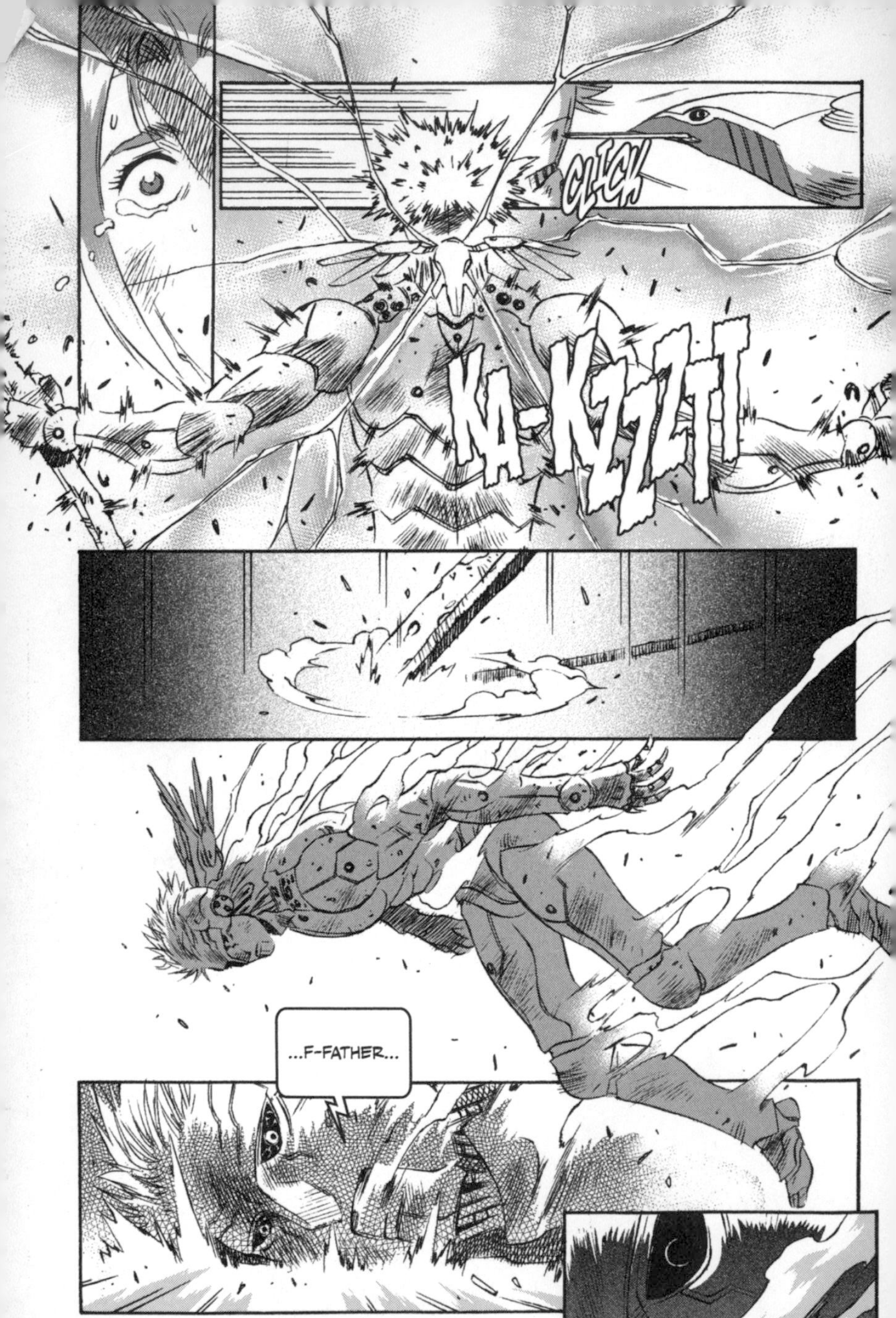
CLICK
KA-KZZZTT
...F-FATHER...

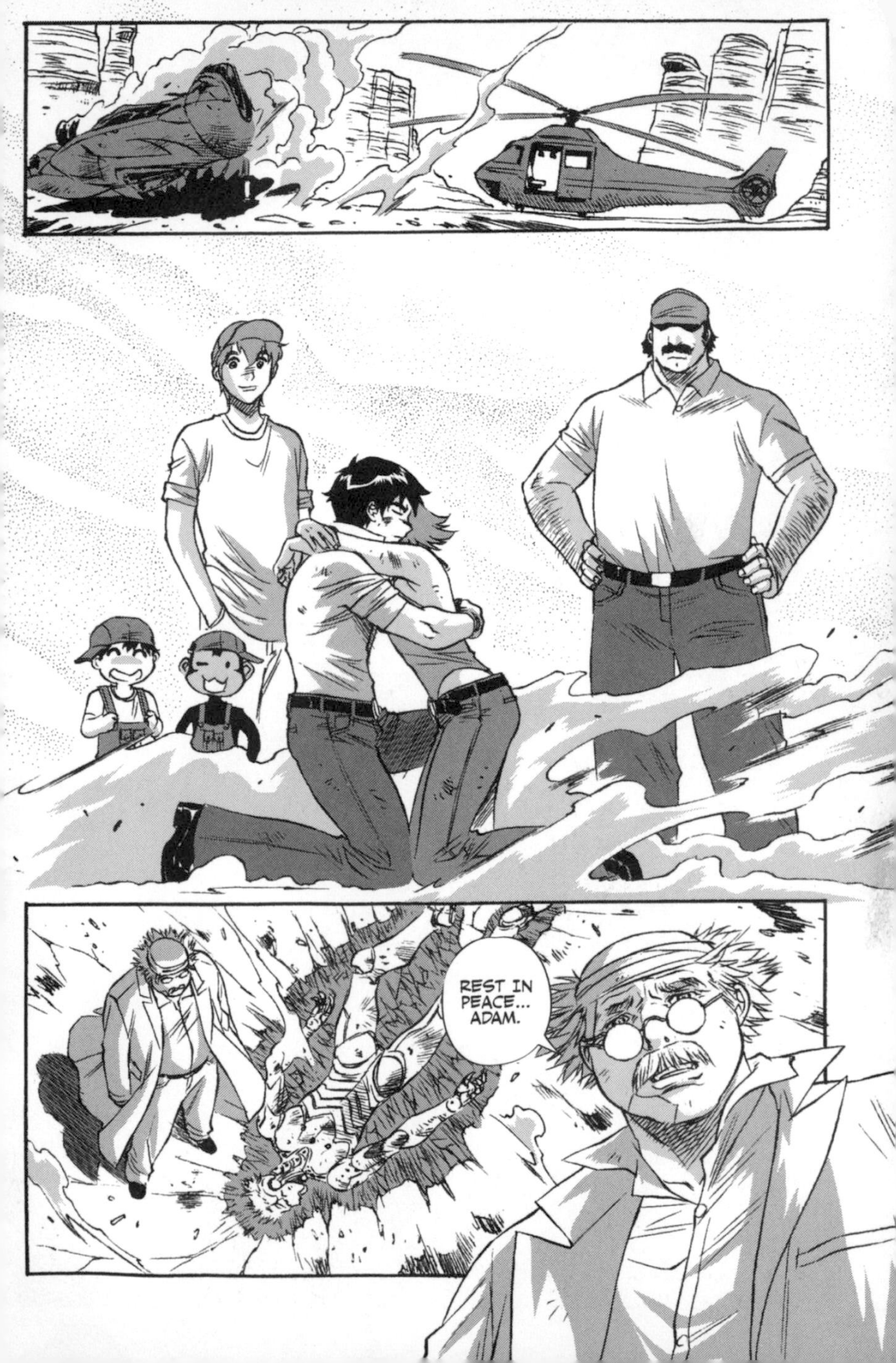
REST IN PEACE... ADAM.

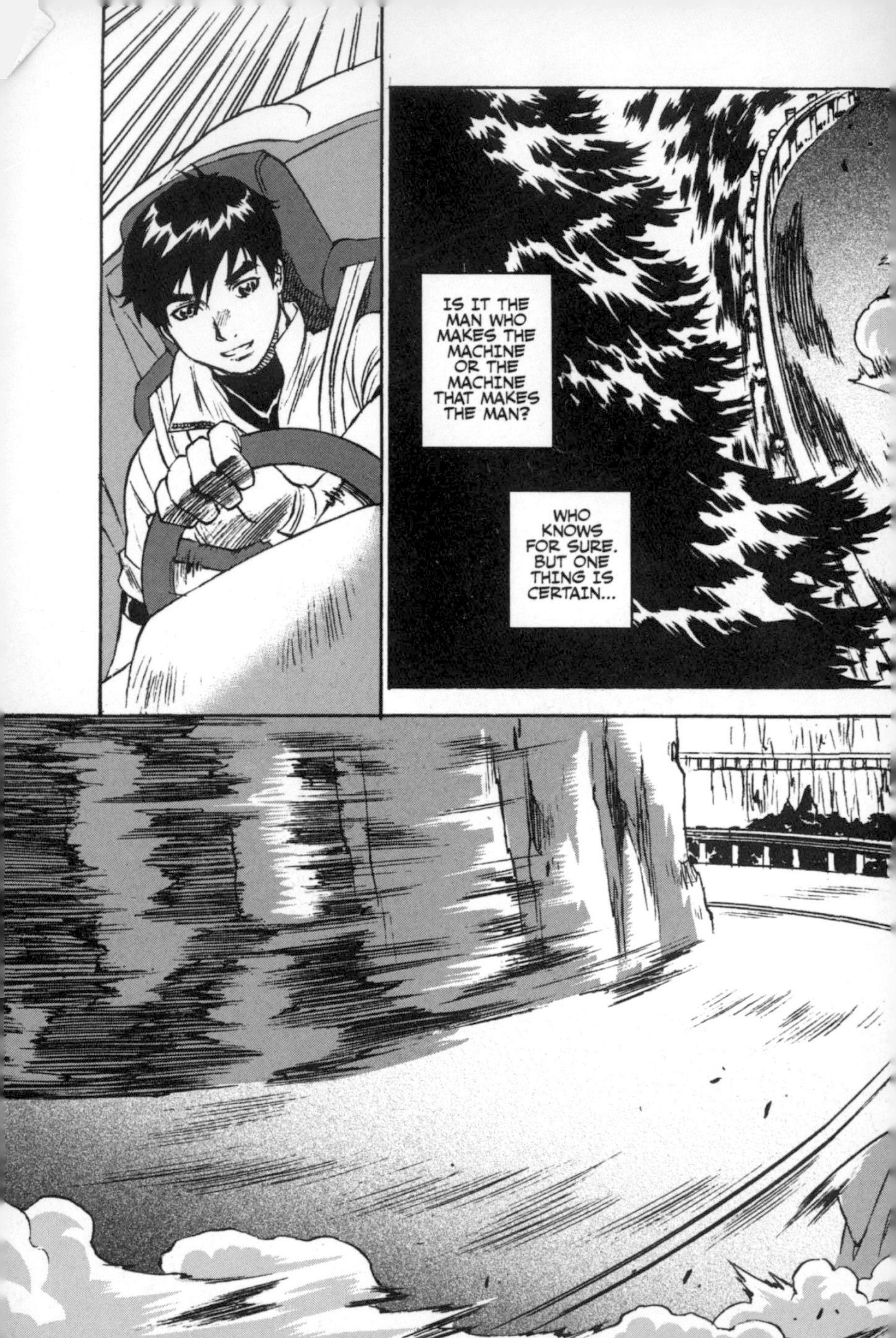
IS IT THE MAN WHO MAKES THE MACHINE OR THE MACHINE THAT MAKES THE MAN?
WHO KNOWS FOR SURE. BUT ONE THING IS CERTAIN...

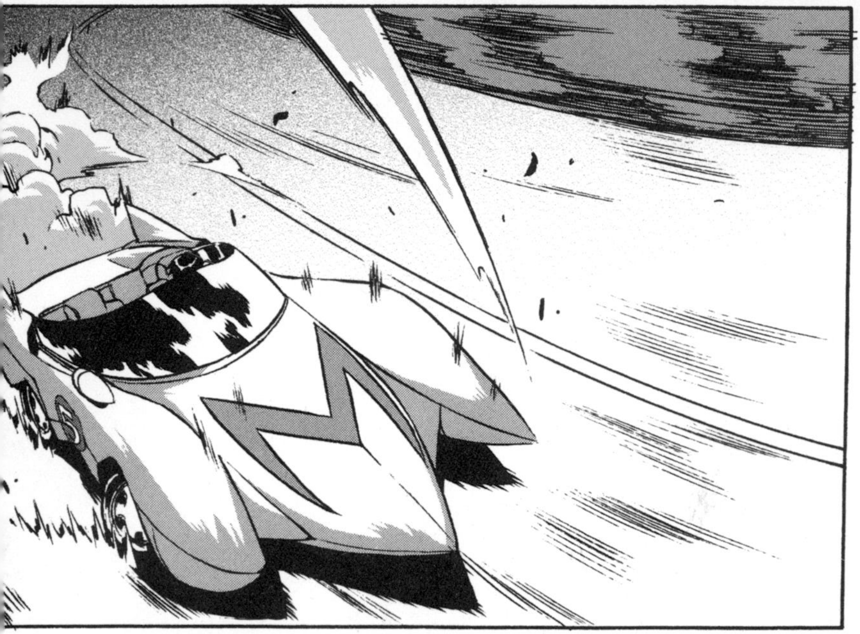
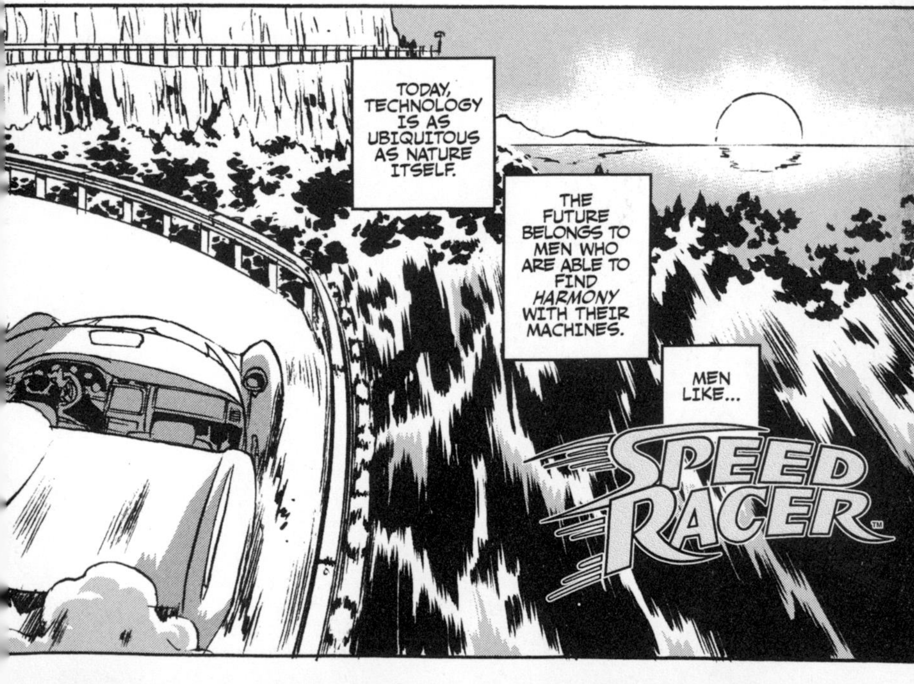
TODAY, TECHNOLOGY IS AS UBIQUITOUS AS NATURE ITSELF.
THE FUTURE BELONGS TO MEN WHO ARE ABLE TO FIND *HARMONY* WITH THEIR MACHINES.
MEN LIKE...
SPEED RACER™

SKETCH PAD

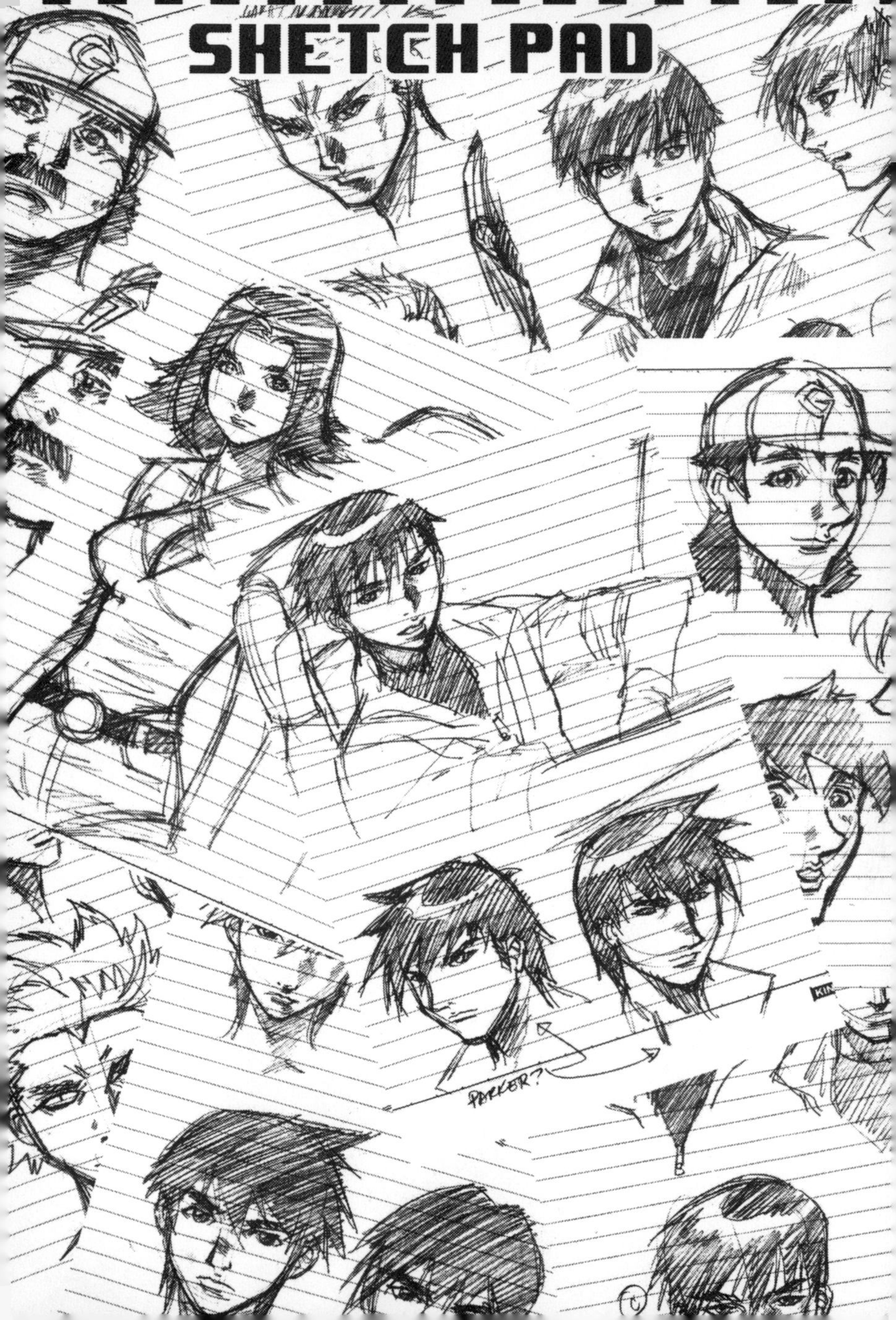
PARKER?

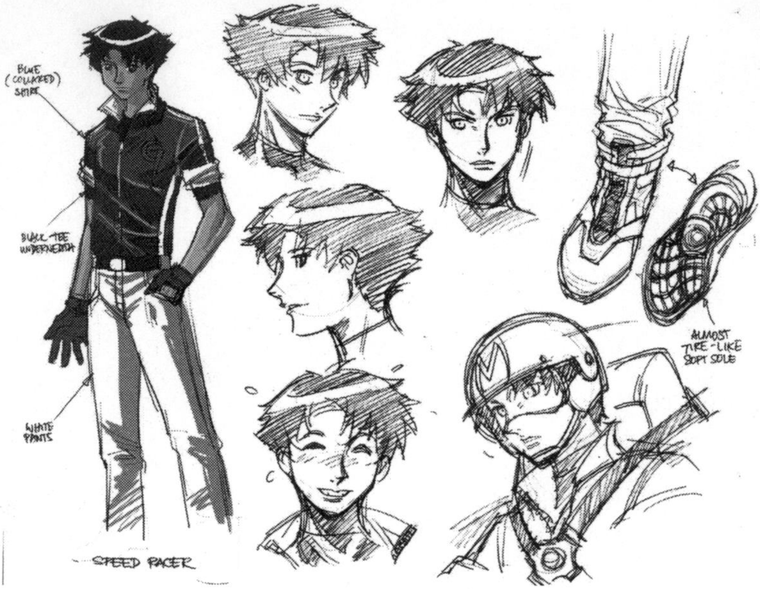
BLUE (COLLARED) SHIRT
BLACK TEE UNDERNEATH
WHITE PANTS
ALMOST TIRE-LIKE SOFT SOLE
SPEED RACER

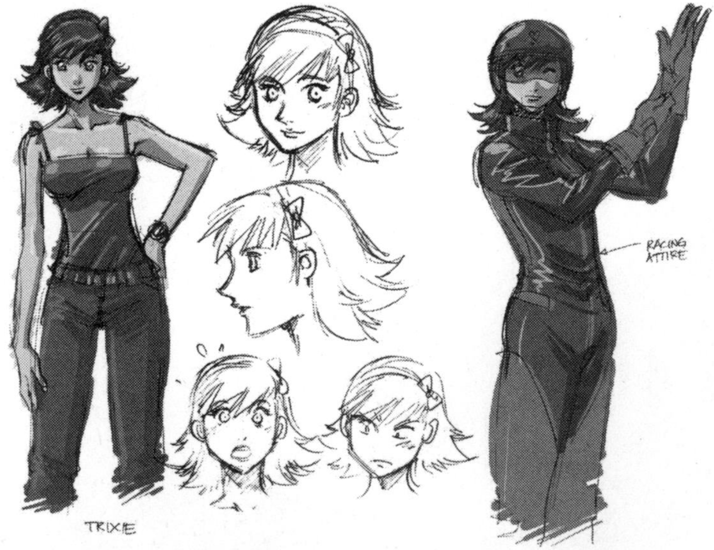
RACING ATTIRE
TRIXIE

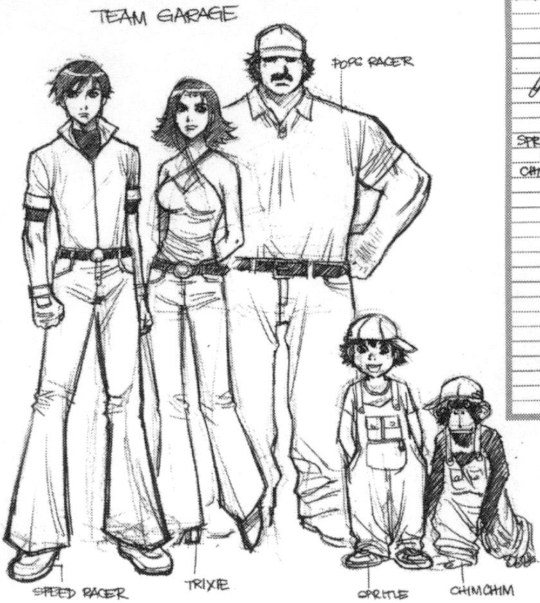
TEAM GARAGE
POPS RACER
SPEED RACER
TRIXIE
SPRITLE
CHIMCHIM

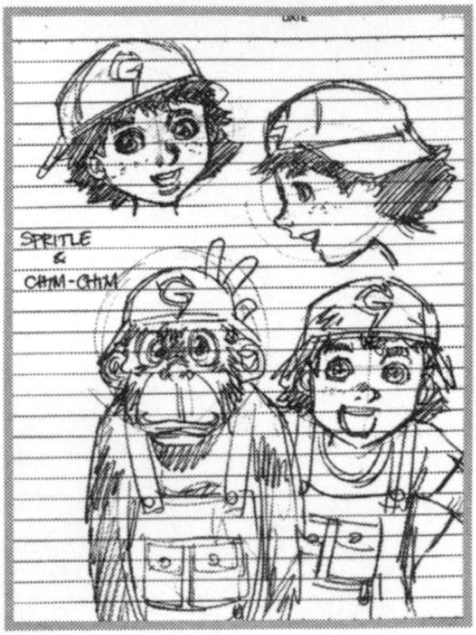
SPRITLE
&
CHIM-CHIM

Mach 5

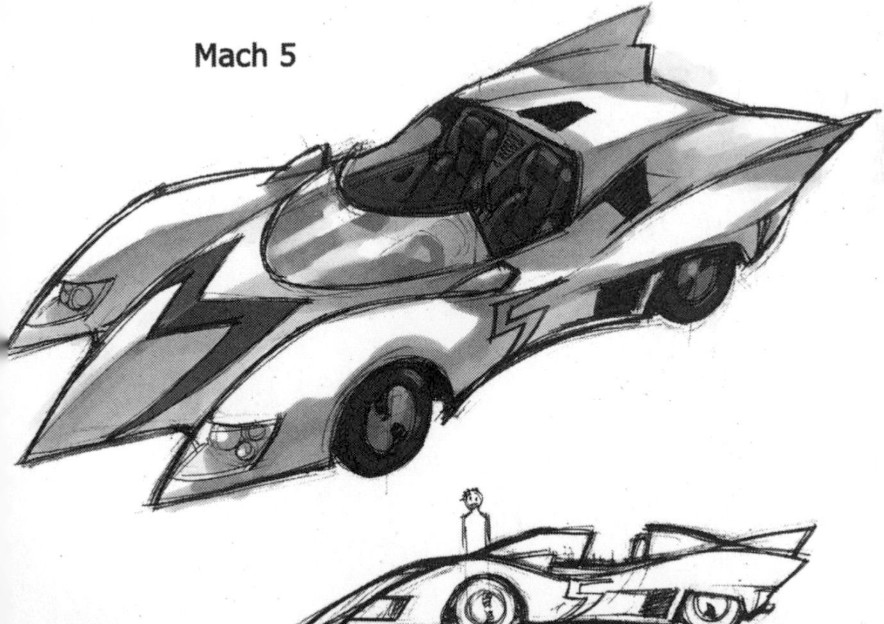

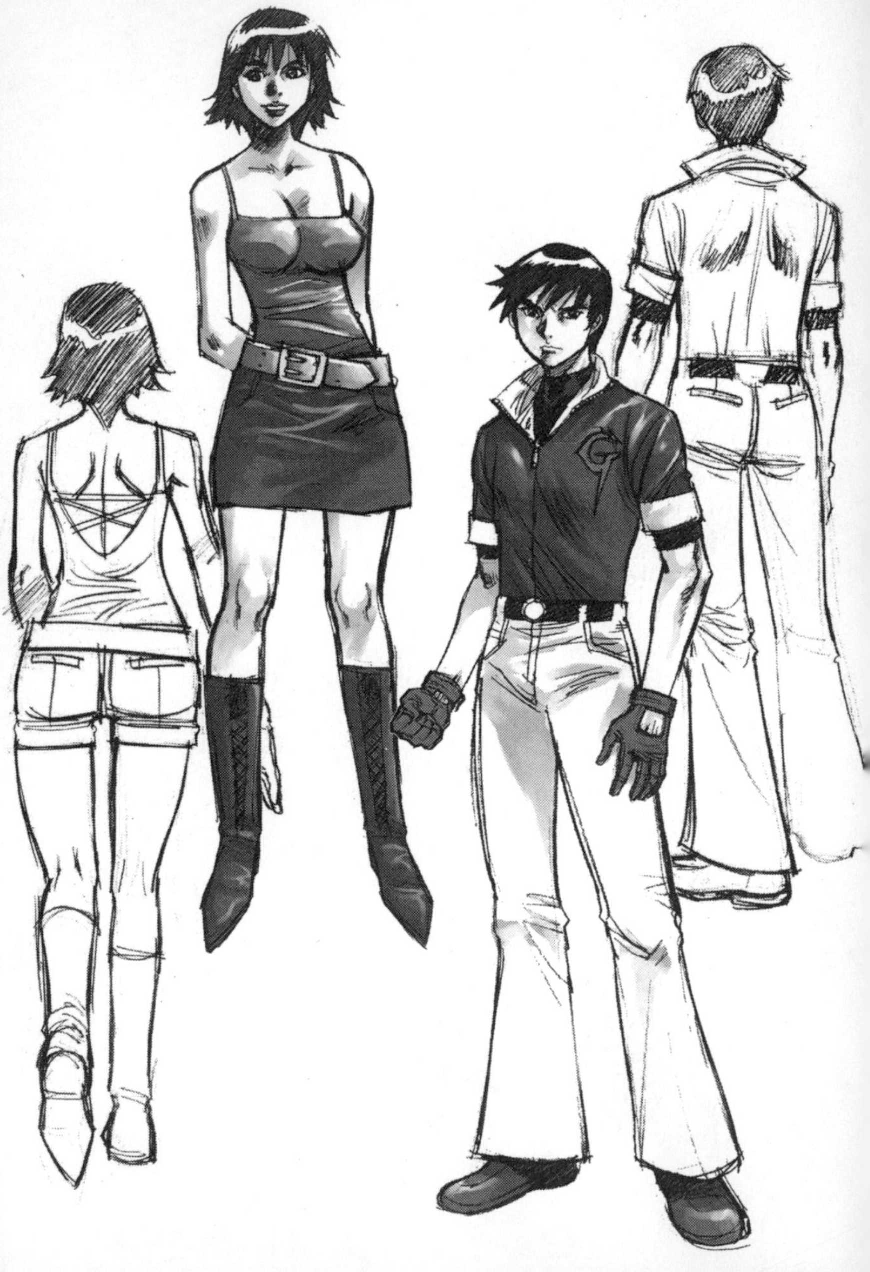

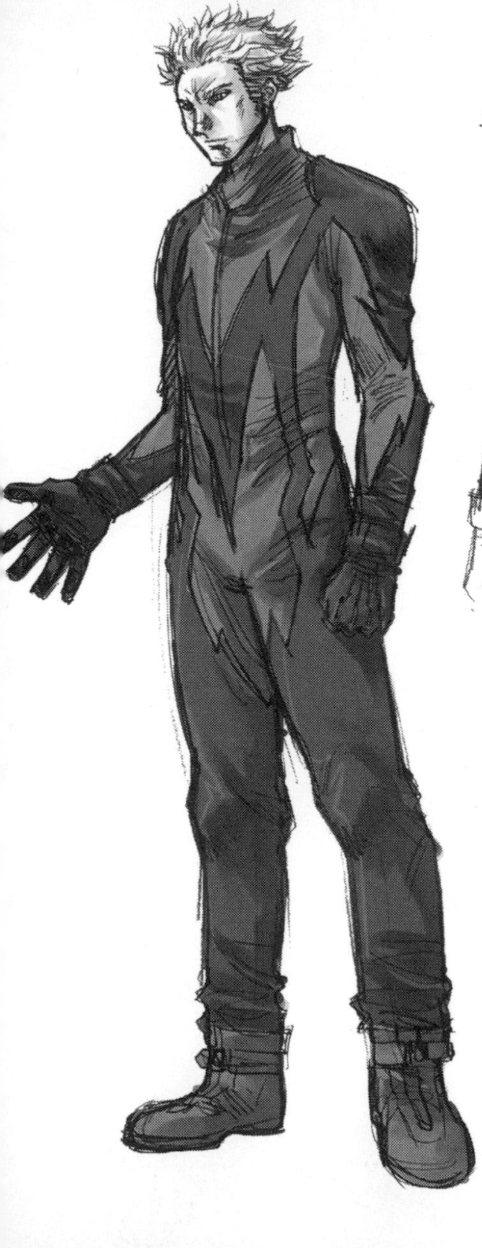

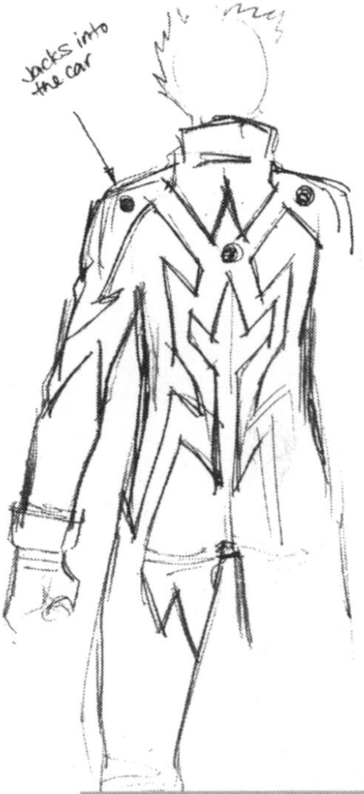
Jacks into the car

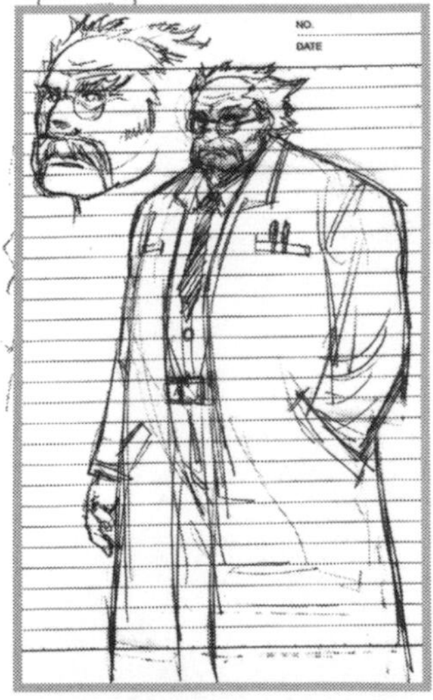
NO.
DATE

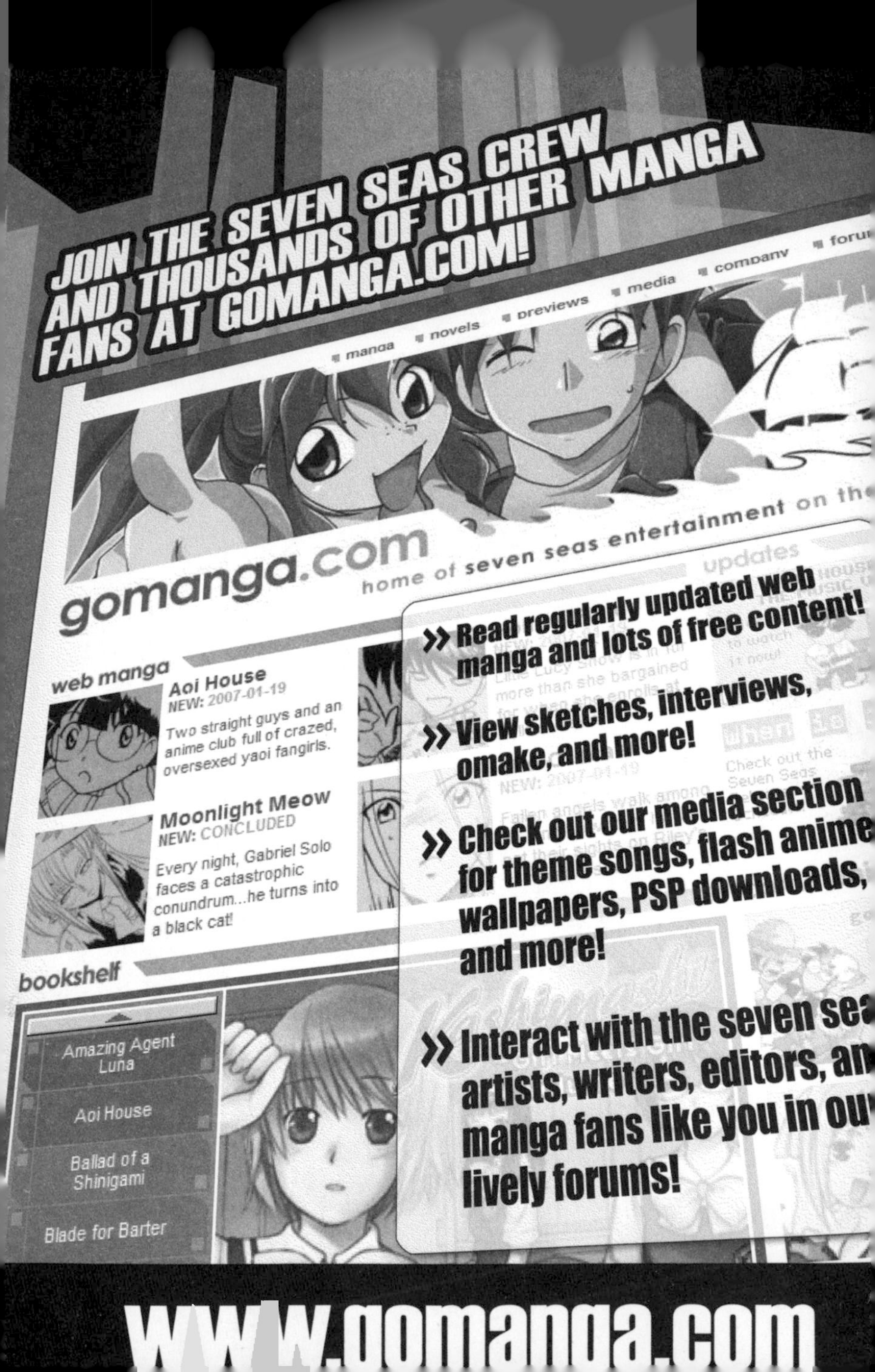
JOIN THE SEVEN SEAS CREW AND THOUSANDS OF OTHER MANGA FANS AT GOMANGA.COM!
manga
novels
previews
media
company
gomanga.com
home of seven seas entertainment on the
updates
web manga
Aoi House
NEW: 2007-01-19
Two straight guys and an anime club full of crazed, oversexed yaoi fangirls.
Moonlight Meow
NEW: CONCLUDED
Every night, Gabriel Solo faces a catastrophic conundrum...he turns into a black cat!
bookshelf
Amazing Agent Luna
Aoi House
Ballad of a Shinigami
Blade for Barter
» Read regularly updated web manga and lots of free content!
» View sketches, interviews, omake, and more!
» Check out our media section for theme songs, flash anime for theme songs, flash anime, PSP downloads, wallpapers, PSP downloads, and more!
» Interact with the seven sea artists, writers, editors, an manga fans like you in ou lively forums!
www.gomanga.com